C and UNIX

Tools for Software Design

Martin L. Barrett
East Tennessee State University

Clifford H. Wagner
The Pennsylvania State University

JOHN WILEY & SONS
New York • Chichester • Brisbane • Toronto • Singapore

ACQUISITIONS EDITOR   Steven Elliot
ASSISTANT EDITOR   Sharon Smith
MARKETING MANAGER   Debra Riegert
PRODUCTION EDITOR   Jennifer Knapp
DESIGN SUPERVISOR   Pedro A. Noa
MANUFACTURING MANAGER   Mark Cirillo
ILLUSTRATION COORDINATION   Gene Aiello
OUTSIDE PRODUCTION   Publication Services, Inc.

This book was set in 10/12 Times Roman by Publication Services, and printed and bound by R. R. Don-nelly/Crawfordsville. The cover was printed by New England Book Components.

AIX is a registered trademark of International Business Machines Corporation. ANSI is a registered trademark of American National Standards Institute, Incorporated. AT&T is a registered trademark of American Telephone and Telegraph Company. BSD is a registered trademark of UUNET Technologies, Incorporated. DEC is a registered trademark of Digital Equipment Corporation. General Electric is a registered trademark of General Electric Company. Hewlett–Packard is a registered trademark of Hewlett–Packard Company. IBM is a registered trademark of International Business Machines Corporation. Mosaic is a registered trademark of Mosaic Systems, Incorporated. Motif is a registered trademark of Open Software Foundation, Incorporated. Multics is a registered trademark of Honeywell Information Systems, Incorporated. Open Software Foundation is a registered trademark of Open Software Foundation, Incorporated. OS/2 is a registered trademark of International Business Machines Corporation. Solaris is a registered trademark of Genisco Technology Corporation. Sun Microsystems is a registered trademark of Sun Microsystems, Incorporated. TEX is a trademark of the American Mathematical Society. Ultrix is a registered trademark of Digital Equipment Corporation. UNIX is a registered trademark of UNIX System Laboratories, Incorporated. WordPerfect is a registered trademark of WordPerfect Corporation

Library of Congress Cataloging-in-Publication Data

Barrett, Martin L.
    C and UNIX: tools for software design
    / Martin L. Barrett, Clifford H. Wagner.
        p.   cm.
    Includes index.
    ISBN 0-471-30927-3 (paper)
    1. C (Computer program language)   2. UNIX
    (Computer file)   3. Computer software—Development.
    I. Wagner, Clifford H.   II. Title.
QA76.73.C15B38   1996
005.13′3—dc20   95-1816
                                                  CIP

Printed in the United States of America

10 9 8 7 6 5 4 3 2 1

To Ellen, Leon, Ruth, and Sam
To Mary Beth, Donald, and Thomas

Preface

Match each word in the left column with a word from the right column:

Salt	Light
Red	Pepper
Mickey	Tobago
Trinidad	Minnie

Some things just naturally fit together. Such is the case for C and UNIX. These software tools have been developed in tandem; C is an excellent programming language; UNIX is an excellent operating system; they work well together; and many software developers choose to take advantage of the symbiotic relationship between C and UNIX.

In *C and UNIX: Tools for Software Design* we introduce the essential features of C and UNIX, and we encourage readers to use them together to write more powerful and more efficient programs. We assume that our readers have some prior programming experience, but we do not require knowledge of any particular language or any specific programming concepts. The text is designed for a one-semester course, and it would be feasible to use this text in a CS1 course for which C is the designated language and where students have prior programming experience. The text is also appropriate for non–computer science majors, particularly those in mathematics, engineering, and science. The UNIX material is self-contained and may be skipped by those who already know UNIX or are using another operating system.

The guiding principles of *C and UNIX: Tools for Software Design* are the following:

- Emphasize software design throughout the text. There are entire chapters devoted to program design (Chapter 6) and data structure design (Chapter 11). Additionally, there are chapter sections devoted to the design of tables and data encapsulation (in Chapter 9) and abstract data types (in Chapter 14).
- Develop C and UNIX simultaneously, so that the reader can more easily develop C programs in a UNIX environment and can write programs that take advantage of UNIX features. This goal notwithstanding, the UNIX topics are presented with sufficient independence from the C topics that an instructor can easily rearrange or omit UNIX topics as appropriate. Moreover, our UNIX coverage is not exhaustive because at least one entire book would be needed to explain the complete UNIX operating system.
- Include a thorough summary, review problems, and several programming problems in each chapter. Some of the programming problems are suitable for use as team projects. As the text progresses, many of the programming problems are less fully specified, permitting the reader a more realistic experience of having to confront design issues as well as the imprecision of many real-life problems.

- Include examples covering scientific problems, applied mathematics, and the precision of floating-point arithmetic. Among topics covered in programming problems are the ideal gas law, the accuracy of summations, root finding, the future value of an annuity, simulation, time series smoothing, image processing, integrals, descriptive statistics, fuzzy sets, and sparse arrays (represented via linked lists). These examples concentrate on numerical and mathematical aspects of scientific programming; they do not consider any theoretical details.
- Lay a foundation for other computer science courses such as those in data structures, analysis of algorithms, numerical analysis, computer graphics, and compiler design.

We concentrate on developing C as defined in the ANSI standard, with occasional references to distinctions that must be made when using other versions of C. Likewise, we concentrate on developing the C shell version of UNIX, with occasional references to the Bourne shell. Because many readers will use the vi editor to write their programs, we include a thorough discussion of both elementary and advanced features of vi.

The chapters of *C and UNIX: Tools for Software Design* are arranged in four parts:

- *Basic program syntax and control.*   Chapters 1 through 3 introduce basic features of C and UNIX, including C program syntax and flow of control, as well as elementary file editing and maintenance. The specific topics are brief histories of C and UNIX, an introduction to writing and executing C programs in a UNIX environment, file and directory maintenance, program syntax, data types, the vi editor, and branching and looping statements.
- *Program design and control of input and output.*   Chapters 4 through 6 discuss both user-defined functions and standard functions, including input/output functions, principles of program design and testing, and UNIX commands that are related to C programming. The specific topics include standard function libraries, user-defined functions, scoping rules, storage classes, simple input/output commands in C and UNIX, text files, program design and testing methods, and UNIX commands to support program development.
- *Data structure design and management.*   Chapters 7 through 11 cover arrays, user-defined static data structures, dynamic data structures, and more advanced editing and UNIX commands. Specific topics include defining, searching (and sometimes, sorting) arrays, strings, structs, unions, binary files, and linked lists; using these structures to implement stacks, queues, and other linked lists; general principles of data structure design; advanced vi editing; pattern searching in UNIX; UNIX programming; and UNIX file utilities.
- *Advanced features of C and UNIX.*   Chapters 12 through 14 include C constants, macros, bit operations, function pointers, low-level file processing, recursion, UNIX parsing tools, UNIX processes, and an introduction to abstract data types, object-oriented design, and electronic mail.

In addition, there are appendices with summaries of C commands, UNIX commands, vi commands, standard function libraries, and C operator precedences. There is also an Instructor's Manual that contains a sample syllabus and answers for review problems.

We thank our families for their encouragement and patient support. We thank our colleagues Peter Gingo, the University of Akron; Stephen J. Hartley, Drexel University; Linda

Hayden, Elizabeth City State University; and Phil Pfeiffer, East Stroudsburg University, for conscientiously reviewing our manuscript and offering many insightful criticisms and suggestions. We thank our secretary, Elsie Wilt, for her cheerful and excellent assistance. We also thank our many students, particularly Rosanne Bender, Yiching Cheng, Raymond Hilderbrand, Dan Nguyen, Nathan Raupach, Gary Rynearson, and Brian Surratt, who by reading the text and solving the problems helped refine preliminary versions of the text.

We encourage our readers to send us comments, suggestions, criticisms, and requests.

Martin L. Barrett
Johnson City, Tennessee

Clifford H. Wagner
Harrisburg, Pennsylvania

Brief Contents

Contents

Chapter 1

Introduction

This chapter introduces the C programming language and the UNIX operating system. Some sample C programs are given. While the details of the programs are partially explained here, full explanations of the features used in these examples are left for later chapters. The introduction to UNIX will explain how to log in to a UNIX system and how to use a few simple commands. Becoming an effective and efficient user of C and UNIX will depend not only on reading the material presented, but also on trying out new concepts on the computer.

Introduction to C

The C programming language is generally considered a *high-level* computer language—that is, a language that operates away from the details of machine characteristics and that is more readable, more organized, and more structured than assembly language. Yet C retains the ability to work at lower levels (bit manipulation is possible, for example) plus the flexibility to represent even higher-order concepts. The current popularity of C in the marketplace and in academia reflects its adaptability to diverse applications and environments.

Other languages, of course, compete with C for use in these areas. To compare another language with C on specific elements of syntax or style, or even to make some overall quality judgment of C versus another language, is to miss the point about programming. Languages are *tools* that a programmer uses. Good programs can be written in any language. Bad programs are also possible regardless of language choice. While some C programs may be difficult to read, debug, and modify, the likely culprit for these problems is the programmer. Good programming methods are an integral part of this book.

Brief History

In the early 1970s, Dennis Ritchie developed the C language in conjunction with the UNIX operating system at AT&T. (See [Kernighan and Ritchie].) Its antecedents were B and BCPL, typeless languages that today are largely forgotten. C was meant to be a small language (as compared to, say, PL/I) in that it contains only basic operations (no operations on arrays as objects, for example); no input or output methods (these are done as function calls); and no provision for multiprocessing (such as the rendezvous in Ada). Flow of control is done via a few control methods and the function call. Over time, libraries of functions have been developed to answer questions of the "Why can't I do *that?*" type.

There are two basic types of C and many subtypes. Traditional C, usually referred to as "Kernighan and Ritchie C" or "K&R C" (after the authors of *The C Programming Language*), continues to be used and supported. ANSI C was developed in the 1980s as a standard for the language. This version of the language is designed to promote *portability* (being able to move an existing program from one machine to another with no changes to the source code itself), reliability, and efficiency of execution of C programs. Part of ANSI C's appeal is due to the similar syntax present in C++, a relatively recent language that is growing in popularity. The ANSI standard is more or less adhered to by compiler vendors, but some differences remain among commercial products, leading to the aforementioned subtypes of C. This book discusses ANSI C and tries to point out where K&R C diverges.

Keep in mind the following features of C:

- C is a *typed* language, that is, the variables declared in a C program must be declared as, say, integer or floating-point. C is not, however, *strongly* typed, in that the values in variables can change type at the whim of the programmer.
- C is a *structured* language. Programs are constructed from well-defined control structures, functions, and modules. Modular programming helps break larger problems into a collection of smaller, more manageable pieces. The use of functions is encouraged in C and often in fact required. For example, input and output, as mentioned earlier, must be done via function calls.
- The use of *pointers* (addresses of variables) is often necessary when passing parameters to functions and when dealing with arrays, strings, and dynamic memory allocation. The beginner in C must make an extra effort to understand pointers.

Writing good programs is less a result of language choice than it is of programmer discipline. This text encourages a uniform programming style that includes full documentation of code. It is possible, even easy, to write unreadable C programs, as is proven again every day by thousands of programmers. Writing readable, maintainable, and error-free programs in C is not only possible, it is not even very hard—it simply takes dedication on the part of the programmer.

Example Programs

The following simple C programs and discussions are meant to give the flavor of programming in C. They are not meant to describe all possible features of the language, nor do they do much in the way of computation. Do not expect to understand every detail, either. Each topic is covered in full later in the text. The examples are ordered approximately by chapter, but not all chapters are represented.

Basic Syntax and Program Format

Each command and operation in C has a specific syntax and set of semantic rules that must be followed in order to construct correct programs. We mention just a few of those rules here, and we also look at the usual format for a C program.

Almost every C statement ends with a semicolon. The few exceptions to this rule include statements that are not truly part of the C language and groups of statements. The following sample program illustrates this and the general program format.

```
#include <stdio.h>
main()
{
    /* Chapter 1 Example 1 */
    /* Comments, like this one, begin with slash-star and end with star-slash */
    printf(
        "Today's temperature is 20 degrees Celsius, 68 degrees Fahrenheit. \n" );
}
```

The program *preamble*, which comprises the first statement of this program, often contains constant and type definitions (there are none in this simple program) and `#include` statements. An `#include` statement is a signal that some information must be added to the program from another file, either a system file (such as, in this case, `<stdio.h>`) or one defined by the programmer. This and some other necessary statements are technically not C, but they are needed to write complete programs.

The remainder of the program is the program *body,* where the action occurs—the C statements that actually *do* something. The braces { and } enclose the main program, which begins with the word `main()`. The only statement in the program body, the `printf()` statement, is an example of a function call. The `printf()` function is defined in the `<stdio.h>` file mentioned in the previous paragraph, which explains why `<stdio.h>` must be referenced. (This is the usual purpose of files whose names end in `.h`, either system files or user-defined files.) The symbols `\n` at the end of the quoted sentence indicate that a carriage return should be used when the quoted sentence is displayed. Note the semicolon at the end of the `printf()` statement. The two lines that precede the `printf()` statement, those surrounded by /* and */, are *comments*: nonexecutable statements that document the program. Neither comments, nor `#include` statements, nor a set of statements in braces (such as the `main()` program) should be terminated by semicolons.

A C program like this would be stored in a UNIX file with a name similar to `prog.c`, where the extension `.c` is mandatory. It could be compiled (made ready to run) with the UNIX command `cc prog.c`, which would produce the file `a.out`. This file could then be executed by typing `a.out`, and the output *should* be

```
Today's temperature is 20 degrees Celsius, 68 degrees Fahrenheit.
```

Note that the compilation command may be different from `cc`. For example, at the authors' site, `acc` is used for the ANSI C compiler, and `gcc` is used for the GNU compiler (available at many universities).

The foregoing example contains an entire (and short) program, but it does not show the authors' preferred style. The next example does. It also illustrates some simple assignment and operation statements. In the programming examples, entire programs will not always be shown, because you will be able to fill in many of the program details easily.

```
/* Title : Chapter 1 Example 2 */
/* Source: ex2.c              */
/* Date  :   /  /             */
/* Author: B&W                */
/* Input : none.              */
/* Output: to screen, temperature values          */
/* Method: use Celsius to Fahrenheit conversion formula */
/* Included header files: */
#include <stdio.h>
main()
{
   /* Variable declarations: */
   int celsius;
   double fahrenheit;
   /* Assign a Celsius value and compute the Fahrenheit value */
   celsius = 20;
   fahrenheit = 1.8 * celsius + 32.0;
   printf(
     "Today's temperature is %d degrees Celsius, %lf degrees Fahrenheit.\n",
     celsius, fahrenheit );
}   /* main */
```

The first few lines are comments that describe the program that follows. Besides a preamble and a program body, this program also has a *variable declaration* section. There are two variables, which show some basic types: the `int` variable `celsius` and the floating-point (`double` for double-precision) variable `fahrenheit`. A value is simply assigned to the former, and the corresponding value is computed for the latter. The output of this program, if it were compiled and executed, would be similar to that of the previous example. The symbols `%d` and `%lf` in the `printf()` statement are place holders for the variables' values: one for an integer value and one for a floating-point value. Chapter 2 discusses variable types and assignments in more detail.

Control Structures

For a program to accomplish its tasks, there must be ways to control the flow of execution. In C, this takes the form of decision statements (`if` and `switch`) and looping statements for repetition (`for` and `while`). The next program shows the usage of a `for` loop, commonly used for repeating a sequence of instructions a fixed number of times.

```
/* Title : Chapter 1 Example 3 */
/* Source: ex3.c              */
/* Date  :   /  /             */
/* Author: B&W                */
/* Input : none               */
/* Output: to screen, table of temperature values   */
/* Method: use Celsius to Fahrenheit conversion formula */
/* Included header files: */
```

```
#include <stdio.h>
main()
{
    /* Variable declarations: */
    int celsius;          /* Integer counter variable                */
    double fahrenheit;  /* Double-precision floating-point variable */
    /* Print a table header. */
    printf( "Celsius | Fahrenheit\n" );
    /* Count from 10 to 20. */
    for ( celsius = 10; celsius <= 20; celsius++ ) {
        /* Compute the Fahrenheit temperature. */
        fahrenheit = 1.8 * celsius + 32.0;
        /* Formatted table entry. */
        printf( "%7d | %6.2lf \n", celsius, fahrenheit );
    } /* for loop */
} /* main */
```

This example program does a simple task: printing a table of Celsius and Fahrenheit temperatures from 10 to 20 degrees Celsius. The for statement has three parts: the initialization of the counter variable (celsius = 10), the boundary check (celsius <= 20) that tests for loop termination, and the counter increment (celsius++) that increases the counter variable by one on each iteration. The effect is to repeat the statements enclosed in braces 11 times as celsius varies from 10 to 20. The for statement itself does not need to be terminated by a semicolon, because it uses braces to contain several statements.

The program would produce the following output if run:

```
Celsius | Fahrenheit
     10 |   50.00
     11 |   51.80
     12 |   53.60
     13 |   55.40
     14 |   57.20
     15 |   59.00
     16 |   60.80
     17 |   62.60
     18 |   64.40
     19 |   66.20
     20 |   68.00
```

The conversion control characters %7d and %6.21f are place holders for an integer value using seven places, and a floating-point (double) value having two decimal places and using six places overall. Formatting details such as these conversion control instructions are explained in more detail in Chapter 5.

Functions

Functions are used to break larger programs into smaller parts. The C language provides many built-in functions, such as printf(), used in the previous examples. Other useful functions include ones for mathematical operations (defined in <math.h>) and for string manipulation (defined in <string.h>). A function's use is defined by its name, the *parameters* it can accept, and the kind of value it returns. For system functions, these specifications are described in .h files. For user-defined functions, the programmer describes the function's attributes in a *prototype* definition before using the function, as shown in the next example.

```
/* Title : Chapter 1 Example 4 */
/* Source: ex4.c            */
/* Date  :   /  /           */
/* Author: B&W              */
/* Input : none             */
/* Output: Celsius and converted Fahrenheit temperatures */
/* Method: use Celsius to Fahrenheit conversion formula  */
/* Included header files: */
#include <stdio.h>
/* Conversion function prototype: */
double convert( int celsius_temp );
main()
{
   /* Variable declarations: */
   int celsius;         /* Integer counter variable              */
   double fahrenheit;  /* Double-precision floating-point variable */
   /* Assign a Celsius value */
   celsius = 20;
   /* Call the conversion function */
   fahrenheit = convert( celsius );
   /* Print the results */
   printf(
     "Today's temperature is %d degrees Celsius, %6.2lf degrees Fahrenheit.\n",
     celsius, fahrenheit );
} /* main */
/* Function: convert                  */
/* Parameters: celsius_temp, int      */
/* Returns: double Fahrenheit value   */
/* Input: none                        */
/* Output: none                       */
double convert( int celsius_temp )
{
   /* Local Fahrenheit variable */
   double fahrenheit_temp;
   /* Compute Fahrenheit value and return it */
   fahrenheit_temp = 1.8 * celsius_temp + 32.0;
   return( fahrenheit_temp );
} /* convert */
```

The convert() function removes the details of converting from one temperature scale to the other from the body of the main program. The function prototype, which describes its parameters and return value, is placed in the program preamble. The function body is placed after main(); its format is similar to main(). The *parameter* passed to convert() is an int value, and the function *returns* a double. Details of parameter passing are covered in Chapter 4.

Input and Output

Input and output in C are handled by system functions. The previous examples have used printf(), which displays information on the screen. The scanf() function retrieves data from the keyboard. There are more specialized functions for character and string input and output, and there are also similar functions available for reading and writing files. The next example shows the use of scanf().

```
/* Title : Chapter 1 Example 5 */
/* Source: ex5.c              */
/* Date  :  /  /              */
/* Author: B&W                */
/* Input : Celsius value from keyboard               */
/* Output: Celsius and converted Fahrenheit temperatures */
/* Method: use Celsius to Fahrenheit conversion formula  */
/* Included header files: */
#include <stdio.h>
main()
{
   /* Variable declarations: */
   int celsius;
   double fahrenheit;
   /* Prompt the user for a celsius temperature */
   printf( "Enter a Celsius temperature to be converted: " );
   scanf( "%d", &celsius );
   /* Compute the Fahrenheit value and display both */
   fahrenheit = 1.8 * celsius + 32.0;
   printf(
     "Today's temperature is %d degrees Celsius, %lf degrees Fahrenheit.\n",
     celsius, fahrenheit );
} /* main */
```

The scanf() function will read an integer value from the keyboard and pass this value back in celsius. In order to do this, scanf() needs &celsius, which is a *pointer* to (that is, the address of) the variable celsius. The programmer is in charge of checking for input errors. Chapter 5 discusses input and output details.

Arrays

An *array* is a list or table of values of the same type. Each entry in the table is *indexed* by a position number. Arrays are accessed either sequentially or in random order. In the next example, Celsius temperatures are stored in an array of int values. These Celsius temperatures might be experimental readings taken at different times.

```
/* Title : Chapter 1 Example 6 */
/* Source: ex6.c              */
/* Date  :   /  /             */
/* Author: B&W                */
/* Input : a list of Celsius values from keyboard      */
/* Output: a table of Celsius and Fahrenheit temperatures */
/* Method: use Celsius to Fahrenheit conversion formula  */
/* Included header files: */
#include <stdio.h>
/* Size of temperature array: */
#define MAXSIZE 10
main()
{
    int celsius[ MAXSIZE ];      /* Celsius temperature array */
    int i;                       /* Loop counter              */
    double fahrenheit;           /* Fahrenheit temperature    */
    /* Have the user fill the Celsius temperature array */
    for ( i = 0; i < MAXSIZE; i++ ) {
       printf( "Enter Celsius temperature #%d:", i );
       scanf( "%d", &celsius[ i ] );
    }  /* for loop */
    /* Print a table header. */
    printf( " Celsius | Fahrenheit\n" );
    /* Display the temperatures */
    for ( i = 0; i < MAXSIZE; i++ ) {
       /* Formatted table entry. */
       fahrenheit = 1.8 * celsius[ i ] + 32.0;
       printf( "%9d | %6.2lf \n", celsius[ i ], fahrenheit );
    } /* for loop */
} /* main */
```

In C arrays are indexed starting from zero and ending at 1 less than the declared size. Thus the for loops that access celsius[ ] use the phrase i < MAXSIZE as the upper bound. Arrays are discussed in Chapter 7.

Also note the #define statement, used to declare a constant MAXSIZE, whose value is 10. Like the #include statement, this is not a C instruction but is necessary for constant declarations. Statements beginning with # are handled by the *C preprocessor*, which interprets such statements prior to compilation. Chapter 12 discusses this topic in more detail.

Strings

Strings are specialized arrays for storing characters. Unlike arrays of other types, strings are usually treated as single objects. For example, a name or an address can be stored in a string. Individual characters can be accessed, since strings are arrays of characters, but more often than not, strings are used as units. The next example uses two strings and one string function.

```
/* Title : Chapter 1 Example 7   */
/* Source: ex7.c                 */
/* Date  :   /  /                 */
/* Author: B&W                    */
/* Input : keyboard, name string */
/* Output: simple message         */
/* Method: none                   */
/* Included header files: */
#include <stdio.h>
#include <string.h>
/* String type definitions: */
#define STRMAX 40
typedef char MyStringType[STRMAX];
main()
{
    /* Variable declarations: */
    MyStringType yourname, mymessage;
    /* Store a message */
    strcpy( mymessage, "This example makes no reference to temperature" );
    /* Get the user's name */
    printf( "Please enter your first name: " );
    scanf( "%s", yourname );
    /* Print a message */
    printf( "%s, %s.\n", mymessage, yourname );
} /* main */
```

Notice that no ampersand is used with string variables in a `scanf()` statement. If the user entered the name Bob in response to the prompt, the output produced by the program would be

```
This example makes no reference to temperature, Bob.
```

The `strcpy()` function is one of a number of string utility functions prototyped in `<string.h>`.

The statement `typedef char MyStringType[STRMAX];` declares a new type, a string of 40 characters. The program uses two variables, `yourname` and `mymessage`, of this type. Chapter 8 discusses strings and string functions in more detail.

Records

A *record* is a group of related variables, possibly of different types. A record in C is called a `struct`. Each part or *field* of the `struct` acts like a separate variable. A record is used to keep data about a real-world object together in one variable. Chapter 9 discusses the details of `struct` variables. In the next example, a `struct` type is declared to hold both Celsius and Fahrenheit temperatures.

```
/* Title : Chapter 1 Example 8 */
/* Source: ex8.c            */
/* Date  :   /  /           */
/* Author: B&W              */
/* Input : Celsius value from keyboard                 */
/* Output: Celsius and converted Fahrenheit temperatures */
/* Method: use Celsius to Fahrenheit conversion formula  */
/* Included header files: */
#include <stdio.h>
typedef struct {        /* Temperature record definition: */
    int celsius;        /*     Celsius temperature         */
    double fahrenheit;  /*     Fahrenheit temperature      */
} TemperatureRec;
main()
{
    /* Variable declarations: */
    TemperatureRec current;  /* Current temperature */
    /* Prompt the user for a Celsius temperature */
    printf( "Enter a Celsius temperature to be converted: " );
    scanf( "%d", &current.celsius );
    /* Compute the Fahrenheit value and display both */
    current.fahrenheit = 1.8 * current.celsius + 32.0;
    printf(
      "Today's temperature is %d degrees Celsius, %lf degrees Fahrenheit.\n",
      current.celsius, current.fahrenheit );
} /* main */
```

One variable, a record of type TemperatureRec, is declared in the main program. It has two fields, which are accessed with the syntax current.celsius and current.fahrenheit. This record can be passed to functions, carrying both pieces of temperature information. Arrays of structs can also be declared. Chapter 9 also discusses the use of binary files to store and retrieve records.

Among the other topics discussed in later chapters are the following. Chapters 6 and 11 cover several software engineering topics, including program design techniques and data structure design. Linked lists and shell script programming are covered in Chapter 10. Chapters 13 and 14 discuss advanced C programming techniques, including processes and inter-process communication. See each individual chapter for definitions of these terms.

Introduction to UNIX

UNIX is an *operating system* for computers—that is, it is a program that manages the computer's resources (the CPU, main memory, input and output channels, and so on) and makes the computer usable by humans. There are many other operating systems in existence—for example, DOS and OS/2 are operating systems for microcomputers. Attributes that make UNIX interesting are its portability (it is used on microcomputers, workstations, and mainframes); the fact that it supports multiple users at a given time (unlike DOS) and *multiprogramming* (in which many programs or *processes* are resident in memory and compete for the machine's resources); and, of course, its current popularity in the marketplace.

The UNIX material in this book can help you become an efficient user of UNIX. What it will not do is teach about networking with UNIX, system internals, or how to be a UNIX system administrator—in short, about how to become a UNIX guru. These are beyond the scope of this text. However, it will enable you to get useful work done on a UNIX system and will familiarize you with the many tools and commands available in UNIX.

Brief History

The ancestor of UNIX was MULTICS, an operating system that was a joint venture of Massachusetts Institute of Technology, AT&T, and General Electric. MULTICS was a large, multiple-user, time-sharing system that did not gain much acceptance outside its development environment. When AT&T withdrew from the MULTICS project around 1969, Ken Thompson set about developing a small version of MULTICS in assembly language on an unused computer at AT&T, calling his system UNIX as a pun on the ancestor. Dennis Ritchie soon joined in the project, and UNIX was rewritten in the C language. UNIX and C have been joined since their beginnings at AT&T [Tanenbaum].

The UNIX system was developed internally at AT&T, but because of legal constraints, AT&T could not market it. Starting in 1974, UNIX was licensed to universities. After the breakup of AT&T in 1984, a subsidiary was created to market UNIX. The result of all this was at least three distinct strains of UNIX: Seventh Edition (and later), from Bell Research; Berkeley or BSD, from the University of California at Berkeley; and System V from AT&T. The latter two, however, were dominant. There were also other commercial versions—AIX from IBM, Ultrix from DEC, and SunOS/Solaris from Sun Microsystems, to name a few. In order to try to unify the market, vendors agreed to merge System V and BSD into one standard UNIX. The attempt was short-lived, however, because the vendors again split into two worlds: the AT&T/Sun version of System V (under various names) versus the Open Software Foundation version, which combines IBM's AIX with DEC, Hewlett-Packard, and others [Tanenbaum]. As pundits have observed, the beauty of standards is in having so many standards to choose from.

What impact does this have on the average user? Fortunately, not much. From the point of view of everyday use, all of these versions will pretty much look and act alike. Differences will arise, however, in choosing hardware (for example, AIX is not available on a Sun workstation); in choosing graphical user interfaces (Motif from the Open Software Foundation products, OpenWindows from Sun); and in choosing application software, which sometimes requires the use of one particular version of UNIX. If any differences apply to the examples in this book, they will be noted. Also, Chapter 14 discusses some system-dependent issues.

Using the UNIX Information

In order to make the best use of the information on UNIX discussed in this and other chapters, the following strategy is suggested. First, read through the material in these sections in its entirety before sitting down at a computer terminal or workstation. After you have thought about the concepts discussed, try out the commands at a computer. This can be done by using the same material as a guide, by using the tutorial review problems at the end of this chapter, or simply by trying out the commands on your own. Be sure to look for possible problem areas (some of which are pointed out in the tutorials).

Keep in mind that there may be differences between this text and your environment. The material presented here assumes that a character-based terminal will be used, which is the traditional UNIX environment. Most systems today, especially workstation systems, are based on some graphical user interface, such as the Sun OpenWindows environment. In such an environment, several windows can be opened, each of which is equivalent to a character terminal. In addition, there are often graphical tools that supersede some of the UNIX commands, making interaction with the system more user-friendly. See Chapter 14 for details, but remember that you are responsible for learning the quirks of the local environment. The local system administrator or other local users can give good advice.

Logging In and Out

UNIX, like other mainframe and workstation operating systems but unlike most personal computer operating systems, requires that users obtain access privileges through the system administrator. A UNIX account is identified by an identification name and a password, which must be entered in order to gain access to the system.

Login

The *login* procedure involves two pieces of information: a *user id* and a *password*. The system administrator assigns the user id when creating an account on a UNIX system. The user id is usually associated with the user's name, as in bob, but it may contain extra information, as in janew112. Note that UNIX commands are *case-sensitive,* and input is normally expected in lower case; this is probably true for most user ids. The password may also be assigned at first by the administrator, perhaps to some generic string like newuser. You can change your password after you log in.

To log in to a UNIX system, the login prompt must be visible on the screen:

```
login:
```

Type your user id on the login line (and press the enter or return key). The following line should then appear:

```
Password:
```

Type your password and press the enter or return key. The password's characters will *not* appear on the screen when they are typed. The system checks the id and password. If it finds a problem, an error message is printed and you can try again. Typing mistakes are common, especially on the password, so don't give up. (If, after several attempts, you are still unsuccessful, talk to your system administrator for help.) If the login is successful, some standard system messages may be printed along with the message of the day. The former doesn't usually change, but the latter often contains important and timely new information for users.

At the first login, you should change your password to a secret word. In general, passwords are from six to eight characters long and may contain special characters such as question marks or parentheses. It is a good idea (for security reasons) to use one or more special characters in a password. Many users use something easy and obvious—a spouse's name, say, or the digits of a birthdate. These may be guessed by unscrupulous outsiders trying to gain illegal access to your system. On the other hand, a password must be remembered, so random characters are not a good idea, either.

Entering Commands

UNIX handles user commands through a *command interpreter*, a special interface program that processes commands entered at the keyboard. After you log in, a *command prompt* (a symbol that indicates the interpreter is ready for a command to be entered) will be shown, which may look like this:

```
%
```

or

```
machine %
```

where `machine` is the name of this particular UNIX system. Note, though, that the command prompt may be different. We will assume that the *C shell* is being used as the command interpreter (the program that UNIX uses to process the commands you type). There are other command interpreters, including the Bourne shell and the Korn shell; if one of these is in use, there will be minor differences in how some commands operate from what is presented here (alternatively, the C shell may be started by typing the command `csh`).

After the command prompt appears, the system is waiting for a command to be typed. Commands usually result in the system doing some work and printing the results on the screen. Unless otherwise noted, when the term "print" is used, it means output shown on the screen, not a printer; sending output to the printer will be discussed later. After typing a command, press the return or enter key.

To change your password, type the command **passwd** (note the spelling and the use of lower case) at the command prompt. The system will respond by prompting for the current password, then for the new password, and finally to repeat the new password as a check. If all is successful, the new password will be in force at the next login.

Special Keys

When typing commands and running programs in UNIX, you must be able to deal with typing mistakes and to interrupt executing programs. There are special keystrokes for handling these operations. They can be set by the user, and therefore may vary in different environments. Each of the three basic operations is associated with a character. With their most common association, they are (see Figure 1.1).

- The *kill* character (control-U, that is, holding down the control key and the U key simultaneously), which removes the current command
- The *erase* character (control-H), which backs up one space in the current command
- The *interrupt* character (control-C), which stops the execution of a running program

To control the associations of keys and operations, the **stty** command is used. Typing

```
stty -a
```

will show the current settings for a terminal. For example, to change the interrupt character to control-Q and the erase character to control-N, the command is

```
stty intr ^Q erase ^N
```

where the caret character represents the unprintable control key on the screen and in Figure 1.1. This line typically is inserted into the `.cshrc` file, which is located in the user's home directory. `.cshrc` stores user preferences and other system commands that customize the user's working environment.

There are two keystrokes for controlling the scrolling of information on the screen. Control-S stops scrolling, and control-Q resumes it. Some terminals react slowly to these commands or may send information to the screen in such a large chunk that the command is too late to have the desired effect. If you press control-S, remember that control-Q must be typed to undo it, even if the scrolling is finished. A terminal can appear "hung" if this is forgotten.

Getting Help

The command line prompt environment of UNIX is not very user-friendly. There are two basic commands to get help, though. The first, **man**, prints the manual page (often referred to simply as the "man page") for a specific command. For example,

```
man passwd
```

will tell how to use the `passwd` command. A manual page can be quite long, containing more than one screenful of information. If so, one screenful will be displayed at a time, and the system will wait for you to press the space bar (to get another screenful), d (to scroll forward one-half page), return (for one more line), b (to scroll backwards one screenful), or q (to quit). Note that it is not necessary to press the return or enter key after the space, d, b, or q.

The information in a manual page is complete for a given command, but it is not always easy to read or digest, and it is assumed that its information can be placed in context—not something that a beginning user can always do. In addition, it is assumed that you know the command itself, so questions like "How do I see what files are in this directory?" are not directly answerable.

Common Control Characters

^U	Kill current line
^H	Erase one character
^C	Interrupt running program
^S	Stop scrolling
^Q	Resume scrolling

Figure 1.1   Some common control settings

The second help command is **apropos**. It also needs a word to work with, but the word need not be an actual command. For example,

```
apropos file
```

will print a list of all commands that deal with files. It is then up to the user to find the specific command. This again may not be all that helpful—a common UNIX word like "file" can produce dozens of lines on files, few of which will be useful or even understandable to a beginner. This state of affairs keeps UNIX guidebook authors busy.

Some systems now offer other methods of obtaining help. For example, GNU's `info` command offers a menu-based help utility, and commercial versions of UNIX often have proprietary help utilities.

Logout

To end a login session, type **logout** at the command prompt. This will cause the login prompt to appear on the screen again. (Note: When you use a graphical user interface such as OpenWindows, a login session is probably inside a window. In this case, the logout command may cause the error message "Not a login shell" to appear. The proper command is then **exit**.)

Working with Files

Manipulating UNIX files is covered in three parts: simple file operations (this chapter), editing files (Chapter 2 and advanced material in Chapter 7), and managing directories (Chapter 3). Since easy access to files is one of the basic organizing principles of UNIX, files will be discussed in other places in this book, too.

There are many files already stored in the file system before you log in for the first time. Over time, a user will create files for various purposes—source files containing program code, data files, executable files, and so on. There are a number of UNIX commands that help manage these files.

The file system is organized in a tree structure (see Chapter 3 for more details), in which a *directory* contains files and may also contain other directories. Associated with each user's account is a part of that structure reserved for personal use, called the *home directory*. The *working directory* (or, equivalently, *current directory*) is the directory that is currently in use. Until we discuss how to change the working directory, your home directory and your working directory will be the same.

Listings of Directories

To see what files exist in a directory, the command `ls` is used. It causes a listing of the names of the files in the current directory to be printed in alphabetical order. For example, after logging in for the first time, `ls` may print nothing, since no files have been created yet.

Almost every UNIX command can be augmented by two things: *flags* (also known as *command options*), which denote optional behavior, and *parameters*, which are actual items of information that the command uses as input. Flags are usually one-letter codes preceded by a dash (or by a plus sign or by no character; this varies by command). Common commands can have many such flags, of which only a few are often used or remembered. For example, `ls` can take the `-a` flag, as in

```
ls -a
```

Note the space between the s and the - and the lack of a space between the - and the a. This option causes all files, including the so-called *hidden files,* to be listed along with the regular files. Names of hidden files start with the period character, such as .cshrc or .login. Such files are not so much secret as just placed out of the way of normal use. They usually contain some information that is initialized once and rarely changed. The file .login is such a file; it contains commands that the operating system runs at each login. The files . and .. are directory files that point to the current directory and the current directory's parent, respectively.

Another flag for ls is -l or long listing. It produces a listing of file names plus extra information about each file, such as who owns it, size, when it was last modified, and permission codes (see Chapter 3 for more details).

Some commands allow option flags to be combined; others do not. For example, ls permits combining the -a and -l flags. Any one of

```
ls -a -l
```

or

```
ls -l -a
```

or

```
ls -al
```

or

```
ls -la
```

will produce a long listing of all files, including hidden files.

Some commands also accept parameters to be acted on. We've seen that man expects a command to look up. The ls command, for example, can be given a directory name as a parameter. The contents of that directory will be printed rather than the contents of the working directory. The lack of any parameters means that the command will use a default value as the argument. In the case of ls, the working directory is the default. The command

```
ls /usr/bin
```

will print the contents of one of the system's directories, called /usr/bin, where some of the system's command files are located.

Contents of Files

To see what's in a file, there are two commands, **cat** and **more**. The cat command prints the contents of a file to the screen. If the file has more lines than the screen can display at once, some of the lines scroll off the screen. The more command prints one screenful at a time, then waits for either the enter key (to get one more line from the file), the space bar (to get one more screenful of lines from the file), d (to scroll one-half screen), b (to scroll backwards one screen), or q (to quit). (Recall that the man command had the same options.) Each command needs a file name as parameter. The line

```
cat .cshrc
```

will show the contents of the file .cshrc, located in your home directory. This file contains commands run by the system when a *shell* is started. (A shell, such as the C shell mentioned earlier, is the system's program to interpret commands; when a user logs in, a shell is started to read and carry out commands. Both .cshrc and .login are read at this time.)

The command

```
more .login
```

will show the contents of the login startup file.

To print the contents of a file on a printer, use **lpr**, as in

```
lpr .cshrc
```

which would print the contents of .cshrc. There are often system-specific details concerning the use of printers. Ask the system administrator for the correct method of printing at your site.

Manipulating Files

In order to have a temporary file to work with, suppose the command

```
man more > myfile
```

has been entered. Rather than putting the man page (manual page) for more on the screen, this creates a file called myfile in the working directory. (Chapter 5 discusses the use of the redirection character > to create files.) To check that it's there, use the ls command, and to see what's in it, use the cat or more command: cat myfile or more myfile.

To rename a file, the command **mv** (move) is used. It takes two parameters: the first is the old name of the file, and the second is the new name. For example, the command to rename myfile to ourfile is

```
mv myfile ourfile
```

The result of this command can be checked with ls. Care should be exercised with mv—for example, don't rename .login or .cshrc, since the system requires files of that name to exist.

To copy a file, the command **cp** (copy) is used. The syntax is the same as in mv. To create a second copy of ourfile, type

```
cp ourfile yourfile
```

A check of the directory using ls -l should show both file names and equal sizes.

The command **rm** deletes a file. Once deleted, files are generally unrecoverable (unless your system has regular backups on tape—but even then, the deleted file must have been saved on the tape, and a request must be made to the system administrator to restore the file), so be careful. The command

```
rm yourfile
```

will delete our second copy of the test file. A useful option for `rm` is the `-i` (interactive) flag. Using this, the system will double-check before removal of the targeted file by prompting `Remove file?`, to which you can answer `y` or `n`. For example,

```
rm -i ourfile
Remove ourfile? n
```

would not remove the original test file.

References

Kernighan, Brian W., and Dennis M. Ritchie, *The C Programming Language,* 2nd ed., Prentice Hall, Englewood Cliffs, NJ, 1988.

Tanenbaum, Andrew S., *Modern Operating Systems,* Prentice Hall, Englewood Cliffs, NJ, 1992.

Chapter Summary

■ UNIX Commands

`login`	Start a shell, such as the C shell (an environment in which the user can execute UNIX commands)
`logout`	Stop the shell program
`ls ToPort`	List `ToPort`; that is, list visible files in the directory named `ToPort`
`ls`	List visible files in the working directory
`ls -a`	List all files in the working directory
`ls -l`	List visible files using long form of listing (include sizes, dates, and other information)
`stty -a`	Show all terminal settings
`cat NMouse`	Show all contents of the file `NMouse`
`more ToCome`	Show contents of the file `ToCome`, allowing the user to scroll forward (space, d, or Enter), scroll backward (b), or quit (q) at any time
`lpr AlphabetSoup`	Print the contents of the file `AlphabetSoup`
`cp oldfile newfile`	Copy the contents of `oldfile` to `newfile`; there will be two files with identical contents
`mv oldfile newfile`	Move the contents of `oldfile` to `newfile`; this is a renaming command, so there will still be exactly one file
`rm WaxBuildup`	Remove the file `WaxBuildup` from the working directory
`rm -i WaxBuildup`	Remove `WaxBuildup` interactively, prompting the user to confirm the action
`man cc`	Allow the user to scroll through the manual page describing the UNIX command `cc`
`apropos passwd`	Show UNIX commands related to `passwd`

Review Problems

1. (Manual and Password Tutorial) Answer each question and complete each instruction by executing the indicated UNIX command(s).
   a) What is the UNIX system response to a request for a nonexistent manual page? (man pass)
   b) What is the UNIX response to a request for a manual page whose command is misspelled? (man password)
   c) How does the manual describe the purpose of passwd? What percentage of the manual is displayed on the first screen? (man passwd)
   d) Change your password, keeping a record of your new password in a secure place. (passwd)
   e) Pressing the b key causes the screen to scroll backward. Try this as you read about the manual command.(man man)
   f) How many system commands deal with passwords? (First try apropos password, then try apropos passwd)
   g) What is the purpose of the cc command? (man cc)
   h) Are there many system commands with the string cc embedded in their name? (apropos cc)
2. (Elementary File Tutorial) Answer each question after executing the accompanying UNIX command(s).
   a) How many files are in the working directory? For each file, what is the file name and the date of the most recent change? (ls and ls -al)
   b) How many visible files are in directory /usr/bin? (ls /usr/bin | more) *Note:* The pipe command (|) is discussed later; in conjunction with the more command, it is useful for scrolling through long directory listings.
   c) Executing the ls command without a parameter to specify the directory produces a listing of which directory? (ls)
   d) What is the UNIX system response to a cat command with a misspelled file name? (cat cshrc)
   e) Why might the cat command not be a good choice for viewing some files? (cat .cshrc)
   f) What is the purpose of the file .cshrc? (more .cshrc and man .cshrc)
   g) What file is added to the working directory by the command man more > myfile? (ls, man more > myfile, and ls)
   h) Are any files added to or deleted from the working directory when the mv command is executed? (ls, mv myfile ourfile, and ls)
   i) Does ourfile contain the same information as the manual page for the command more? (more ourfile)
   j) If the file name parameter is missing, does the rm command remove any file(s) from your working directory? (rm, ls, rm -i, and ls)
   k) Does rm ourfile remove any file(s) from the working directory? (rm -i ourfile and ls)
   l) What happens if you attempt to remove a nonexistent file? (rm nonexistentfile and ls)
3. (Special Keys Tutorial) Execute the following commands related to the terminal settings for special keys.
   a) Enter the command stty -a and carefully record the current terminal settings for the kill, erase, and interrupt keys.
   b) Practice using kill, erase, and interrupt keys.
   c) Reset the erase key to control-N.
   d) Verify that control-N (upper case) is now an erase key.
   e) Determine whether the previous erase key still works.
   f) Determine whether the control-n (lower case) works as an erase key.

g) Log out and log in again; then determine whether the system has kept track of your terminal setting for the erase key. If it has, change the erase key back to its original setting and verify this change.

4. These questions discuss visible and hidden files.
   a) What is the purpose of beginning a file name with a period?
   b) What UNIX command produces a listing of all files (both visible and hidden) in the working directory?
   c) What UNIX command produces a listing of only the visible files in directory `/usr/bin`?

5. In each part of this exercise the command `cp .cshrc ShellCopy` is followed by two additional commands. Execute each command sequence, but first predict and explain the system response (recalling that UNIX is case-sensitive).
   a) Execute the sequence

      ```
      cp .cshrc ShellCopy,  cp shellcopy AnotherCopy,  rm AnotherCopy.
      ```

   b) Execute the sequence

      ```
      cp .cshrc ShellCopy,  cp shellcopy AnotherCopy,  rm shellcopy.
      ```

   c) Execute the sequence

      ```
      cp .cshrc ShellCopy,  cp ShellCopy AnotherCopy,  more AnotherCopy.
      ```

6. (Computer Investigation) Perform this investigation to determine what happens when the copy command is executed twice.
   a) Find a relatively short file in your working directory (use `ls -al`).
   b) Make a copy of this file, using `temp` as the name of the copy.
   c) Execute the command `cp temp duplicate`, and then use `ls -l` and `more` to verify that the two files, `temp` and `duplicate`, have the same length and the same content.
   d) Again execute the command `cp temp duplicate`, and then use `ls` and `more` to determine whether the two files, `temp` and `duplicate`, still have the same length and the same content.

7. (Computer Investigation) Investigate flags for the commands `ls`, `rm`, and `more`:
   a) Find all flags for the commands `ls` and `rm`.
   b) Determine whether the command `more` has any flags.

8. Consider the following C program:

   ```
   /* Included header files: */
   #include <stdio.h>
   main()
   {
     for ( i = 1; i <= 10; i++ )
       printf( "%2d", i );
   }
   ```

   a) What is missing from this program?
   b) If missing parts were added to the program, what would be the output?
   c) Write a well-documented program whose output is the integers from 1 to 4, with each integer on a single line.

9. Name four kinds of C statements that are not terminated by a semicolon.

Chapter 2

Programs

Every programming language has a set of rules, called the *syntax* of the language, that govern how legal programs are constructed. This chapter discusses the syntax of C, showing the basic layout of programs and the use of variables, assignment statements, and arithmetic operations for simple calculations. UNIX topics include the use of the vi editor to create programs and the cc command to compile C programs.

Program Format

A program in C can be made up of many components, sometimes spread over several files. Here we will look at the format of simple programs that are small enough to be contained in one file. No definite rule governs whether one file or many files are used for a C program. One rule of thumb is to break large programs into smaller pieces; another is to group program pieces by functionality. Later chapters will discuss this more fully.

The following short program is used to illustrate program format. You may also refer to the programs presented in Chapter 1 for further examples. Figure 2.1 shows the three main parts.

```
/* Title : Chapter 2 Example 1 */
/* Source: ex21.c             */
/* Date  : __/__/__           */
/* Author: B&W                */
/* Input : none.              */
/* Output: The string "Hello world!" is printed 10 times. */
/* Method: Simple loop */
/* This is the preamble section of the program. */
/* Included header files: */
```

```
#include <stdio.h>
/* Next comes a constant definition: */
#define MAXSIZE 10
/* main is next. */
main() {
   /* Variable declarations go here: */
   int count;   /* Counter variable. */
   /* Some sample statements: */
   for( count = 0; count < MAXSIZE; count++ ) {
     printf( "%d : ", count );
     printf( "Hello, world!\n" );
   }
   printf( "All done.\n" );
   /* The closing brace is the end of main. */
}
```

— Preamble —
   #include statements
   #define statements
   Type declarations

— Main Program —
   main()
   {

     Variable declarations

     C code]

   }

— User-Defined Functions —
   (each has same format as main())

Figure 2.1   General C program format

The preamble to a program—the lines that come before the main section—is used to make declarations. If a program will need to use definitions found in another file, the name of that file is given in an `#include` statement. Such files are either standard, such as `stdio.h`, or user-defined. The format for standard header files is shown in

```
#include <stdio.h>
```

where the angle brackets signal the compiler to look for `stdio.h` in a predefined directory (usually `/usr/include`). Chapter 4 further discusses the use of standard header files. For now, you should always use the preceding `include` statement, which is needed to do simple input and output.

For *user-defined* header files, the name is given in quotes, as

```
#include "defs.h"
```

which is correct when the header file is in the same directory as the program file. Pathnames, which give directory names and the file name, may be used, as in

```
#include "../defs.h"
```

which is one directory higher than the program file's, or

```
#include "/usr/home/jane27/prog1/defs.h"
```

which uses an absolute pathname to locate the file. (See Chapter 3 for a full discussion of the file system and its naming techniques.) Chapter 4 discusses when and why to create such files; they are not needed here, except to note that the rest of the preamble (see next paragraph) is sometimes put into include files.

Other types of statements usually placed in the preamble are the `#define`, used to declare constants (discussed later in this chapter); function prototypes, which tell the compiler what user-defined functions will be used (discussed in Chapter 4); and type declarations (discussed in Chapter 7).

The rest of a C program consists of functions, each of which has a similar structure. One of these is usually called `main()` and is executed before any others. It is customary for this special function to be placed before the others, although this is not a requirement.

A function header, even `main()`, may contain parameter declarations, but details of this are left to Chapter 4. The body of the function is enclosed in braces (`{` and `}`). Inside the function, variable declarations are made first, followed by the C statements that do the function's job. A simple C statement is terminated with a semicolon. Some statements, such as `if`, may have a group of statements following them. Each statement in the group ends with a semicolon. The group is enclosed in braces and does not have a terminating semicolon.

No special statement is needed to terminate a program. Functions often contain a `return` statement, which is the last statement executed in the function, but `main()` does not. The closing right brace is the end of `main()`, and it may be the end of the program file if no user-defined functions follow. If there are such functions, they come next in whatever order the programmer wants.

Simple Syntax

Each C language construct, such as `for` and `switch`, has specific syntax rules that will be covered when the construct is introduced (mostly in Chapter 3). This section discusses basic syntax rules common to all C statements.

Statements

Several kinds of statements can occur in a C program. Simple statements in the C language, as we have seen, must be terminated by a semicolon:

```
printf( "All done.\n" );
```

Simple statements are usually placed on separate physical lines in a program file. Because the semicolon is the actual terminator, though, it is legal *but not recommended* to place more than one statement on the same physical line, as

```
count++; printf( "%d\n", count );
```

Some commands, such as `for`, may be followed either by a single statement or by a group of statements (grouping is discussed in the next section). In the former case, the statement is again terminated with a semicolon:

```
for ( i = 0; i < 10; i ++ )
  printf( "%d \n", i );
```

A common mistake is to end the `for` statement with a semicolon, too:

```
for ( i = 0; i < 10; i ++ );
  printf( "%d \n", i );
```

This is legal but has a very different effect from the previous example: the `printf` statement is no longer a part of the `for` construct, which now has no body.

Another type of simple statement is that handled by the *C preprocessor.* Any statement that uses the # prefix, such as `#include` and `#define`, is of this type. Thus, these statements are not technically C statements and are *not* terminated with a semicolon. The statement

```
#define MAXSIZE 10;
```

is incorrect and results in an error message.

Comments in a C program are surrounded by /* and */. Any text inside these markers is ignored by the C compiler and not executed. Comments are used to explain the program to the reader. A comment may be placed on a line by itself, such as

```
/* Variable declarations go here: */
```

or may occur at the end of a C statement, such as

```
int count;    /* Counter variable. */
```

or may be embedded inside a C statement, as in

```
int count,    /* Loop counter variable. */
   amount,    /* Number on hand.        */
   total;     /* Summation variable.    */
```

where what might appear to be three C statements is actually just one spread over three lines. Nesting of comments, as

```
/* This is a /* nested */ comment (and is illegal). */
```

is illegal.

Comment statements are part of the *documentation* of a program. Documentation styles vary among individuals and institutions. In software engineering, program development follows several distinct stages, and each stage is recorded in its own set of documents, such as Software Requirements Specifications and Test Plan Specifications (see [Pressman] for more details). We now present some general guidelines for documenting software.

An entire program should be preceded by *external* documentation, telling who wrote the program and when, what changes have been made, what the purpose of the program is, the general outline of the program's design, what input the program expects, what output it produces, and what limitations are known about the program. Each function contained in the program should have a similar but shorter preliminary section telling what the function does, what parameters will be passed in and out, and when and why the function is called.

Internal documentation describes specific sections or lines of code. Type and variable declarations should be explained. Consecutive lines of code are often related to each other in purpose; these groups should be preceded by a comment. Individual lines that are important or tricky may need a comment devoted solely to them. What code needs documentation and how much of it is not always clear, but we will provide examples of documented code where possible. Generally, long examples of C code in this book will contain proper comments, but short examples may not.

Grouping

As mentioned above, C statements are sometimes grouped together inside braces. Certain C constructs either require this or allow it. For example, C functions (including `main()`) must be delimited by braces. The `for` construct may be followed either by a single statement or by a group of statements in braces. Recall that the final right brace is not terminated with a semicolon.

Data Types

The C language includes several basic data types. Variables can be declared in these types, and composite data structures may be constructed from these basic types. These simple types are discussed subsequently. To declare a variable of a certain type, the syntax is `typename variablename`. For example

```
int count;
```

was used in the foregoing example. This will allocate a memory location associated with the name `count` that can be used to store an integer. Assignment of values to variables is discussed in a later section.

Because many different kinds of computers have C compilers, there is no standard for the size and precision of the data types. Common sizes will be mentioned. A standard function, `sizeof()`, can be used to determine the actual amount of memory allocated for a data type on a given machine. Figure 2.2 shows the standard types (with sizes in bytes); see [Tanenbaum] and the review problems for more details.

Integer Types

There are four basic types of integer variables: `char`, `short`, `int`, and `long`. The first, `char`, when used without modifiers (see the discussion of `unsigned` in the following paragraph), denotes a character variable rather than an integer. The name `short` is an abbreviation for `short int`, and `long` is an abbreviation for `long int`, although these longer names are rarely used. The `int` type usually conforms in size to the word size of the computer being used, often two bytes (16 bits) or four bytes (32 bits). The `short` type is then shorter, if possible, or the `long` type is longer. On machines that use two-byte words, `short` and `int` are usually two bytes and `long` is four bytes; on machines using four bytes, `int` and `long` are usually four bytes but `short` is two bytes. The number of bits determines the precision of the type, because integers are stored in binary format.

The modifier `unsigned` may precede each of the basic integer types, and additionally the modifier `signed` may precede type `char`. Without the `unsigned` modifier, the first bit is reserved for the sign (positive or negative) of the variable. Types using `unsigned` represent only nonnegative numbers.

Type	Usual size	Range (signed)
char	1	$-128 \ldots 127$
int	4	$-32{,}768 \ldots 32{,}767$
float	4	$10^{-38} \ldots 10^{38}$
double	8	$10^{-308} \ldots 10^{308}$

Modifiers	
signed	short
unsigned	long

Figure 2.2   C types and modifiers

This means, for example, that a two-byte short integer would have sixteen bits, one of which is used as a sign bit. The remaining fifteen bits allow 2^{15} possible combinations and could be used to represent numbers in the range from -32768 to 32767. On the other hand, an unsigned short uses all sixteen bits to represent the nonnegative number and has a range from 0 to 65535. The precision of the others can be computed similarly. The type char, when used as an integer, should be preceded by either signed or unsigned. The former allows values in the range from -128 to 127, and the latter gives the range 0 to 255. The signed modifier can be used in front of the other types, but it rarely is, because it is redundant. Finally, note that when unsigned is used alone, it is an abbreviation for unsigned int.

Float Types

Three data types are used to represent floating-point (real) numbers: float, double, and long double. As with the integer types, the size of each type depends on the machine and may in fact be the same on some machines. Unlike the integers, though, a floating-point number requires two quantities to be stored. When the number is written in standard exponential form, the quantities are the mantissa (decimal part) and the exponent. For example, the number 78.412 would be written as 0.78412×10^2. Of course, the mantissa is stored as a binary fraction, and the exponent is stored as a binary integer.

The float type often uses four bytes, of which three bytes are allocated to the decimal part and one byte to the exponent. In decimal (not binary) terms, this gives about six significant digits in the mantissa and a range of about -38 to $+38$ in the exponent. The double type usually uses eight bytes, giving more precision and range. The double is the type used for most standard functions in the mathematics library, described in Chapter 4. The long double type is often implemented using the same size as the double.

Character Types

The char type has already been mentioned with the integer types. By itself, it is used to represent single-character values, not integers. The connection here is that the char type actually stores an integer code for the character. The coding scheme (called the *collating sequence* for that character set) usually used is the ASCII set (for American Standard Code for Information Interchange). It associates the numbers 0 through 127 (which can be stored in seven bits) with various letters, numerals, punctuation marks, control characters, and the like. (Using the eighth bit to extend the size of the set from 128 to 255 is often supported, but we will ignore these characters here.) For example, the letter A is coded as 65, and + is 43.

String variables will be discussed in full in Chapter 8, but we mention them here in order to use them in simple examples. A *string* is an ordered collection of single characters (that is, an array of characters). The length of this collection must be specified using the square bracket notation of arrays. For example, a 10-character string is declared

```
char str[10];
```

The variable str has a useful length of *nine* characters, not 10, however, since one character will be used by the *string terminator* character, \0. (See the discussion of assignment later in this chapter.) Strings can be thought of as units rather than as collections of single characters, or the individual characters can be the focus of attention as well, according to what is needed at a given time in a given program.

Constants

Constants are numeric or character values used in a program. *Literal* constants are actual numbers or characters such as 10 or a. *Symbolic* constants are named constants associated with literal constants. Literal constants are sometimes necessary in programs, but their use should be minimized in favor of symbolic constants.

Literal constants are of the basic types discussed in the preceding section. Character constants must be enclosed in single quotes, as 'a'. String constants are delimited by the double quote character, as in "dog". The floating-point constants can have either regular decimal notation or exponential notation. Thus, the constant 78.412 can also be expressed as 0.78412e+2 or as 784.12e-1. Floating-point constants are treated as type double. Integer constants have their usual form (such as 10). Several minor points apply to integers:

- Do not use commas in any numeric constants (this applies to floating-point numbers, too).
- Octal (base-eight) constants are preceded by a zero, as in 071.
- Hexadecimal (base-sixteen) constants are preceded by the characters 0x, as in 0x4A2, using digits A through F to represent 10 through 15.

Symbolic constants can be declared in two ways. The first method, which was illustrated in the earlier example, uses the #define statement. This associates a logical name with a value, as in

```
#define MAXSIZE 10
```

which defines the name MAXSIZE as the integer 10. Symbolic constants are often in upper case to differentiate them from variables, but this is not required. Note that there is no way of telling what the type of this constant is other than the way the number 10 was written. If the value had been written as 10.0, then MAXSIZE would be considered double. Symbolic character and string constants are possible, too, as shown in

```
#define RESPONSE 'C'
#define PROMPT   "Enter C to continue:"
```

A useful set of definitions is

```
#define FALSE 0
#define TRUE  1
```

which associate symbolic constants with the C boolean values, 0 to indicate false and 1 to indicate true (although any value other than 0 indicates true).

The second way of declaring a constant looks similar to a variable declaration, but uses the keyword const as a modifier. For example,

```
const int MAXNUM = 10;
```

declares a constant and assigns it an initial value. This method, not supported in K&R C, assigns constants a type, unlike the `#define` method. However, the first method remains the more popular of the two.

Assignment and Operators

Once a variable has been declared, it can be assigned a value. This might be a constant, literal or symbolic, or it might be the value of an arithmetic expression. Variables can be reassigned many times over the course of a program's execution. We first discuss the arithmetic operators used to construct expressions.

Arithmetic Operators

C supports the usual arithmetic operations via the following operators. Except where noted, these operators can be applied to variables of either integer or floating-point types.

The sign operators + and - work on a single variable or expression. The plus operator is not really needed, since x and +x have the same meaning. The plus operator usually occurs in front of literal constants, as in +1.41 to highlight that the constant is positive. The minus operator has the effect of multiplying the following expression by -1, so the x and -x have opposite signs. Again, this operator is often used in literal constants, as in

```
#define MINNUM -10
```

Addition, subtraction, and multiplication of the expressions x and y are expressed as x + y, x - y, and x * y, respectively. The division operator / applies as usual to floating-point expressions, as in 14.2/1008.08. When applied to two integer operands, this operator yields the whole number part of the quotient, and the remainder is discarded. For example, 14/4 evaluates to 3. Another division-related operator is used to capture the remainder. 14%4 evaluates to 2, the remainder when 4 is divided into 14. It is an error to apply the % operator to floating-point expressions. In any division expression, a run-time error results if the denominator is zero.

Two other operators, ++ and --, may only be applied to integer variables. The first is the increment operator, which adds 1 to the current value of the variable to which it is applied. For example, if `count` is an `int` and currently has the value 5, then `count++;` increases the value of `count` to 6. Similarly, the decrement operator -- decreases a variable's value by 1. If we now write `count--`, then `count` will decrease to 5. These operators may either follow or precede the variable they are applied to, so that the effects of `count++;` and `++count;` are equivalent. However, if these operators are used within expressions, we must pay attention to how they are evaluated. The prefix version, `++count`, causes `count` to be incremented *before* it is used in the expression, while the postfix version, `count++`, uses the *original* value of `count` and then increments its value. For example, if `count` has the value 10, the expression `result = ++count;` will store 11 in `result`, but the expression `result = count++;` will store 10 instead. Both versions, of course, increment `count` to 11. To avoid confusion, we adopt two conventions:

- The increment operators will not be used inside expressions.
- Only the postfix version will be used.

Expressions can contain more than one operator, as in 4 * 5 + 8. Two questions arise when considering such expressions:

- In what order are the operators evaluated?
- What is the effect of mixed types in the expression?

The first question will be answered shortly in the section on grouping and precedence. The answer to the second is that an expression's type is determined by the component of greatest *order*.

The standard data types are ordered in the following way:

```
unsigned char
signed char
short
int
long
unsigned long
float
double
long double
```

Usually, expressions are *promoted* from lesser types to greater types according to this ordering. The first promotion that would take place is to convert unsigned char, signed char, and short to int. This takes place regardless of mixing; integer arithmetic is performed on ints at a minimum. Promotions to higher types then take place as needed, and the entire expression has the highest needed type. Note that these conversions are temporary and do not affect the values stored in any variables in the expression. For example, suppose these declarations were made:

```
short s;
int   i;
float f;
double d;
```

The following expressions would then have the indicated types:

```
s * d           double
i + s           int
d - f           double
s + i + f + d   double
```

It is possible to force a type conversion when needed; this process is called *type casting*. A cast is forced by placing the desired type in parentheses in front of the expression to be cast. A common example occurs in division problems. Recall that integer division using / results in an integer answer. We can force floating-point division to occur by casting the numerator, denominator, or both to a floating-point type. For example, if both i and j are ints, the expression i / j results in an integer answer. The expression i / (float) j casts j to float, which forces a promotion of i to float, and the operation is then floating-point division. Be careful with parentheses, though. A type cast has a lower precedence than any of the arithmetic operators. For example, in the expression (float) i / j, the division is performed first, so it is integer division, and then this whole number answer is cast to a `float`.

Variable Assignment

The simplest method for assigning a value to a variable is to use the = assignment symbol. The statements

```
int count;
count = 43;
```

store the value 43 in the integer variable `count`. Variables may be used to assign values to other variables, as in

```
float x, y;
x = 43.2;
y = x;
```

which first assigns 43.2 to x, then copies this same value into y. Character variables are assigned character constants in a similar way:

```
char letter;
letter = 'h';
```

String variables, however, must be assigned constant values using the `strcpy()` function, which requires the statement `#include <string.h>` at the beginning of a program. Its use is

```
char name[ 10 ];
strcpy( name, "Leon" );
```

These statements declare a string variable, `name`, which can hold a string of nine or fewer characters, and then copy the string `Leon` into `name`. Recall that the effective length is nine characters, not ten, because one character must be reserved for the string terminator mentioned earlier. The `strcpy()` function automatically places the terminator after the `n` in `Leon`. Failure to account for the space needed by the terminator is a common cause of program errors, as in `strcpy( name, "Goldilocks" );` since `strcpy()` fails to detect such improper assignments. In fact, `strcpy()` will not detect an error even if a string constant more than 10 characters long is assigned to `name`. The statement

```
strcpy( name, "Rumpelstiltskin" );
```

will destroy six bytes of information somewhere without the programmer knowing anything about it.

As a short cut, initial values may be specified when variables are declared. The = operator is used here, also. For example, the declaration statement

```
int total = 0,
    count = 100;
```

assigns each of the declared integers a starting value.

When an expression, not just a constant, occurs on the right-hand side of an assignment statement, that expression is evaluated first, and the resulting value is assigned to the variable on the left side. Only a single variable is allowed on the left-hand side of an assignment statement. Recall that expressions of mixed type are allowed on the right-hand side, necessitating promotion of values to higher types. It is possible that the resulting expression's type may not match that of the variable being assigned. In this case, either a promotion or a demotion is necessary. If the right side is of lesser type than the left, the promotion follows the previously described rules. In the opposite case, the right side needs to be demoted to a lesser type, and some loss of precision may occur. For example, the statement `count = 34.2 * 1.981;`, where `count` is an `int`, requires that the right-hand side be cast into an `int`. This is accomplished by *truncation*: the floating-point expression's fractional part is discarded. Note that rounding does *not* take place; `count` will be set to 67, not 68. It may occur that the variable does not have enough precision to accept the expression, as in `s = 40000;` where `s` is of type `short`. In this case, a run-time error results.

There are several shortcut assignment operators in C. Recall the integer increment operator ++. Because this simply adds 1 to a variable, the statement `count++;` could be written as `count = count + 1;`. The shortcut assignment operators have a similar flavor. The `+=` operator is used to add a value to a variable (`count += 5;` is equivalent to `count = count + 5;`). This operator is not restricted to integer types; it can be used on floating-point types, too. Examples of the shortcut operators and their equivalent expressions are

Increment: `count += 2;` equivalent to `count = count + 2;`
Decrement: `count -= 8;` equivalent to `count = count - 8;`
Multiplication: `count *= 10;` equivalent to `count = count * 10;`
Division: `count /= 2;` equivalent to `count = count / 2;`
Remainder: `count %= 20;` equivalent to `count = count % 20;` (integer types only)

Precedence and Grouping

The expressions used in previous examples were fairly simple. Arbitrarily complex expressions can be constructed, but recall that to evaluate them, the order of evaluation of operators must be specified. Each operator must be given a priority with respect to the other operators. Also, when operators having the same priority occur more than once in an expression, the expression must be scanned either from left to right or from right to left. These *precedence rules* are presented in full in an appendix; only a simplified version is given here.

For the most part, precedence rules follow the rules of algebra. For example, multiplication is higher in priority than addition, so the expression 3 * 4 + 5 evaluates to 17, not 27. Division has the same priority as multiplication. Assignment is also considered an operation, and it has lowest priority.

Rather than trying to learn the precedence rules, it is better to show explicitly the order of operation by using grouping. Grouping in expressions is done with parentheses, which have the highest priority. For example, (3 * 4) + 5 shows that the multiplication will occur first; that form is preferred over the same expression without parentheses even though both evaluate to 17. At times, grouping is necessary rather than optional. For example, the expression 3 * (4 + 5) forces the addition to take place first, so that this expression evaluates to 27. Similarly, x + y / z is different from (x + y) / z, because the addition is done first in the latter expression.

Programs in UNIX

C programs need to be created via a text editor, then compiled and executed. In this section, we present how to create a program file, how to use the C compiler to create an executable version of the program, and then how to execute that program.

Using vi to Create Programs

A text editor is used to create a C program. A common editor on UNIX systems is **vi**, usually pronounced "vee-eye" and short for *visual*. vi is a full-screen editor with a large collection of commands, so large that most keystrokes have special meanings. Most commands are cryptic, often single keystrokes. A few are mnemonic, but most are not. While this makes it difficult to learn the commands, it is convenient for touch typers once the commands are mastered, because their hands rarely need to leave the home position. The novice user should try out all the commands on a sample file. This section presents an introduction to vi, with enough material to create and modify C programs. Chapter 7 contains material on advanced vi topics.

To start vi to create a C program file called `prog1.c`, type

```
vi prog1.c
```

The extension `.c` is required for C files. If this file did not exist before, you will now create it. If it did exist, then you will be editing the previously saved version.

When vi is running, it is in one of three states (see Figure 2.3):

- *Input mode,* in which text is typed into the file
- *Command mode,* where keystrokes are interpreted as commands, not text, and are not echoed on the screen
- *Ex mode,* indicated by a line at the bottom of the screen and used for certain commands inherited from vi's predecessor, ex

The startup state is command mode. To change from command to input mode, use any of the commands i, I, a, A, o, O; to return to command mode, press the escape key. To change from command to ex mode, type :; to return, either press the escape key (to abort the ex command) or press the return key (to execute the command). Typing the colon causes a colon to appear on the bottom line, and any text typed after that is echoed on that line. When ex commands are shown, we will always show the colon.

To quit from vi, several ex commands can be used. :wq will save the current version of the file, under the same name that was used when starting up vi, and then quit. To save the

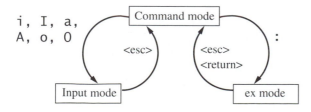

Figure 2.3 Changing states in vi

file without quitting, use :w. To save the file under a new name, type :w newname, which still leaves you editing the original file. To just plain quit without saving, :q will work only if you have not made any changes to the file. If you had changes, a warning message will appear. To quit without saving your modifications, type :q!. This is sometimes called the panic quit, and it is useful when there are incorrect changes. Figure 2.4 summarizes the write and quit commands.

When input mode is entered, any text that is typed shows up on the screen until the escape key is pushed. On some systems, the cursor changes shape or blinks while in input mode. The commands to change to input mode differ in where new text is inserted:

i begins insertion at the current cursor position.
I inserts at the beginning of the current line.
a begins immediately after the current position.
A appends at the end of the current line.
o opens a new line under the current line.
O opens a line above the current line.

In a new file these distinctions do not matter, but in existing files the cursor usually has to be positioned (see the next paragraph) before characters are inserted. While in input mode, pressing the return key will end the current line at the current position and start a new one. An existing line can be split by positioning the cursor in mid-line, then typing i followed by pressing return and escape. Also, typing control-H will backspace the cursor one position, allowing for retyping of errors.

When the file contains some text and the state is command mode, the cursor can be moved around the screen by various commands. On most keyboards, pressing the arrow keys will move the cursor one position in the indicated direction. There are other ways, too. To move the cursor one character to the right, either press the space bar or type the letter l (recall that in command mode these keystrokes are not echoed). Yes, the letter l moves the cursor to the right. The letter h effects a move to the left. The letter k moves up one line, and either the letter j or pressing the return key moves down one line. (In the days before most keyboards had arrow keys, these commands constituted an "arrow key cluster" around the home position of the right hand.) A beep usually sounds if you try to move beyond the limits of the screen. Note, though, that a file may grow in length beyond what a screen can show. In

Command	Action
:w	Save current file
:w *filename*	Save as *filename*
:q	Quit if no changes
:q!	Quit, no update
:wq	Save current file and quit

Figure 2.4   Saving files and quitting vi

this case, when a downward movement is attempted, the text will scroll up one line, showing a new line at the bottom of the screen. Similar scrolling can be done upwards in a file. To move up or down a screenful at a time, the commands control-B (for back) and control-F (for forward) are used.

In command mode, text can be deleted. After you position the cursor under a character, typing x will delete it, and any text to its right will move one space to the left to fill in. The command dd will delete the current line, and dw will delete the current word from the cursor position to the end of the word. Preceding one of these commands with an integer will cause that number of objects to be deleted. For example, typing 5x deletes five characters, and 8dd deletes eight lines. Deleted material can be recovered using p if you type it immediately after the deletion (you can move the cursor first). The deleted material is put at the current cursor location. Chapter 7 mentions other methods for recovery.

Commands can be undone by typing u, which restores the previous change, or U, which restores the current line to its initial state, undoing all changes to that one line. The command J is used to join the next line onto the end of the current line, in effect deleting the end-of-line marker.

Using cc and a.out

The C compiler is a program that converts a C program file into either an executable file or an object module that must be processed further (linked) to produce an executable file. There are many versions of C compilers sold by various vendors for different machines and operating systems. We will discuss using a C compiler in a UNIX environment according to the ANSI standard for C. Some details may differ on your particular system.

The C compiler is run on the file prog2.c by the command

```
cc prog2.c
```

This will attempt to compile the C program, reporting any warnings or errors found in the attempt. If successful, the compile will produce an executable file with the default name a.out. This file is executable, so it can be run by simply typing its name. *Recall that your system may use* acc, gcc, *or some other command to call an ANSI C compiler.*

There are two common options invoked when compiling. The first allows another name to be provided for the executable file. This is done using the -o *filename* option. The usual name for this file is the C program file's name without the .c extension, as

```
cc prog2.c -o prog2
```

producing the executable file prog2 rather than a.out. The second common option is to include one of the standard library files. This is done with the -l*name* option. The mathematics library is a likely candidate, as in

```
cc prog2.c -lm
```

Most standard libraries have abbreviations that are used in the name part of this option; m is the abbreviation for the math library. Recall that the program itself must also contain the statement #include <math.h>, a necessary redundancy. To combine the two options, type

```
cc prog2.c -lm -o prog2
```

which compiles prog2.c, links it with the math library, and produces the executable file prog2.

References

Pressman. Roger S., *Software Engineering: A Practitioner's Approach,* McGraw-Hill, New York, 1992.
Tanenbaum, Andrew S., *Structured Computer Organization,* 3rd ed., Prentice Hall, Englewood Cliffs, NJ, 1990.

Chapter Summary

■ **Sample Program (to illustrate syntax introduced in this chapter)**

```
/* Title : Sample Program for Chapter Two */
/* Source: sample2.c                      */
/* Date  : __/__/__                        */
/* Author: B&W                            */
/* Input : After a prompt, the user must enter one character   */
/* Output: The individual characters of a string,              */
/*         the values of two numerical expressions,            */
/*         a prompt, and a line count.                         */
/* Description: Illustrates various constructs of a C program  */
/* Note: To compile, enter "cc sample.c -lm -o sample"         */

/* Header Files: */
#include <stdio.h>
#include <math.h>   /* This file includes the cosine function   */
#include <string.h> /* This file includes the strcpy function   */

/* Symbolic Constants: */
#define INTCONST 28                /* Integer constant        */
#define OCTCONST 012               /* Integer(octal) constant */
#define HEXCONST 0x1A              /* Integer(hex) constant   */
#define DBLCONST 1.23e2            /* Double constant         */
#define CHARCONST 'C'              /* Character constant      */
#define PROMPT "Enter C to continue" /* String constant       */

main ()
{
  /* Declare local variables */
  int i,                  /* i is an index variable        */
    linecount = 0;        /* linecount is initialized to zero */
  char response;
```

```
char phrase [ INTCONST ];   /* phrase is a string having      */
                            /* at most 27 characters          */
double expression = OCTCONST * HEXCONST;

/* Copy a string into phrase */
strcpy( phrase, "'Once more!,' Tom iterated." );

/* Print the individual characters of phrase, one at a time    */
for (i = 0; i < INTCONST; i++){
  printf( "phrase[%d]: %c, \n", i, phrase [ i ] );
            /* On the previous line, %c specifies a char       */
  printf( "    a character whose integer value is" );
  printf( "%3d.\n", phrase[ i ] );
  linecount += 2;

}


/* Print a numerical expression using doubles */
printf( "%2d * %2d = ", OCTCONST, HEXCONST );
printf( "%2.01f.\n", expression );
            /* On the previous line, %lf specifies a double    */

linecount++;

/*Print another numerical expression using doubles             */
printf( "cosine( %4.31f ) = ", DBLCONST );
printf( "%4.31f.\n", cos( DBLCONST )  );
            /* On the previous lines, %lf specifies a double    */

linecount++;
/* Prompt the user */
printf( "%s: ", PROMPT );              /* %s specifies a string */
scanf( "%s", response );
linecount++;         /* The user's response causes a linefeed */
/* Accept any user response and report total line count */
printf( "Total line count (including this line): " );
printf( "%2d.\n", ( linecount + 1 ) );

}
```

■ **UNIX Commands**

`cc filename.c`	Compile the C program in the file named `filename.c` and produce an executable file named `a.out`
`cc filename.c -o filename`	Compile the C program in the file named `filename.c` and produce an executable file named `filename`

`cc filename.c -lm -lf`	Compile the C program in the file named `filename.c`; include the `<math.h>` and `<float.h>` libraries, and produce an executable file named `a.out`
`a.out`	Execute the C program that has been compiled into the executable file named `a.out`

■ vi **Commands**

Mode Changes

`vi filename.c`	Start the `vi` editor in normal command mode and view `filename.c`
`i`	Change from command to input mode, insert at cursor
`a`	Change from command to input mode, insert after cursor
`I`	Change from command to input mode, insert at beginning of current line
`A`	Change from command to input mode, insert at end of current line
`o`	Change from command to input mode, open new line below current line
`O`	Change from command to input mode, open new line above current line
Escape key	Change from input to command mode
`:`	Change from command to ex mode
Escape key	Abort ex command and return to command mode
Return key	Execute ex command and return to command mode
`:w`	Save file (using the name given when `vi` was started)
`:w newname`	Save file using the name `newname`
`:q`	Quit `vi` without saving file (assumes no changes have been made)
`:q!`	Quit `vi` without saving file, even if changes have been made
`:wq`	Save (revised) file and then quit

Input Mode Actions

Return key	End current line and begin a new line
i, return key, escape key	Split current line into two lines
`^H`	Backspace one position
Escape key	Change from input to command mode

Command Mode Actions

Arrow key	Move cursor one character/line in indicated direction
`l` (`h`)	Move cursor one character to right (left)
Space bar	Move cursor one character to right

k (j)	Move cursor one line up (down)
Return key	Move cursor one line down
^B (^F)	Move one screen backward (forward)
x	Delete current character
dd	Delete current line
dw	Delete current word (from cursor to end of word)
2x	Delete 2 characters (current character and character to right)
2dd	Delete 2 lines (current line and next line)
p	Put back most recently deleted text
u	Undo most recent change
U	Undo all recent changes on current line
J	Join current line and next line

Review Problems

1. Expand the following code fragment into a fully documented program. Then execute the program to observe what happens when a string of 10 characters is printed in fields of size 5, 10, or 15 characters. Note the use of the option s for printing strings with printf(). Add comments to the program to point out that a colon and a period are used to show the limits of each printed field.

```
char digits[ 11 ];

strcpy( digits, "1234567890" );
printf( "A field of length 5:%5s.\n", digits );
printf( "A field of length 10:%10s.\n", digits );
printf( "A field of length 15:%15s.\n", digits );
```

2. What output is produced by the following two statements? Note that there are two semicolons, hence two statements.

```
for ( i = 0; i < 10; i++ );
    printf( "%d\n", i );
```

3. Express each number as a floating-point constant using both regular decimal notation and exponential notation.
   a) 1,234
   b) 1,234.5
   c) 0.1234
   d) 1.234×10^2

4. Express each number as an integer constant, an octal constant, and a hexadecimal constant.
   a) 1,234
   b) 2
   c) 8
   d) 16
   e) 1,024

5. Evaluate each expression and indicate the resulting type (in the context of the given declarations).

```
int i1 = 1, i2 = 2, i3 = 3, i4 = 4;
float f1 = 1.0, f2 = 2.0, f3 = 3.0;
double d1 = 1.0, d2 = 2.0, d3 = 3.0;
```

a) i1 + f1
b) d2 / i1
c) i2 / i3
d) i2 % i3
e) i3 % i2
f) (double) i2 / i4
g) i2 / (double) i4
h) f3 / d3
i) d3 / f3

6. Consider a 24-hour clock, where hour 0 is the first hour after midnight and hour 23 is the last hour of the day. Suppose that the integer variable h has a value in the range $0 \ldots 23$ and represents an hour of the day on a 24-hour clock. Write two expressions for converting h to the corresponding hour on a 12-hour clock.

7. Write a program to report the total (and all partial sums) of each summation. Display all values with four decimal places.

a) $1 + \frac{1}{2} + \frac{1}{3} + \cdots + \frac{1}{20}$

b) $\frac{1}{20} + \frac{1}{19} + \cdots + \frac{1}{2} + \frac{1}{1}$. For this summation, use a for loop where the index is decremented.
Note: Although the two summation totals are equal in this problem, there are other summations in which rounding errors are so large that one version of a summation may be more accurate than another.

8. Write a proper C expression to represent each of these algebraic expressions. Assume that the declaration double x1, x2, a, b, c; has been made.

a) $\dfrac{x_1 + x_2}{2}$

b) $x_1 + \dfrac{x_2}{2}$

c) $ab - c$

d) $a(b - c)$

e) $\dfrac{ab}{c}$

f) $a\left(\dfrac{b}{c}\right)$

9. Write a program to determine the number of bytes your computer system uses to store variables of type char, int, long int, float, and double. Your program should be based on the following code fragment and should include the header files <stdio.h>, <limits.h>, and <float.h>. For types int, long int, float, and double, use constants INT_MIN, LONG_MIN, FLT_MIN, DBL_MIN, INT_MAX, and so forth; these constants are from the header files <limits.h> and <float.h>.

```
int size;

/* Find storage size of characters */
size = sizeof ( char );
```

```
printf( "Size of each character: %2d bytes, ", size );
printf( "Minimum character: %d, ", CHAR_MIN );
printf( "Maximum character: %d\n", CHAR_MAX );
```

10. (vi and compiler tutorial) Enter and execute the sample program as follows.
    a) Create a file sample.c, containing the declarations, definitions, and executable statements (but no comments) of the program given at the beginning of the chapter summary. Save this file and quit vi.
    b) Reopen sample.c for editing and add the comments exactly as given in the chapter summary. Save this file, but do not quit the vi editor.
    c) Continue editing this file, replacing the date comment with a new comment line to state that the code was entered by you and to give the current date. Add a second comment line to state that the program is taken from this textbook (give a complete and correct reference for the textbook).
    d) Compile and execute the program.

Programming Problems

Note: In each of these problems, you may wish to create a new program by modifying the program given in the chapter summary.

1. Write a program to display the integer values of the characters 'a'...'z', the characters 'A' ...'Z', and the characters '0' ... '9'. First display a table with four columns: the lower case characters, the integer values of the lower case characters, the upper case characters, and the integer values of the upper case characters. Then display a table with two columns: the numerical characters and the integer values of those characters. Use appropriate column labels in each table.

2. Write a program to display powers of 2 from 2^0 to 2^7. Define constants MIN = 0 and MAX = 7, and write a loop based on these control constants to print the powers of 2. Express each power in both integer and floating-point form.

3. (Finite Geometric Series) A finite geometric series is a summation of the form $a + ar + ar^2 + \cdots + ar^n$. If r is not 1, this sum is equal to

$$a\left[\frac{1 - r^{n+1}}{1 - r}\right].$$

Write an interactive program that allows the user to demonstrate this result. (Refer to Chapter 1 and the Chapter 2 Summary for examples of interactive programs.) Have the user input two doubles (a, r) and one integer (n), and then produce output such as

```
For a = 4.0, r = 2.0, and n = 3:
Accumulated sum: ar + a(r^2) + ... + a(r^n) = 60.0, and
Formula: a { [ 1 - r^(n+1) ] / [ 1 - r ] } = 60.0.
```

where the caret symbol (^) indicates exponentiation.

Calculate the first summation value using a for loop to accumulate the sum; calculate the second summation value using the given formula. In both calculations use another for loop to evaluate exponentials such as r^2, r^n, and r^{n+1}. For the second and third output lines, use strings for the expressions on the left of the equal signs.

4. (Sales Tax) Write an interactive program to prompt the user to input a price amount, then calculate and display the associated sales tax (use the retail sales tax rate for your locality.) Use the strings

"What is the price?" and "The sales tax is" to prompt for input and to label output. The output sentence must end with a period. Refer to Chapter 1 and the Chapter 2 Summary for examples of interactive programs.

5. Write an interactive program that asks the user to input a positive integer a and then calculates the largest integer b for which a*b <= INT_MAX, where INT_MAX is the maximum representable integer as defined in the header file <limits.h>. Refer to Chapter 1 and the Chapter 2 Summary for examples of interactive programs.

Chapter
3
Flow of Control

In Chapter 2 simple C statements, such as declaration of variables and assignment of values, were discussed. This chapter discusses some basic constructs available in C for ordering the execution of statements when a program is run. Two types of constructs are available: branching statements, for conditional processing, and loop statements, for repetitive processing. In the UNIX portion of this chapter the file system structure is discussed.

Branching: `if, switch`

Once a variable has been assigned a value, that value can be tested using several operators. Depending on the results of the test, a *branch* to one of several sections of code may then occur: that is, one group of statements is executed, and another group may not be executed. This decision making gives programs flexibility, an ability to react to different states in appropriate ways. We first discuss the available test operators, then cover the branching constructs.

Boolean Operators

The operators used to make decisions return *boolean* values: that is, either the value *true* or the value *false*. Recall that although C does not have a separate `boolean` data type (unlike other languages, such as Pascal), it does use the integer values 0 for false and any nonzero value for true. In Chapter 2 the symbolic constants TRUE and FALSE were defined to make it easier to use these values. (Note that the boolean value TRUE was defined there to be exactly 1 rather than "not 0"; therefore an expression should not be compared to TRUE for testing.) The boolean operators are all binary (taking two operands) except for !, which is unary. For now, the operators discussed here are assumed to work on operands of the simple data types: integer, floating-point, or character. We will enclose boolean expressions in parentheses, their most common format. Operators for comparing string, record, and array values will be discussed later.

The boolean operators (sometimes called *relational* or *comparison* operators) ask simple comparison questions about the operands. The < operator asks whether the first operand is less than the second operand. For example, consider the following assignments:

```
int operand1, operand2;
operand1 = 10;
operand2 = 5;
```

The phrase (operand1 < operand2) evaluates to false in this case, since 10 is not less than 5. The other inequality operators have similar meaning. The > operator tests for "greater than," as in (operand1 > operand2), which evaluates to true in this case. The <= and >= operators test "less than or equal to" and "greater than or equal to," as in (operand2 <= operand1) and (operand1 >= operand2), which both evaluate to true in this case.

The operands need not be variables. Constants, either literal or symbolic, can be used in either or both operand positions. In the example in the previous paragraph, (operand1 <= 100) is true and (-5 > operand2) is false. It is legal but unusual to have constants for both operands, because presumably the programmer would know the values of the constants and thus the boolean expression. An exception occurs when a symbolic constant is used, since its value may not be obvious because it is defined elsewhere (as in an #include file). For example, if the constant operand1 is locally defined and MAXVALUE is defined in an #include file, one might write (operand1 >= MAXVALUE). Note also that both variables are boolean values and can stand alone: (operand1) and (operand2) are both true.

To test for exact equality, C uses the operator ==. For example, (operand1 == operand2) is false. Note the similarity of this operator with the assignment operator, =. A common mistake (even for experienced programmers) is to use = in place of ==. Programmers who also know Pascal are particularly vulnerable, because Pascal uses = as its equality test operator (and uses := for assignment). Unfortunately, while this is a logical error, it is not a syntax error. The operator != is used to test for nonequality. For example, (operand1 != operand2) is true in the example given previously, because the operands have different values.

Compound boolean statements are possible using the operators for logical *and* (&&), *or* (||), and *not* (!). The *and* operator evaluates to true only if both its operands are true; if either or both are false, the entire expression is false. The *or* operator evaluates to true if either or both its operands are true and to false only if both operands are false. Note that this is sometimes called *inclusive or* to distinguish it from the common English usage of "or" to mean that one of the operands is true but not both (called *exclusive or*). The unary *not* operator evaluates to true if its operand is false and to false if the operand is true. Using these operators, compound statements are constructed by interpreting "operand" as any legal boolean expression.

The following tables (Figure 3.1) show the usage of these operators and corresponding boolean values. Note the use of parentheses for grouping. As was the case with arithmetic expressions, there is a precedence assigned to each operator, ordering the evaluation when an expression is mixed. Parentheses should be used to clarify the ordering. In the tables, operand1 and operand2 use the previously assigned values, 10 and 5.

Expression	First Value	Second Value	Expression Value
`((operand1 > 2) && (operand2 == 5))`	True	True	True
`((operand1 != 2) && (operand2 < 2))`	True	False	False
`((5 < 3) && (operand2))`	False	True	False
`((!operand1) && (!operand2))`	False	False	False
`((operand1) || (operand2))`	True	True	True
`((operand1) || (operand1 == operand2))`	True	False	True
`(!(operand1) || (2 <= operand1))`	False	True	True
`((!operand1) || !(operand2))`	False	False	False

Expression	Expression Value
`(!operand1)`	False
`(!0)`	True
`(!(!operand1))`	True

Figure 3.1 Binary operators (upper table) and unary operators (lower table); `operand1` = 10 and `operand2` = 5

When the first operand in an *and* statement is false, the result is false, regardless of the value of the second operand. Likewise, when the first operand in an *or* statement is true, the result is true. C uses this information to do *short-circuit evaluation* when possible for these operators. The second operand is not evaluated in these cases.

It is possible to create even larger boolean expressions, as in

```
((( operand1 > 2 ) && ( operand2 == 5 )) || ( !operand1 ))
```

Working from the inside out, the expression using *and* is true, which is then used as the operand for the *or* expression, making the result true (by a short-circuit evaluation).

The examples above used only `int` expressions, but recall that any simple type may be used. For example, using the statements

```
float x  = 7.23;
char  ch = 'X';
```

the boolean expressions (`x < 10.0`), (`ch == 'y'`), and (`x > operand2`) are legal and have values of true, false, and true, respectively. Note that the last expression is of mixed type. As with arithmetic expressions, values of lower types are promoted to higher types before evaluation occurs. Here, operand2's value would be promoted to a float and then the expression would be evaluated, but operand2's type would not change.

The comparison of floating-point values is less clear-cut than the comparison of integer values, because of roundoff errors. Recall that decimal values are converted to binary fractions. When computations using floating-point values are done, the results can only be considered approximate. Comparisons must take this into account in the form of *tolerance tests* rather than exact equality tests. For example, consider the boolean expression (4 * x + 2 == 0.12). If the first operand differs from the second by even one bit, the result is false, but that one bit may not be significant. For example, the expression (1.0 == 9 * (1.0 / 9.0)) may evaluate to false because of rounding in the evaluation of 1.0 / 9.0. The appropriate test is to declare first a tolerance value, such as #define TOLERANCE 0.00001, then to test whether the two operands are this close to each other. The algebraic statement that does this is

$$|(4x + 2) - 0.12| < \text{TOLERANCE}$$

Translated to C, this is

```
(((( 4 * x + 2 ) - 0.12 ) < TOLERANCE )
   && ((( 4 * x + 2 ) - 0.12 ) > -TOLERANCE ))
```

which asks if the difference between the two operands is less than the tolerance in absolute value. (The absolute value function, abs(), and its variants are discussed in Chapter 4.)

if **Statements**

Boolean values are used to help make decisions about which of several sections of code to execute. The simplest branching construct is the **if** statement, which can have several forms. The syntax for if statements is of either the form

if (*condition*) *group 1*;

or

if (*condition*) *group 1*; else *group 2*;

In both cases, *condition* is a boolean expression, and the *groups* are either single C statements or groups of C statements surrounded by braces. (In fact, some writers suggest surrounding even a single statement with braces, in order to maintain a uniform style and to facilitate the addition of other statements to the group.) Note that, unlike mathematical logic statements and other programming languages, the word "then" is not used. When if statements are executed, the condition is evaluated according to the rules discussed in the preceding section. If this expression is true, the group following the condition is executed.

If the condition is false, the group that follows the condition is not executed. In the first format (without the **else** clause), *group 1* is simply skipped. In the second format (with the else clause), *group 1* is skipped but *group 2* is executed.

It is legal to use other if statements as part of either group. These rules are illustrated in the next few examples.

The following program fragment asks the user to enter a floating-point number. If this number is greater than zero, its square root is printed.

```
double number;
printf( "Enter a real number: " );
scanf( "%lf", &number );              /* lf is the input code for double */
if ( number >= 0.0 )
  printf( "The square root of %lf is %6.4lf.\n", number, sqrt( number ));
```

(The square root function `sqrt()` is discussed in Chapter 4.) Note that the second `printf` is on its own line and is indented. This is not required, but it is the recommended style. The conditional code is set off from the remainder of the program. When this code is executed, suppose the user enters 5.79. Since this is larger than zero, the `printf` is executed:

```
The square root of 5.79 is 2.4062.
```

If the user enters -104.2, no output would be produced.

The above example would be better if an error message were printed when negative input was encountered. This can be rectified by using an `else` clause, as in

```
if ( number >= 0.0 )
  printf( "The square root of %lf is %lf.\n", number, sqrt( number ));
else
  printf( "The number you entered was negative; no square root computed.\n" );
```

If the user now enters -104.2, then the output is

```
The number you entered was negative; no square root computed.
```

The next example uses several C statements in a group as the "then" clause. The user is asked if help is needed, and the program either prints help instructions or not, depending on the answer.

```
char answer;
printf( "Do you need help instructions? Answer y or Y: " );
answer = getchar();    /* This function is discussed fully in Chapter 5. */
getchar();             /* Clear the input buffer (read over "newline")   */
if (( answer == 'y') || ( answer == 'Y' )) {
  printf( "     HELP INSTRUCTIONS\n" );
  printf( "This program is designed to do the following operation:\n" );
  printf( "1. Compute the square roots of real numbers.\n" );
  printf( "2.   ... and so on ...\n" );
} /* if (answer) */
```

A compound boolean condition is used to test `answer`. If the user enters either an upper case or lower case y, the instructions will be printed; all the `printf` statements will be executed or none will. Note that, for documentation purposes, the closing brace is commented, identifying what it closes.

To illustrate the use of `if` statements inside the conditional statement groups (called *nested* `if` statements), consider the following examples. For the first, suppose that `count` of type `int` has been assigned some value, and MAX is the integer constant 100.

```
if ( count > 0 )
  if ( count > MAX )
    printf( "Count is larger than %d.\n", MAX );
  else
    printf( "Count is positive but smaller than %d.\n", MAX );
```

The second `if` statement, including the `else` clause, is part of the first `if` statement. Suppose that `count` has the value –5. Neither `printf` statement will be executed. If `count` is 200, the first `printf` is executed; if `count` is 22, the second is executed. This construct may appear ambiguous, especially if it is written as

```
if ( count > 0 )
  if ( count > MAX )
    printf( "Count is larger than %d.\n", MAX );
else
  printf( "Count is positive but smaller than %d.\n", MAX );
```

which has the same syntax as the previous example. Indentation is optional as far as the compiler is concerned, so the lack of it here does not force the `else` clause to belong to the first `if`, even if it looks so to a human reader. If such an `else` clause is to be matched with the first `if`, it must be forced using braces, as in

```
if ( count > 0 ) {
  if ( count > MAX )
    printf( "Count is larger than %d.\n", MAX );
} else
  printf( "Count is nonpositive.\n" );
```

The syntax rule governing `else`s states that an `else` clause belongs to the most recent unmatched `if` statement, unless braces are used to alter the structure. Incorrect usage of `else` clauses is sometimes called the *hanging* `else` problem.

Recall that C uses short-circuit evaluation of boolean *and* and *or* expressions. This allows the `if` construct in the next example to be valid. Suppose that `int count` and `double sum` have been assigned values and that MIN is an integer constant.

```
if (( count != 0 ) && ( sum/count > MIN ))
  printf( "Average is greater than %d.\n", MIN );
```

If short-circuit evaluation were not used and `count` were zero, the boolean expression would result in a run-time error because the division expression would have a zero denominator. Short-circuiting causes the first operand to be evaluated; if true, the second is not evaluated and no error occurs. A logically equivalent construction is

```
if ( count != 0 )
  if ( sum/count > MIN )
    printf( "Average is greater than %d.\n", MIN );
```

Both the foregoing problem and the earlier example on computing a square root show the usefulness of `if` statements in handling error conditions. Both dividing by zero and attempting to find the square root of a negative number are arithmetic errors. More generally, `if` statements can be used to check that variables contain values within legal boundaries, where "legal" depends on the application. For example, suppose that a user is asked to enter an exam score. To determine that this score is within the range zero to 100, one could write

```
#define MINSCORE 0      /* Smallest legal score for exams. */
#define MAXSCORE 100    /* Largest legal score for exams. */
int score;              /* Holds test score. */
/* Get test score from user. */
printf( "Enter a test score: " );
scanf( "%d", &score );
/* Check for illegal score. */
if (( score < MINSCORE ) || ( score > MAXSCORE )) {
  printf( "Error: test score should be between %d and %d.\n",
    MINSCORE, MAXSCORE );  ]
} else {
  /* Processing of correct score goes here. */
  /*  ...                                    */
}
```

A common problem in processing numeric data is sorting that data. The next example solves a simple version of this problem: sorting three integer values and printing the sorted list. Since three integers can be ordered in six different ways, there are six different `printf` statements. Only two numbers can be compared at a time. The decisions that need to be made can be organized in a *decision tree,* showing the two paths that can result from each comparison of pairs of numbers. See Figure 3.2. In this decision tree, a triple such as 3, 1, 2 indicates the correct ordering of the three variables.

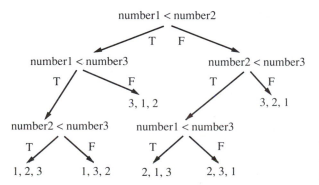

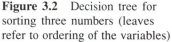

Figure 3.2 Decision tree for sorting three numbers (leaves refer to ordering of the variables)

```
int number1, number2, number3;
/* Ask the user for three integers. */
printf( "Enter three integer values to be sorted.\n" );
printf( "First  integer: " );
scanf( "%d", &number1 );
printf( "Second integer: " );
scanf( "%d", &number2 );
printf( "Third  integer: " );
scanf( "%d", &number3 );
if ( number1 < number2 )
  if ( number1 < number3 )
    if ( number2 < number3 )
      printf( "%d, %d, %d\n", number1, number2, number3 );
    else
      printf( "%d, %d, %d\n", number1, number3, number2 );
  else
    printf( "%d, %d, %d\n", number3, number1, number2 );
else
  if ( number2 < number3 )
    if ( number1 < number3 )
      printf( "%d, %d, %d\n", number2, number1, number3 );
    else
      printf( "%d, %d, %d\n", number2, number3, number1 );
  else
    printf( "%d, %d, %d\n", number3, number2, number1 );
```

The indentation of the statements in this example shows how `else` clauses are paired with appropriate `if` statements, but again remember that the indentation itself is no guarantee of correct pairing. We will reconsider sorting problems in subsequent chapters.

The next example shows how repeated `if` statements can be used to classify a value according to given criteria. The user is asked to enter an integer representing a test score. After checking that the value is legal, the program classifies the score according to a grading scale and prints a message appropriate for this grade. The same definitions used previously are repeated for convenience.

```
#define MINSCORE 0     /* Smallest legal score for exams. */
#define MAXSCORE 100   /* Largest legal score for exams.  */
/* Grading scale constants. */
#define MIN_A    90   /* Lowest possible A grade. */
#define MIN_B    80   /* Lowest possible B grade. */
#define MIN_C    70   /* Lowest possible C grade. */
#define MIN_D    60   /* Lowest possible D grade. */
int score;            /* Holds test score. */
/* Get test score from user. */
printf( "Enter a test score: ");
scanf( "%d", &score );
/* Check for illegal score. */
```

```
if (( score < MINSCORE ) || ( score > MAXSCORE )) {
  printf( "Error: test score should be between %d and %d.\n", MINSCORE, MAXSCORE );
} else {
   /* Classify score according to grading scale. */
   if ( score >= MIN_A )
     printf( "Congratulations, your grade is an A.\n" );
   else if ( score >= MIN_B )
     printf( "Not bad. Your grade is a B.\n" );
   else if ( score >= MIN_C )
     printf( "Average. Your grade is a C.\n" );
   else if ( score >= MIN_D )
     printf( "Caution! Your grade is a D.\n" );
   else
     printf( "Failing. Your grade is an F.\n" );
}
```

After an exam score is entered, it will fit one of these classifications. Even though a score, say 73, is larger than both `MIN_C` and `MIN_D`, since it is tested against `MIN_C` first and fits that category, it will not be tested against `MIN_D`. Notice that the last classification does not need an `if` condition. An alternative to this construction would be to list explicitly each letter grade's range. For example, to test if the score is a C, the condition would be

```
if (( score >= MIN_C ) && ( score < MIN_B ))
  printf( "Average. Your grade is a C.\n" );
```

Conditional Assignment

Consider the following situation. We want to make an assignment to a variable, and the value we will assign depends on whether a certain condition is true or false. For example, suppose that we want to compute and store the square root of a real number only if it is nonnegative, but we want to store zero if the number is negative. The code to do this is

```
if ( number >= 0.0 )
  SquareRoot = sqrt( number );
else
  SquareRoot = 0.0;
```

assuming that `number` and `SquareRoot` are defined as type `double` and that `number` has been assigned a value.

There is a shorthand method for this kind of *conditional assignment*. C provides a construct with the syntax

variable = (*condition*) ? *value1* : *value2* ;

where *condition* is a boolean condition. If it is true, then the *variable* is assigned *value1;* otherwise, it is assigned *value2*. Both values may be expressions.

Using conditional assignment, the previous example can be rewritten as

```
SquareRoot = ( number >= 0.0 ) ? sqrt( number ) : 0.0;
```

To explain the syntax of conditional assignment further, we note that

(*condition* ? *value1* : *value2*)

is an expression that evaluates to either *value1* or *value2*. This expression can be assigned to a variable, as just shown, or it can be used in any other context where an expression is appropriate. For example, $y = |a - b|/2$ can be evaluated by the following statement:

```
y = (( a > b ) ? ( a - b ) : ( b - a )) / 2;
```

This construct will be used occasionally and will be important in the section on macros in Chapter 12.

switch **Statements**

When an integer variable needs to be checked for equality against several values, a series of `if` statements can be used. Because this is frequently needed, a separate C construct, the `switch` statement, exists to handle it. Only integer variables (including the `char` variants) may be used in a `switch`. Neither strings nor any real type may be used.

The syntax for a `switch` is

```
switch ( variable ) {
  case value1 : group1 ;
                break;
  case value2 : group2 ;
                break;
  /* Repeat case's as needed. */
  /*           ...            */
  case valueN : groupN;
                break;
  /* The next part is optional. */
  default     : groupD ;
                break;
}
```

where each *group* is either a single C statement or a group of C statements (oddly, braces need *not* surround the group), the *value*s are constants that *variable* may have as a value, and **break** is used to delineate **case** sections. The execution of a `switch` is based on matching: If the *variable* is equal to *value1,* then the statements in *group1* are executed; if equal to *value2,* then *group2* is executed, and so on. The optional **default** section matches *variable* if it did not match any previous value. At most one group is executed. No group will be executed if *variable* does not equal any value and the **default** section is not present. Another variation of the `switch` construction, where one or more sections do not include **break**, is discussed later.

As an example, suppose that the `char` variable `LetterGrade` has been assigned a character value, and this value is used to report what test score must have been received to justify this letter grade. This is the reverse of the previous example, which assigned a letter grade based on a test score.

```
switch ( LetterGrade ) {
  case 'A': printf( "Test grade was between %d and %d.\n", MIN_A, MAXSCORE );
            break;
  case 'B': printf( "Test grade was at least %d and less than %d.\n",
              MIN_B, MIN_A );
            break;
  case 'C': printf( "Test grade was at least %d and less than %d.\n",
              MIN_C, MIN_B );
            break;
  case 'D': printf( "Test grade was at least %d and less than %d.\n",
              MIN_D, MIN_C );
            break;
  case 'F': printf( "Test grade was at least %d and less than %d.\n",
              MINSCORE, MIN_D );
            break;
  default : printf( "Illegal letter grade.\n" );
            break;
} /* switch ( LetterGrade ) */
```

Since the `switch` variable here is of type char, the values are character constants and are surrounded by single quotes. If an integer variable were used, the integer constants would not need quoting. The final brace is identified as the match to the `switch`'s opening brace.

When a group of statements applies to several values of the `switch` variable, the group need not be repeated. Instead, several `case` statements can be made to apply to a single group. For example, suppose that, in the previous example, `LetterGrade` may have either upper case or lower case values for grades. The `switch` would be modified as

```
switch ( LetterGrade ) {
  case 'a':
  case 'A': printf( "Test grade was between %d and %d.\n",
              MIN_A, MAXSCORE );
            break;
  case 'b':
  case 'B': printf( "Test grade was at least %d and less than %d.\n",
              MIN_B, MIN_A );
            break;
  /* ... and so on for the other grades. */
```

Here, if `LetterGrade` has either value a or A, the first `printf` is executed.

It is not required that a `case` group end with a `break` statement. If `break` is missing and this `case` is selected, the next `case`'s group is also executed, continuing until either a `break` or the end of the `switch` is found. The fragment

```
  case 8 : printf( "Case 8 was chosen.\n" );
  case 17: printf( "Case 17 was chosen.\n" );
            break;
```

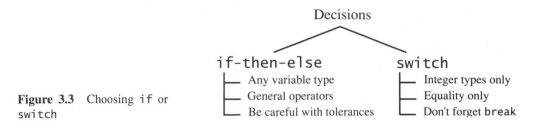

Figure 3.3   Choosing `if` or `switch`

prints both messages if the `switch` variable is 8, but only the second if it is 17. Also, it is sometimes useful to include a `case` option, but to take no action if it is chosen. The fragment

```
case MAX_A: break;
```

shows this.

When deciding to use `if` or `switch`, keep in mind that `switch` operates only on integer types (including `char` types), but `if` can operate on any variable type. The `if` construct is also more general in the operators it can handle; `switch` uses only equality. See Figure 3.3.

Looping: `for`, `while`, `do while`

The previous discussions of the `if` and `switch` constructs showed how to use branching to control the flow of execution in a program. A special type of branching construct allows groups of statements to be executed repeatedly, until some boolean condition is met. This *looping* behavior is built into the C language in the **for** and **while** loop constructs. A `for` loop is often used to repeat the execution of some statements a given number of times—that is, by counting the number of repetitions. A `while` loop is often used to repeat some processing code until some condition is met or some state is achieved—for example, reading data from a file until the end of the file is reached. However, both types of loops are flexible enough that each could replace the other.

`for` Loops

We first discuss the use of `for` loops for their traditional job as counter loops. The steps in setting up a `for` loop are as follows: Given a *counter* variable (usually, but not necessarily, of an integer type), decide on an initial value to assign the counter (often 0 or 1), and decide on a maximum value that the counter can have (the number of repetitions). Also decide on the increment to be added to the counter on each step (usually 1). Finally, decide on the statement or group of statements to be repeated. As long as the final value has not been reached, this group will be executed repeatedly.

The general syntax of `for` is

```
for ( initialization; continue check; change ) group;
```

where *initialization* is an assignment statement that sets the initial value of the counter, *continue check* is a boolean statement that tells what condition to check for before each iteration of the loop, and *change* is an assignment statement that tells how to change the loop variable at the end of each iteration. The *group* of C statement(s) is executed zero or more times—zero if the continue condition immediately fails. Several examples follow to illustrate the syntax and semantics of `for`.

To print ten blank lines, for example, the code

```
int counter;
for ( counter = 1; counter <= 10; counter++ )
  printf( "\n" );
```

will suffice, since `counter` is initialized to 1, `counter` is incremented by 1 on each iteration, and execution stops after `counter` reaches 10. The `printf` statement is executed 10 times; `counter` has value 1 the first time the `printf` is executed, 2 the second time, and 10 the final time. Starting at 1 and counting up to 10 is logical, but the code

```
for ( counter = 0; counter < 10; counter++ )
  printf( "\n" );
```

has the same effect but begins counting at zero and stops at 9. This style of counting will be important when array processing is discussed in Chapter 7.

It is legal to reference the counter variable inside the loop, but not to change its value (since it is being used to run the loop). The following code

```
for ( counter = 1; counter <= 10; counter++ )
  printf( "%d\n", counter );
```

prints ten lines numbered 1 through 10, and

```
for ( counter = 1; counter <= 10; counter++ )
  printf( "%d", counter );
printf( "\n" );
```

prints one line with the numbers 1 through 10.

A useful application of `for` loops is to sum a list of values. For example, to find the sum of the integers between -50 and 50, we first declare an *accumulator variable,* called `sum`, and initialize it to zero. At each iteration of the `for` loop, the value of `sum` is updated, adding the counter to the previous value of `sum`.

```
int counter, /* Loop counter. */
    sum;        /* Accumulator.  */
/* Always initialize accumulator to zero. */
sum = 0;
for ( counter = -50; counter <= 50; counter++ )
  sum += counter;   /* Accumulation step. */
/* Print the total. */
printf( "The final sum is %d.\n", sum );
```

If only even integers were to be counted in this example, we could change the increment statement to `counter += 2`. There is no requirement that the counter equal the final value stated in the second part; for example, if the above loop counted by threes instead, changing the increment to `counter += 3`, the final value of `counter` would be 49, since one more increment, to 52, would be over the maximum.

The next example shows the accumulation of integer test scores received from the keyboard. It assumes that the number of scores, NUMTESTS, is known in advance, and it prints out both the total of the scores and the average score.

```
int counter,   /* Loop counter. */
    sum,       /* Accumulator.  */
    score;     /* Test score.   */
/* Print general directions. */
printf( "Test score summation and averaging. \n" );
printf( "  Enter test scores as prompted.\n" );
/* Always initialize accumulator to zero. */
sum = 0;
/* Main loop: get scores from user and sum them. */
for ( counter = 1; counter <= NUMTESTS; counter++ ) {
  /* Prompt the user to enter a test score. */
  printf( "Enter score: " );    /* Note that the \n is provided by */
  scanf( "%d", &score );        /*    the user's input.            */
  sum += score;
}  /* for counter */
/* Print the total. */
printf( "The final sum is %d.\n", sum );
printf( "Average score = %f.\n", sum / (float) NUMTESTS );
```

This code could be changed in several ways to make it more useful. The prompt inside the `for` loop could print a slightly different message on each iteration of the loop, giving the user a more informative prompt, as in

```
printf( "Enter score #%d: ", counter );
```

The first time this statement is executed it prints `Enter test score # 1:`, the second time produces `Enter test score # 2:`, and so on, changing the number in the message on each iteration.

Rather than count to a predefined maximum, NUMTESTS, the program could prompt the user for the number of test scores to enter. The two lines for this are

```
printf( "How many test scores will be entered? " );
scanf( "%d", &numtests );
```

assuming `numtests` is an `int`. These lines would precede the `for` loop, which itself would have this new continue condition: `counter <= numtests;`. Finally, in the computation of the average, `numtests` must be substituted for the constant NUMTESTS.

One thing that could not be done easily is to find the difference of each score from the average. Since the variable `score` is being overwritten on each iteration of the loop, old scores are lost. To overcome this problem requires that either the scores be reentered or an array be used to store the scores. The latter approach is discussed in Chapter 7, along with other examples of array processing.

This section ends with an example of a `for` loop that does not use an integer counter variable. Suppose that, given the mathematical function $y = x^3 - 2x$, we wish to print a table of values for that function over the domain $[-5.0, 5.0]$. The counter here will be of type `double` and will be incremented by the symbolic constant DELTA. The function's value will be recomputed at each iteration of the loop, and a table will be output.

```
#define DELTA  0.5     /* Increment for x.        */
#define MINX  -5.0     /* Minimum of the domain. */
#define MAXX   5.0     /* Maximum of the domain. */
double x,      /* The free variable to run the loop. */
       y;      /* The value of the function.         */
/* Print a table title and column headings. */
printf( "Table of Function Values\n\n" );
printf( "   X    |   Y      \n" );
printf( "--------------------\n" );
/* Loop over the domain. */
for ( x = MINX; x <= MAXX; x += DELTA ) {
  /* Compute function value. */
  y = x*x*x - 2 * x;
  /* Write one row of the table. */
  printf( " %8.2lf | %10.4lf\n", x, y );
} /* for x */
```

The first three iterations of the loop produce

```
    X    |   Y
--------------------
 -5.00   | -115.0000
 -4.50   |  -82.1250
 -4.00   |  -56.0000
```

and the other rows are similar.

Other variable types and other kinds of initialization, continuation checks, and increment sections are possible. Characters may be used, for example, where the increment operator is ++. Decrementing the loop variable is legal, so that counting backwards is possible. Also, it is possible to construct compound statements in the `for` header. This is done by separating the statements by commas. For example, the initialization section might set two variables, `i` and `j`, to be 0 and 1. This is done by writing

for (i = 0, j = 1; *continuation check*; *change*)

while **Loops**

The logical construction of a while loop is quite similar to that of the for loop, with the same three parts. A loop control variable is initialized before the first iteration of the loop. The value of this variable is checked at each iteration, and the loop is exited when some boolean condition is met. Unlike the situation with the for loop, the loop variable can have its value changed inside the while loop.

The syntax of while loops is different than for. The initialization is done outside the loop and so is not technically part of the structure. Changing the value of the loop variable is done inside the loop but is optional. Only the continuation condition check is required. Like for loops, while loops may execute the loop body zero times. This happens if the continuation condition is initially false.

The formal syntax for while is

while (*condition is true*) *group*;

where, as usual, *group* is one C statement or a group of C statements enclosed in braces. The actual syntax for while, incorporating the logical structure just shown, is

```
initialize loop variable;
while ( boolean condition is true ) {
        body of loop, possibly including
        change of loop variable
}
```

Changing the loop variable, more often than not, involves a conditional statement reflecting whether the loop should be exited or not.

For example, recall the previous example, in which the user is asked whether help is needed. A while loop can be used to verify that an appropriate answer has been entered before processing that answer. Note that the prompt to the user has been changed.

```
char answer;
printf( "Do you need help instructions? Answer y or n: " );
answer = getchar();    /* This function is discussed fully in Chapter 5. */
while (( answer != 'y' ) && ( answer != 'n' )) {
  printf( "Please answer only y or n.\n" );
  printf( "Do you need help instructions? Answer y or n: " );
  answer = getchar();
  getchar();  /* Clear the newline from the input buffer */
}  /* while answer */
if ( answer == 'y' ) {
  printf( "     HELP INSTRUCTIONS\n" );
  printf( "This program is designed to do the following operation:\n" );
  printf( "1. Compute the square roots of real numbers.\n" );
  printf( "2.   ... and so on ...\n" );
}  /* if (answer) */
```

This simple example illustrates a common usage of `while` loops: checking user input for errors before continuing.

As a second example, recall the `for` loop example used for summing test scores. In both versions of that problem, we needed to know the number of tests that were being entered, either from a fixed constant or from the user's response to our query. This was necessitated by the counting nature of the `for` loop. The following example uses a *flag* or *sentinel* value, rather than a counter, to run the `while` loop. A flag value is a constant used as a marker for some condition. It must be in the range of values for a variable's type (an `int`, for example) but outside the range of logical values for that variable. In this case, we need an integer constant that cannot be used as a test score. The symbolic constant `FLAG` is used for this.

```
#define FLAG    -999      /* Safely outside 0..100 */
int counter,  /* Loop counter. */
    sum,      /* Accumulator.  */
    score;    /* Test score.   */
/* Always initialize accumulator to zero. */
sum = 0;
/* Print general directions. */
printf( "Test score summation and averaging. \n" );
printf( "   Enter test scores as prompted.\n" );
printf( "   Enter %d as the last score when done.\n", FLAG );
score   = 0;     /* Initialize the loop variable.  */
counter = 0;     /* Keep a counter, too.           */
/* Main loop: get scores from user and sum them.   */
while ( score != FLAG ) {
  /* Prompt the user to enter a test score.      */
  printf( "Enter score #%d: ", counter + 1 );
  scanf( "%d", &score );
  /* Before summing, check for a legal score.   */
  if ( score != FLAG ) {
    sum += score;      /* Accumulate the score   */
    counter++;         /* Add one to the counter */
  } /* if score */
} /* while score */
/* Print the total. */
printf( "The final sum is %d.\n", sum );
printf( "Average score = %f.\n", sum / (float) counter );
```

In the prompt to enter a score, the variable `counter` is off by 1, because it was initialized to zero. The alternative is to initialize `counter` to 1, then decrement it by 1 after exiting the loop. Note that in this example, as in the `for` version, we do not check the input for errors.

A flag variable may be separate from input values in the program. In the following example, the flag is set depending on the input but is not itself an input value. This example is a program that simulates the children's game in which a person thinks of a number between 1 and 100, and a second person (simulated by the program) tries to guess the number. The first person must answer (truthfully) whether the guess is larger, smaller, or equal to the secret number.

```c
#include <stdio.h>
#define LOWER     1      /* Smallest acceptable number */
#define UPPER   100      /* Largest acceptable number  */
#define TRUE      1
#define FALSE     0
main() {
int lower, upper,      /* Limits of the current range  */
    guess,             /* The next guess to make       */
    count,             /* Counts the number of guesses */
    done;              /* The flag variable            */
char answer;           /* The user's answer about the guess. */
/* Print directions */
printf( "Number Guessing Game\n" );
printf( "Think of a number between %d and %d\n", LOWER, UPPER );
printf( "   and I'll guess it!\n" );
/* Initialize the limits, counter, and flag variables. */
lower = LOWER;  upper = UPPER;
count = 0;      done  = FALSE;
/* Loop until the user's number has been guessed. */
while ( !done ) {
  /* Compute the next guess. */
  guess = ( lower + upper ) / 2;
  printf( "Is your number <, >, or = to %d? \n", guess );
  answer = getchar();
  getchar();  /* Clear the newline from the input buffer */
  /*  Classify the user's answer. */
  switch ( answer ) {
    case '=':  printf( "Gotcha!\n" );   /* Guessed correctly      */
               done = TRUE;             /* Set flag to quit loop  */
               break;
    case '<':  upper = guess - 1;       /* Too high: reset upper bound */
               count++;                 /* Add one to counter          */
               break;
    case '>':  lower = guess + 1;       /* Too low: reset lower bound  */
               count++;                 /* Add one to counter          */
               break;
    default :  printf( "Answer only <, >, or =.\n" );
               break;
  } /* switch answer */
} /* while !done */
printf( "It took %d guesses to find your number.\n", count );
}  /* main */
```

There is a variant of the `while` construct, called **do while**. It differs in that the loop condition is tested at the bottom of the loop rather than at the top of the loop. The boolean condition is tested in the same fashion, executing another iteration if the condition is true. (Note that this is different from alternative loop structures in other languages, such as the **repeat-until** loop in Pascal, which *exit* the loop if the condition tested is true.) The logical difference between the `while` and the `do while` loop is that a `while` loop does not execute at all if the condition is initially false, but the `do while` loop always executes at least once, because the condition is not tested until the end.

As an example of `do while`, consider playing the previous number-guessing game several times. In its current form the user must execute the program each time the game is played. To allow the user to continue playing, we need to surround the code with a `do while` structure, using another flag variable called `play_again` based on the user's response to a "Play again?" query. The following example does not repeat all of the game code:

```
/* Add this variable to the previous code. */
int  play_again;        /* Flag for playing the game again */
/* Surround the entire game with a do while loop. */
do {
  /* Print directions */
  printf( "Number Guessing Game\n" );
  /* And so on ... */
  } /* while !done */
  printf( "It took %d guesses to get your number.\n", count );
  /* Prompt user to play again. */
  printf( "Play again? y or n: " );
  answer = getchar();
  getchar();  /* Clear the input buffer */
  /* Classify the answer, assuming that not y means n. */
  if ( answer = 'y' ) play_again = TRUE;
  else play_again = FALSE;
} while ( play_again );    /* End of do while loop */
}  /* main */
```

Note that the `while` condition is equivalent to writing `while ( play_again == TRUE );`. Also, observe that `play_again` was not initialized outside the `do while` loop.

Loop Design

Given that C has three loop constructs, the programmer must decide which of the three to use. In general, the following rules should be observed (see Figure 3.4).

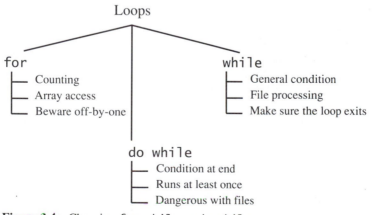

Figure 3.4 Choosing `for`, `while`, or `do while`

Loops that depend on counting, where the number of iterations is known beforehand, should be `for` loops. Important examples of this are array processing, discussed in Chapter 7, and file processing when the number of records is known.

If the loop depends on a more general condition, use a `while` loop. This includes file processing when the number of records is not known (that is, processing until end of file is reached), continuing until the user indicates "all done," as in the foregoing game example, in menu-driven applications, and in certain numerical problems in which computing is to continue until an answer is within a tolerance.

The `do while` loop should be used with caution because of the way it checks the exit condition. In particular, file processing with this kind of construct is a common mistake; assuming that a file contains at least one record can lead to disaster.

Some programmers tend to fix on one of the loop constructs and write all their loops using it. It is easy enough to equate the `for` construct to `while`:

```
for ( initialization ;  continuation check;  change  )
      loop body;
```

is equivalent to

```
initialization;
while ( continuation check ) {
   loop body;
   change ;
}
```

The `for` loop is more compact: all of the control statements appear together, so it is more easily read or modified.

Using `break` and `exit()`

Two other C commands that can be used with loop structures as well as in other contexts are `break` and the `exit()` function. The `exit()` function is defined in `<stdlib.h>`.

We have already seen the `break` command used to delineate the `case` alternatives in a `switch` statement. Recall that the effect of a `break` was to exit the `switch` statement. When `break` is used inside a loop, the same effect is achieved: The loop is exited immediately, regardless of the state of the exit condition. The `exit()` statement has a more global effect: When it is executed, the program is aborted. The `exit()` takes an integer parameter of the programmer's choice, which is returned to the operating system. In UNIX a return value of zero signifies normal termination of a command or program, and any other value signifies abnormal termination.

It is generally considered bad programming style to write loops that contain more than one exit point. Given the way `for`, `while`, and `do while` are described, there is only one way to quit a loop: when the exit condition is met, which is tested either at the top of the loop (`for` and `while`) or at the bottom (`do while`). We mention here two cases where this rule might be broken.

The first concerns error handling. When a program detects an error situation such as illegal input (out of range, perhaps) or a potential division by zero, some special action should be taken. If such an error occurs while a loop is being executed, this action may necessitate exiting the loop or even the program. Thus, either a break (with an error condition flag set) or a call to the function exit() (preceded by a printf with an error message to the user) needs to be included.

The second case occurs in a style of programming known as *event-driven programming*. A program of this kind usually waits for input events, such as keystrokes or mouse button clicks. Upon detecting an event, an appropriate action is taken, perhaps via a switch statement that delineates the possible event values. One way to construct such a program is to write an infinite loop—that is, one that at least appears to continue forever. In fact, some event may cause execution to cease, and this is done using a break or exit() statement. The format for an infinite loop is either

```
for ( ;; ) {
  loop body
}
```

or

```
while ( TRUE ) {
  loop body
}
```

In the for loop, no initialization, change, or, more importantly, exit check is stated. The exit check never becomes true, so the loop iterates forever. Similarly, the while loop's exit condition is always true, because the symbolic constant TRUE is used.

The UNIX File System

UNIX uses a hierarchical structure to organize files and directories. There is one global file structure, in which an individual user is assigned a home directory. As a rule, a user may create files, directories, and subdirectories from that home directory but from no one else's. The following sections describe how to manage files and directories and how to navigate the UNIX file system. The reader should recall the discussion of basic file commands from Chapter 1.

File System Tree

The UNIX file system is organized as a tree. The root of the tree, called / or the *root* directory, is owned by the system. There are typically several standard subdirectories under /, such as usr, bin, and etc. These are used by the system to organize the programs and data needed to maintain the system efficiently. For example, the subdirectory /bin usually contains the executable (binary) files for UNIX commands. Depending on the organization of your particular UNIX system, your home directory will be located as a subdirectory at some level below root. For example, a typical setup may place your home directory as a subdirectory of /usr/home, and the actual pathname of the home directory for a user whose login name is bob might be /usr/home/bob. Figure 3.5 shows part of the UNIX file tree.

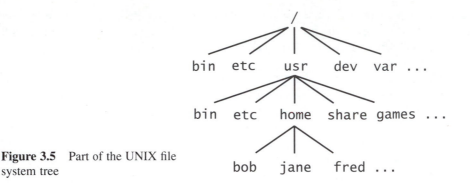

Figure 3.5 Part of the UNIX file system tree

Directory names and file names are written in two styles: either by referencing them from the current working directory or by using a full (absolute) pathname from the root. For example, if the working directory is currently `/usr/home/bob`, a file named `employee.data` (created, perhaps, using the `vi` editor discussed in Chapter 2) can be referred to as either simply

```
employee.data
```

or

```
/usr/home/bob/employee.data
```

There is also a shortcut method for referring to your home directory. The tilde character before your login name will be expanded by the system to the full pathname for your home directory. If, in the previous example, `bob` was the user's home directory, then

```
~bob/employee.data
```

is yet another way to refer to the same file. Similarly, the tilde represents your own home directory, as in

```
~/employee.data
```

which, for user `bob`, references a file in `bob`'s home directory.

The **cd** command is used to navigate the file structure—that is, to move up and down the levels of the tree. Without any parameters, `cd` returns to the home directory. The tilde character may also be used; `cd ~` also returns to the home directory. To move up one level from the working directory to its parent directory, the command `cd ..` is used. If the working directory is currently `/usr/home/bob`, then `cd ..` changes the working directory to `/usr/home`. To move down one level, give `cd` the subdirectory name as a parameter. Moving from `/usr/home` back to `/usr/home/bob` is accomplished by `cd bob`. Full pathnames can also be used: `cd /usr/bin` changes the working directory directly to `/usr/bin`, and `cd ~bob` changes directly to `bob`.

To make new subdirectories, the command **mkdir** is used. For example, if the home directory is `/usr/home/bob` and is also the working directory, then to create a subdirectory called `project1`, the command is `mkdir project1`. This subdirectory will now show up when the `ls` command is run. Now, `cd project1` will change the working directory to this new subdirectory. Subdirectories are a useful way to organize files. Rather than collect many unrelated files in the home directory, subdirectories should be created according to logical divisions—projects, homework assignments, and so on.

Recall that the `mv` command, discussed in Chapter 1, is used to rename files. It has two other uses. The command `mv` *dirname newdirname* changes the name of the directory *dirname* to *newdirname,* assuming that `dirname` is a subdirectory of the current working directory. To relocate files from one directory to another, the `mv` command can be used with just a directory name as the target. For example, suppose that the user `bob` has created the subdirectory `project1` as described in the preceding paragraph and wishes to move a file named `mydata` from the home directory into `project1`. From the home directory, `bob` would type

```
mv mydata project1
```

Then typing `ls project1` shows an entry for `mydata`.

Subdirectories may have subdirectories, too, as seen from the overall file tree. Suppose that `project1` has data, code, and output to manage. After `bob` makes `project1` the working directory, the commands

```
% mkdir data
% mkdir code
% mkdir output
```

set up the appropriate subdirectories. After `bob` types `cd code`, the full pathname of the working directory is `/usr/home/bob/project1/code`. To return to the home directory, either `cd` (return directly to the home directory), `cd ..` followed by `cd ..` (moving up one level twice), or `cd ../..` (move up two levels at once) will work.

When navigating the file tree, it is easy to lose track of what the current working directory is. The command **pwd** returns the full pathname of the working directory.

Directories can be removed with the command **rmdir**, provided the subdirectory being removed is empty. In the above example, the command `rmdir output`, if the working directory is `~bob/project1`, removes the subdirectory `output`.

Protection Modes

In order to protect the file system and to ensure some minimal privacy, UNIX files and directories have *protection modes* associated with them. There are three modes: read, write, and execute. When applied to a file, these have the obvious meaning. For example, if a user has read permission on a file, then `cat` or `more` may be executed by that user on the file to see its contents. Without read permission, the file's contents will not be displayed. Write permission allows a user to alter a file, and execute permission allows a user to run a file (used for compiled and linked C files, for example).

For directories the same modes are used but with slightly different meanings. Read permission allows a user to display directory contents—that is, to see what files and subdirectories it contains. Write permission allows files to be created, modified, and deleted in this directory. Execute permission allows one to `cd` to this directory.

Each of the three protection modes may be granted or denied to each of three sets of users: the owner of the file or directory; the *group* that the user belongs to; and everyone else (*others*). When a file or directory is created, it is given a default set of permissions. To see what these permissions are, the command `ls -l`, the long directory listing, is used (see Figure 3.6).

This command displays each file and subdirectory in the following format:

<protection mode> <number of links> <owner> <size> <date and time> <file name>

The protection mode is a set of 10 characters. The first indicates whether this is a file, a directory, or a *link,* using -, d, or l, respectively. The term *link* refers to the fact that a file that physically resides in one directory may be listed in other directories (by name only); these other directory entries are called links and are identified by the l. The other nine characters are the read, write, and execute permissions, indicated by r, w, and x for granted permissions or - if denied. There are three sets of three characters, one each for user, group, and others. After the protection mode the integer number of links indicates a real file with virtual files pointing to it. The owner's id appears next, followed by the size of the file in bytes, the date and time of the last modification to the file, and the file's name.

For example, if the file `employee.data` were created with `vi` in the directory `/usr/home/bob`, the command `ls -l` might reveal

```
-rw-rw----   0   bob   28   April 15   8:22   employee.data
```

The protection mode indicates that this is not a directory; that the owner has read and write but not execute permission (because it is probably a data file, not an executable file); and that the group has the same permissions, but others have no permissions. There are no links to this file; it belongs to `bob`, has 28 bytes, and was last modified on April 15 at 8:22; and its name is `employee.data`.

The permissions on a file or directory may be changed using the **chmod** command. It accepts two parameters: the protection mode changes and the file or directory name. The changes are represented in one of two styles. In the first, one or more of the letters u, g, or o

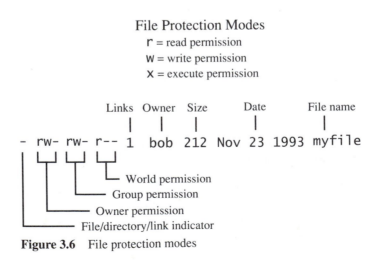

Figure 3.6   File protection modes

(for user, group, others) are given, followed by either + (to grant the permission) or – (to deny the permission), and finally, one or more of the modes r, w, or x. For example, the command

```
chmod o+rw employee.data
```

will add read and write permissions for others to the file `employee.data`. The second style is more cryptic than the first but is commonly used. It encodes the permissions into a three-digit octal number. The digits correspond to user, group, and others permissions. The individual digits are formed by adding the following codes for each permission chosen: 4 for read permission, 2 for write permission, and 1 for execute permission. For example, to give read and write permission to the user but only write permission to the group and others,

```
chmod 0622 employee.data
```

will do the job. The first digit is zero to signify an octal constant; the second is 6 because 6 = 4 (read) + 2 (write); the others are 2 for write permission.

Chapter Summary

■ C Commands

Binary Boolean Operators

`<, <=, >, >=`	$<, \leq, >, \geq$
`==, !=`	Equal, not equal
`&&, ||`	And, or (inclusive or)

Unary Boolean Operator

`!`	Not (negation)

Branching Statements

```
if ( condition )
    statement;
```
condition is a boolean expression, *statement* is a simple or compound statement (enclosed in parentheses), and *statement* is executed if and only if *condition* is true.

```
if ( condition )
    statement1;
else
    statement2;
```
statement1 is executed if and only if *condition* is true; *statement2* is executed if and only if *condition* is false.

```
switch ( variable ) {
    case value1:   statement1;
                   break;
    case value2:
    case value3:   statement2;
                   break;
    default:       statement3;
                   break;
} /* end of switch */
```
variable is of integer type. Each *statement* is a simple or compound statement (*not* enclosed in parentheses); each *value* is an integer constant. If *variable* contains *value1*, then *statement1* is executed; if *variable* contains *value2* or *value3*, then *statement2* is executed; if *variable* contains anything else, then *statement3* is executed.

Conditional Expressions

(*condition*) ? *value1* : *value2*   *condition* is a boolean expression; the expression has *value1* if and only if *condition* is true; the expression has *value2* if and only if *condition* is false

Loops

```
/* a loop to output the first 10 positive integers */
for ( count = 1; count <= 10; count++ )    /* Initialization,  */
                                /* Continuation check, Change   */
  printf( "%d\n", count );      /* Loop body                    */
/* a second loop producing the same output */
count = 1;                      /* Initialization              */
while ( count <= 10 ) {         /* Continuation check          */
  printf( "%d\n", count );      /* Loop body                   */
  count++;                      /* Change loop control variable */
}

/* a third loop producing the same output */
count = 0;                      /* Initialization              */
do {
  count++;                      /* Change loop control variable */
  printf( "%d\n", count );      /* Loop body                   */
} while ( count < 10 );         /* Continuation check          */
```

Stopping Commands

`break;`   Stop the loop or `switch` statement and execute the next statement

`exit( 0 );`   Stop the program and return 0 as the status parameter

■ UNIX Commands

Directory Names

`/`   Root directory

`/usr`   Pathname of user directory, a subdirectory of root

`/usr/bin`   Pathname of `bin`, a subdirectory of `/usr`

`/usr/home/prog1.c`   Pathname of `prog1.c`, a file contained in the directory `/usr/home`

`~bob`   Home directory of a user named `bob`

`pwd`   Have the operating system report the full pathname of the working directory

Directory Maintenance

`mkdir sub1`   Make a new directory, `sub1`, a subdirectory of the current working directory

`rmdir sub1`   Remove the subdirectory, `sub1`, an *empty subdirectory* of the working directory

mv myfile sub1	Move myfile to the subdirectory sub1
cd sub1	Change the working directory to sub1
cd ..	Change the working directory to the parent of the current working directory
cd ../..	Change the working directory to the grandparent of the current working directory
cd	Change the working directory to the home directory

File Permissions

chmod o+rw file1	Grant others (o) permission to read (r) and write (w) to file1, a file in the working directory
chmod o-w file1	Deny others (o) permission to write (w) to file1
chmod o+r-w file1	Grant others permission to read file1, and deny others permission to write to file1
chmod o+x file2	Grant others permission to execute (x) file2

Review Problems

1. Look for serious flaws in each of the following loops. In each case, assume that MyNumber is an integer variable that has been assigned a value between 1 and 10 and that the user is trying to guess that value. Also assume that constants TRUE (1) and FALSE (0) have been defined, that integer variables guess and finished have been declared, and that finished has been initialized to FALSE.

a)

```
while ( !finished ) {
  printf( "\nTry to guess my number: " );
  scanf( "%d", &guess );
  if( guess == MyNumber )
    printf( "You are correct." );
}
```

b)

```
while ( !finished ) {
  printf( "\nTry to guess my number: " );
  scanf( "%d", &guess );
  if( guess == MyNumber ) {
    printf( "You are correct." );
    finished = TRUE;
  }
}
```

c)

```
int attempts = 0;
printf( "You are allowed three tries to guess my number.\n" );
while (( !finished ) && ( attempts <= 3 )) {
  printf( "\nTry to guess my number: " );
  scanf( "%d", &guess );
  if( guess == MyNumber ) {
    printf( "You are correct." );
    finished = TRUE;
  }
  attempts++;
}
```

d)

```
int attempts = 0;
printf( "You are allowed three tries to guess my number.\n" );
do {
  printf( "\nTry to guess my number: " );
  scanf( "%d", &guess );
  if( guess == MyNumber ) {
    printf( "You are correct." );
    finished = TRUE;
  }
  attempts++;
} while ( !finished ) && ( attempts < 3 );
```

2. Replace the following code fragment by an assignment statement, as instructed in each part.

```
if ( answer == 'y' )
  play_again = TRUE;
else
  play_again = FALSE;
```

   a) Use a conditional assignment of the variable play_again.
   b) Use an unconditional assignment of the variable play_again.
3. Predict the number of iterations (this is also the number of lines of output) for each of the following loops. In each loop, i is an integer variable.
   a)

```
for( i = 0; i <= 10; i++ )
  printf( "%d\n", i )
```

   b)

```
for( i = 1; i < 10; i++ )
  printf( "%d\n", i )
```

c)

```
    for( i = 1; i <= 10; i++ )
      printf( "%d\n", i );
```

d)

```
    i = 0;
    while ( i <= 10 ) {
      printf( "%d\n", i );
      i++;
    }
```

e)

```
    i = 1;
    while ( i < 10 ) {
      printf( "%d\n", i );
      i++;
    }
```

f)

```
    i = 1;
    do {
      printf( "%d\n", i );
      i++;
    } while ( i < 10 );
```

g)

```
    i = 10;
    do
      printf( "%d\n", i );
    while ( i > 1 );
```

4. A programmer carelessly wrote the following code to display the the decimal values of $1/7$, $2/7, \ldots, 7/7$. The intent was to produce seven lines of output, but there were actually eight lines.

```
double x = 0.0, delta = 1.0/7.0;

do {
  x += delta;
  printf( "%8.7lf \n", x );
} while ( x < 1.0 );
```

a) Explain why this code produced eight lines of output.

b) Write a loop that has a loop control variable of type `double` and correctly displays the decimal values of $1/7, 2/7, \ldots, 7/7$.

5. Write a program to illustrate that if *expression1* is FALSE, then (*expression1* && *expression2*) is determined to be FALSE without evaluating *expression2*.

6. Write a program to find and report the largest power of 20 that can be expressed as a long integer.

7. (UNIX Directory Maintenance and File Permission Tutorial) After logging on to UNIX, perform the following directory and file changes, confirming each change with frequent listings of the appropriate directories.

a) Determine the full pathname and contents of your home directory.

b) Create a file `TempFile0` in your home directory.

c) Create a subdirectory `TempDir1`.

d) Create a file `TempFile1` in the directory `TempDir1`.

e) Create a subdirectory `TempDir2` in the directory `TempDir1`.

f) Create a file `TempFile2` in the directory `TempDir2`.

g) Grant others permission to read from and write to `TempFile0`.

h) Grant others permission to write to but not read from `TempFile2`.

i) Determine the name and contents of the working directory.

j) Deny others permission to read from or write to `TempFile1`.

k) List all files in your home directory.

l) Delete `TempDir2` and its contents.

m) Determine the name and contents of the working directory.

n) Remove all remaining files and directories created during this tutorial session.

Programming Problems

1. Write a program that asks the user to input a single integer and then reports back to the user whether the integer is positive, negative, or zero. In addition, if the integer is positive, report whether it is even or odd. If it is even, find and report the largest power of 2 that evenly divides the integer.

2. (Phone Number) Write a program that asks the user to input a telephone number as a sequence of 10 integers and then prints the given phone number in the form (987)-654-3210. Have the user input the digits individually, reading each digit into an integer variable and verifying that it is indeed a one-digit nonnegative integer. Do not accept zero for the first digit of the area code or for the first digit of the three-digit exchange.

Instructions for Problems 3 to 8: In each of the following problems, write an interactive program based upon a master menu. Repeat the cycle of presenting the master menu and obeying the user's response until the user chooses to stop. Whenever the user is prompted for a menu selection or for specific information, allow up to three attempts to provide a suitable response. Carefully document input values that may cause the program to malfunction.

3. (Factorials) Ask the user to provide a nonnegative integer n and then print either (1) the value of $n!$ or (2) a table showing all factorial values from 0! to $n!$ (let the user choose the type of output). Repeat this process until the user chooses to stop. *Note:* The factorial function is defined for nonnegative integers by $0! = 1$, and $n! = n(n-1)!$ for $n > 0$.

4. (Data Summations and Products) Ask the user for a positive integer n, then ask the user to enter n real numbers, and then calculate (and report) the sum and product of these numbers. Repeat this process until the user chooses to stop.

5. (Divisors) Ask the user to provide an integer n that is greater than 1, and then print the divisors of each integer from 2 to n. Also report whether each integer is a prime or composite number, using the following format for the output. Define an appropriate constant to limit the largest allowable value of n; otherwise the amount of output could be overwhelming.

```
The divisors of integers 2 to 4:
The divisors of 2 are 1 and 2; the integer 2 is prime.
The divisors of 3 are 1 and 3; the integer 3 is prime.
The divisors of 4 are 1, 2, and 4; the integer 4 is composite.
```

6. (Cash Register) Simulate a supermarket cash register. The master menu of this program should present the options: Bakery, Dairy, Deli, Frozen, Grocery, Meat, Produce, NonFood, Subtotal, Total, and Stop. If the user selects one of the first eight options, request a monetary amount (the price of one item) and return to the master menu. If the user selects Subtotal, print the subtotal of all entries thus far and return to the master menu. If the user selects Total, print the final total, including 5% tax on all NonFood Items, ask for the Amount Tendered, calculate and print the Change, clear all variables, and return to the master menu.

7. (ATM) Write a program to simulate an automatic teller machine transaction (ATM) at a bank. (*Note:* In the context of computer network communications, ATM is also used as an abbreviation for "asynchronous transfer mode.") The master menu of this program should present the options: Deposit, Withdraw, Report Balance, and Stop. For each of the first two options, offer a submenu that asks the user to identify an account (Savings or Checking), have the user enter an amount, and then return to the master menu. For Report Balance, ask the user to identify an account, report the current balance of that account, and then return to the master menu. Continue presenting the master menu until the user chooses to stop. (To simplify this problem, assume that the user has one Savings account and one Checking account, and initialize both account balances to zero when the program begins to execute.)

8. (Ideal Gas Law) A well-known physical relationship is the ideal gas law: For a given amount of gas, the pressure P, volume V, and absolute temperature T must satisfy the equation

$$\frac{PV}{T} = k,$$

where k is a constant. Note that this formula requires that temperature be measured on an absolute scale, such as the Rankine scale, where Rankine temperature is Fahrenheit temperature plus 459.67.

Write a program that allows the user to solve problems based on the ideal gas law in the following manner:

1. Ask the user to input values of P (in pounds per square inch), V (in cubic inches), and T (in degrees Fahrenheit).
2. Calculate the constant k corresponding to these three values.
3. Ask the user to specify new values for two of the quantities (P and V, or P and T, or V and T).
4. Calculate the new value the remaining quantity must have in order to satisfy the ideal gas law.
5. Print this new value with a precision of 1 decimal place.

The master menu should then allow the user to repeat the entire sequence of steps, to repeat just steps 3 through 5, or to quit.

For example, on a winter morning an automobile tire might have a pressure of 30 lb per sq. in., a volume of 280 cu. in., and a temperature of 10 degrees Fahrenheit; from this information we can calculate

$$k = (30 \times 280)/(10 + 459.67) = 17.8849.$$

If we want to know the pressure later in the day, when the temperature has increased to 45 degrees Fahrenheit and the volume has increased to 285 cu. in., the program would calculate the new pressure as

$$P = kT/V = (17.8849 \times (45 + 459.67))/285 = 31.7 \text{ lb per sq. in.}$$

Chapter
4

Functions

Breaking down a large problem into smaller component parts is a powerful problem-solving method. In C programming, this method is aided by the availability of *functions*: subprograms that can be *called,* or invoked, by the main program or by other functions in order to do some specific job. In this chapter, we look at the mechanics of creating and calling functions. Chapter 6 will discuss in more detail the use of functions in program design.

A function is like a small program in itself; it can have variable declarations as well as code. When a function call occurs, that function's code is executed. Optionally, functions in C can accept input from the *caller* (the calling program or function) and return a value to the caller.

Built-in functions are available to perform a number of basic chores. For example, the printf() function, already introduced, is a system function that handles the details of producing output. Although these functions are not part of the C language, they are always provided in the *libraries* that come with C compilers. Libraries allow one kind of code reuse: once a library of functions is written, those functions can be used by many programs. This chapter discusses some useful standard functions.

On the other hand, functions may be defined by the user for special purposes. A program can be thought of as a collection of functions, each of which handles some part of the program's processing. We will also look at how to write such functions to do special tasks not handled by the built-in functions.

UNIX commands can be called from inside a C program. This chapter's UNIX section discusses how to accomplish this and introduces some useful UNIX commands that can be used in this context.

Function Calls

A function is used by being called, either from the main program, from another function, or possibly from itself (called a *recursive* call; see Chapter 13 for more details). To call a function, its name is used as a command (if the function return value is not needed) or as an arithmetic or logical expression (whose value will be returned by the function). Conventions that govern function call syntax depend on the definition of the function but not on the internal specifics of the function. In fact, the internal code of the function need not be known to the caller. As will be discussed in Chapter 6, hiding internal details is usually considered a good thing. As long as a function behaves the way it should by returning a correct answer, it can be considered a *black box* (that is, its inner workings are unseen) that can be used as a tool. For this reason, knowing the *interface,* or *prototype,* of a function is enough to use it. The prototype for a function tells what type of value (if any) the function returns and the number and types of the *parameters* to the function. The parameters in the prototype (sometimes called *formal* parameters) are dummy variables, ones whose values will be filled in when the function is called. Those actual values that are substituted for the parameters in the function call are called the *arguments* to the function (sometimes referred to as the *actual* parameters to the function). (See Figure 4.1.)

For example, the `sqrt()` function, used in examples in Chapters 1 and 3, has this prototype, given in `<math.h>`:

```
double sqrt( double x );
```

The type name `double` on the left indicates that this function returns a value of that type. This implies that the returned value must be assigned to a variable of type `double` when `sqrt()` is called. The parameter to the function is also a `double` value. The name of this parameter, `x`, is unimportant; it is simply a place holder. In fact, `x` can even be left out of the prototype. Either a `double` constant or variable may be used as the argument in the call to `sqrt()`, as in the following fragment:

```
double value, answer;
answer = sqrt( 2.0 );
/* The next two lines assign the same value to answer as above. */
value  = 2.0;
answer = sqrt( value );
```

Note that the algorithm for computing the square root is not given. The `sqrt()` function simply accepts an input value and produces an output value. The issues of using incorrect arguments (by type or by value) are discussed later.

Function Prototypes and Calls

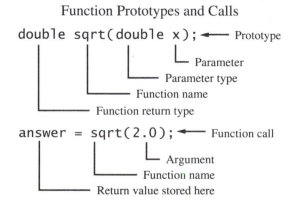

Figure 4.1 Function terminology

If multiple parameters are required, they are separated by commas in both the prototype and the call. For example, provided proper variable definitions are made, the following prototype and call are legal:

```
int myfunction( int first, double second, char third );
result = myfunction( intval, doubleval, charval );
```

If no parameters are used, the special type `void` is used in the prototype, as in

```
int rand( void );
```

which is a pseudorandom number generator defined in `<stdlib.h>`, and the call statement uses empty parentheses, as shown by

```
value = rand();
```

A function need not return any value. The type `void` is used in ANSI C to signify this case. For example,

```
void srand( unsigned seed );
```

defined in `<stdlib.h>` seeds the pseudorandom number generator `rand()` with the parameter `seed`, and no return value is needed (see below for more details).

In addition, there are two ways to pass parameters. The method used in the examples so far is the first method, called *pass by value*. These values are input only to the function. (Internally, the argument value is copied into the function's memory space; the mechanics of the process are unimportant for this discussion.) In other words, the value of each argument is unchanged after the function call. Even if a variable (not a constant) is used for the argument and the function changes the parameter value in its own code, the caller will know nothing of the change.

In the second method, called *pass by address* (or *pass by reference*), the function may change the value of one or more input arguments in addition to providing a return value. Pass by address may be used to send input values and receive output values apart from the function's return value. The pass-by-address method is also used when arrays (discussed in Chapter 7) or large structures (discussed in Chapter 9) are the parameters. Except in these latter two cases, a different kind of syntax is used in both prototype and call to apply pass by address. The prototype

```
void myfunc( int *param );
```

is called in the fragment

```
int myparam;
myfunct( &myparam );
```

Note the asterisk before `param` in the prototype and the address operator & in the calling statement before the argument `myparam`. The function may use the value stored in `myparam`, if any. It also may return a new value in `myparam`. In this example, the function is actually receiving the memory address of `myparam`, rather than a copy of the value stored in `myparam`.

These issues are covered further in the section on user-defined functions. In order to use the standard functions, discussed next, we need to know the prototype and must pay attention to the return type and kinds of parameters.

Standard Functions

A number of libraries are provided with ANSI-compatible C compilers. These contain standard functions that make some tasks easier. A few have already been introduced. Each library has a corresponding header file, which must be included via an `#include` statement, and some additionally require that they be linked to a user program by the compiler. We discuss a few libraries here (see Figure 4.2). See Appendix B for a list of all the common libraries and header files.

The Mathematics Library

The mathematics library contains common functions needed in doing computations. The function prototypes and several constants are defined in the file `<math.h>` (remember to compile using the `-lm` flag whenever using the mathematics library). Each math function returns a value of type `double`. With a few exceptions each also accepts one `double` parameter as input. When `float` or `int` parameters or return variables are used, automatic promotion or truncation takes place. For most floating-point numerical computations, though, the type `double` is recommended. Examples of usage for these functions are given, but it is beyond this book's scope to explain the meaning of the functions fully. Also note that several integer functions are located in `<stdlib.h>`, described in a later section.

The square root function `sqrt()` has been used in several previous examples. Its prototype is

```
double sqrt( double x );
```

The square root of a negative number is undefined. When `sqrt()` is passed a negative argument, a run-time error occurs.

There is no function to square a number (this can be done by multiplication), but a more general power function is available:

```
double pow( double base, double power );
```

Header Files of Standard Libraries

`<ctype.h>`	Character functions
`<math.h>`	Mathematical functions
`<stdio.h>`	Input/output functions
`<stdlib.h>`	Memory allocation, general functions
`<string.h>`	String functions

Figure 4.2 Header files of some standard libraries

returns the value (base)^power. For example,

```
double base  = 5.0,
       power = 3.15,
       answer;
answer = pow( base, power );
```

will produce the value 159.1312644 in answer. Often, integer values are given for the power; recall that such values will automatically be promoted to double at run time.

The functions given by

```
double ceil( double x );
double floor( double x );
```

are used to change a double into an integer (though not, as can be seen in the prototype, an int) by elevation to the smallest integer greater than or equal to the parameter and by truncation to the largest integer less than or equal to the parameter, respectively. Thus, the fragment

```
double first, second;
first = floor( 5.75 );
second = ceil( 10.002 );
```

will store 5.0 in first and 11.0 in second. No standard function is provided for rounding off.

Absolute value can be computed using

```
double fabs( double x );
```

The f in fabs() indicates that a floating-point absolute value is returned. Note that both the parameter and return value are double; to compute integer absolute value, see abs() in the section on <stdlib.h>.

Three trigonometric functions are provided. Each assumes that the parameter is an angle measured in radians. The prototypes are

```
double sin( double theta );
double cos( double theta );
double tan( double theta );
```

for the sine, cosine, and tangent functions of theta, respectively. For example, to store the sine of a 30-degree angle in variable result, we might write

```
double theta, result;
/* Compute the value of 30 degrees in radians. */
theta  = 30.0 * ( 3.14159 / 180.0 );
result = sin( theta );
```

The inverse trigonometric functions, arcsine, arccosine, and arctangent, are given next.

```
double asin( double value );
double acos( double value );
double atan( double value );
```

Unlike the trigonometric functions, the arcsine and arccosine functions expect the input parameter to fall in the domain -1 to 1. A run-time error results otherwise.

For engineering applications the *hyperbolic* functions are often needed. Three functions are defined by the prototypes

```
double sinh( double x );
double cosh( double x );
double tanh( double x );
```

Besides the more general pow() function, there is a specialized power function defined as

```
double exp( double power );
```

which computes the value e^{power}. The inverse of this function is

```
double log( double x );
```

which computes the natural logarithm of x. Note that this function is *not* named "ln," its standard mathematical name. For convenience, there is a base-ten logarithm function,

```
double log10( double x );
```

which again is not correctly named (it should be simply "log"). Both log() and log10 expect the input parameter to be positive. A run-time error occurs if the argument is not positive.

We omit here some less commonly used functions provided in the mathematics library. For the complete listing, see Appendix B.

The stdlib Library

The stdlib library contains a collection of useful, albeit miscellaneous, functions. The header file <stdlib.h> must be included in your program to use it.

As mentioned above, several integer functions are defined here rather than in the mathematics library. The functions

```
int abs( int i );
long labs( long l );
```

compute the absolute values of int and long values, respectively.

A pseudorandom number generator is provided in the function

```
int rand( void );
```

The integer returned is in the range 0 to RAND_MAX, a large system-dependent constant defined in `<stdlib.h>`. The randomness (or lack thereof) of a sequence of numbers produced by any such generator should be verified before it is used in simulation problems. For "everyday" use, `rand()` is adequate. Repeated calls to `rand()` produce what appears to be a sequence of randomly distributed integers. Before the first call, the generator can be *seeded* by a call to

```
void srand( unsigned seed );
```

with the default seed equal to 1 if no such call is made. The parameter to `srand()` causes `rand()` to start its sequence in a different place. One common method of seeding is to use the current time of day, as in

```
srand( ( unsigned ) time( NULL ) );
```

This requires that both `<stdio.h>` (for the definition of NULL) and `<time.h>` be included. The `time()` function returns a long integer; see Appendix B for proper usage.

Several conversion functions defined in `<stdlib.h>` take string arguments and return numeric values. The following three functions,

```
int atoi( char *str );
long atol( char *str );
double atod( char *str );
```

convert strings to `int`, `long`, and `double` values, respectively. For example,

```
int intval;
intval = atoi( "458" );
```

stores the integer value `458` in the variable `intval`. These functions are useful when soliciting character input from a user. Use of the other two functions is similar.

The function call `system()` provides access to operating system commands from within C programs. Its prototype,

```
int system( char *str );
```

shows that the command is given as a string parameter. For example, the function call `system( "ls" );` produces a directory listing. It is up to the operating system to execute the command. The return `int` value is the exit status of the command. For more examples and discussion, see the UNIX section of this chapter.

The programs we have discussed so far have assumed that program execution ends when the last command of `main()` is executed. There is a way to exit a program at any point using the function defined by

```
void exit( int status );
```

The `status` parameter is used to pass a value back to the operating system and indicates a successful termination if `status` is 0 and unsuccessful if `status` is 1. This function is best used to handle error conditions, as in the fragment

```
if ( denominator == 0 ) {
  printf( "Error: denominator is zero.\n" );
  exit( 1 );
} else {
/* ... rest of the code ... */
```

The `ctype` Commands

The file `<ctype.h>` contains a number of useful *macro* and function definitions related to character testing and conversion. A macro is similar to a function in that it can accept parameters and execute code; the difference is in how these are carried out. Macros are handled by the C preprocessor, like the `#include` statements, rather than by the compiler. The preprocessor replaces the macro name with the macro's code and makes parameter substitutions. Macros are not as powerful as functions, especially in their use of parameters; Chapter 12 discusses this topic in more detail. For now, we can treat the `ctype` macros as if they were actually function calls.

The character-testing commands return a true (nonzero) or false (zero) value. Each tests whether the character parameter belongs to a certain set of characters. For example,

```
int isalpha( int ch );
```

tests whether or not `ch` is a letter of the alphabet. Note that `ch`'s type is `int`, not `char`, but recall that in practice `char` is implemented as an integer value. The other test commands are

```
int isdigit( int ch );
int isalnum( int ch );
int isprint( int ch );
int isupper( int ch );
int islower( int ch );
int ispunct( int ch );
int isspace( int ch );
```

which test whether `ch` is a member of the following sets, respectively:

- Digits, 0 through 9
- Letters plus digits
- Printable characters (this excludes control characters, for example)
- Upper case letters
- Lower case letters
- Punctuation characters
- White space characters (space `' '`, newline `'\n'`, carriage return `'\r'`, form feed `'\f'`, tab `'\t'`, and vertical tab `'\v'`)

See Chapter 8 for an example that uses some of these commands.

There are two character conversion commands for changing from upper to lower case or the reverse. Their prototypes are

```
int tolower( int ch );
int toupper( int ch );
```

If the parameter ch's value is in the set of upper case letters, `tolower()` returns the lower case version of that letter. If, however, ch is not in that set, `tolower()` simply returns ch. Similarly, `toupper()` returns the upper case version of ch (or just ch if the character is already upper case). For example, the fragment

```
char ch = 't';
printf( "%c %c\n", ch, toupper( ch ) );
```

will display

```
t T
```

as its output.

User-Defined Functions

When there is no standard function to do a needed job, a user-defined function can be created. Such functions by necessity have a single purpose, but with care and the use of parameters multipurpose, reusable functions can be written. A function that displays a menu whose choices are sent as parameters, for example, is more general than a menu function that displays some specific (*hard-coded*) choices. As the discussion of use defined functions progresses, keep in mind that as a general rule, the more generic a functio. is, the more reusable it is, and that less code will need to be written and tested as a result. Further design issues regarding functions will be discussed in Chapter 6.

Writing functions and calling them are straightforward in C. We will always write prototypes for the function examples in this text, following the style of the standard functions previously discussed. Issues in parameter passing, especially those parameters that must return values, are less straightforward. You should take special notice of the syntax rules governing such parameters, as will be discussed.

Also note that in C, unlike in other languages, functions may not be nested inside one another. This is true of `main()`, too—it cannot contain the definition and body of another function. All C functions, then, are at the same lexical level: No function contains another function.

Function Format

As noted in the chapter introduction, functions are like small, self-contained programs. Their code follows the same pattern as the full program examples in the previous chapters. A pair of braces encloses the function's code. Variable declarations and initializations are given next, followed by whatever C code is needed to implement the function's job. Functions usually follow `main()`.

Recall from the discussion of the standard libraries that each function has a type, usually one of the simple C types, or the special type `void`. The type tells what kind of value (none in the case of `void`) the function returns; the value is returned using the `return` statement, illustrated below. The function name is used to call the function from another function (recall that even `main()` is itself a function). A function name may be used like a variable in an expression, or it may appear as a lone command, but it may not appear on the left side of an assignment statement. Consider these three statements using standard functions:

```
x = 4 * sqrt( y );        /* Legal function call */
srand( 1 );               /* Legal function call */
sin( theta ) = 0.172;     /* Illegal function call */
```

The `sqrt()` function is called within a numeric expression, and the return value (a `double`) will be used as if it were a constant. The `srand()` function returns no value, so it may be used alone. The statement using `sin()` is incorrect, because it attempts to assign a value to the function as if it were a variable.

The function prototype is a restatement of the first line of a function. Prototypes are often placed immediately before the start of `main()` to ensure that the compiler knows of the existence of the functions as it processes `main()`'s code. This relates to the need to define a term before using it, since the function body follows `main()`.

A Simple Example

The following simple example will illustrate the basics of function writing and calling. The function used in this example, called `banner()`, clears the screen and prints an identification banner for an inventory program. We show the entire program to illustrate function and prototype placement, even though the main program itself does nothing but call the `banner()` function.

```
#include <stdio.h>
void banner( void );      /* The prototype for the banner function */
main()
{
  banner();      /* Call to the banner function */
  /* The inventory processing would go here. */
}
void banner( void )
/* banner clears the screen and prints a header */
/* for an inventory program.                     */
{
  system( "clear" );
  printf( "\n" );
  printf( "    ********************\n" );
  printf( "    *                  *\n" );
  printf( "    * INVENTORY PROGRAM *\n" );
  printf( "    *                  *\n" );
  printf( "    ********************\n" );
  printf( "\n" );
}
```

Note that the `banner()` function does not return any value; thus it is declared as type `void` and contains no `return` statement. It also accepts no parameters, as indicated by the word `void` in the parentheses. Later examples will show functions that accept parameters and return values.

Pass-by-Value Parameters

Recall the two methods for passing information to a function discussed earlier: pass by value and pass by address. We briefly covered the syntax necessary to use each method; here we review that syntax and give further examples.

Pass-by-value parameters are used to send input to a function. Most of the standard functions discussed in the first part of this chapter used pass-by-value parameters. Inside the function they act like local variables—they can be used in expressions and be assigned new values, for example. There is no reverse connection back to the argument associated with that parameter, however, so an assignment is not reflected in an updated value in the calling function or program. Several short examples will illustrate these ideas.

The following function `CelToFahr()`, given a Celsius temperature, computes a Fahrenheit temperature using the conversion formula $F = \frac{9}{5}C + 32$. The only parameter is a `double` that represents the input Celsius temperature and is a pass-by-value parameter. The Fahrenheit temperature is printed by the function. No value is returned, so type `void` is used.

```
void CelToFahr( double celsius )
/* CelToFahr computes the Fahrenheit equivalent of the */
/* input Celsius temperature and prints that value.    */
{
    double fahr;     /* Holds the Fahrenheit temperature */
    fahr = ( 9.0 / 5.0 ) * celsius + 32.0;
    printf( "%lf Celsius equals %lf Fahrenheit.\n", celsius, fahr );
}
```

The prototype of this function may take one of three legal forms: as a direct copy of the definition, as a copy but with the parameter name changed, or without the parameter name:

```
void CelToFahr( double celsius );     /* Direct copy style         */
void CelToFahr( double c );           /* New-parameter-name style */
void CelToFahr( double );             /* No-parameter-name style  */
```

The first form is the safest to use, provided that you use the cut-and-paste facility in the editor being used to create the program. Recall that the prototype would normally precede `main()`. The purpose of a prototype is to give the compiler information about the function before it is used. The compiler needs to know the type of the parameter, but at this point the name of the parameter is not needed—thus we have a variety of allowable prototype styles.

The call to `CelToFahr()` from `main()` could take the form

```
CelToFahr( 98.6 );
```

if a constant value were used as the argument, or as

```
double temperature = 98.6;
CelToFahr( temperature );
```

to pass a value stored in a variable. See Figure 4.3.

Pass-by-Value Parameters

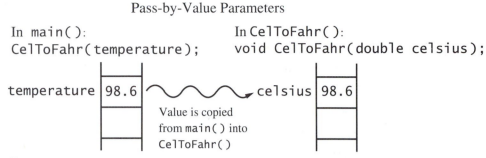

In main( ):
CelToFahr(temperature);

In CelToFahr( ):
void CelToFahr(double celsius);

temperature 98.6 ⟶ celsius 98.6

Value is copied
from main( ) into
CelToFahr( )

Figure 4.3 Parameter passing: by value (copy)

Return Values

Often a function needs to send a value back to the calling function. To do that, the return statement is used, and the function must be declared as the proper type, not void. We illustrate the return statement by rewriting the previous example.

If we change the specification of CelToFahr() so that the Fahrenheit value is returned to the calling function rather than printed, we would write the following:

```
double CelToFahr( double celsius )
/* Version 2:                                    */
/* CelToFahr computes the Fahrenheit equivalent of the */
/* input Celsius temperature and returns that value.   */
{
    double fahr;      /* Holds the Fahrenheit temperature */
    fahr = ( 9.0 / 5.0 ) * celsius + 32.0;
    return( fahr );
}
```

Note the use of the return statement. The value to be returned, which may be any expression that evaluates to the function's type (in this case double), is stated after the reserved word return. The parentheses are optional. That is, the last statement in the preceding code could be written as

```
return fahr;
```

The use of parentheses is only a matter of style here.

In main() the return value could be printed directly, as in

```
printf( "%lf Celsius equals %lf Fahrenheit.\n", 98.6, CelToFahr( 98.6 ));
```

or we could capture the return value in a variable, as in

```
double temperature = 98.6, converted;
converted = CelToFahr( temperature );
printf( "%lf Celsius equals %lf Fahrenheit.\n", temperature, converted );
```

Either style is acceptable, and the choice depends on whether the returned value will be needed later or not.

We look at two other possible implementations of the `CelToFahr()` function. Note that the local variable `fahr` is not really necessary, because, as we noted, the `return` statement can be given an expression. Thus, the body of the function could simply be the one line

```
return(( 9.0 / 5.0 ) * celsius + 32.0 );
```

Not only is the code shorter, but the storage space for the local variable is not needed. For such a simple function, this style is acceptable.

Finally, suppose that instead of using a local variable to hold the Fahrenheit temperature, we use the parameter itself.

```
double CelToFahr( double celsius )
/* Version 3:                                           */
/* CelToFahr computes the Fahrenheit equivalent of the */
/* input Celsius temperature and returns that value.   */
{
    celsius = ( 9.0 / 5.0 ) * celsius + 32.0;
    return( celsius );
}
```

Now consider the following code from `main()`:

```
double temperature = 98.6, converted;
converted = CelToFahr( temperature );
printf( "%lf Celsius equals %lf Fahrenheit.\n", temperature, converted );
```

From the way that this version is coded, you might expect that the value of `temperature` will be changed, but in fact it remains the same. `temperature`'s value of 98.6 will be copied into the parameter `celsius`, but although a new value is assigned to `celsius`, that value is not stored in `temperature`. This is the essence of pass-by-value parameters. The parameter acts like a local variable that receives an initial value when the calling function's corresponding value is copied in. No new value is copied out.

One final comment about the third version of `CelToFahr()` is in order. The use of the variable `celsius` to store a Fahrenheit temperature is risky, because it is potentially confusing to someone reading this code. This fragment is presented here only to illustrate the essence of pass-by-value parameters.

One Way In, One Way Out

For functions more complicated than the `CelToFahr()` example, there may be choices of several values to return according to a boolean expression. In this case, several `return` statements may be required. However, it is good programming style to use only one `return` statement so that the function has only one entrance point (the function's first statement) and one exit point (the `return` statement). This simplifies the task of tracing the flow of the function when trying to decode complicated programs.

For example, consider a function that returns the larger of two input `double` values. A simple inequality test is needed to accomplish this.

```
double maximum( double first, double second )
/* maximum() returns the larger of the two */
/* input parameters first and second.     */
{
double bigger;     /* Holds the larger of the values */
if ( first > second )
  bigger = first;
else
  bigger = second;
return( bigger );
}
```

To call this function, one might write

```
printf( "The larger of %lf and %lf is %lf.\n,
    firstval, secondval, maximum( firstval, secondval ));
```

provided that `firstval` and `secondval` are properly declared and initialized.

In order to illustrate the one-entrance-point, one-exit-point rule, compare the following less desirable alternative to the previous example.

```
double maximum( double first, double second )
/* Version 2:                              */
/* maximum() returns the larger of the two */
/* input parameters first and second.     */
{
if ( first > second )
  return( first );
else
  return( second );
}
```

This version has two exit points, because there are two occurrences of `return`. In such a simple example, it can be argued that violating the one-entrance-point, one-exit-point rule is inconsequential. Of course, multiple exit points in larger functions will make code harder to understand and debug, but why worry about it here? It is a matter of discipline: Writing good code when it is critical to do so demands that standards be followed, and this is one such standard.

Pass-by-Address Parameters

There are situations when a function parameter needs to carry some new value back to the calling program. In this case a pass-by-value parameter is not appropriate. Instead, a pass-by-address parameter is needed. However, keep in mind that pass-by-value parameters should be used when they can be used; use pass-by-address parameters only when they are absolutely necessary.

The syntax for pass-by-address parameters is, unfortunately, less than straightforward in C as compared to other languages. Recall from the chapter introduction that two steps are involved. First, the function definition must indicate that a parameter is actually an address by using * in front of the parameter name. Second, in the calling function, the argument matched with this parameter must be preceded by the & symbol. This argument *must* be a variable; it cannot be a constant. The * operator is sometimes called the *dereferencing* operator, while the & is called the *address* operator. Inside the function, the dereferencing operator must be used to extract a value from or store a value in the parameter. Matching up & in the calling program with * in the function is not inherently difficult. The use of the parameter inside the function, though, is a common source of errors.

As an example, consider the three-way exchange of values necessary when we want to swap the contents of two `int` variables. A temporary variable is needed to hold one of the values to ensure it does not get erased. To accomplish this using a function, consider first the function header

```
void exchange( int *first, int *second );
```

This shows that two `int` * parameters are used. Both parameters are pass-by-address, as indicated by the * prefix. Our intent is to return new values in each of these parameters. The function body will contain the aforementioned temporary `int`, and the code is simple:

```
void exchange( int *first, int *second )
/* exchange swaps the values of the two pass-by- */
/*    address parameters.                         */
{
  int temp;      /* Holds one value temporarily */
  temp    = *first;
  *first  = *second;
  *second = temp;
}
```

Pass-by-Address Parameters

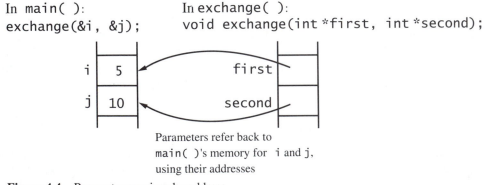

In `main( )`:
`exchange(&i, &j);`

In `exchange( )`:
`void exchange(int *first, int *second);`

i | 5   first

j | 10   second

Parameters refer back to
`main( )`'s memory for `i` and `j`,
using their addresses

Figure 4.4 Parameter passing: by address

The expression *first within the function dereferences the address stored in first—that is, it finds the value that first refers to (or *points to*, as is sometimes said). See Figure 4.4.

Note the difference in the syntax for referring to temp, which is of type int, and first and second, which are of type int *. It would be an error to write

```
temp = first;
```

since these variables are of different types: first will contain an address when this function is called at run time.

The prototype of the exchange() function may be written in any of three styles, but each of them must include the * to indicate pass-by-address parameters. The three methods are

```
void exchange( int *first, int *second );    /* Direct copy style        */
void exchange( int *a, int *b );             /* New parameter name style */
void exchange( int *, int *);                /* No parameter name style  */
```

and again the prototype should appear before main().

To show how to call the exchange() function, we give an entire program that shows the values of i and j before and after the call to exchange():

```
#include <stdio.h>
void exchange( int *first, int *second );    /* Function prototype */
main()
{
    int i = 5, j = 10;
    printf( "The values of i and j are %d and %d\n", i, j );
    /* Call to exchange() is next. */
    exchange( &i, &j );
    printf( "The values of i and j are %d and %d\n", i, j );
}
/* The exchange() function goes here. */
```

Note the use of the & address operator on both i and j. This requests that the addresses of i and j be passed to exchange(), whatever those addresses may be, but not the values of these variables—at least not directly. The exchange() code will access these values indirectly, by use of the * dereference operator.

As a second example, consider the following purchasing problem. Given a number of items purchased and the unit price of the item, we need to compute the total price to charge for this transaction, plus the sales tax on the items using a constant sales tax rate. The following function purchase() does these tasks.

```
void purchase( int NumItems, double UnitPrice, double *total, double *tax )
/* purchase computes total and tax given the NumItems and UnitPrice */
/* and uses the global constant TAXRATE.                            */
```

```
{
   /* Compute the total price, not including tax, of the items. */
   *total = NumItems * UnitPrice;
   /* Compute the tax on the total. */
   *tax = TAXRATE * ( *total );
}
```

Provided that the constant TAXRATE has been defined using a `#define` statement, the following fragment would call this function:

```
int    items = 10;
double price = 1.45, total, tax;
purchase( items, price, &total, &tax );
printf( "The total price for %d items at %d per item is %lf.\n", items,
   price, total );
printf( "The sales tax is %lf.\n", tax );
```

Note that the first two arguments need not be variables in the calling function; constants could be used. However, the latter two arguments must be variables, because the address operator is needed.

There are occasions when pass-by-address parameters may be used in a function without dereferencing. Suppose that in the foregoing `purchase()` function we change the `NumItems` parameter to be pass-by-address, and that the function prompts the user for what value to use. We would change the function to

```
void purchase( int *NumItems, double UnitPrice, double *total, double *tax )
{
   /* Ask the user to enter the number of items purchased. */
   printf( "Enter the number of items purchased: " );
   scanf( "%d", NumItems );
   /* Compute the total price of the items. */
   *total = ( *NumItems ) * UnitPrice;
   /* Compute the tax on the total. */
   *tax = TAXRATE * ( *total );
}
```

Note the usage of `NumItems` in the `scanf()` statement. As we have seen in other examples, the `scanf()` function normally requires that & be used before the variable that a value is being read into. Here, the parameter `NumItems` is already a pointer value, because it is a pass-by-address parameter. Dereferencing it with * would be an error. However, in the computation of the total, it *is* dereferenced in order to obtain the value stored in it by the `scanf()` call. To call this from `main()`, we would write

```
purchase( &items, price, &total, &tax );
```

noting that now `items` must be used with the address operator to match the new parameter definition in `purchase()`.

Scoping Rules

We have referred to local variables, those declared inside functions, in some of the examples in this chapter. The idea of the *scope* of a variable or identifier is related to the notion of locality. Where a variable is declared defines where it can be used.

A *block* of code is a series of statements enclosed inside braces. The body of a function, for example, defines a block. The function's parameters and the variables it declares are inside the block defined by the function. Other blocks are usually associated with control structures like `if` and `while`. When a variable is declared inside a block, it cannot be referred to from outside the block—that is, it cannot be "seen" outside its block. This scoping rule is why we called function parameters and variables declared inside a function "local". They cannot be referenced from outside the function. Similarly, those variables declared inside `main()` are local to `main()`, for the same reason. Other functions cannot access the local variables of `main()`.

The basic scoping rule places walls between functions. Functions may communicate with one another only via their parameters. This makes debugging functions easier, since all references are local—or should be. There is another scoping rule to consider, however. Variables may be declared outside of any function. Physically, they would be placed before `main()`, in the same place as function prototypes. When the variables are declared here, all the functions in the file may "see" them—that is, they are *global* to the file. See Figure 4.5.

Although there are times when global variables may be needed, it is generally inadvisable from the point of view of program design to use such variables. The reason is the converse to the locality-of-reference idea. If a function manipulates a global variable, managing and debugging the program become harder, because it is difficult to track all references made to a global variable. Assignment of a value to a global variable in a function

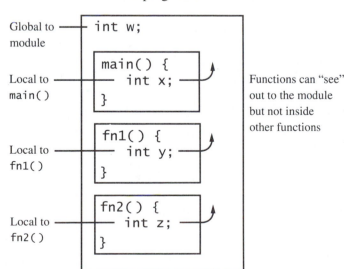

Figure 4.5   Scoping rules

is called a *side effect* of the function—that is, the function is affecting something other than its parameters and local variables. Another factor that makes global variables a bad idea is that they might have the same names as local variables or parameters. Although the compiler keeps this straight by assuming that the local variable is the one being referenced, this is one more rule that can cause confusion for the programmer.

Finally, for the sake of completeness, we note that it is legal to create blocks using braces for no particular reason inside otherwise normal-looking code, and then to declare variables inside the block. The scoping rules say that these variables are local to their block and cannot be seen from outside. The fact that "outside" means the rest of the function is potentially confusing if the new variables have the same names as variables used in the outer block. For example, consider the fragment

```
int i = 2, j = 4;
printf( "i, j = %d, %d\n", i, j );
{
   /* This is a new block, nested inside the outer block. */
   int j = 6, k = 8;
   printf( "i, j, k = %d, %d, %d\n", i, j, k );
}
```

which would produce the output

```
i, j = 2, 4
i, j, k = 2, 6, 8
```

Because j is used twice, the second `printf()` refers to the local version and prints 6. The reference to i inside the interior block is also legal, because i's scope includes that block. It would be illegal to refer to k after the closing brace, because the inner block cannot be seen from the outer block. A reference to j there would be legal, though, and would refer to the version of j declared in the outer block. This kind of code is unnecessarily confusing and should be avoided.

If, however, new names are used in the inner block, much of the confusion is cleared up. For example, if l were used instead of j in the inner block of the previous example, there would be no ambiguity. The variables l and k, used only within the inner block, would go out of existence after control passed back to the outer block (assuming there were more statements following the closing brace, for example). Such inner blocks, while sometimes useful, will not be used in our examples.

Storage Classes

The scope of variables just discussed is complicated by the fact that there are several kinds of *storage classes* for variables. These classes have associated rules that determine when memory is allocated for the variables and when it is released. We discuss these storage classes next.

The auto Class

The **auto** or automatic class is the default class for variables—if nothing is said about a variable's class, it is assumed by the compiler to be auto. A variable can be explicitly declared to be of this class by prefacing its type with the reserved word `auto`, as in `auto int count;`. The variables we have discussed so far have all been of class `auto`, because the class was omitted.

A local `auto` variable in a function has memory space allocated for it when the function is called at run time. This space is lost when control passes from the function back to the calling routine—that is, the `auto` variable lives only while the function does. This is also true for variables defined in arbitrary blocks as described in the preceding section.

Variables of class `auto` are not necessarily initialized to zero when memory is allocated for them. Whatever value happened to be stored in that memory location is inherited by the variable. Thus it is wise to initialize `auto` variables to zero or another default value. It should be noted, however, that many C compilers do initialize `auto` variables, even though it is not required.

The `static` Class

The class **`static`** is used for variables that need to retain values from one function call to the next. Unlike an `auto` variable, the memory allocated for a `static` variable and the value stored there are retained under the variable's name after execution of the function is finished. Thus, a `static` variable may be accessed the next time the function is called. The variable is still local to the function, though. Precede the variable's declaration with the reserved word `static` to make it of this class.

For example, suppose that we needed a function that kept track of how many times it was called. Suppose also that it is not feasible to keep a counter in `main()` and increment it when the function is called, because the function might be called from other functions. Therefore, a `static` counter should be declared inside the function, as in the fragment

```
void example( possibly some parameters here )
{
    static int count = 0;      /* Declaration of counter variable */
    count++;                   /* Increment counter at each call  */
    /* Rest of function code */
}
```

The initialization of `count` to zero is done only once, when the function is first called—recall that this is when space is allocated for `count`. The next line increments `count` to one. Subsequent calls to `example()` ignore the initialization. The previous value of `count` is retained, so the increment statement will correctly count the calls to the function, as was desired.

Global variables may be declared as class `static`. In this case they are not truly global but only global to the file in which they are declared. Global variables, `static` or not, are usually declared at the beginning of a file in order to be visible to the functions that follow.

The initialization of `count` to zero was actually unnecessary, although initializing a variable always makes the code more readable. Variables of class `static` are initialized to zero when they are first encountered.

The `extern` Class

Recall that in discussing global variables we noted that they were usually declared before `main()`. Such variables are by default of type **extern**. However, the usual application of this class occurs when multiple C files are used. This will be discussed further in Chapter 6, but we show a simple example here.

Suppose that the file `part1.c` contains the following code:

```
int x = 10;     /* x is a global extern int */
main() {
/* Some code here ... */
```

and that the file `part2.c` contains the fragment

```
void fn( void ) {
extern x;
/* Processing goes here ... */
```

Inside the function `fn()` the variable x is declared as `extern`. This tells the compiler to look elsewhere for the actual definition of x—in this case, in `part1`. The linker will do the work of resolving the reference after the compiler is done. The point to remember here is that in order to reference x from inside `part2.c`, it must be declared as `extern`.

Like `static` variables, `extern` variables are automatically initialized to zero at compile time.

The `register` Class

In a computer's memory, *registers* are the fastest kind of storage available; they are typically located on the same chip as the processor. Some registers are needed to handle basic operating system or program chores, but some are allocated by the compiler. The programmer can suggest that some variables be allocated registers by declaring them to be of class **register**. Note that this is *only* a suggestion—the compiler may choose to ignore it.

Usually, a variable that is critical to the speed of execution of a program is declared as `register`. For example, a loop counter could be declared as `register int index`. Also, a variable may be declared simply as `register` without mentioning a type, in which case the type defaults to `int`. Variables of class `register` are not automatically initialized.

Overuse of this class is no guarantee of improved performance, because registers are few and the compiler can ignore a `register` request. For that reason, we will not use the `register` class in any examples.

The `volatile` Class

The **volatile** class is used for variables that will be accessed by a physical device, such as a disk drive or printer. This class is used in programs, including some network communications programs, that have direct access to devices. Additionally, a `volatile` variable is protected from certain optimizations that a compiler may make to compress code by eliminating statements such as repeated assignments. For example, assuming the definition `int i;` the sequence

```
i = 0;
i = 1;
```

might be reduced by an optimizer to the single statement

```
i = 1;
```

since, without any intervening statements, that is the net effect of the two original statements. If, however, i were declared as

```
volatile int i;
```

the reduction would not take place. If i were being used to control a physical device, that device might note the alternation of values in the original format and react to each new value of i. Reducing the code to the single line removes the "strobing" effect on i and could result in different behavior by the device. That is, each individual assignment may have an effect on a device that the compressed, optimized version may lack.

Some Useful UNIX Commands

The UNIX commands discussed up to this point have dealt with file and directory management and basic editing. In this chapter, we look at several utility commands that provide file information, user information, and general information.

File Information

Counting Lines, Words, Characters

Recall that the command `ls -l` shows the long listing for files in the current directory. This includes information about the file size in bytes, its creation date, and the permissions for the file. The command **wc**, which stands for *word count*, tells the size of the file in three different ways: the number of lines, words, and characters. Suppose that the file `example.dat` is created and contains the lines

```
My dog has fleas.
My cat requires constant attention.
```

The command

```
wc example.dat
```

will produce the output

```
    2    9    54 example.dat
```

showing that the file contains two lines, nine words, and 54 characters (including two newline characters). Flags may be used to show just one or two of these quantities; they are -l for lines, -w for words, and -c for characters. The command `wc -lw example.dat` produces

```
    2    9 example.dat
```

for example. The wc command can also be used to produce summaries of multiple files. The command `wc -l *.dat` will report the line counts for each file ending in `.dat` and then tell the total number of lines in all such files.

Finding Strings in Files

To find an occurrence of a word or string in a file, the command **grep** can be used. grep takes two arguments (the search string and the file to be searched) and displays all lines of the file that contain that string. The command grep cat example.dat, using the same file as above, produces

```
My cat requires constant attention.
```

Note that the command grep ca example.dat would produce the same output. The -n flag tells grep also to report the line number: grep -n ten example.dat would show

```
2:My cat requires constant attention.
```

This command is especially useful when the file is too long to use cat or more to examine the output visually. For example, the system file /etc/termcap is a long file containing entries describing all the terminals that a system recognizes. On the authors' system, the command

```
grep -n xterm /etc/termcap
```

produces the output

```
1867:xterm|vs100|xterm terminal emulator (X Window System):\
1883:xterms|vs100s|xterm terminal emulator, small window (X Window System):\
1884:    :co#80:li#24:tc=xterm:
1885:xterm-bold|xterm with bold instead of underline:\
1886:    :us=\E[1m:tc=xterm:
1890:xterm-ic|xterm-vi|xterm with insert character instead of insert mode:\
1891:    :im=:ei=:mi@:ic=\E[@:tc=xterm:
```

The grep command has other flags and can handle many kinds of string patterns. See Chapter 8 for a further discussion of these features.

Obtaining a Sorted Version of a File

To retrieve information from a file in sorted order, the **sort** command is useful. The sort program treats the contents of a file line by line and, within each line, as space-delimited words. By default, sort sorts in ascending order according to the first word on each line and using the ASCII collating sequence. (Note that Z comes before a in this sequence.) Flags that alter the behavior of sort will be discussed subsequently.

Files used as input to sort often contain tables of data. The following file mydata contains temperature and humidity data for several cities:

```
Chicago 98 63
Phoenix 102 25
Boston 85 66
Minneapolis 78 88
```

The command `sort mydata` would produce

```
Boston 85 66
Chicago 98 63
Minneapolis 78 88
Phoenix 102 25
```

To sort on another word rather than the first, the flags `+start` and `-end` are used, where the integer `start` indicates the first word to use, counting from zero, and **end** means to stop just *before* that field. A list sorted on temperature would be produced by `sort +1 -2 mydata`:

```
Phoenix 102 25
Minneapolis 78 88
Boston 85 66
Chicago 98 63
```

Note that, as stated, the ASCII sequence was used to sort the temperatures, so that 102 is less than 78 because 1 precedes 7. To treat the temperatures numerically, use the `-n` flag, as in `sort -n +1 -2 mydata`:

```
Minneapolis 78 88
Boston 85 66
Chicago 98 63
Phoenix 102 25
```

Another difficulty arises when a data item contains a space, as in `New York`, which would be treated as two words. To remedy this, either delete the space (`NewYork`), use an underscore (`New_York`), or use a nonblank field separator such as a colon. The `-t` flag, used in conjunction with the separator symbol, alerts `sort` to the alternative separator. For example, the data file `newdata`

```
Minneapolis:78:88
Boston:85:66
Chicago:98:63
Phoenix:102:25
New York:73:66
New Rochelle:68:65
```

uses a colon separator, and the command `sort -t: +0 -1 newdata` sorts this file by city.

Other flags include `-f` to treat upper and lower case equally; `-r` to reverse the order (that is, to sort in descending order); `-u` to suppress repeated lines; and `-o myoutfile` to send the output to a file named `myoutfile`.

User Information

UNIX is a multiuser operating system, so many users may be logged in at one time. There are several commands that show information about users. **who** lists the ids of the users currently logged in plus some information about their current session—usually what terminals they are using and when they logged in. A variant of this command, **whoami**, shows your own user id. A related command, **w**, shows the same information as who and includes the current command being executed by each user. The information produced varies by system, so try each command on your own system.

The **finger** command produces similar information but usually includes the actual names of users. This command will accept a user id as a parameter, as in finger johnd. This will print information about johnd including whether he is currently logged in. If this user has a file named .plan in his home directory, this file's contents are displayed, too. The .plan file is used to let others know of personal information like telephone numbers and schedules. For example, finger johnd might produce

```
Login name: johnd                 In real life: John Doe
Directory: /home/users2/johnd     Shell: /bin/csh
No mail.
Plan:
Work: (555) 948-6083
Home: unlisted
Office Location: 112E Computer Building
Office Hours:  MWF 12-1
Host          Login at      Idle  TTY Console Location
bigcomputer   Tue 11:55am   0:01   p0 ttyp1
```

where the information after Plan: and before Host is the contents of .plan and the rest is generated by the system.

General Information

Several commands produce useful general system information. The **date** command shows the current time and date according to the system's clock; this is normally accurate but not foolproof. The **cal** command prints the current month's calendar. It also accepts either one or two numeric parameters. If only one argument is given, that argument is interpreted as a year, and the entire calendar for that year is displayed. For example, cal 95 shows the calendar for the year 95 A.D., while cal 1995 shows 1995's calendar. If two arguments are used, the first must be in the range 1 to 12 and is used as the month; the second is again the year. Thus cal 6 1995 displays

```
    June 1995
 S  M Tu  W Th  F  S
              1  2  3
 4  5  6  7  8  9 10
11 12 13 14 15 16 17
18 19 20 21 22 23 24
25 26 27 28 29 30
```

A full-year calendar may partially scroll off the screen.

When logged into a UNIX system, a program called a *shell* is running. There are several kinds of shells, and the variants are discussed in Chapter 10. Which shell you are running is a matter of choice, either yours or the system administrator's. The finger command tells which one you are using. The shell keeps track of some information about your environment, such as the kind of terminal you are using and your home directory. In the Bourne shell (sh), the command **set** will display a list of all environment variables and their settings for your current session. In the C shell (csh) there are both shell variables, shown by set, and environment variables, shown by **setenv**. We discuss only the C shell (not the Bourne shell) here and ignore environment variables.

The list of shell variables may be long, depending on your system. To show the setting of one particular variable, use the **echo** command. For example, the command echo $term might display vt100. Note the use of the dollar sign here; the command echo term will display term rather than the value stored in this variable.

As another example, echo $prompt shows the current prompt string. To change the prompt to myprompt>, type set prompt = "myprompt> ". Similarly, echo $term displays the current terminal type. To change the value of term to vt100, type set term = vt100. See Chapter 10 for more details on using shell variables.

UNIX System Calls from C Programs

UNIX commands can be executed from within C programs using the system() function defined in <stdlib.h>. It accepts a string parameter, used to denote the command to be executed. For example,

```
system( "ls -l /etc" );
```

will print the long directory listing of /etc. A string variable may be used as well, as in

```
char cmd[40];
strcpy( cmd, "ls -l /etc" );
system( cmd );
```

A common argument to system() is clear, which clears (erases) the screen. This might be used before printing a menu, for example:

```
system( "clear" );
printf( "1. Menu choice one.\n" );
/* and so on */
```

Be careful of the placement of this command in loops—a common mistake is clearing the screen at every pass of a loop rather than once before the loop begins.

Chapter Summary

■ **Sample Program (to illustrate syntax and constructs introduced in this chapter)**

```
/* Title : Sample Program for Chapter Four */
/* Source: sample4.c                       */
/* Date  : __/__/__                         */
/* Author: B&W                              */
/* Input : none                                    */
/* Output: Discussed in the Chapter 4 Review Exercises */
```

```c
/* This program illustrates function prototypes,   */
/* function headers with both pass-by-value and    */
/* pass-by-variable parameters, function calls      */
/* with arguments, and the use of recursion.       */

#include <stdio.h>

/* The three styles of function prototypes are shown here: */
void Increment ( int val, int *add );
void PrintLine ( int, int, int );
int f( int x );

main( )
{
  /* These variables are used as ARGUMENTS in function calls: */
  int count, int_1 = 0, int_2 = 0;

  /* Print header: */
  printf( "   Instruction  count  int_1  int_2\n\n" );
  for ( count = 1; count <= 2; count++ ) {
    /* Call to standard function: */
    printf( "Before Call %d:", count );
    /* Call to user-defined function: */
    PrintLine( count, int_1, int_2 );
    Increment( int_1, &int_2 );
    printf( " After Call %d:", count );
    PrintLine( count, int_1, int_2 );
    printf( "\n" );
  }
  /* Calls to both a standard and a user-defined function: */
  printf( "f( %d ) = %d", count, f( count ));
}

void Increment( int val, int *add )
/* This function increments each PARAMETER.   */
/* val is a pass-by-value parameter           */
/* while add is a pass-by-address parameter.  */

{ static int count = 0;
  /* This variable counts the number of calls to Increment. */
  /* Reusing the name "count" is legal but confusing.       */

  printf( " Inside Call :" );
  PrintLine( count++, val++, ( *add )++ );
  printf( " Inside Call :" );
  PrintLine( count, val, *add );
}
```

```
void PrintLine( int inta, int intb, int intc )
/*  The parameters of PrintLine are inta, intb, and intc.  */

{ printf( "  %d       %d       %d\n", inta, intb, intc );
}

int f( int i )
/*  This function may make a recursive call to itself.  */
{
  if ( i < 10 )
    return( i );
  else f( i / 10 );    /* A recursive call */
}
```

■ C Variables and Parameters

Variables (and sometimes, parameters) may be classified by *scope, referencing method,* and *storage class.*

Scope

A *program variable* (defined outside any function, including `main()`) may be referenced by any instruction following its declaration. A *function parameter* (defined in the function header) may be referenced by any instruction inside the function. A *function variable* (defined inside a function body, as delineated by function brackets) may be referenced by any instruction that is inside the function and that follows the variable declaration. When a function is called, each parameter must be replaced by an *argument*—that is, by a variable whose scope includes the given function call.

Referencing Method

All variables and parameters may be referenced by either their value or their address (location where stored in memory). In the following declarations, `val` is the *value* of an integer variable and `add` is the *address* of an integer variable:

```
int val, *add;
```

The address of `val` is `&val` and the value of `add` is `*add`.

Storage Class

The storage class of a variable determines the storage location or the length of time during which storage space is allocated for the given variable. Memory is allocated for an `auto` (automatic) variable only during the time when its block is being executed. Memory for a `static` variable is allocated from the first time the variable's block is executed until the program terminates. Memory for an `extern` variable is allocated before and/or after a given file is executed; in this way an `extern` variable can be shared with another program file. A `register` variable is one the compiler is asked to store in a register in order to reduce the time required to access the variable. A `register` variable may be `auto`, `static`, or `extern`.

■ **C Commands**

Standard Functions

`#include <math.h>`	Include standard mathematics functions in the current source code file
`doublea = fabs( doubleb )`	Assign the absolute value of `doubleb` to `doublea`; each variable should be a `double`
`#include <stdlib.h>`	Include miscellaneous functions from the standard library `<stdlib.h>`
`inta = abs( intb );`	Assign the absolute value of `intb` to `inta`; each variable should be an int
`longa = labs( longb );`	Assign the absolute value of `longb` to `longa`, each variable should be a `long`
`system( "ls" );`	Invoke the UNIX command `ls` to print a listing of the current directory
`exit( 0 );`	Stop the program and return 0 as the status parameter
`#include <time.h>`	Include timing functions from library `<time.h>`
`srand( (unsigned) time( NULL ));`	Use the value of `time( NULL )` to seed the random number generating function `rand( )`
`inta = rand( );`	Assign a random integer to the variable `inta`, assuming that `inta` is an integer variable
`#include <ctype.h>`	Include character macros or functions from the library `<ctype.h>`
`isdigit( ch )`	An integer expression whose value is true (nonzero) if the character variable `ch` is a digit and false (zero) if `ch` is not a digit

■ **UNIX Commands**

File Information

`wc MyFile`	Display the counts of lines, words, and characters in `MyFile`
`sort MyFile`	Display the lines of `MyFile`, sorted by the first field on each line and using the ASCII sequence
`sort +1 -4 MyFile`	Display the lines of `MyFile`, sorted by the second through fourth fields on each line and using the ASCII sequence
`sort -n +5 -6 MyFile`	Display the lines of `MyFile`, sorted by the numerical value of the sixth field on each line
`grep myword MyFile`	Display the lines of `MyFile` that contain the string `"myword"`

User Information

who	Display the ids of users currently logged in
w	Display the ids and current commands of users currently logged in
whoami	Display your own id
finger nail	Display a variety of information about the user whose id is nail

General Information

cal 2 1900	Display the calendar for February 1900 (try to predict the result of this particular command)
echo $SHELL	Display the current shell
echo $term	Display the current terminal setting (C shell)
echo $path	Display the current directory search path (C shell)
set	Display all shell variables (C shell)
set term = vt100	Temporarily reset term to vt100 (C shell)
set	Display all environment variables (Bourne shell)
TERM=vt100	Temporarily reset TERM to vt100 (Bourne shell)

Review Problems

1. Consider the sample program given in the Summary for this chapter.
   a) Predict the output of the sample program.
   b) What is the difference between the expression (*add)++ and the expression *add++ ? Note: *add++ produces the same result as *(add++).
2. Suppose the sample program given in the Summary for this chapter is modified by inserting a semicolon after the for instruction. The modified line is

   ```
   for ( count = 1; count <= 2; count++ ); {
   ```

   What is the output of the modified program?
3. a) Write a program to test the behavior of the function f( ) given in the Chapter Summary. Also write documentation to describe this function.
   b) Write a function, g( ), that has one int parameter for input and returns the first digit of that integer. For example, the call g(123) should return 1, g(-321) should return 3, and g(0) should return 0.
4. Write a program that asks the user to input 20 characters, one at a time and with a newline after each character. Test each character as it is entered, and terminate the program immediately if any nonalphabetic character is entered. Write two versions of the program, as follows:
   a) Version A should use both for and exit.
   b) Version B should use neither for nor exit.
5. Write a function to read (from the standard input) the first character that is not a white space character.
6. Write a program to compute three approximations of π using the three inverse trigonometric functions from <math.h>. Test and report whether there are any differences in the approximations.

7. (Rounding) Write a program that accepts a sequence of doubles for input and for each double reports two integers: the truncated value of the double and the integer nearest to the double. Use user-defined functions to find the truncated value and the nearest integer.

8. Describe the value(s) of each expression:
   a) `rand() / RAND_MAX`
   b) `( 1.0 * rand() ) / RAND_MAX`
   c) `( 10.0 * rand() ) / RAND_MAX`

9. Write a program to print 10 random numbers, each random number being a double in the interval from 100.0 to 200.0. Before printing the numbers, offer the user the option of providing a seed integer (to be used by the function `srand()`).

10. Why does the following code fragment fail to print a table of the 26 upper case letters (assume that `'A'` is less than `'a'`, that ch is a char variable, and that `<ctype.h>` is included)?

```
for ( ch = 'a'; ch <= 'z'; ch++ ) {
   ch = toupper( ch );
   printf( "%c\n", ch );
}
```

11. Write a program to demonstrate that the evaluation of a trigonometric function, such as `sin()`, takes much longer than the evaluation of a character conversion function, such as `toupper()`.

12. (UNIX Tutorial) Execute the appropriate UNIX command to answer each of the following questions. Try to predict the output in advance.
   a) What is your id?
   b) What are your login name and directory?
   c) Who are the other current users of your system?
   d) How many days were there in September 1752? Note: The calendar for September 1752 is very unusual. For an explanation, read about the Gregorian calendar and its adoption in an encyclopedia or similar reference.
   e) What is the calendar for September 1752 when sorted according to the first character of each line? *Hint:* First create a text file Sept1752, containing the calendar for September 1752, by executing the command `cal 9 1752 > Sept1752`.
   f) What are the dates for the week of 14 September in the year 1752?
   g) How many lines are in the file Sept1752?
   h) What is the name of your shell?
   i) What are the directories in your current search path?
   j) What are the current settings for the environment variables and the shell variables (if applicable)?

13. Write a function to
   1. Print the existing file TempFile to the screen
   2. Print TempFile again, sorted by the second word on each line
   3. Print counts of the lines, words, and characters in TempFile

Programming Problems

1. Write a program to convert four-digit alphabetic codes into four-digit numeric codes, as would occur in entering an alphabetic code via a telephone keypad or dial. For example, the alphabetic code string "BUBA" uses only two telephone keys and translates to the integer 1811.

2. (Values of Inverse Trig Functions) Write a program to display values of each of the three inverse trigonometric functions from `<math.h>`. Evaluate `asin( x )` for 101 values evenly spaced on the interval $-1 \le x \le 1$, but rather than printing all 101 values, print a table showing the 11 values `asin( -1.0 )`, `asin ( -0.8 )`, ..., `asin( 1.0 )`. Analyze `acos()` in a similar manner. For

the function `atan()`, use 101 values from the interval $-100 \le x \le 100$ and print the 11 values `atan( -100.0 )`, `atan( -80.0 )`, ..., `atan( 100.0 )`. In addition to printing selected values, verify that all values are within the appropriate range for the given function.

3. (String Conversion) Write a program that asks the user to input a sequence of characters representing digits in a number. The characters should be input one at a time (the user should press the return key after each character) with `'x'` to mark the end of input. Allow at most one period to signify a decimal point; the occurrence of any other nonnumeric characters in the input should be detected and declared an error. Accept at most four digits in the integer part of the number, and if a decimal point is given, allow at most three digits in the fractional part of the number. When proper input is obtained, the program should represent the given number as a `double` and then report back to the user the number, its square, and its cube. Do not use any of the conversion functions such as `atod()`. Use the `getchar()` function, as shown in the following code fragment, to read a character and then read the return key, which must also be pressed for each digit of input:

```
ch = getchar();
getchar();
```

4. (Substitution Cipher) Write a program to encode and decode brief messages using a substitution cipher, in which each alphabetic character is shifted by a fixed number of characters in the alphabet. For example, if the shift amount is -2, then each character is replaced by the character that comes two places before it in the alphabet (`'a'` is replaced by `'y'` and `'b'` is replaced by `'z'`). Your program should ask the user for a shift integer and then prompt the user to enter one line of text. Use a loop based on `getchar()` to read each character, changing only the alphabetic characters. Print the coded message with alphabetic characters shifted and in upper case. For example, if the user indicates a shift of $+1$ and enters the line My name is HAL, then your program should print the line, NZ OBNF JT IBM. Use the format specification `%c`, as in `printf( "%c", ch );`, to print one character at a time.

   Use this program to find the shift used to produce the coded palindrome XFBE LTP T LEBFX.

5. (Name Check) Write a program that asks the user to enter a surname (such as `"Black"` or `"Smith-Jones"`) and then checks to determine whether standard English capitalization rules are followed (including these: The first character and any character following a hyphen should be upper case; all other characters should be lower case; there should be at most one hyphen). Have the user input the name on one line of text; assume that each character is alphabetic, a hyphen, or an end-of-line character. Print a correctly capitalized version of the name and report the number of case errors as well as the number of misused hyphens. *Hint:* First write a function that reads a sequence of characters until a nonalphabetic character is read, prints each alphabetic character (the first in upper case, the others in lower case), updates a count of case errors, and returns the last character read. Call this function from the main body of the program.

6. (Future Value of an Annuity) An annuity is an investment in which the investor invests a fixed amount (P) at the beginning of each time period and accumulates interest at a fixed rate (i) for each period. The future value of the annuity (A) at the beginning of the nth time period (the total amount accumulated through direct investment and reinvestment of interest) is given by the formula

$$A = \frac{P[(1 + i)^n - 1]}{i}.$$

For example, investing \$10.00 at the beginning of each month, at a rate of 1% per month and for a period of 12 months, yields a future value (in dollars) of

$$A = \frac{10[(1 + 0.01)^{12} - 1]}{0.01} = \$126.83$$

at the beginning of the twelfth month.

Write a program that allows the user to calculate values of A, P, or n based on inputs of the other three variables. Report answers with two decimal places.

7. (Sorting Integers) Write two functions that sort three integers into numerical order.
   a) For the first function, use the header `void sort1( int a, int b, int c )`. This function should print the integers in numerical order and should not use any local variables.
   b) For the second function, use the header `void sort2( int *a, int *b, int *c )`. The last three instructions of this function should assign new values to a, b, and c in such a manner that

   ```
   a <= b <= c
   ```

   Write a program to test both functions. Use a `printf()` instruction inside `main()` to display the values returned by `sort2()`.

8. (Root Finding—Bisection Method) Write a program that executes up to 10 steps of the *bisection method*, which is a simple iterative algorithm for finding a root of an equation of the form $f(x) = 0$, subject to the requirement $a \leq x \leq b$.

   The following is a description of the bisection method: Start with an equation of the form $f(x) = 0$ and an interval of the form $[a, b]$. Assume that $f(x)$ is continuous and that $f(a)f(b)$ is negative; this ensures the existence of at least one root x for which $f(x) = 0$ and $a \leq x \leq b$. Begin by estimating the root to be the midpoint $c = (a + b)/2$. Improve the initial estimate by zooming in on either the half interval $[a, c]$ or the half interval $[c, b]$ and using the midpoint of that subinterval as the next estimate of the root. This zooming process is accomplished by the following instructions:

   1. If $f(a)f(c)$ is negative, replace b by c and find the new estimate by $c = (a + b)/2$.
   2. Else, if $f(c)f(b)$ is negative, replace a by c and find the new estimate by $c = (a + b)/2$.
   3. Else stop and declare c as the final estimate; $f(c)$ must equal zero in order to reach case 3.

   These instructions are repeated until case 3 is reached or until a specified number of estimates have been calculated.

   Include a user-defined function to evaluate $f(x)$. For example, in solving $x - \cos x = 0$, for $0 \leq x \leq 1$, use the function

   ```
   double f( double x )
   {
      return ( x - cos( x ));
   }
   ```

   The values for a and b should be input by the user. At each step of the iterative process, report the current values of a, c, b, and $f(c)$.

9. (Finding Vowels) Write a function, `int IsVowel( int *ch )`, to determine whether a character is a vowel. Return the argument ch as a lower case character, and return a constant, TRUE or FALSE, for the function value. The common rule for vowels is that the vowel characters are a, e, i, o, u, and sometimes y. Accordingly, have your function randomly declare y to be a vowel half the time. Write a test function that generates a list of random upper and lower case characters and reports the status of each character, letting the user specify the length of the list. Summarize the percentage of cases where Y and y were declared to be a vowel, in the manner of the following output, which shows the final lines from a list of 500 random characters. (*Note:* The instruction `printf( "%%" );` displays a single percent symbol.)

   ```
   500. C is NOT a vowel.

   Y and y were declared vowels 8 out of 22 times.
   This represents 36% of the time.
   ```

10. (Simulation) If x is a pseudorandom integer between 0 and RAND_MAX, then

```
r = ( (double) x ) / ( RAND_MAX );
```

assigns to r the value of a pseudorandom real number between 0.0 and 1.0. If r1, r2, ..., r12 are twelve such pseudorandom numbers, then a pseudorandom standard normal value can be generated by calculating

```
z = ( r1 + r2 + ··· + r12 ) - 6;
```

Write a program to generate 100 pseudorandom standard normal values. Report the average of the 100 values (this average should be close to 0.0) and the percentage of values between -3.0 and 3.0 (this percentage should be quite high).

11. Test the following function and determine what it does.

```
int f( double x )
{ int y;
  y = floor( log10( x ));
  return ( y );
}
```

Chapter
5

Input/Output

This chapter discusses the basics of input and output in both C programs and in UNIX. Formatted control for keyboard input and screen output is discussed first. The processing of text files comes next. We leave the discussion of random access files (binary files) to Chapter 9. The UNIX topics for this chapter include how to redirect input from files and output to files and how to use pipes to provide output from one UNIX command as the input to another.

Simple Input and Output

We have already seen how to use the `printf()` and `scanf()` functions in their simple forms. The next sections discuss these commands again and cover the basic formatting arguments accepted by each.

C programs have three standard files available for use. These are **stdin**, associated with the keyboard; **stdout**, associated with the screen; and **stderr**, used for displaying error messages and also associated with the screen. Input from the keyboard comes from `stdin` when `scanf()` is used. Output produced by `printf()` is sent to the screen via `stdout`. Error output must be sent explicitly to `stderr`; see the file functions later in this chapter for details.

In Chapter 4 standard functions were discussed in general. Both `printf()` and `scanf()` are standard functions with prototypes given in `<stdio.h>`. These functions are somewhat different from those previously discussed in that they can accept *any* number of parameters of *any* basic type rather than being restricted to parameters of fixed number and type. This capability might seem unusual at first glance, but it is essential that input and output operations be supported in this manner. Otherwise, separate functions would be required for each basic type, and a new function call would be needed for each value being input or output.

Using `printf()`

The `printf()` function, as we have seen in many examples, is used to write output on the screen. Arguments to `printf()` generally begin with one or more string constants delineated by the double quote character, as in `"string constant"`, which may contain special format symbols, such as %d, and carriage control characters, such as \n, which we have encountered before. The string constants may then be followed by expressions that match the format symbols in type. The format symbols may contain values to control the field in which the expressions' values are placed.

Each string argument passed to `printf()` is, except for the format and carriage control characters, printed literally. A beginner's mistake is to include a variable name inside the double quotes; this prints the variable name, not the variable's value:

```
printf( "Total so far = count\n" );
```

Even if `count` is, say, an `int` variable, this statement prints the phrase `Total so far = count` without substituting the value of `count`.

It is usual to have only one string constant, followed if necessary by the list of expressions matching the format characters. It is legal, however, to use several strings. For example, the statement

```
printf( "count = %d\nsum = %d\n", count, sum );
```

produces the same output as

```
printf( "count = %d\n", count, "sum = %d\n", sum );
```

If both `count` and `sum` are of type `int` and have values 5 and 275, respectively, either statement will produce

```
count = 5
sum = 275
```

as its output. Since two lines of output are being printed, it would be more appropriate, and more readable, to code the example using two `printf()` statements.

Format Control

Format controls are special character sequences designed to place output values within user-defined fields. They form a sort of target space within which the expression associated with the format string will be placed. We have seen simple examples previously. Each format control sequence has the general form

%*<flag><field int><.precision int><size prefix><conversion char>*

The format control sequence must begin with %, an "escape" character signaling that subsequent characters are to be treated specially, and it must end with one of the conversion characters:

```
d, i, u, o, x, X, f, e, E, g, G, c, s, p, n, %.
```

The internal (machine) representations of values of the standard types must be converted to text for output; these conversion characters alert `printf()` to the type being used. The conversion characters d, i, u, o, x, and X specify that a whole number is being printed; the characters f, e, E, g, and G specify floating-point numbers; c and s specify characters and strings; and p, n, and % are special-purpose conversion characters to be discussed subsequently (see Figure 5.1).

Between the two required characters, there may be several optional characters to specify the format in more detail. The *<flag>* characters specify justification to the right or left (that is, moving an item to the left or right when the item is smaller than the minimum field, described next) and padding the unused area with blank spaces or zeros. The *<field int>* characters specify minimum output length (that is, the minimum number of characters to be printed). The *<.precision int>* characters specify the precision of an approximation. Finally, the *<size prefix>* character specifies a `long` or `short` type (for example, a `long` float specifies a `double`). Thus, the instruction

```
printf( "Pi = %10.2lf", 3.14159 );
```

contains a format control sequence for printing a `double`. It also specifies no flag, a minimum of 10 spaces after the equal sign, and an approximation with two decimal places. The resulting output is

```
Pi =       3.14
```

Conversion Characters

d, i, u	Integer
o	Octal integer
x, X	Hexadecimal integer
f	Floating-point number
e, E	Exponential notation
g, G	Shorter of f, e, or E
c	Character
s	String
p	`void *`
n	`int *`
%	%

Figure 5.1   Conversion characters

The *<flag>* characters are chosen from the set

```
-, +,  , #, 0
```

and appear most often with numeric conversions (see Figure 5.2).

The minus sign, -, indicates that the expression should be left-justified in its field rather than right-justified, which is the default. A plus sign, +, forces nonnegative values to be preceded by a plus sign; the default is no sign for such values. A space forces positive values to be preceded by a blank space. If both a plus sign and space are used, the plus sign takes precedence. A pound sign, #, when used with format characters o or x, prefixes nonzero values with 0 or 0X, respectively. When # is used with e, E, f, g, or G, a decimal point is used in the value (the default is to use a decimal point only if digits follow it); additionally, the g and G have trailing zeros printed. Finally, a zero, 0, causes leading spaces to be padded instead with zeros.

The first integer value field width defines the minimum length of the field in spaces. The expression's value is placed in this field right-justified; that is, if there are any extra spaces, they appear to the left, unless the - flag is used. The second integer value (separated from the first by a period) defines the precision with which the expression is printed. For floating-point types f, e, and E, this is the maximum number of digits to the right of the decimal point. For integer types this value is the minimum number of digits to print. For s string formatting, the precision indicates the maximum number of characters to print from the string. If a string has more characters than this maximum amount, the extra characters are not printed.

The prefix character modifies the format character by indicating which variant, if any, to use. The h prefix indicates a short type and may modify d, i, o, u, x, and X. The l prefix indicates long and may modify the same integer formats as h as well as the floating-point formats e, E, f, g, and G, where it indicates a double instead of the default float. The L prefix indicates that an e, E, f, g, or G is of type long double (see Figure 5.3).

Flags

-	Left justify
+	Print sign
<space>	Force blank
#	Force 0 or 0x (with o, x, X) Force decimal point (with floats)
0	Pad with 0s

Figure 5.2 Flag characters

Prefixes

h	short (integers only)
l	long (integers only) double (floats only)
L	long double (floats only)

Figure 5.3   Prefix characters

The integer format characters are d and i, decimal integers; u, unsigned integer; o, unsigned octal integer; and x or X, unsigned hexadecimal integer.

Suppose that we have defined short i = 15; int j = -275; and consider the statements

```
printf( "1234567890\n" ); /* Space counter for the following output */
printf( "%5d\n", i );
printf( "%9.6d\n", j );
printf( "%+d\n", j );
printf( "%+8hd\n", i );
```

These produce the following output:

```
1234567890
   15
  -000275
-275
      +15
```

Floating-point formats come in the following varieties. The printf() function is lenient about the difference between the float and double types; that is, the l prefix is not required. The f format character is used to print decimals in the style <-*whole number.decimal*>, where the number of digits in the whole number part is determined by its magnitude, and the number of digits in the decimal part is determined by the precision width, if present, or 6 as the default. Decimal values are rounded, not truncated. The e format is used for exponential notation style <-*digit.decimal*> e <*sign*><*integer*>, where only one digit is used before the decimal point, the decimal part follows the same rules as for the f format, and the e signals that the following integer is the power of ten in exponential notation. The E format simply substitutes a capital E for the lower case e. The g format chooses the more compact of the f and e formats, but chooses e only if the exponent is less than −4 or is greater than or equal to the precision. In addition, the precision is interpreted as the number of significant digits, but trailing zeros are removed and a decimal point is printed only if it is followed by a digit. The G behaves similarly and chooses between f and E.

For example, given the declarations

```
float   x = 300.586;
double y = -0.44718;
```

the statements

```
printf( "1234567890\n" ); /* Space counter for the following output */
printf( "%8.2f\n", x );
printf( "%8.2e\n", x );
printf( "%8.2g\n", x );
printf( "%8.4g\n", y );
printf( "%8.4E\n", y );
printf( "%8.4lf\n", y );
```

produce the output

```
1234567890
  300.59
3.01e+02
     3e+02
 -0.4472
-4.4718E-01
 -0.4472
```

The string formats are c for a single character and s for strings. In the latter case, the associated string value is printed up to the first \0 character found or until the precision is reached.

Three other format characters are available. The p is used for an argument of type void *, a pointer to a void type. The pointer (address) is printed in hexadecimal format. The n is used with a pointer to an integer. The value of this integer is not printed; rather, the number of characters printed so far by this call to printf() is stored in the argument. (Refer to Chapter 7 for more on pointer variables.) Finally, the format % is used to print a percent sign, and it is not matched to any expression. Thus, printf("%%\n"); prints a single percent sign.

Carriage Control

Carriage control characters send special instructions to the output device. Although most of these instructions make sense when applied to the screen, some can be recognized as printer controls. These control characters should be tested on one's screen device. Figure 5.4 lists the carriage control characters, which will be described subsequently.

Many previous examples have used one of the carriage control characters: \n, the new-line character. This causes a new line to be started. As with the other control characters, the newline must be typed as two characters, the backslash followed by n. Internally, though, this is stored as a single character, because the newline command corresponds to one ASCII character.

Carriage control

\n	Newline
\t	Horizontal tab
\v	Vertical tab
\b	Backspace
\r	Carriage return
\f	Form feed
\\	\
\"	"
\'	'
\0	String terminator (null)

Figure 5.4   Carriage control characters

Some other common control characters are \t, the horizontal tab character; \v, the vertical tab; \b, the backspace character; \r, which causes a carriage return (but not a line feed); and \f, the form feed character.

If a character that has another special meaning is to appear as itself within a string literal such as a `printf()` statement string, a backslash must precede the character. For example, to print a double quote, use \"; otherwise, the double quote will be taken as terminating the string. Similarly, \' produces the single quote, \\ represents the backslash character, and \0 stands for the null character. For example, to check whether a character variable `ch` contains the single quote character, use the expression (`ch == '\''`). Likewise, the statement `ch = '\"'`; assigns the double quote to `ch`.

As another example, consider the commands

```
printf( "One\'s quotes (\") should, in the long run,\n" );
printf( "never exceed one\'s backslashes (\\).\n" );
```

which produce the output

```
One's quotes (") should, in the long run,
never exceed one's backslashes (\).
```

However, recall that %%, not \%, is used to print a single percent sign. The reason for the difference is that the characters introduced by the backslash have special meanings (such as '\'') or are unprintable (such as '\r') anywhere a string literal is used, but the percent sign has special meaning only in a `printf()` or `scanf()` format string.

Using `scanf()`

As with `printf()`, the basics of `scanf()` have been seen in previous examples. The two commands share similar format characters, but `printf()` is more flexible—it can accept expressions, not just variables, for example. One major difference between the two commands is that `scanf()` requires the *addresses* of the variables it is accessing. This should make sense in light of Chapter 4's discussion of pass-by-value versus pass-by-address parameters for functions. The `scanf()` function needs to return values in its parameters, so it needs their addresses. This is the cause of many problems because of the need to remember when it is appropriate to use the & address operator (needed for simple variables) and when not to use it (for strings and in functions where a parameter is pass-by-address). Refer to Chapter 4 for a discussion of these topics.

The string argument passed to `scanf()` may contain the format control characters, plus other control information. The latter is optional and is interpreted literally, as in `printf()`. Thus, white space in the string matches white space in the input (including a carriage return). It is not necessary to match the same number of spaces exactly, however. Non–white space characters not preceded by % are likewise matched to their counterparts in the input. For example, if we need to read an `int` and a `float` that are either on the same line separated by spaces or on two separate lines, the command

```
scanf( "%d %f", &i, &f );
```

will do the job (provided the appropriate declarations have been made). This will successfully read a data line such as 102 5.441. If the data items are instead separated by a comma, then the command

```
scanf( "%d, %f", &i, &f );
```

is needed and will successfully read the input line 102, 5.441 typed at the keyboard. It is important to note that the two examples are incompatible. The comma on the second example's input line is significant. If the first `scanf()` is used to read the second line, the comma is matched to f, the `float` variable, causing an error to occur. However, the second `scanf()` successfully reads the *first* line of input.

There is no simple way to control type mismatches when using `scanf()` with format characters. If a `float` is expected but the user types letters, the corresponding `float` variable will be filled with something, but no error will be reported. This is one reason that some programmers write their own input conversion functions instead of using `scanf()`. The `scanf()` call does, however, return an `int` value that indicates the number of successful conversions made. This value can be used to make a simple error check, as in

```
count = scanf( "%d %f", &i, &f );
if ( count < 2 ) {
  printf( "Error in reading the values." );
  exit();
}
```

The returned value from `scanf()` is stored in `count`, which is then checked for the correct number of conversions: two. This check can tell that *something* went wrong, but not what.

Format Control

The `%` is used to indicate that what follows is control information. In its simplest form, the format control character is simply the analog of the `printf()` characters previously described. We briefly revisit those characters here.

The integer family contains `d` and `i` for signed integer types, `u` for unsigned decimal integers, `o` for unsigned octal integers, and `x` and `X` for unsigned hexadecimal integers.

The floating-point family contains `f` for decimal floating-point types, `e` and `E` for exponential notation, and `g` and `G` for either style.

The character family contains `c` for single characters and `s` for strings. Care must be used in reading characters and strings. For example, it is assumed that string variables have enough space to store the input string plus the end-of-string terminator, `\0`. If this is not true, a run-time error may occur when that string is printed later. Also, the string matched by `%s` cannot contain white space; an equivalent statement is that `%s` matches a string delimited by white space. For reading single characters, it is usually advisable to declare a string of length 2 and use the conversion string `%1s`, or to use the `getchar()` function discussed in the following section.

A prefix character may modify the basic type character, as in `printf()`. These are `h` to indicate a `short` integer type, `l` to indicate a `long` integer type and a `double` float type, and `L` to indicate a `long double` type. The `scanf()` function is less enient than `printf()` when these prefix characters are omitted. In order to get the correct value into a variable, the type of the variable must be matched exactly by the format characters. The most common error made in this regard is to use the `%f` format for a `double` variable instead of the required `%lf`. This has no serious effect in a `printf()` but is wrong for a `scanf()`:

```
double x;
scanf( "%lf", &x );     /* Correct match       */
scanf( "%f",  &x );     /* Incorrect match     */
printf( "%lf", x );     /* Correct match       */
printf( "%f",  x );     /* Incorrect but works */
```

Other Input and Output Commands

Several other functions may be used to receive input from the keyboard and to produce output on the screen. The functions in this set are used less frequently than `printf()` and `scanf()` because they have very specific uses.

The following prototypes show two output functions, defined in `<stdio.h>`:

```
int putchar( int ch );
int puts( char *str );
```

The first function is used to output single characters to the standard output. The prototype declares the parameter `ch` as type `int` rather than `char`. This is feasible, because `int` is the underlying type of `char`s. This allows more flexibility because an `int` can represent special character codes such as `EOF` (end-of-file). The second function is used to write strings to the screen. The next code fragment illustrates the use of these functions.

```
char *sentence = "Life is good.";
int  count;
/* Write the string, one character at a time. */
for ( count = 0; sentence[count] != '\0'; count++ )
  putchar( sentence[count] );
printf( "\n" );
/* Write the string all at once. */
puts( sentence );
```

Each part writes the string `sentence`:

```
Life is good.
Life is good.
```

The corresponding input functions are defined by these prototypes:

```
int getchar( void );
char *gets( char *str );
```

As with `putchar()`, the **getchar()** function uses the underlying type `int` instead of `char`. A call to this function takes the form

```
char ch;
ch = getchar();
```

where the necessary type cast to `char` is automatic. Use of the `getchar()` function is complicated by the fact that the standard input, normally the keyboard, uses a buffer to hold characters. Thus, a call to `getchar()` will wait for input until the return key is pressed. The return key press is also interpreted as a character, which can complicate input processing. A second call to `getchar()` will remove the return press character if necessary.

The **gets()** function is useful for reading strings that may contain white space characters. Recall that white space is significant to the `scanf()` function when reading strings. One or more spaces are used to delimit strings and other data for `scanf()` and are then ignored. A call to `gets()` will retrieve one line of input, regardless of internal white space. The fragment

```
char str[20];
gets( str );
```

may be used to receive, for example, the string `Life is good.` or the single word `Life`, whereas a `scanf()` call would need to use three string variables to handle the first string and one for the second. On the other hand, recall the problem with `getchar()` mentioned earlier in handling the return press character. If a call to `getchar()` is used to read one character on a line, and a call to `gets()` to read the next line, then `gets()` receives the return press character and an empty string value for its argument. A second call to `getchar()`, as already noted, takes care of this.

It is important to note that when reading strings, neither `gets()` nor `scanf()` is fool-proof. Neither checks to make sure that enough memory has been allocated to store the string being read. Since you will not know what the user will actually type in response to a prompt, any variable's size limit can be overrun. This is one facet of the larger problem of obtaining and verifying input by size and type. Prompting the user to enter an integer, for example, is no guarantee that the user will follow the instructions. If the code

```
int number;
printf( "Enter an integer: " );
scanf( "%d", &number );
```

is executed, the user might respond by typing `Life`, and something will go wrong. A C program may not crash at this point, but invalid information would be stored in the variable `number`.

Text File Processing

When data is stored using variables, that data is lost when the program exits unless something special is done to save it. It is possible to use the `printf()` function, which normally writes data on the screen, in conjunction with the UNIX redirection commands to save data in a file, as will be described later in the chapter. This section discusses other methods for writing data directly to files. Only text files are covered here. Chapter 9 discusses the use of binary files to store records for direct access file applications.

Opening and Closing Files

The `<stdio.h>` header file contains the definition of a record type that is used by the operating system to keep track of open files. The name of this record type is **FILE**. The data in a record of type FILE is managed by the operating system and can be accessed by the user, but we will not need to know this information. To open and read from or write to a file, we only need to use the FILE type name to declare *file pointer* variables. A file pointer is declared in the following manner:

```
FILE *fptr;    /* fptr is a file pointer variable */
```

Once a `FILE` * variable is declared, it can be used to reference the file in other commands. For example, the function to open a file is **fopen()**, which has the prototype

```
FILE *fopen( char *name_string, char *mode_string );
```

The parameter `name_string`, either a literal string such as `"prog1.dat"` or a string variable, contains the name of the file to be opened. In UNIX this may be a full pathname, such as `"/usr/home/myuserid/prog1/prog1.dat"`. The second parameter indicates what kind of access is being requested on the file. There are three basic access modes: read, write, and append. Read access requires that the file already exist. Write access will create a new file if the file does not exist, but if the file does exist, write access will erase the contents of the file on opening. Append access will create a new file if necessary but will not destroy the contents of an existing file, because the intent of append is to add information to a file. Certain combinations of these modes are also possible, indicated by using a plus sign. Legal mode strings include:

"r", for read-only access
"w", for write access
"a", for appending to a file
"r+", read and write access; file must exist
"w+", write and read access; existing file contents erased or new file created
"a+", append and read access

One other character, "b", may be included in the mode string to indicate a binary file. Interleaving of reads and writes is usually done only on binary files, not text files. Binary files are illustrated in Chapter 9.

The value returned by the fopen() function is a file pointer. If an error occurs when opening the file, the value of this pointer is NULL, a constant declared in <stdio.h>. Always check for this possibility. Moreover, even if a file pointer is·not NULL, the file may be empty. Robust programs guard against reading from empty files.

For example, the following fragment shows how to open the file prog1.dat for read access.

```
FILE *fptr;


fptr = fopen( "prog1.dat", "r" );
if ( fptr == NULL ) {
  printf( "Error opening prog1.dat\n" );
  exit( 0 );
}
```

When the name string parameter is a character string variable whose value was obtained from the user, and fptr returns a NULL, it is more appropriate to prompt the user for the file name again, because a simple misspelling may have caused the error. The next fragment prompts the user for a file name until a file is successfully opened.

```
#define LIMIT 40
FILE *fptr;
char  filename[LIMIT];   /* filename may have up to 39 characters, plus */
                         /* a NULL character to terminate the string.   */
do {
  printf( "Enter name of file: " );
  scanf( "%s", filename );
  fptr = fopen( filename, "r" );
  if ( fptr == NULL ) {
    printf( "Error opening %s\n", filename );
    printf( "Please try again.\n" );
  } /* if ftpr */
} while ( fptr == NULL );
```

For the sake of completeness, the next example shows a shortcut method for assigning and checking the file variable. It is possible, but not desirable because of possible confusion, to combine the assignment of `fptr` and the test of its value for NULL. The trick (and it *is* a trick) is to enclose the assignment in parentheses inside the test statement, as the following fragment shows:

```
if (( fptr = fopen( filename, "r" )) == NULL ) {
   printf( "Error opening %s\n", filename );
   printf( "Please try again.\n" );
} /* if ftpr */
```

Although the syntax appears to indicate a test of parenthetical phrase (`fptr = fopen( filename, "r" )`) for equality with NULL, the actual test is of `fptr` with NULL. Thus, this version appears to use one less line of code, having combined the assignment statement with the test. However, the compiler still views this as two lines. More importantly, compressing the code makes it less readable and thus more prone to errors and misunderstanding. Therefore, our examples will not use this style, but the reader should be alert to it in other programmers' code.

When processing of a file is finished, the file should be closed using the **fclose()** command, whose prototype is

```
int fclose( FILE *fptr );
```

The parameter passed to `fclose()` is the same file pointer variable that was returned from the `fopen()` function call. The return value from `fclose()` is zero if the file was successfully closed, and the constant **EOF** if an error occurred. EOF is defined in `<stdio.h>` and is used to indicate that either an error occurred (its use here) or the end-of-file was reached, which will be illustrated subsequently.

We will assume in the following examples that a sequence of statements similar to one of the fragments just given is used to open files. Note that such "safe" file opening code could easily be placed in a separate function to hide the details of prompting for a file name and testing for existence of the file.

Reading and Writing Text Files

The usage of the functions discussed in this section, **fprintf()** and **fscanf()**, corresponds directly to the related functions `printf()` and `scanf()`. Refer to the earlier sections of this chapter dealing with those functions to see the full list of options for each. This section shows how to use the new functions to read and write text files.

The `fprintf()` function writes information to an open text file. It returns an integer telling how many bytes were actually written. This integer can be used for error checking. The first parameter to `fprintf()` is the file pointer obtained from the `fopen()` call. The other parameters are a combination of literal strings, containing formatting information, and variables or expressions that match the format characters.

As a simple example, suppose we want to write the even integers from 2 to 20 to a text file, one integer per line. We assume that the file pointer variable `fptr` has been properly assigned via the `fopen()` statement for writing.

```
int count;    /* for loop counter */
for ( count = 1; count <= 10; count++ )
   fprintf( fptr, "%d\n", 2 * count );  /* Write twice the count to the file. */
fclose( fptr );    /* Close the file */
```

As with screen output, the integers being printed will be in character format, as opposed to binary or internal format. This means that the file containing these integers could be edited using, say, vi, or it could be displayed using `cat` or `more`. We return to this issue when discussing binary files in Chapter 9.

Recall that the standard file `stdout` is opened by the system when a program starts. The output from `printf()` statements is by default directed to `stdout`, normally associated with the screen. The `fprintf()` function can also be used to send information to the screen using the syntax `fprintf( stdout, …`*some message*`…);`. Similarly, `stderr`, intended for error messages, may be used by statements of the form `fprintf( stderr, …`*some message*`…);`.

The `fscanf()` function reads information from an open text file. The first argument to `fscanf()` is again the file pointer variable. The other parameters follow the same form as `scanf()`, where formatting characters are matched by type to the addresses of variables. Again, see the earlier discussion of `scanf()` for more details.

To read the file written in the previous example, the following fragment will suffice. Assume that the file referred to by `fptr` has been successfully opened for reading.

```
int item;    /* To hold the value read from the file */
for ( count = 1; count <= 10; i++ ) {
   fscanf( fptr, "%d", &item );   /* Read one value.               */
   printf( "%d\n", item );        /* Print the value on the screen. */
}
fclose( ftpr );   /* Close the file */
```

Although this example is quite simple, it illustrates the use of `fscanf()`. It also hints at an important yet subtle idea in file processing. There must be agreement on the format of the data stored in a file. Unlike an interactive program, where the user is being prompted for information and the program can be constructed to handle a variety of responses, file-processing programs must rely on a given structure of the file. Some steps can be taken to recover from format mismatches, but such problems must be avoided at the program requirement and design stages. The examples in the next section show some simple file-processing strategies.

The standard input file, `stdin`, from which `scanf()` receives keyboard input, may also be used with `fscanf()`. The syntax used is `fscanf( stdin, `*format,*` `*variables*` );`. It is also possible to assign any of the standard input or output files to a FILE * variable. For example, consider a program that asks the user whether input will be read from a file or from the keyboard. The variable `whichone` is then set to 1 to indicate that a file is to be used or 0 to indicate the keyboard. Assuming the correct definitions, the fragment

```
if ( whichone )
   infile = fopen( userfile, "r" );
else
   infile = stdin;
```

assigns `infile` as either `stdin` or as the user's file. After this initialization, input is received using `fscanf( infile,...);` statements, regardless of which value was assigned to `infile`. The other file commands described subsequently may make use of this technique, too.

Other File Input and Output Commands

We mention briefly here several other functions available for reading and writing text files. Each has an analog among the interactive input and output functions discussed earlier in this chapter.

To write a single character to a file, the equivalent functions **putc()** and **fputc()** may be used. Their prototypes are

```
int putc( char ch, FILE *fptr );
int fputc( char ch, FILE *fptr );
```

where `fptr` is the file pointer for an open file. Similarly, to read a single character from a file, the functions **getc()** and **fgetc()** are available and have similar prototypes:

```
int getc( FILE *fptr );
int fgetc( FILE *fptr );
```

All four functions return EOF in case of error. An additional function, **ungetc()**, is used to push back a character that has already been read (but not EOF). Its prototype is

```
int ungetc( int ch, FILE *fptr );
```

The functions **fputs()** and **fgets()** are used to write and read strings. Their prototypes are

```
int fputs( char *str, FILE *fptr );
char *fgets( char *str, int num, FILE *fptr );
```

Note that `fgets()`, unlike `gets()`, has an integer parameter. This is used to indicate that at most `num` − 1 characters are to be read, terminating at end-of-line or end-of-file. The end-of-line character will be placed in `str` before the string terminator. If end-of-file is encountered as the first character, EOF is returned; otherwise `str` is returned. The `fputs()` function returns EOF if unsuccessful.

File Processing Examples

The following examples show three simple ways to process data files. Many file-processing methods have been developed, most of which attempt to speed up access to data in the file by some clever storage scheme. Sorted files, index files, and B-trees are a few of the well-known methods; see, for example, [Sedgewick]. This section's examples are not nearly so smart, but they share one characteristic with the other methods: the processing method and the file structure are intertwined with each other.

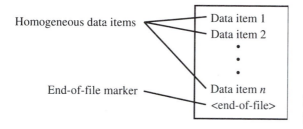

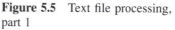

Figure 5.5 Text file processing, part 1

Read until EOF

The simplest method for file processing is simply to read until the end of the file is reached. In C, this means checking until the EOF flag is returned by the `fscanf()` function. As in any file, the data to be read must be of a known type. Chapter 9 contains examples of reading and writing records to files. In the next example the file is *homogeneous:* All the file contents are of the same type. In this and the following examples only simple data types are used (see Figure 5.5).

In addition, the function **feof()** can be used to check whether the end of a file has been reached. Its prototype is

```
int feof( FILE *fptr );
```

which returns a nonzero value if the end has been reached and zero otherwise. The `feof()` function is used in the next example. Beware that a file may exist and yet be empty.

This example illustrates a simple yet powerful file operation: merging two sorted files into a new, third, sorted file. The size of neither input file is known beforehand, so the read until end-of-file technique must be used on each. The algorithm used is this: Read one data item from each input file and compare them. Put the smaller (assuming the sort order is smallest to largest) into the output file and read a new item from the input file from which that smaller item was read. Repeat this process until the end-of-file condition is reached in one of the input files. Then copy the remaining data items from the other input file into the output file. For simplicity, we will use files of integers and will assume that each of the three files has been successfully opened—two for reading and one for writing—and that each input file is not empty.

```
#define FALSE 0
#define TRUE  !FALSE

FILE *infile1,    /* First input file pointer   */
     *infile2,    /* Second input file pointer  */
     *outfile;    /* Output file pointer         */
int  inval1,      /* Input value from first file */
     inval2,      /* Input value from second file */
     done;        /* Flag for stopping the merge */
```

```
/* Loop until processing of one of the files is finished */
done = FALSE;
fscanf( infile1, "%d", &inval1 );
fscanf( infile2, "%d", &inval2 );
while ( !done ) {
  if ( inval1 < inval2 ) {
    fprintf( outfile, "%d\n", inval1 );
    if ( fscanf( infile1, "%d", &inval1 ) == EOF )
      done = TRUE;
  } else {
    fprintf( outfile, "%d\n", inval2 );
    if ( fscanf( infile2, "%d", &inval2 ) == EOF )
      done = TRUE;
  }
}
/* Decide which file finished first and copy the other to the outfile */
if ( feof( infile1 )) {
  /* File 1 is finished, so copy the rest of file 2. */
  fprintf( outfile, "%d\n", inval2 );
  while ( fscanf( infile2, "%d", &inval2 ) != EOF )
    fprintf( outfile, "%d\n", inval2 );
} else {
  /* File 2 is finished, so copy the rest of file 1. */
  fprintf( outfile, "%d\n", inval1 );
  while ( fscanf( infile1, "%d", &inval1 ) != EOF )
    fprintf( outfile, "%d\n", inval1 );
}
```

Note the several tests for EOF: when reading from either input file and when deciding which file was exhausted first. We assumed that both input files contained at least one integer; that is, we did not test for EOF in the initial `fscanf()`s for each file.

Header Information

Files often contain information about their contents in a *header section* that precedes the actual file data. This header may specify the data types of the data records and format used to store those records. In the next example, we show a very simple kind of header: The first line of the file contains an integer telling how many lines of data follow it. Note that the use of a header makes a file *heterogeneous*—the header is a different kind of information from the file data itself (see Figure 5.6).

Suppose that floating-point test scores have been entered in a text file, one score per line, and that we want to compute the average of those scores. The header information, an integer on the first line, tells how many test scores follow in the file. We can use a `for` loop to read the scores one at a time until there are no more scores left. We assume the file has been correctly opened for reading and that it will be correctly closed.

Read Header

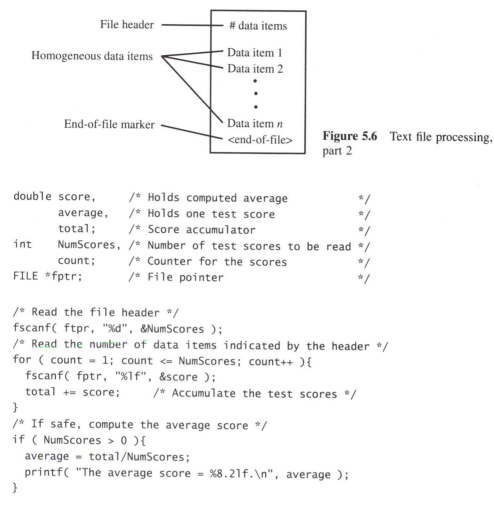

Figure 5.6   Text file processing, part 2

```
double score,    /* Holds computed average      */
       average,  /* Holds one test score        */
       total;    /* Score accumulator           */
int    NumScores, /* Number of test scores to be read */
       count;    /* Counter for the scores      */
FILE *fptr;      /* File pointer                 */

/* Read the file header */
fscanf( ftpr, "%d", &NumScores );
/* Read the number of data items indicated by the header */
for ( count = 1; count <= NumScores; count++ ){
  fscanf( fptr, "%lf", &score );
  total += score;       /* Accumulate the test scores */
}
/* If safe, compute the average score */
if ( NumScores > 0 ){
  average = total/NumScores;
  printf( "The average score = %8.2lf.\n", average );
}
```

Several things can go wrong when the foregoing code is executed. If the file is empty, the first `fscanf()` fails. If `NumScores` is larger than the number of scores actually stored, the second `fscanf` will also fail. A robust program should handle these situations. We will not pursue these issues at this point.

Flag at End

The final file-processing method uses a *marker* or *flag* value to indicate the end of the data rather than relying on EOF. Obviously, the marker is redundant information if it simply indicates the end of the file. A common usage is for the marker to indicate the end of a section of data. Several sections may then be contained in one data file (see Figure 5.7).

For this example, suppose that a store keeps track of its daily sales transactions by writing each individual sales amount into a data file. At the end of each day, a marker is written

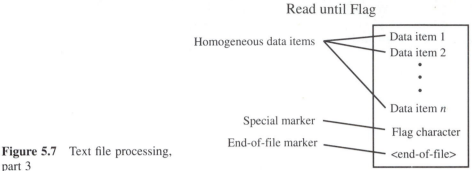

Read until Flag

Homogeneous data items

Special marker

End-of-file marker

Data item 1
Data item 2

•
•
•

Data item *n*

Flag character

<end-of-file>

Figure 5.7 Text file processing, part 3

to separate this day's sales from the next day's sales. Since sales amounts will be positive real numbers, we choose the value -1.00 as the marker to separate days. The following program fragment finds the total sales for each day and the total sales for the entire period stored in this file. Again assume that the input file has been opened correctly.

```
#define MARKER -1.00


double CurrentSale,
       DailySale,
       TotalSale;
FILE   *fptr;


TotalSale = 0.0;
/* Loop until end of file */
while ((( fscanf( fptr, "%lf", &CurrentSale )) != EOF ) {
  /* Reinitialize DailySale each day. */
  DailySale = 0.0;
  /* Read one day's sales amounts */
  while ( CurrentSale > MARKER ) {
    /* Accumulate this day's sales */
    DailySale += CurrentSale;
    fscanf( fptr, "%lf", &CurrentSale );
  }
  printf( "Daily Sales = %8.2lf\n", DailySale );
  /* Accumulate today's sales into total */
  TotalSale += DailySale;
}
printf( "Total Sales for period = %8.2lf\n", TotalSale );
```

Note that the test for the marker value is not an equality test. As usual with floating-point numbers, you should test for equality with respect to a tolerance value, as discussed in Chapter 3. The test here does not need a tolerance value, because sales amounts should be positive values, and the marker is negative. We leave it to the reader to devise a method that also tests for and excludes negative sales amounts.

UNIX System I/O

UNIX maintains a consistent philosophy about input and output by using the concept of a *stream* of bytes. A stream is simply a sequence of data. In UNIX this data, regardless of its meaning, is treated as raw data in one-byte units. Thus, when the `cat` operation is performed on a file, the file is retrieved and sent to `stdout` byte by byte. Keyboard input, printer output, and data from communications devices are all treated in this uniform way. Note that this is a logical view of input and output. For example, the physical details of how a file is retrieved from a hard disk are conveniently ignored. Using a logical view rather than a physical view simplifies a task by removing (or at least delaying consideration of) smaller details.

The metaphor of a flowing stream of bytes has given rise to other related concepts: *pipes* of data, *tee* connections, and *redirection* of streams to and from files. A UNIX command that uses the stream concept to simplify its input and output is called a *filter*. The remainder of this chapter discusses streams, redirection, pipes, and filter commands.

Redirection

Both UNIX commands and user-written C programs often require input or produce output. When the input is expected from the keyboard or the output is sent to the screen, it is possible to use redirection commands to substitute a file's contents as the source of input or to send the output to a file. The basic redirection commands for this are < to redirect input and > to redirect output.

The output of a UNIX command may be captured in a file using redirected output. For example, the command `ls > listing` will send the output of the `ls` command into the file `listing`, which is created when the command is executed. Likewise, `sort datafile > newdatafile` will send a sorted version of the file `datafile` into the new file `newdatafile`.

Most often, UNIX commands are used with output redirection, since most commands take a command line parameter indicating the file to be used as input. For example, the `cat` command is usually used in conjunction with a file name, as in `cat myfile.c`, which will show the contents of `myfile.c` on the screen. However, if the `cat` command is issued with no parameter, it waits for input typed at the keyboard, echoes whatever is typed, and ends when control-D is typed. In fact, input can be redirected to the `cat` command. The command `cat < myfile.c` will achieve the same effect as `cat myfile.c`.

If a file already exists by the name used in a redirection command, UNIX will either complain with an error message or erase the existing file and overwrite it with the new file; the choice depends on the settings of certain environment variables. If, however, you wish to append an existing file with redirected output, the command >> does the trick. For example, suppose that the file `mydata` already exists. Then `sort datafile >> mydata` will append a sorted version of `datafile` on the end of `mydata`.

To create a user-written example using redirected input, suppose that the following C program were compiled to the executable file `example`:

```
#include <stdio.h>
```

```
main() {
  int    age;
  double salary;
  printf( "Enter the employee age: " );
  scanf( "%d", &age );
  printf( "Enter the employee salary: " );
  scanf( "%lf", &salary );
  if ( age > 0 )
    printf( "Salary per year of age = %8.2lf\n", salary/age );
}
```

When `example` is executed, the input for the two `scanf()` statements is obtained from the keyboard. Suppose that instead we first use `vi` to create a file named `example.dat` containing the data

```
39
31500.0
```

Then we can execute the command `example < example.dat`. The input data for the two `scanf()` statements is now obtained from the file `example.dat`.

Note, however, that the previous example's prompts for input and the label for the output would still be printed on the screen. In order to create a program that behaves like a UNIX command, prompts must not be used. Programs that behave in this way are discussed next.

Filters and Pipes

A UNIX *filter* is a command that accepts a stream of bytes as input and produces a stream of bytes as output. No intervention or interaction is needed once a stream is directed to a filter. Many UNIX commands are filters. Some common examples previously discussed are `sort`, `wc`, and `cat`. Each accepts an input stream, possibly formatted in some way (such as records on a line for `sort`), and produces an output stream, also optionally formatted (such as the three integers produced by `wc`). Some commands are not filters. `more`, for example, produces a prompt and requires input from two sources: a file and the keyboard. The `mv` command simply renames files, without dealing with input and output at all.

User-defined programs can be designed to work like filters too. As seen in the last example, the use of prompts in a program violates the spirit of a filter. Input to a filter is unprompted, although it may be formatted in some way. For example, to change the previous example to act like a filter, we might write

```
scanf( "%d%lf", &age, &salary );
```

to collect the input and

```
printf( "%8.2f\n", salary/age );
```

to produce the output. In order to work like other UNIX commands, though, this program might be designed to check the command line for a file name. If one were present, that file would be used as input. Otherwise, the standard input would be used, and redirection of input could be handled. Command line parameters are discussed in Chapter 8. An output file could be handled similarly.

Besides redirection, UNIX filters can receive their input and route their output another way. A *pipe* sends the output of one command to the input of another. A pipe is represented by the character | and is used after the command that produces output and before the command that awaits input, all on one command line.

Suppose, for example, that we needed to produce a list of files in the current directory, sorted by the number of lines contained in each. Recall that the UNIX command to count lines is wc -1 and that the sort command will do the sorting. To combine these two commands, we write

```
wc -1 * | sort
```

which pipes the output of wc into the input of sort and shows the sorted list on the screen. The * symbol is a special character that matches any string, in this case any file name. See Chapter 7 for more details about this and other special characters.

Piping can be combined with redirection to get input from a file or save output in a file. To send the output of the previous example to the file outfile, one would write

```
wc -1 * | sort > outfile
```

The contents of outfile could then be viewed using more.

When user programs are written as filters, piping can be used on them as well. Suppose that the code fragment in the preceding section were made into a complete program that computed salary per age for any number of inputs, and that the executable file produced using cc is called agesal. Further, suppose a data file named infile exists, where each

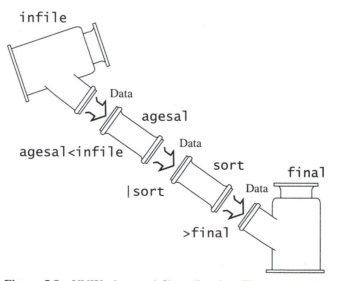

Figure 5.8 UNIX pipes and file redirection. The command is
agesal < infile | sort > final

line of `infile` contains an integer age and a floating-point salary. To process `infile` using `agesal`, sort the output, and save the results in `final`, one would write (see Figure 5.8)

```
agesal < infile | sort > final
```

Sometimes output needs to be seen on the screen as well as sent to a file. In such a situation the **tee** command is needed. For example,

```
agesal < infile | sort | tee  final
```

will show the results of the previous command on screen and send them to the file `final`. Note that this example also illustrates the use of two pipes in one command. In general, any number of pipes may be used to link commands to provide customized functions.

Reference

Sedgewick, Robert, *Algorithms in C,* Addison-Wesley, Reading, MA, 1990.

Chapter Summary

■ **Sample Program (to illustrate syntax and constructs introduced in this chapter)**

```c
/* Title : Sample Program for Chapter Five */
/* Source: sample5.c                       */
/* Date  : __/__/__                         */
/* Author: B&W                             */
/* Input : From keyboard, a file name,        */
/*          two characters, an integer, and a double  */
/* Output: Four data items to a file and to screen   */

/* Open a file, interactively read and store four items */
/* in the file, close the file, reopen it for reading,  */
/* and then write file contents to screen               */

#include <stdio.h>

#define LIMIT 40
/* Maximum number of characters in filename is (LIMIT - 1) */

void WriteFile( FILE *file_ptr );
void ReadFile ( FILE *file_ptr );

main( )
{ FILE *file_ptr;         /* Pointer to a text file          */
  char filename[ LIMIT ]; /* Name of the text file           */
  int fclose_status;      /* Remember if closing is successful */
  /* Open a file for writing */
```

```
   printf( "Name the file, using at most " );
   printf( "%d characters: ", ( LIMIT - 1 ));
   scanf( "%s", filename );
   /* Read over the Return key from above */
   getchar();
   file_ptr = fopen( filename, "w" );


   /* If successful so far, write to file, */
   /* then close it and reopen for reading */
   if ( file_ptr != NULL ) {
     printf( "\n\nComplete each instruction by " );
     printf( "pressing <Return> key.\n" );
     WriteFile( file_ptr );
     fclose_status = fclose( file_ptr );
     if ( fclose_status != EOF )
       file_ptr = fopen( filename, "r" );
     else {
       printf( "Error occurred trying to close file: " );
       printf( "%s\n", filename );
     }
   }
   else {
     printf( "Error occurred in trying to open file: " );
     printf( "%s\n", filename );
   }


   /* If successful so far, write file  */
   /* contents to screen and close file */
   if (( fclose_status != EOF ) && ( file_ptr != NULL )) {
     printf( "\n\nContents of file: %s\n", filename );
     ReadFile ( file_ptr );
     if ( fclose( file_ptr ) == EOF ) {
       printf( "Error occurred trying to close file: " );
       printf( "%s\n", filename );
     }
   }
   else {
     printf( "Error occurred trying to reopen file: " );
     printf( "%s\n", filename );
   }
}


void WriteFile( FILE *file_ptr )

/* Read four items from the keyboard and store them */
/* in the specified file.  scanf() reads over any   */
/* white space before a number but not a character. */
```

```c
{ char ch1, ch2;    /* First two items */
  int i;            /* Third item      */
  double x;         /* Fourth item     */

  /* One way to read and write a character: */
  printf( "Enter a single character: " );
  ch1 = getchar();
  getchar();  /* Read over the <Return> character */
  fputc( ch1, file_ptr );

  /* Another way to read and write a character: */
  printf( "Enter another character: " );
  scanf( "%c", &ch2 );
  fprintf( file_ptr, "%c", ch2 );

  /* Read and write two numbers */
  printf( "Enter an integer, some white space, and a double: " );
  scanf( "%d %lf", &i, &x );
  /* Note:The next command prints a space between the numbers */
  fprintf( file_ptr, "%d %lf", i, x );
}


void ReadFile ( FILE *file_ptr )
/* Read four items from the specified file and print    */
/* them on the screen.  fscanf() reads over any white   */
/* space before a number but not before a character.    */

{ char ch1, ch2;    /* First two items */
  int i;            /* Third item      */
  double x;         /* Fourth item     */

  /* One way to read and write a character: */
  ch1 = fgetc( file_ptr );
  printf( "Characters: " );
  putchar( ch1 );

  /* Another way to read and write a character: */
  fscanf( file_ptr, "%c", &ch2 );
  printf( "%c\n", ch2 );
  /* Read and write two numbers */
  fscanf( file_ptr, "%d %lf", &i, &x );
  printf( "Integer: %d\n", i );
  printf( "Real: %lf (decimal form), or ", x );
  printf( "%E (exponential form)\n", x );
}
```

■   **C Commands**

Opening and Closing Text Files

```
FILE *fptr
```

`fptr = fopen( "file1", "r" );`	Open the text file for reading; return a pointer to `file1` if opening is successful, otherwise return NULL
`fptr = fopen( "file1", "w" );`	Create (overwrite if necessary) a text file, open the file for writing
`fptr = fopen( "file1", "a" );`	Open the text file for writing, set file position pointer at the end of the file
`fptr = fopen( "file1", "r+" );`	Open the text file for reading and writing; return a pointer to `file1` if opening is successful, otherwise return NULL
`fptr = fopen( "file1", "w+" );`	Create (overwrite if necessary) a text file, open the file for writing and reading
`fptr = fopen( "file1", "a+" );`	Open the text file for writing and reading, set file position pointer at the end of the file
`fclose( fptr );`	Close the file to which `fptr` is pointing
`feof( fptr );`	Return TRUE if EOF has been read

Text Input

`ch = getchar( );`	Read the next character from the standard input stream and assign it to the variable `ch`
`ch = fgetc( file_ptr );`	Read the next character from the text input stream to which `file_ptr` is pointing and assign it to the variable `ch`
`gets( str );`	Read the next line of characters from the standard input stream and assign it to the string variable `str`
`fgets( str, n, file_ptr );`	Read the next (n-1) characters from the text input stream to which `file_ptr` is pointing and assign them to the string variable `str`
`scanf( "%c %s %d %lf", &ch, str, &i, &x );`	From the standard input stream, read and convert from text format to the specified formats, the next character, a string, an integer, and a `double`, and then assign these to the variables whose addresses are &ch, `str`, &i, &x. The function reads over any white space (usually spaces and newlines) preceding the string, integer, or `double`, and terminates conversion of each of these when a white space is reached.
`fscanf( file_ptr, "%c %s %d %lf", &ch, str, &i, &x );`	From the text input stream to which `file_ptr` is pointing, read a character, a string, an integer, and a `double` as described above

Text Output

`putchar( ch );`	Write the character `ch` to the standard output stream
`fputc( file_ptr, ch );`	Write the character `ch` to the text output stream to which `file_ptr` is pointing
`printf( " %c%7s% 7d%-7.2lf", ch, str, i, x );`	To the standard output stream, write a space, the character `ch`, the string `str`, the integer `i`, and the `double` `x`. The string, integer, and `double` will be converted to text format and printed in a field of at least seven columns. If the integer is positive, it will be preceded by a space. The `double` will be left-justified in its field and will be printed with two decimal places.
`fprintf( file_ptr, " %c%7s% 7d%-7.2lf", ch, str, i, x );`	To the text output stream to which `file_ptr` is pointing, write a space, a character, a string, an integer, and a `double` as described above

■ **UNIX Commands**

`MyProg < in_file`	Redirect *input* to the program `MyProg` from the file `in_file`, rather than from the standard input stream
`MyProg > out_file`	Redirect *output* from the program `MyProg` to the file `out_file`, rather than to the standard output stream. If `out_file` already exists, it is overwritten or an error message is given.
`MyProg >> out_file`	Redirect *output* (and append, if necessary) from the program `MyProg` to the file `out_file`, rather than to the standard output stream
`FirstProg	SecondProg`	Execute the programs `FirstProg` and `SecondProg`; *pipe* the output stream from `FirstProg` to the input stream for `SecondProg`
`FirstProg	tee SecondProg`	*Tee* output of the program `FirstProg` to the program `SecondProg` *as well as* to the standard output stream

Review Problems

1. Write a code fragment that uses format controls to produce the following output on the screen. Do not assume that the printing position is already established at the left margin.

```
12345678
========
3.14159
   3.14
  +3.14
 3.1E+00
```

2. Write a code fragment to print a string of at most 10 characters, left-justified within the first 10 columns on the screen, followed by three blank columns, followed by an integer right-justified within a field that accommodates integers of absolute value at most 999. Do not use any blank spaces within the format control sequence.

3. Are the following code fragments equivalent?
   a) Code Fragment 1:

   ```
   double y, z;
   scanf( "%lf %lf", &y, &z );
   ```

   b) Code Fragment 2:

   ```
   double y, z;
   scanf( "%lf", &y );
   scanf( "%lf", &z );
   ```

4. Consider the following code fragment.

   ```
   FILE *file_ptr1, *file_ptr2;
   double a, b, c;

   file_ptr1 = fopen( "file1", "w" );
   file_ptr2 = fopen( "file2", "w" );
   fprintf( file_ptr1, "1 2.01 -3E20" );
   fprintf( file_ptr2, " -1.0\n1.000\n3.14159E02" );
   if ( fclose( file_ptr1 ) == EOF )
     printf( "Error occurred trying to close file: %s\n", "file1" );
   if ( fclose( file_ptr2 ) == EOF )
     printf( "Error occurred trying to close file: %s\n", "file2" );

   file_ptr1 = fopen( "file1", "r" );
   file_ptr2 = fopen( "file2", "r" );
   printf( "12345678901234567890 1234567890\n" );
   fscanf( file_ptr1, "%lf %lf %lf", &a, &b, &c );
   printf( "%10g%10g%10g\n", a, b, c );
   fscanf( file_ptr2, "%lf %lf %lf", &a, &b, &c );
   printf( "%10.1E%10.1lf%10.1lf\n", a, b, c );
   if ( fclose( file_ptr1 ) == EOF )
     printf( "Error occurred trying to close file: %s\n", "file1" );
   if ( fclose( file_ptr2 ) == EOF )
     printf( "Error occurred trying to close file: %s\n", "file2" );
   ```

   a) How many characters (including \n but not EOF) are stored in file1 and file2 following execution of the two fprintf() instructions?
   b) What output is produced?

5. The purpose of the following function, PrintFile1(), is to prompt the user for a file name, open the given file, and write the file contents to the screen.

```
#define NAME_LIMIT 40

void PrintFile1 ( void )
{ char ch, filename[ NAME_LIMIT ];
  FILE *file_ptr;

  printf( "Enter file name " );
  printf( "(limit of %d chars): ", NAME_LIMIT - 1 );
  scanf( "%s", filename );
  file_ptr = fopen( filename, "r+" );
  while ( ch != EOF ) {
    ch = fgetc( file_ptr );
    printf( "%c", ch );
  }
}
```

   a) Find at least two major shortcomings of the given function.
   b) Find at least five other shortcomings of the function as given.
   c) Write a corrected version of the function.

6. Give the UNIX command to execute the programs `Prog1`, `Prog2`, and `Prog3` in consecutive order, with input to `Prog1` coming from the file `in_file`, output from one program used as input to the next program, and output from `Prog3` going to the file `out_file`.

7. Write a program to show the tab settings on your system.

8. Check your manual to determine whether `tee` overwrites or appends by default, and find the flag that changes from the default to the alternate mode.

Programming Problems

1. (File Scan) Write a function to scan a file (specified by the user) and count the number of occurrences of upper case characters, lower case characters, decimal digits, white spaces, and other characters. In addition, give the user an option of specifying one character to be counted separately. Echo the file contents to the screen, using <EOF> to mark the end of file, then print a table of character counts, and then report the special character count (if appropriate) and the line count, as in the following sample output (where the newline character was designated as the special character).

```
HERE ARE THE FILE CONTENTS:
 This line begins with a space.
This line has a tab character before the period
The third line has 0 newline characters.<EOF>

CHARACTER    COUNT
=================
Uppercase       3
Lowercase      92
Digit           1
White Space    23
Other Chars     3

=================
TOTAL         122
```

```
The character '\n' occurred 2 times.
There are 3 lines in this file.
```

2. (Directory Count) Write a function that returns the number of visible files in the current directory. Do this by redirecting the directory listing to a temporary file and basing the count on the number of lines in the temporary file. Remove the temporary file before terminating the program.

3. (Sorting) Write a program to sort a user-maintained directory that is stored in a text file having lines of the form

    <name> *<size>* *<month>* *<day>*

    where *<name>* is string of 29 or fewer characters (but not an empty string, and not containing any white space), *<size>* is a nonnegative integer, *<month>* and *<day>* are integers that indicate the date of the last change, and there are one or more white spaces between entries. Allow the user to sort by name, by size, or by date. Print the sorted files using upper case for all file names, even though the original directory file may contain names in lower, upper, or mixed case.

    Base the sorting program on three user-defined functions:

    - The first function should copy the directory file to a temporary file wherein each name is converted to upper case and each date is coded by a single integer (have larger integers represent later dates). Assume that the last two elements in the directory file are '\n' and EOF.
    - The second function should be a filter that calls the UNIX `sort` command (to sort the temporary file) and redirects the output of `sort` to a second temporary file.
    - The third function should display the contents of the second temporary file, decoding the date to the original month and day.

    Each function should return an error code. Remove both temporary files before terminating the program.

4. (Variation of `wc` function) Write a program that scans a text file and counts the number of lines, words, characters (excluding white space characters), average word length, and average number of words per line. Treat any characters between the last '\n' and the EOF marker as a final line of text. Count punctuation characters in the total character count, but not in the calculation of average word length. Do not use the UNIX function `wc`.

5. Write a filter program to read a text file and produce an output stream that echoes the input but changes capitalization so that the only upper case characters in the output are

    - The initial character in the file
    - Any character that is the first alphabetic character after a period, a question mark, or an exclamation mark

6. (Reformatting) Write a filter program to read a text file and produce an output stream that reformats the input in the following manner:

    - All original spaces and newline characters are deleted.
    - Newline characters are inserted after every 25th remaining character.
    - Spaces are inserted on each line of output after the fifth, tenth, fifteenth, and twentieth characters.
    - All alphabetic characters are printed in upper case.

    Coded text is sometimes displayed in this manner to make it harder to recognize word and line breaks from the original text. For example, this sentence is reformatted as shown here:

    ```
    FOREX AMPLE ,THIS SENTE NCEIS
    REFOR MATTE DASSH OWNHE RE:
    ```

7. (ATM—Login) Write a program to simulate the login process of an automatic teller machine. Base the program on a function that asks the user first for an identification number (an actual ATM would automatically read this from the magnetic strip on the user's plastic card) and then, if the id number is valid, asks for a Personal Identification Number (PIN). The function should return an integer to indicate either a successful login or an appropriate error code. Use two associated files. The first file should contain messages to inform the user of a successful login or any errors; the program should offer to log the user in only after successfully opening this file. Each line of the message file should contain a message corresponding to one of the codes that might be returned by the login function. All other messages presented to the user should be coded as string constants within the program. After reading the user's identification number, the login function should attempt to open a second file containing valid pairs of ids and PINs. Each line of this file should contain one such pair. If the user's id appears in the second file, the user should be prompted to enter a PIN, and this response should be compared with the PIN from the file. Ids should be nine-digit positive whole numbers; PINs should be four-digit positive whole numbers.

8. (Cumulative Sales Report) Write a program to read individual sales data from a file and print a report of total sales for each day, total sales overall, and average daily sales (rounded to the nearest cent). Assume that each datum in the file represents either an individual sales amount, an end-of-day marker or an end-of-data marker. Report an error if any sales datum (other than a marker) is not positive or if an end-of-day marker does not immediately precede the end-of-data marker.

Chapter 6

Program Design

In this chapter we discuss methods for designing programs. The programs discussed up to this point have been quite small. In order to progress to writing larger programs, care must be taken to control the added complexity of such programs. "Larger" does not merely mean more lines of code; it also implies more functionality, more computation, perhaps more user interaction, more data, and more interconnections among all these elements.

There are formal methodologies for designing programs. These require a commitment by the program developer in time and effort to learn specific notations and terminology. Although such formal methods are beyond the scope of this text, we will discuss some general principles for program design and will look at a decomposition method for breaking up larger problems into smaller ones. Chapter 11 discusses issues in data structure design, a necessary component of program design. The UNIX topics for this chapter include tools for helping manage and debug programs.

Design Concepts

The field of *software engineering* applies engineering practices to the design of programs that are efficient, reliable, and economical. These practices include identifying the various stages of the software development process (sometimes called the *software life cycle*); applying systematic, repeatable methods to each stage; developing and incorporating reusable code; and verifying that software achieves its stated goals of performance. This process includes maintenance activities, because software used over a long period of time will require repairs to fix errors and modifications to add new functionality. One model of the software life cycle is the *iterated waterfall* model (refer to Figure 6.1).

At each phase in this model, errors inherited from previous phases require modifications at previous phases (where the error was introduced). The development process must repeat or iterate earlier phases until each part is correct. The phases are described subsequently in this chapter; see [Pressman] or [Sommerville] for more details.

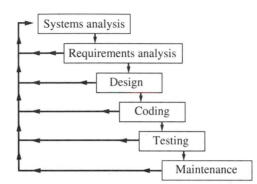

Figure 6.1 Iterated waterfall model of software development

In order to illustrate the concepts in this chapter, we will use a simplified check-in/check-out system (CICOS) for a small hotel. The desired system will automate the check-in process, produce itemized bills on check-out, keep track of current occupancy, and maintain records of recent transactions (see Figure 6.2).

The system is not totally realistic, because it contains many simplifications that would not be acceptable for a real hotel. However, it should show some concrete applications of the ideas presented in this chapter.

The statement that a new system is needed is the first step, called the *systems analysis* phase, in any software life cycle model. A company or other organization must identify its current and future needs and show why the current system is no longer adequate. Possible solutions, such as updating the current system, buying off-the-shelf software, or developing new software, are explored. Costs and risks for each are analyzed. Hardware and staffing needs play a part in this, of course, but here we focus only on the software aspects. If the decision is made to develop a new software package, then either internal resources are lined up for the project or an outside software development company is retained. For our hotel example, room management is currently done by hand, using a set of file cards with room information, customer forms filled out by hand, and a filing system organized by floor. It is the desk clerk's responsibility to search manually for unoccupied rooms when a customer is checking in. The process is time-consuming, is error-prone, and lacks adequate backup records. Also, its efficiency is highly dependent on the clerk's knowledge. Therefore, it is decided to automate the system on a UNIX workstation using C as the development language.

The *requirements analysis* phase determines the functional and performance specifications of the software precisely. Some of the work in this phase is social and psychological, because the eventual users of the software must be queried about their needs. This may take the form of user interviews or market research. Once the requirements are known, they are reformulated into precise, verifiable statements detailing what the software will do and how

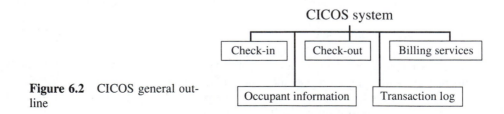

Figure 6.2 CICOS general outline

the user will interact with it. Specifications may be written in a formal specification language or simply in technical English, but they are usually organized into a logical structure. For example, one of the requirements for our hotel system, CICOS, is stated as, "An itemized bill will be produced for the customer at check-out." The related specifications in technical English are the following.

An itemized bill will be produced for the customer at check-out:

- An itemized bill will be displayed on the screen.
- This display will include fields for:

    Customer name and address, check-in date, *check-out date, method of payment, credit card number, room number, daily room rate, *number of days stayed, *room charges, telephone charges, other charges, *tax, *total.

- This display will allow the clerk to change information in nonstarred fields.
- Fields marked with a star will be computed automatically.
- This display will contain an option for printing a hard copy (printer) version of the itemized bill on a carbon form.

This is only a partial list. For example, the designs of the check-out screen and the hard copy display need to be specified. In this book, specifications are usually given for problems and examples, and we do not discuss the details of requirements gathering and specification any further.

The *design* phase can be broken into parts. In the first part, a high-level design is developed, indicating how the program will be organized on a broad scale. Modules and their component functions are specified, thereby forming a structure or skeleton of the program. Also, the data structures necessary to the program are identified. The interactions between functions are determined by the structure of the program and by the interface definition (the prototype) of each function. The program structure includes how functions are grouped into modules (collections of functions, sometimes called *units*) and which functions will call other functions. The interface definition of each function determines what data items are passed as parameters. The second part, known as *detailed design,* gives each function its own structure, providing an outline for the eventual code. *Pseudocode* (a mixture of English and generic computer code) is often satisfactory for this part and forms the basis for code documentation.

Our CICOS might be made up of a central control module, which calls as needed the modules for check-in, check-out, searching the guest list for a particular customer, and showing occupancy information. The occupancy module may be broken down by room, by floor, and by entire hotel functions. The design for the check-out module is as follows:

Check-out module

- Obtain room number from user
- Query system date
- Compute number of days stayed
- Compute room charges
- Compute total charge
- Display check-out screen

- While not done do
  - Update fields
  - Process new entries
- If printed bill is desired
  - Print itemized bill
- Write bill to transaction file

Some lines of this design need further refinement, and some refer to other functions. The interface between the check-out module and the functions it calls must be clearly stated. For example, "compute room charges" depends on the number of days stayed, the type of room, and any discounts or surcharges applicable. The latter two need to be looked up in the room data structure and passed to the function that computes room charges. The section on top-down design has more on the design of the hotel program.

The next phase, the *coding* phase, involves writing the program based on the chosen design. Provided the detailed design was carefully constructed, this should be a straightforward task. Knowledge of data structures, algorithms, and implementation techniques drives the design phase more than the coding phase. Coding should simply implement the desired structures and algorithms in the development language. For example, in the CICOS check-out process, the room information needs to be looked up based on the room number. A two-dimensional array (that is, a table; see Chapter 7 for a discussion of arrays) of room records might be considered appropriate, and queries on this structure could be implemented.

The *testing* phase is usually considered as a distinct phase following coding, but many testing activities are performed at each of the other phases. Errors can occur in specifications and design as well as in code. The need for productivity requires that such errors be detected as early as possible before they are propagated to (and usually enlarged in) later phases. Even so, there are several testing activities to do after code is produced; some of these are discussed in this chapter. The check-out module for the hotel example requires that room charges be computed. This was designated as a separate function whose parameters are number of days stayed, type of room, and discounts or surcharges. To test the room charge function, a table of possible values for each of these parameters is constructed. Especially important among these values are boundary values. For example, if the number of days stayed can be any positive integer, we would test (at least) values 0, 1, and 2. If we also decide to bound this parameter from above, say at 365 days, then we would also test values 364, 365, and 366.

The final test for a system is the acceptance test, in which the customer decides whether or not the delivered system is satisfactory. Regular contact with the customer and careful checking of the program against the system specifications eliminate rude surprises at this point.

Once the program is delivered, the *maintenance* phase begins. Bugs that are discovered as the program is subjected to normal use, shortcomings of the original requirements, desired new functionality, and new hardware or operating system environments all lead to requests for changes to the existing program. A program can last many years through incremental changes and major releases. In CICOS, for example, suppose that the computation of the number of days stayed did not handle leap years correctly. Whether this was an error at the requirements specification, design, or coding stage can be argued, but the bug could be fixed as part of the maintenance activities. Also, suppose that later the system needs to support a reservation system. The program could be expanded to support concurrent access to the room data, more storage to support future occupancy, and an ability to run on different hardware platforms. For major changes, of course, we are back to the systems analysis phase. The existing program may need to be scrapped and a new one built.

The use of engineering practices gives a different flavor to software development, and as a result, some people view software engineering as distinct from computer science. Consider the following analogy. The proof of a theorem in mathematics, while quite logical, is unique to that theorem and cannot be transferred to another theorem. Some techniques are reusable, but in general each proof is a unique creation. Computer science is sometimes viewed in this manner, producing programs the way mathematical proofs are constructed. Software production, seen in this manner, requires a unique solution for each new problem. Again, while some reuse of methods (data structures, algorithms, and tricks of the trade) is possible, each new program is a unique creation. Software engineering, on the other hand, emphasizes *repeatable* processes that can be applied across problem domains and measured for efficiency and success. Careful specification and documentation at each phase play a large role in the overall process, but producing them is sometimes seen as unproductive activity because no lines of code are directly produced. This is a more mundane view of program development, perhaps, yet it still allows room for creative solutions through innovative designs and algorithms. For the production of large programs by teams of programmers, the methods of software engineering appear to be essential.

Components

The ability to break up programs into smaller parts, both code and data, is an important tool for managing the complexity of a program. Designing a program can be driven by the data components or by the code components. As noted above, Chapter 11 discusses data structures and the consequences those structures imply for program design. Here, we discuss the code components needed for design.

Blocks, Functions, and Modules

What should be the building blocks of the design of a program? When larger tasks are decomposed into component subtasks, the decomposition stops when the designer feels confident that a subtask is small enough to be codable—but that is a subjective judgment. When the design is translated into code, some tasks might correspond to modules, some to functions, some to blocks of code, and some to individual lines of code.

The latter two cases are associated with the detailed design, whereas the former two correspond to high-level design. In previous chapters, detailed design has been shown in examples that have used given specifications and have shown methods of implementing solutions for small problems. For high-level design we focus on functions and how functions can be grouped together into modules.

Chapter 4 emphasized the principle of "one job, one function." Each function in a design is associated with one task or component subtask. The interface to a function—its name, return type, and number and type of its parameters—defines how other functions interact with it. Its job should be precisely defined. The details of how the function accomplishes its job are left to the detailed design and the implementation. This is one aspect of the concept of *information hiding,* in which a high-level description of a function ignores its internal workings. This allows design to concentrate on the large scale and ignore the small scale, decreasing the immediate complexity of the problem.

From the hotel example, consider the need to act on the initial choice obtained from the clerk. Once the clerk chooses a legal option, a controller module must take the appropriate action: check a new customer in, check a customer out, search the rooms for patron information, and so on. Each of these tasks should be a separate function or module, called from the controller module. The controller module does not need to know, for example, how the itemized bill is produced, and the code that produces the bill does not need to reference the details of the controller module.

A related concept is *modularity*. A large program broken into units and functions is modular. Each named unit and function can be treated as an *object:* something that can be dealt with as a whole. Units, being collections of functions, can be rated on two properties: cohesion and coupling. The functions within a unit should be related to each other by the tasks they perform; ideally, each should perform a subtask of the unit's task.

How the functions relate to each other is called the *cohesion* of the module. Cohesion varies from high to low and is stated by types, which include (from highest to lowest) *functional* (subtasks of a larger task), *communicational* (functions share common input or produce common output), *temporal* (functions are called at approximately the same time), and *coincidental* (unrelated functions placed in a module for convenience). High cohesion is a desirable property of a program, because ideally a module should try to do one thing, and the component parts should all relate to that goal.

Interunit connections are rated by the *coupling* of units. *Tight* or *content* coupling means that units share data or control information; *loose* coupling means that units are self-contained; and there is a graduated scale between these extremes. Loose coupling of modules is more desirable than tight coupling. Tight coupling implies that two or more modules must work together on a task and must be understood (and debugged) jointly. This adds complexity to a program from a purely structural (as opposed to problem-induced) aspect. Another aspect of information hiding—that data and control information are kept within a function or module and should not be visible from outside—is a cousin to loose coupling and is also desirable. (See [Sommerville] for more details.)

In the CICOS example, recall the task of producing an itemized bill. Our pseudocode design indicated several component tasks were required, such as "Compute number of days stayed" and "Print itemized bill." If these tasks were designed as functions, they would be placed together in one module to ensure high cohesion. If instead we placed the "Print itemized bill" in a module with, say, the function that searches for a patron and the function that displays the main menu, we would be guilty of coincidental cohesion. Producing the bill is logically separate from keeping track of current occupancy information. These tasks should be placed in separate, independent modules to ensure loose coupling.

High cohesion and loose coupling are ideal goals, but they are sometimes difficult to achieve. The design of data structures, and which modules need to share these structures, often complicates reaching these goals. Good design requires forethought and experience.

Function Parameters

As noted above, a function helps simplify code by handling one specific job, although that job may be modified by the arguments which are substituted for the function's parameters.

A function may be used simply to remove some task from the main body of a program. For example, the task "Display the header information on the screen" might be implemented by a series of `printf()` calls. When placed in a function, the task of displaying the header is replaced by one statement, such as `DisplayHeader();`. Even if this task is needed only once, the function call simplifies the main program.

More generally, there are tasks that need to be done at several points in a program. For example, "Display the main menu" may need to be done many times. To repeat the code for this task would unnecessarily complicate the program, even though it is accomplished by a few `printf()` statements.

Sometimes the task requires input information or returns values other than the function's return value. The main menu function could be generalized to print any menu, for example. The generic menu function could then be called with the main menu stored in strings as the arguments to the function. Later, when a submenu must be displayed, the generic function could be called with a submenu's strings as the arguments. If careful attention is paid to the parameters, the function may be made as generic as possible, not only reusable from within the current program but suitable for storage in a library so that other programs can use it. *Reusability* of code is one way to increase programmer productivity.

From the discussion of function parameters in Chapter 4, recall that pass by value and pass by address are the two methods for parameter passing in C. The fact that parameters can be passed in these two ways implies that there are two uses for parameters in functions. A pass-by-value parameter is used only as input to a function. This may be an argument to some computation, as in `sqrt( x );` for example. Pass-by-address parameters, on the other hand, can be used both to send data into a function and to return new values from a function.

Without parameters, a function must either operate on global data (visible throughout the program or unit) or contain program-specific information. Global variables may appear to be a simple solution to what some see as the "problem" of using parameters. This problem is aggravated by C's syntax for pass-by-address parameters. Nevertheless, the use of globals prohibits reusability of functions, not only in the case of library functions but also in the case of user-defined functions. A more subtle problem also arises when using global variables. Since the global is not mentioned in the function prototype, the calling function is invoking two sets of actions by the act of calling the function: what is promised with regard to the parameters and arguments and whatever happens to the globals. Especially when more than one person is developing the program, these second, implicit actions may be overlooked. Oversights also occur when one person works on a program over time—without stringent discipline, the developer may forget these implicit actions. Manipulation of globals inside a function is sometimes called a *side effect* of the function. Even though global variables are legal in C, their use is discouraged except where absolutely needed.

As an example where a global variable might be justified, consider the hotel program. The array of room records is a likely candidate to be a global variable, because several functions will need to access it, either to update information stored there or to retrieve information. On the other hand, it is easily passed as a parameter, thereby maintaining control over the structure. "A global is easier" is rarely a valid excuse for bypassing the use of parameters.

Potentially reusable functions from the hotel program are hard to identify. Designers and programmers must use extra effort to make functions reusable. The menus, as noted earlier, can be handled by a generic display function. Computing the room charge, however, is specific to this program and unlikely to be reused.

Design Methods

Program design methods are differentiated by what they consider first (and thus as most important) about a system. The following brief descriptions (which follow [Northrop and Richardson]) do not tell the whole story about each method but instead indicate the focus of each. For each method there exist formal methodologies, which often consist of graphical representations, step-by-step techniques, and design style rules. Refer to Figure 6.3 and see [Pressman] or [Sommerville] for details.

Kinds of Design

The *function-oriented* method breaks larger tasks into smaller ones. This is a special case of a design process known as *top-down design* or *stepwise refinement.* Tasks are decomposed until each task is the right size for implementation as a function. The resulting program structure is a hierarchy or tree of functions. Grouping of functions into modules or units is done largely by proximity in the tree. The method ignores, to a large extent, what data structures are being used. The CICOS function that computes the number of days stayed, called by the function for computing the room charge, is an example of function-oriented design.

Data flow design models a program as a series of processes that accept data as input, process it, and produce data as output. Data structures necessary to model the flow are designed first, followed by design of the processes (modules). The modules a' refined by decomposing them into component functions. Data flow diagrams are used to ˜how the flow of data from one process to the next graphically and are often useful as an organizational method regardless of the design method being used. For example, check-out information in CICOS is input for the check-out function, is modified, and then becomes output. This information is in turn input for the transaction history module.

The *data structure–oriented* model at first takes a database approach to design. Data is seen as highly structured, perhaps according to a formal model such as the relational model

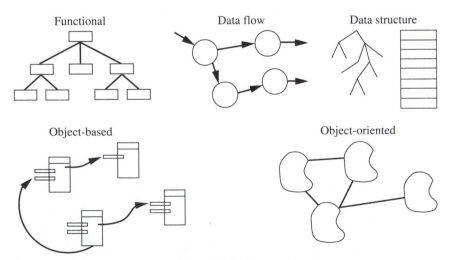

Figure 6.3   Design methods and sample diagrams

(where data is stored in tables). Operations on the data structures are defined. These operations constitute the functions and modules of the program and affect the program design: sequential data leads to repetition structures, hierarchies lead to trees, and so on. Less emphasis is placed on program structure, however, than on the modeling of entities with appropriate data structures. For example, our hotel could be modeled by first designing the room record. An array of room records, plus fields for other hotel information, could model the hotel itself. This program might also need data structures for files and file indexes to speed lookup of rooms and tenants.

In *object-based* design, data structures and operations on them begin to merge to produce modules centered around *abstract data types,* or ADTs. An ADT is meant to model a real-life object. The use of "abstract" indicates that the ADT, as a module, presents to other modules only an idealized view of itself. The only possible operations on the ADT's data are defined by the ADT's external interface (that is, its function prototypes). No outside module can directly access the ADT's data, and knowledge of the internal workings of the ADT is not necessary. In this way, information hiding is achieved. For the hotel example, a Rooms ADT could be used. Operations on Rooms would then include entering tenant information, retrieving tenant information, querying a particular room, and so on. The check-in function would interface with the user to gather the necessary information, then call the necessary function to enter it into Rooms. The check-in function would pass parameters to the ADT and would not need to know whether the tenant information is stored in an array, a list, or a file.

Finally, *object-oriented* design takes the ADT concept and builds new abstractions on it. An *object,* like an ADT, is a model of a real-life entity. Objects contain internal data structures, a public interface in the form of function prototypes, and private functions. A *class* is an object template, and objects are variables of their class type. In addition, a class can be derived from another class, inheriting the features of the parent class. Such classes are the main design unit. Objects that are derived from the various classes communicate with each other via function calls but hide their internal workings from other objects. Object-oriented programming languages, such as Smalltalk and C++, are used to implement this design method. One class in CICOS could be defined for room information. Since most languages provide basic classes for common data structures, we would probably be able to reuse an array class, tailoring it to hold our objects with room information.

In summary, note that function-oriented design focuses on the control structures of a program, using a hierarchical model for the interactions between functions. Data flow design looks at both how data moves through a system and what control mechanisms are needed to process that data. The remaining three methods are all data-oriented. Data structure–oriented design focuses on the logical structure of the data and how to implement it. Object-based design constructs modules around the data, providing access to the data via the module interface (the functions defined on the data). Object-oriented design takes this one step further by generalizing modules to objects that can interact with other objects and by abstracting common properties of objects to create classes. Practitioners of each method might argue for the superiority of their method over the others, but the fact that there are practitioners of each method indicates that a clear-cut choice of a "best" method is far from obvious.

Top-Down Design

Top-down design is a useful technique regardless of the design method used. This decomposition technique is often contrasted with *bottom-up* design, which we discuss here briefly. Libraries of related functions, such as the <math.h> library, are typical of bottom-up design. We can construct larger functions or units by combining basic functions from the library. For example, using the sqrt() and pow() functions we can write a new function that finds the roots of a quadratic equation. Similarly, recall the discussion of UNIX filters in Chapter 5. Filters can be combined to form more complex commands. Also, note that the library of functions need not be a standard one; user-defined collections of functions may be used too.

In practice, neither the top-down nor bottom-up design methods are used alone. When trying to decompose a large problem into components, it is useful to keep an eye toward both existing and easily implemented low-level functions as a target. Similarly, combining small functions into larger components requires some model of what is being built.

We now consider CICOS as an example of the top-down design method. Again, many details about the necessary data structures are omitted. Chapter 11 discusses design of data structures.

Our first pass design will be a two-level hierarchy (*tree*). A controller module, which asks the user (the clerk) what to do next, is the root of the tree. Each of the major functions of CICOS (check-in, check-out, occupancy information, and transaction history) is a child of this parent (see Figure 6.4*a*).

The controller module will, for the most part, simply call these modules to do the actual work. To obtain input from the clerk, a main menu will be presented, displaying numbered choices. This belongs in a function, using the idea for generic menu display discussed earlier, so we decompose the controller into its main part and the menu function.

The check-in module will require input from the clerk, based on the customer's needs; from this information an empty room needs to be found. Therefore, we break the check-in module into an information procedure and a find-room procedure. Similarly, the check-out module can be broken into two pieces. The display function will allow the clerk to enter and modify data at the screen, and the billing function will print the itemized bill on a printer. These subhierarchies are shown in Figure 6.4*b*.

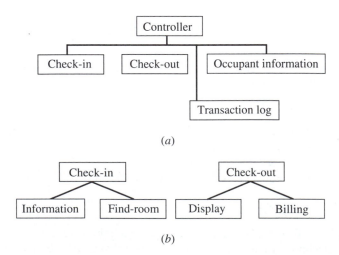

Figure 6.4 Top-down design for part of CICOS

For the occupancy module, we will add the following specifications. Queries about occupancy will be of four types:

- Given a room number, print information about that room.
- Given a floor number, print information about that floor.
- Print summary information for the entire hotel.
- Given a name, find the room (if any) in which that customer is staying.

The occupancy module, like the controller module, will ask the clerk to enter a choice, so the generic menu display can be used here, too.

For the transaction history, useful operations would include entering a new transaction, searching previous transactions for a particular customer, and summarizing recent transactions. Since transactions will accumulate over time, this is probably best handled using files. Each of the component functions will rely on file functions, which will be adapted to handling the file formats we use. For example, the records could be stored sequentially by time, along with an index based on customer names to speed searching.

Now our hierarchy has several levels. Because functions such as the generic menu display are reused, it is really a graph, not a hierarchy, but for organization purposes we will treat it as a tree.

Each node in the tree needs to be inspected for further decomposition. New component functions will be identified for each module. Recall that, for example, the check-out function was broken up into steps:

Check-out module

- Obtain room number from user
- Query system date
- Compute number of days stayed
- Compute room charges
- Compute total charge
- Display check-out screen

(and so on)

If any of these steps is complicated, it is a candidate for being implemented as a separate function. Earlier, for example, we suggested that "Compute room charges" was such a candidate. However, the step "Obtain room number from user" is probably simple enough to be coded directly. There is a point at which further decomposition is not useful because the overhead of writing many small functions, passing many parameters, and calling these functions at run time will be overwhelming. There are no strict rules about when to stop the refinement process. A common rule of thumb is that a function should be about a page of code in length. Of course, at the design phase we are not writing code, but we can estimate how much code a function will need.

Separate Compilation in C

C programs do not have to be contained within one file; user programs can be spread across many .c files. The fact that we can link our own programs to library routines is proof of this. In previous chapters, our C programs were small examples, and there was no reason to place code in separate files. For larger programs such as CICOS, this technique, called *separate compilation,* will be useful in helping organize and manage the component modules and functions. Separate compilation involves three steps: partitioning a program into various `.c` files; compiling these files into `.o` (for "object") files; and linking all `.o` files into one executable file.

The partitioning step has less to do with C programming than it does with the software design principles discussed in this chapter. Any `.c` file may contain one or more functions. Typically, a `.c` file is used to contain what we have called a module—a collection of related functions. The decomposition tree is used to identify these modules. Recall that the concepts of cohesion and coupling are important design principles; using the tree will help place functions related by purpose in the same module. In CICOS, for example, we might consider the check-in process as one module containing functions for obtaining user information and the find-room function. This latter may call specialized functions for finding rooms based on various criteria. All these functions would be placed in one `.c` file.

There are, however, a few C details to be aware of when designing modules and separate `.c` files. Visibility is the main issue. Functions within a module should have prototypes, and these prototypes need to be in a user-defined `.h` file. This header file is then included (using `#include`) into any `.c` files that use its functions. Other global definitions, such as `#define` statements and type declarations (discussed in later chapters), are also candidates for inclusion in `.h` files. Another issue is the scope of variables. A variable may be declared at the beginning of a `.c` file, making it global (visible) to the functions within that file but not outside it. When these variables are used, they are often declared as `static` to preserve their values over the life of the program. For example, an ADT can be implemented in C by making the data structure for the ADT static and global to the `.c` file containing the ADT code.

The procedures for compiling programs that use more than one `.c` file differ slightly depending on the compiler and operating system being used. *Object files* are usually produced first. These files contain compiled code, but not all constant, variable, and function references are defined, because the definitions of these things may occur in other files. The object files are then linked together into an executable file, resolving all the unknowns. Some of the details can vary across machines. Compilers in the DOS operating system, for example, use the `.obj` extension for object files, whereas UNIX uses the `.o` extension. The details for separate compilation are discussed later in this chapter in the section on design and debugging tools.

Testing Methods

Methods for testing code range from common-sense caution to formal generation of test plans and test data. Software engineering life cycle models include provisions for testing. Recall that the iterated waterfall method considers testing as a separate phase following the coding phase. There are three parts to the testing phase:

- *Unit testing,* where the functions and modules are tested individually
- *Integration testing,* to ensure that modules work together correctly
- *System testing,* an overall test including verification that the system requirement specifications have been met

Testing involves planning. Most of the planning involves test case construction, as will be described subsequently, but other parts include documentation of what is being tested, how the tests are to be run, and the criteria for successful and unsuccessful outcomes.

One strategy for testing code is to identify all possible paths throughout the code and then to devise data that "exercises" each of these paths and checks for errors. We will not discuss any formal methods for path testing, but this strategy should be followed as much as possible. As discussed below, reasonable selection of test data will help with this problem.

We will focus on testing functions rather than smaller sections of code. If the decomposition of the program into functions is handled well, the functions will be small and manageable. The methods discussed here can be applied to code fragments, as long as there is some control over executing those fragments apart from the rest of the code.

Black Box Testing

When testing a function, we can look at the internal workings of the function's code, the results produced by the function, or both. *Black box* testing ignores the internal details of a function and attempts to verify that, given some set of input parameters, the output parameters produced by the function are correct. Careful choices of the input parameters must be made for this strategy to work. Both pass-by-value and pass-by-address parameters can be used to send values to a function, but only the latter, plus the function's return value, are used to send values back from a function (see Figure 6.5a).

For parameters of standard types, the valid range of input values must be determined first. For example, consider the CICOS function that computes the number of days a customer stayed at the hotel. Let the input parameters to this function be the current date and the check-in date, where each is given as three `int` values: month, day, and year. Valid values for a month parameter are between 1 and 12, inclusively. Similarly, a day parameter must be between 1 and 31. For a year parameter, there will be other constraints. For example, the legal inputs might be limited to the current year and the previous year.

Range testing considers the set of valid input values as broken into various intervals, some legal and some not. For example, the month parameter mentioned in the previous

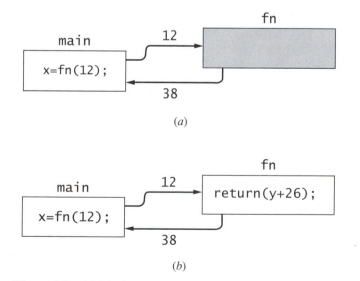

(*a*)

(*b*)

Figure 6.5   (*a*) Black box testing (*b*) White box testing

paragraph divides the set of `int` values into those less than or equal to 0, those between 1 and 12, and those greater than or equal to 13. Test values are then selected as representatives of each range. For a month, that might be 0, 3, and 15.

Boundary testing also considers the valid input values, but it selects additional test values at the boundaries of each interval. For our month example, 0, 1, and 2 could be selected at the bottom of the legal range and 11, 12, and 13 at the top of that range. Other intermediate values could also be used, but the focus here is the common "off by one" error.

All combinations of test values for the various parameters must be tried. These combinations can be listed in tabular form, including the expected output values and the actual output values. When these output values do not agree, the function must be examined for the cause of the error. Black box testing does not directly pinpoint errors but only gives clues to them.

To manage black box testing, it is often necessary to write *driver modules* that do little more than call a particular function using the test parameters. A driver may be a gutted shell of the actual function that will call the test functions. Also, when the function under test calls other functions that have not yet been tested (or perhaps not even coded), those functions must be simulated. Each must provide reasonable output to the test function; this is sometimes provided by lookup tables. For example, if the CICOS function for room charge computation is tested before the function that computes the number of days stayed, this latter function could return a positive constant, or it could subtract the day parameters and return the absolute value of the difference. Such functions are called *stubs*. Since the stub function is not currently being tested, it must be relied on to give correct output, even if that output is (temporarily) bogus.

White Box Testing

White box testing focuses on code execution and intermediate computed values in functions. Despite its name, which might better be "clear box testing," it is not the opposite or an alternative to black box testing, but is instead a complementary method (see Figure 6.5*b*).

Intermediate results can simply be printed out using `printf()` statements placed at strategic points in code. Labeling of this output is necessary and often includes the name of the function and the part of the code being tested. For example, a `printf()` inside a `for` loop might identify which `for` loop, the value of the counter variable, and the values of any other variables of interest. Using the function's name is helpful when several functions are being worked on simultaneously, although it is good practice to concentrate on one function at a time.

As with black box testing, correct values must be determined beforehand to match against computed values. Printouts of test values can become quite long and can be difficult to follow and interpret. Output is often collected in a file for inspection later.

The `printf()` statements added for testing must, of course, be removed before the final version is released. Chapter 12 discusses a useful technique (conditional compilation) for managing this.

Integration Testing

Once the individual functions are working correctly, they must be combined and tested together. This is the job of integration testing. The hierarchy of functions and modules is used to coordinate integration testing, and two strategies are possible.

Top-down testing tests the upper levels of the hierarchy before the lower levels. A controller function is tested, usually using stubs rather than actual functions to provide correct return values. Once this function passes, the next level of functions is added in, replacing the stubs. If the controller again passes, the next level can be added, and so on. Such level by level testing is called *breadth-first* traversal of the tree. An alternative is *depth-first* traversal, which takes a path from root to leaf, returns up a level, finds the next leaf, and so on, recursively.

Bottom-up testing begins at the leaf level and works up the tree. After a group of leaf functions passes its tests, a function one level up that calls this group is tested. Other groups of leaves are tested, followed by their parents. When a group of parents has passed, the function that calls them is tested, and so on to the root of the tree.

It is often useful to use the `printf()` strategy mentioned in the discussion of white box testing here, displaying the name of the function that is executing. `printf()`s can also be used at the very beginning and very end of each function to indicate entry to and exit from the function. This is related to the idea of a *traceback stack,* used in error handling. A traceback stack is a printout of the current function's name, the name of the calling function, its calling function, and so on back to `main()`. When an error is detected, such as "file does not exist," an error is printed, then a flag is returned to the calling function, which prints its own error message, and so on.

Whether top-down or bottom-up, integration testing eventually tests the entire program. The fact that the program works at this point is not the end of testing. As noted earlier, system testing compares the program's interface, output, and performance characteristics against the requirement specifications. Finally, where applicable, the user will test the program to ensure customer satisfaction.

Design and Debugging Tools

UNIX provides several tools to help with separate compilation and debugging of programs. Separate compilation can be done manually by asking the C compiler to compile .c files first, then linking the results together.

In order to compile programs that are spread across two or more .c files, *object files* must be produced. The compiler is instructed to produce an object file rather than an executable file by using the -c flag, as in

```
cc -c prog1.c
```

In this case, a new file called `prog1.o` will be created. This step is repeated for each .c file. Note that the compiler at your site may require a different command rather than cc.

The final linking step combines the object files into one executable file. All of the object files are given as arguments to the cc command. As usual, the default executable file is named a.out, unless the -o flag is used with a name for the executable file. Suppose, for example, that the CICOS program has been placed in the following files:

cicos.h	Constants, type definitions, and function prototypes
cicos.c	Main controller
checkin.c	Check-in module
checkout.c	Check-out module

```
occupancy.c      Occupancy statistics module
transact.c       Transaction history module
```

We would compile this with the following steps:

```
cc -c cicos.c
cc -c checkin.c
cc -c checkout.c
cc -c occupancy.c
cc -c transact.c
```

The current directory would now have five .o files, named cicos.o, checkin.o, and so on. To create an executable program called cicos, we would type the linking command

```
cc cicos.o checkin.o checkout.o occupancy.o transact.o -o cicos
```

As changes are made to a program, it is necessary only to recompile files with changes, along with any files that include changed header files. Unchanged source files do not need to be recompiled. Linking to produce the executable must be redone as well. Suppose that a change was made in checkout.c. We would recompile only that function with cc -c checkout.c, followed by the same linking command already shown.

Using make

Over the course of developing a large program, many individual .c files will need recompilation as changes and fixes are made. To help keep track of this process, and to help organize a project, the make utility is used. The make program looks at the dates of .c files and compares the dates of the corresponding .o files. If the .c file is later, then make takes action to recompile .o files and recreate the executable file.

The make utility uses a special *make file*, created by the developer and usually given the name makefile. The dependencies of .o files on both .c files and .h files is stated in this file, along with instructions for what to compile when date mismatches are noted. The format for a make file is to state pairs of lines. The first line, which begins in the first column, states the dependencies. The second line *must* begin with a tab, followed by the compilation instructions.

For example, using our CICOS example, the instructions for compiling checkin.o would be these lines:

```
checkin.o: checkin.c cicos.h
    cc -c checkin.c
```

Note the format on the dependencies line. We assume that the definitions file, cicos.h, is needed by checkin.c; that is, the statement

```
#include "cicos.h"
```

would appear near the beginning of checkin.c. Also note the use of quotes rather than angle brackets; the quotes indicate that the file is user-defined rather than a system file. The two notifications regarding `cicos.h`, once in the make file and once in `checkin.c`, are both needed since the former notifies `make` and the latter notifies `cc`. Finally, standard `.h` files, such as `<stdio.h>`, do not need to be listed in the dependencies line.

The following is the entire make file of commands for compiling CICOS.

```
cicos: cicos.o checkin.o checkout.o occupancy.o transact.o cicos.h
  cc cicos.o checkin.o checkout.o occupancy.o transact.o -o cicos
cicos.o: cicos.c cicos.h
  cc -c cicos.c
checkin.o: checkin.c cicos.h
  cc -c checkin.c
checkout.o: checkout.c cicos.h
  cc -c checkout.c
occupancy.o: occupancy.c cicos.h
  cc -c occupancy.c
transact.o: transact.c cicos.h
  cc -c transact.c
```

The first pair of lines shows the executable file's dependencies and compilation instructions. The other pairs are needed for each object file.

To produce the executable file from a make file, the `make` utility is run. If the `make` command is typed without parameters, `make` looks in the current directory for a file `makefile`; if none exists, `make` will next look for `Makefile`, the alternative default command file. As `make` runs, the `cc` commands are echoed to the screen. The usual diagnostic messages produced by `cc` are also displayed if there are errors, in which case `make` stops execution.

If neither default make file exists, an error message is displayed. It is allowable to name the make file something other than `makefile`. To have `make` find an alternative make file, the `-f` *filename* option is used. For example, if our file were named `cicos.make` instead of `makefile`, we would start compilation by typing

```
make -f cicos.make
```

Comments are allowed (and encouraged) in a make file. Each comment line begins with the pound sign. For example,

```
#  checkin.c is the source file for check in processing.
#    It uses definitions in cicos.h
checkin.o: checkin.c cicos.h
  cc -c checkin.c
```

documents the dependencies for `checkin.o`. When lines are long enough to spill over to a new line, the first line must end with the backslash character. This most often happens for the executable's compilation instructions for large programs.

Several shortcuts are available for `make`. We list a few of them here, but suggest that the make file be explicit where possible. The shortcuts utilize a feature of `make` that allows a variable to be defined with file names. For example, we could assign the variable `OBJECTS` to hold the names of our object files by writing

```
OBJECTS = cicos.o checkin.o checkout.o occupancy.o transact.o
```

near the beginning of our make file. Another shortcut allows the compiling commands to be omitted and forces make to use the default compiler, presumably cc. Dependencies are still listed. Incorporating these shortcuts, we can write the make file as

```
cicos: $(OBJECTS) cicos.h
  cc $(OBJECTS) -o cicos
$(OBJECTS): cicos.h
```

Note the way our shortcut uses parentheses and the dollar sign to reference OBJECTS inside the make file.

One additional note on make: Other actions besides compiling can be added to a make file. Two common ones are printing and removal of object files. Each action is specified on a line starting with a tab, as the following example shows.

```
cicos: $(OBJECTS)
  cc $(OBJECTS) -o cicos
$(OBJECTS): cicos.h
print:
  lpr *.c
clean:
  rm $(OBJECTS)
```

These new actions must be specified as parameters to make, as in make print and make clean. Neither of these causes recompilation; instead, they just activate the command(s) given after the tab.

Using dbx

Interactive debugging is possible on UNIX systems using the dbx utility. Other debuggers, some more sophisticated and using graphical interfaces, exist and may be available on your system. Using dbx is a bit frustrating after you have been exposed to friendlier tools, but we discuss it here because of its widespread availability.

In order to use dbx, source files and the executable file must be compiled with the -g flag, which can be added to the cc instructions by hand or in a make file, as in

```
checkin.o: checkin.c cicos.h
  cc -c -g checkin.c
```

Once this compilation is accomplished, dbx is typed with the executable file name as a parameter, as in

```
dbx cicos
```

The dbx prompt is usually

```
dbx>
```

Within `dbx` a number of commands are available. We discuss only a few here, but typing `help` at the `dbx` prompt will show the entire list of available commands, and typing `help` *command* will give brief help on that command.

The `run` command, typed at the `dbx` prompt, begins execution of the program being debugged. Execution will look the way it would if `dbx` were not involved, until the program finishes, crashes, or is interrupted by typing ctrl-C. In the latter two cases, typing `where` will show a traceback stack, indicating function names and line numbers for the current statement being executed. The `list` command will show 10 lines of source code beginning at the current line. Typing `list` *first, last* will list the specified range of lines, as in

```
dbx>list 10, 25
```

which shows lines 10 through 25.

To suspend execution at key points, called *breakpoints,* variants of the `stop` command are used. For example, `stop at 25` suspends execution when line 25 is reached. Similarly, `stop in checkin` suspends execution when the function `checkin()` is called. The command `stop when x == 4` causes a stop when the variable x is equal to 4; beware, however, that this third style of breakpoint can be quite slow. The command `status` shows the current breakpoints, numbered in a list. The command `delete` *number,* where *number* is the number of a breakpoint from a `status` display, deletes that breakpoint. The `cont` command resumes execution after a suspension.

When execution is suspended, the `print` command is used to display the values of variables. For example, `print x` will display x's value. This may also be used to display the value of an expression, address, or structured variable (array or `struct`).

Using `dbx` effectively takes some practice. Knowing which are the key variables and where to place breakpoints depends on the program and on particular functions. System code, such as the math library, is not available to `dbx`; only user code compiled with the `-g` flag can be referenced.

Using `lint`

As you may well know by now, the `cc` command's diagnostic error and warning messages are not always helpful. The lines of code referenced by these messages are often the wrong ones because of the way compilers work. The actual source of an error is often somewhere before the flagged line.

The `lint` utility is used to check compilation problems before using `cc`. Like `cc`, `lint` takes a source file as a parameter, as in `lint checkin.c`. It reports suspicious lines of code that the compiler normally accepts. For example, `lint` will report that a line is unreachable because of a condition that is never met. In the fragment

```
x = 1;
if ( x > 1 )
  printf( "This line\n" );
```

the `printf()` will be flagged by `lint` as unreachable. Some type mismatches are also reported, as are function parameters that are never referenced in the function's code. Because `lint` is much stricter than `cc`, many potential "problems" it reports are warnings that you may choose to ignore.

References

Northrop, Linda M., and William E. Richardson, "Design Evolution: Implications for Academia and Industry," in *Software Engineering Education,* ed. J. E. Tomayko, Springer-Verlag, New York, 1991, pp. 205-217.

Pressman, Roger S., *Software Engineering: A Practitioner's Approach,* McGraw-Hill, New York, 1992.

Sommerville, Ian, *Software Engineering,* 4th ed., Addison-Wesley, Reading, MA, 1992.

Chapter Summary

■ Software Life Cycle

Systems analysis phase	Describe the need and purpose for the software along with the costs and risks
Requirements analysis phase	Determine precise specifications for software function and performance
Design phase	Design the software, incorporating design concepts such as those mentioned in the following lists, to plan the modules, interfaces, and data structures
Coding phase	Write source code to implement the given design and create the executable code
Testing phase	Test the software, incorporating testing concepts such as those mentioned in a subsequent list, to verify that the software satisfies the given specifications
Maintenance phase	Correct postrelease errors in the software and add new features

■ Concepts of Code Design

Modularity	Design units (a unit being a function or a module of functions) based on shared functional, communicational, temporal, or coincidental concerns
Information hiding	Design the interfaces between units so that only essential data is passed back and forth
Reusability	Write source code so that it can be adapted to other purposes
Side effects	Permanent variable changes should be made only through pass-by-address variables that are declared in function interfaces; do not create side effects by assigning values to global variables in any other way
Function-oriented design	A software design method that concentrates first on organizing the software's tasks and subtasks
Data flow design	A software design method that concentrates first on organizing the passage of data between program units
Data structure design	A software design method that concentrates first on structures for storing data and operations for manipulating data

Object-based design   A software design method that enforces strict information hiding through the use of interfaces and abstract data types

Object-oriented design   A software design method that extends object-based design by combining algorithms as well as abstract data types into defined classes and that allows operations on these classes

Top-down design   An approach, recommended for all of the design methods listed here, that first analyzes the software using an outline having a few major parts and then analyzes each separate part in the same manner, continuing the process of breaking each part into smaller parts until the smallest parts are quickly and easily accomplished

■ Testing Methods

Black box testing   Test each function separately by executing the function for suitable ranges of input parameters, giving special attention to boundary parameters, and comparing the results with the expected output

White box testing   Test each function separately by observing intermediate values of variables during the execution of the function

Integration testing   Test parts of a program, starting with one level of functions and working up or down until the entire program is tested

■ UNIX Commands

cc -c prog1.c   Compile the C code contained in the file prog1.c and create an object file named prog1.o

cc prog1.o prog2.o -o LinkedCode   Link the object files prog1.o and prog2.o and create an executable file named LinkedCode

cc -c -g prog1.c   Compile the C code contained in the file prog1.c and create an object file prog1.o that is also suitable for analysis by the dbx command

cc -g prog1.c -o buggy   Compile the C code contained in the file prog1.c and create an executable file named buggy that is also suitable for analysis by the dbx command

dbx buggy   Use the interactive debugging utility dbx to analyze the executable file named buggy

make   Compile and link separate source code files according to the instructions contained in the file makefile (or Makefile, if makefile does not exist)

make -f MyMakeFile   Compile and link separate source code files according to the instructions contained in the file MyMakeFile

lint filter.c   Use the debugging utility lint to analyze the source code file named filter.c

Review Problems

1. The following program computes length of stay for hotel transactions that have been recorded in a text file.

```
/* Title: DaysStayed                                          */
/* Input:  Name of file (this file must contain               */
/*           three positive integers per line)                */
/* Output: A report of days of occupancy for each transaction */

/* NOTE: The three integers per line represent a transaction  */
/* number, check in day, and check out day for guests at hotel. */
/* Possible transaction numbers are 1 to 999, possible day     */
/* numbers are 1 to 365. The final line should NOT terminate   */
/* with '\n'. These DATA RESTRICTIONS MUST BE CHECKED before   */
/* executing the program.                                      */

#include <stdio.h>

#define LIMIT 40   /* Max number of chars in filename is 39 */

FILE *OpenFile( char filename[ LIMIT ] );
void PrintLine( FILE *file_ptr );

FILE *file_ptr;            /* Pointer to data file */
char filename[ LIMIT ];   /* Name of data file    */
int count = 1;            /* Transaction index    */

main()
{ /* Identify data file and open it */
  file_ptr = OpenFile( filename );

  /* If successful in opening file, print a report */
  if ( file_ptr != NULL ) {
    printf( "\n%10s%10s\n", "Entry", "Stay" );
    while ( !feof( file_ptr ))
      PrintLine( file_ptr );
  }
  /* Otherwise, report error and quit */
  else
    printf( "Unable to open data file." );
}

FILE *OpenFile( char filename[ LIMIT ] )
/* Ask user to name a text file;         */
/* attempt to open the file for reading */

{ FILE *file_ptr;   /* Pointer to data file */
```

```
    /* Open a file for reading */
    printf( "Name the file, " );
    printf( "use at most %d characters: ", ( LIMIT - 1 ));
    scanf( "%s", filename );
    /* Read over the Return key from above */
    getchar();
    file_ptr = fopen( filename, "r" );

    return( file_ptr );
}
void PrintLine ( FILE *file_ptr )

/* Read transaction number, in_day, out_day from file; compute  */
/* length of stay and print it on next line in table.           */

{ int ch,            /* One character from data file           */
  transaction,       /* Transaction number for a single entry */
  in_day, out_day;   /* Dates for a single transaction         */

    /* Scan one line from the data file */
    fscanf( file_ptr,"%d %d %d", &transaction, &in_day, &out_day );

    /* Read to end of line or end of file */
    while ( !feof( file_ptr ) && ( ch != '\n' ))
      ch = fgetc( file_ptr );

    /* Make an adjustment if guest stayed over new year's day */
    if ( out_day < in_day )
      out_day += 365;

    /* Print one line */
    printf( "%10d%10d\n", count, ( out_day - in_day ));
    count++;
}
```

a) Although the program performs as desired, each user-defined function violates an established principle of software design. What changes should be made to correct these errors?

b) Write a test data file that contains a minimal set of data for black box testing of the function PrintLine().

c) How would you modify PrintLine() for white box testing?

d) Is any of the code easily reusable?

e) Describe the kinds of data files that would cause an error with this program.

2. An executable file DoJob is to be built upon program modules contained in the files MainController.c, GetInput.c, AnalyzeInput.c, and PrintReport.c and with definitions in the file SpecialDefinitions.h.

a) Which UNIX command(s) would you use to check the syntax and logic of these files?

b) Which UNIX command(s) would you use to compile and link these files in a manner that allows interactive debugging of the complete program?

c) Which design method seems to have been used for this program?

d) Which UNIX command(s) would be used to debug this program after compilation?

Programming Problems

For each of the following programming projects, carefully prepare a written report with sections devoted to requirements analysis, software design, source code, and testing.

1. (Address Book) Write a program that allows a user to keep track of the following information concerning various individuals: name, address, telephone number, birthday. Do not sort the individual entries (for example, do not attempt to keep the entries in alphabetical order according to last name).

2. (String Comparison) Write a function to compare two strings as indicated by the following function header.

```
int StrComp( char *s1, char *s2 )
/* Compare the two strings s1 and s2 and     */
/* return 0 if strings are equal, 1 if not.  */
```

3. (Generic Menu Function) Write a function for presenting a list of menu options based on the header

```
int GenericMenu( char filename[ LIMIT ], int n, int t )
```

where n is the number of options to be presented, t is the maximum number of tries, and filename contains a description for a single option on each line; e.g., the first line of filename describes option number 1, etc. The function should return an integer between 1 and n to indicate the user's choice, or 0 to indicate that the user failed to make a suitable response within t tries. The function may assume that n does not exceed the number of lines in filename.

4. (Program File Viewer) Write a program for viewing all or part of a text file, whose contents are assumed to be a C program listing. Allow the user to choose from the following viewing options: (1) display the entire text; (2) for each user-defined function, show only the prototype, the function header, and comments immediately following the header; (3) for each user-defined function, show only the prototype and the function header. Before each function header, insert a line such as

```
<< Function 1: >>
```

where the functions are numbered in consecutive order. *Hint:* For options 2 and 3, count pairs of brackets ({ ... }), being careful not to count any bracket that occurs inside a comment or inside quotation marks.

Chapter

7

Arrays

The ability to collect separate pieces of information into a list or table is a useful way of organizing data. An *array* is a C construct for this purpose. This chapter discusses how to use arrays in C programs, including the relationship between arrays and pointers. This chapter's UNIX topic is advanced editing techniques in vi.

Meaning of Arrays

Many applications use lists of data elements. For example, a point in space can be represented by an ordered list of three real numbers—that is, a vector whose elements are the x-, y-, and z-coordinates of the point. A chessboard is a two-dimensional grid whose nonempty elements are chess pieces. In a relational database, a relation is a two-dimensional table whose rows are elements (or records) of the relation and whose columns are the relation's attributes or record fields. For example, student records might consist of name, age, student identification number, and class standing. One row of the table then holds one student's record. An array is the data type used in C to represent these lists. Three important properties of arrays in C are as follows.

The *type* of an array is the base type of the elements stored in the array. (Refer to Figure 7.1 for illustrations of this and the following terms.) The type can be one of the predefined C types such as int or double, or it can be a more complicated type such as a user-defined data type (such as a struct, discussed in Chapter 9, which is a C record), or even another array. Each individual element of an array can be treated as a single variable of the base type and operated on in the same way as other variables of that type, including being passed as an argument to a function. In the examples above, a point's type is double; the chessboard is either an int code for the piece types or a struct representing chess pieces; and the relation, while logically two-dimensional, is best thought of as a one-dimensional array of records (structs) holding the relation's rows of data.

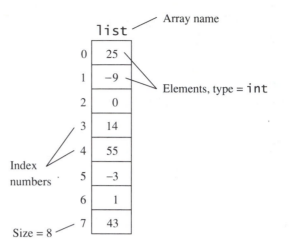

Figure 7.1 Array terminology
for a one-dimensional array

The *size* of a one-dimensional array is the finite number of elements that array contains. Each element is stored in a numbered position; that number is the element's *index*. The index number is an integer and is distinct from the type of the element. Index numbers start at 0 and count up to one less than the declared size—an important difference to note between C and other languages such as BASIC or Pascal. The size is stated in the type declaration of the array and cannot be changed (although there is some flexibility in size when an array is passed as a parameter). For multidimensional arrays, "size" has several meanings; for example, for a two-dimensional array the size may be the size of a row, the size of a column, or the size of the entire array. Elements in multidimensional arrays are referenced by pairs (or triples or quadruples and so on) of index numbers.

Finally, the *dimension* of an array tells what kind of list it is—one-dimensional arrays are linear lists, two-dimensional arrays are tables, and three-dimensional arrays are layers of tables. After three, one can think in terms of copies: four-dimensional arrays are collections of layers of tables, and so on. The dimension, like the size, is declared once and for all. Each dimension declared has its own independent size. The total number of elements allowed in an array is limited by the amount of data space a program is granted, and this can vary by machine. Using the above examples, the point has one dimension, size 3; the chessboard has two dimensions, each of size 8; the relation has one dimension (recall that its base type is a struct) whose size is the total number of records to be stored.

An array need not be completely filled with data. Normally, all three elements of the example point would be filled or none would. A relation, though, might have some of its elements unfilled (due to deletions, perhaps), or it might have the first few elements filled and the remainder empty. A *subarray* is a sequence of consecutive elements in an array, and it is typically that part of the array that has been filled with data. Often, a subarray must be processed instead of the entire array.

A function cannot be declared to return an array, although it can be written to return a pointer to an array (this distinction is described more fully in the section on arrays and pointers). Normally, arrays are passed as parameters to functions.

In initializing or processing an array, the individual elements are the focus. However, treating an array as a unit—a single entity—that can be operated on or passed as a parameter is a powerful concept. A string is one example: a collection of characters that can act perhaps as a name or an address. (Strings are important enough to have the entire next chapter devoted to them. Nevertheless, we should observe now that a string is almost but not quite the same as an array of characters.) Arrays are also the first example we will see of data structure design, the logical grouping of data into useful combinations—an important step in the abstraction process.

One-Dimensional Arrays

The syntax for declaring a one-dimensional array is to give the base type, then the array name followed by the size in brackets:

```
basetype ArrayName[ Size ];
```

The size is usually declared as a constant, as are references to the size in loops, so that later changes in the size do not affect previously written code. The point example from the previous section would be declared as

```
#define SIZE 3
double point[ SIZE ];
```

To access the elements of an array, the array name is used along with the index number in square brackets. Recall that arrays start at index number 0 and run up to one less than the size. So to access the three elements of `point`, we would use `point[ 0 ]`, `point[ 1 ]`, and `point[ 2 ]`.

As one might suspect, one-dimensional arrays are stored in memory in sequential fashion. The starting memory location for an array, where element 0 is stored, is followed by the location of element 1, and so on. How much memory is needed for each element is determined by the array's type: one byte for `char`, for example. *The array's name, when used alone, is treated as a pointer (address) rather than as representing a value of the base type.* This has important consequences for passing an array as a function argument, as will be seen later.

Examples

The following examples are code fragments rather than complete programs. They are meant only to show how to manipulate arrays, not to solve large problems. Each example should be embedded in a function or inside a full program. See the subsequent section on arrays as parameters for other ways of structuring this code.

Filling and Spilling the Contents

The simplest operations on an array are to fill it with data and to extract that data. This example uses an array of test scores for that purpose, first prompting the user to enter the test scores and then printing the whole list.

```
/* Example: Fill an array, then print its contents */
#define NUMSCORES 5          /* Number of test scores expected */
double score[ NUMSCORES ]; /* Array to hold test scores */
int    count;               /* Index variable            */
/* This loop prompts for each test score. */
for ( count = 0; count < NUMSCORES; count++ ) {
  printf( "Enter test score %d: ", count );
  scanf( "%lf", &score[ count ] );
}
/* This loop prints a table of the test scores entered. */
printf( "List of test scores entered:\n" );
for ( count = 0; count < NUMSCORES; count++ )
  printf( "score[ %d ] = %8.2lf\n", count, score[ count ] );
```

Note how the array `score` is defined. It can contain five elements, each of type `double`, indexed from 0 to 4. The first `for` loop takes this indexing into consideration, quitting when the loop index variable `count` reaches 5. The second `for` loop is similar. Note the use of the loop index variable in the `printf()` statements to make a more understandable message to the user.

A sample run of the program might produce

```
Enter test score 0: 42.6
Enter test score 1: 8.17
Enter test score 2: 92.52
Enter test score 3: 44.4
Enter test score 4: 75.0
List of test scores entered:
score[ 0 ] =    42.60
score[ 1 ] =     8.17
score[ 2 ] =    92.52
score[ 3 ] =    44.40
score[ 4 ] =    75.00
```

The fact that C arrays count from 0 is sometimes confusing, especially to users (as opposed to programmers). It might be a good idea to compensate for this by letting the messages above count from 1 to 5 while the actual index `count` is counting from 0 to 4. The reader can decide how best to accomplish this.

When accessing arrays, `for` loops are often used because of the necessity of processing the array sequentially. Exceeding the upper bound on the array index (size minus 1) is incorrect, but it *may not* result in an immediate run-time error. Array references are not necessarily checked during execution (some compilers allow this feature to be turned on or off), for efficiency reasons. An error such as `score[ 5 ]` or the harder-to-debug error

```
count = 5;
/* Some intervening code ... */
score[ count ] = 70.0;
```

may actually execute. The effect is to change the value of a location in memory that is not within the array—surely a dangerous practice that will have dire effects when that position is referenced correctly.

Finally, note the simple output produced in the foregoing example. Each element of the array is printed on a single line. Some arrays will be so large that this style is impractical because of scrolling the video screen or excessive consumption of printer paper. Recall a similar discussion in Chapter 3 on printing inside `for` loops. A review problem at the end of this chapter discusses this topic.

Summing Up

The previous example did no processing on the array of test scores. Suppose now that we wish to compute the average test score. We need to sum the scores and then divide by the total number of scores. Accordingly, two variables, `total` and `average`, are declared to do the summation and average computation, and the following is added to the previous code:

```
/* Example: Find the average of an array of int's */
double total = 0.0, average;
for ( count = 0; count < NUMSCORES; count++ )
  total += score[ count ];
average = total / NUMSCORES;
printf( "The average score is %8.2lf.\n", average );
```

The variable `total` is initialized to zero before summation begins. Inside the `for` loop, the test scores are added successively into `total`. Note that the summation statement could have been included inside the previous `for` loop where the data was entered.

This example may look familiar. In Chapter 3, a similar loop was used to enter scores and compute their average. No array was needed then, so is one needed now? Not really— provided that *only* the average is to be computed. However, without the array `scores` the second `for` loop in the first example—printing the test scores out in a separate list—would not be possible. On the other hand, this problem could be avoided by echoing the scores as they were entered, and doing all three operations (input, computing the average, output) in one `for` loop.

When deciding whether or not to use an array, the key criteria are *memory* and *modularity*. Arrays allow individual data values to be remembered for later use, and arrays serve as convenient data structures for passing information between program modules. Suppose that in the foregoing example we need to know the difference between each test score and the average (that is, the *deviation* from the mean). Then the `score` array could be reprocessed by a second `for` loop:

```
/* Example: Compute deviation from the mean */
for ( count = 0; count < NUMSCORES; count++ )
  printf( "score[ %d ] - average = %lf\n", count, score[ count ] - average );
```

Furthermore, if we wished to structure our program carefully, ensuring that distinct tasks were performed in distinct program modules, an array would be an excellent structure for passing information between the functions, which might have the names `InputScores`, `FindAverageAndDeviations`, and `PrintReport`.

Searching an Unordered One-Dimensional Array

Two important operations on arrays are *searching* for a particular element and *sorting* the entire list of items. A search is initiated with a *key,* the element to be found, and results in either success (the key is found, and its index number is reported) or failure (the key is not present in the array). The method used for searching depends on whether the array is sorted or not, since we can make use of the ordering of a sorted array to speed the search process. A sort (from smallest to largest, although the opposite is also permissible) depends on being able to order the elements according to some rule. For integers and floating-point numbers, this is no problem. Characters are ordered by the collating sequence in use, usually the ASCII code. Strings are sorted alphabetically. Records (or `struct`s) are sorted on one of the fields of the record. There are many algorithms for sorting, ranging both from simple to complicated and from slow to fast, with the two scales being roughly correlated. In this section, we consider searching an unordered array; the next section looks at one sorting method, and then finally we consider searching a sorted array.

For these examples, assume that the array `list`, declared by

```
#define SIZE 10        /* Size of the array list */
int     list[ SIZE ];  /* Array of int's         */
```

has been completely filled with integers, perhaps interactively as in the previous examples. (Chapter 9 will show how to search an array of records given a key field.) The constants TRUE and FALSE, discussed in Chapter 2, are redeclared here. After some variable declarations, the key to be searched for is requested:

```
/* Example: Search an unordered array of int's */
#define FALSE 0
#define TRUE  1
int key,    /* Search key                        */
    index, /* Array index                        */
    found; /* Flag to tell when to quit searching */
/* Get the search key from the user. */
printf( "Enter the key to be found: " );
scanf( "%d", &key );
```

And then the search is made:

```
/* Initialize the index and the flag. */
index = 0;
found = FALSE;
/* Search until found or end of array is reached. */
while (( index < SIZE ) && ( !found ))
  if ( list[ index ] == key ) found = TRUE;
  else index++;
/* Was it found? */
if ( found ) printf( "%d was found at position %d\n", key, index );
else printf( "%d was not found\n", key );
```

The `while` loop has two stopping conditions. The first prevents `index` from growing too large, as will occur if `key` is not in `list`. The second stops the search when `key` is located (when `found` is set to TRUE). Since either condition can terminate the loop, the last `if` statement checks which one actually occurred.

Sorting a One-Dimensional Array

Before presenting a sorting algorithm, let's first look at the simpler problem of finding the smallest element in an array. This is not the same as searching for a key, because we cannot find the smallest element without looking at every element in the list. The algorithm used here keeps track of the smallest element found so far and compares each succeeding element to it. If a smaller one is found, it becomes the new smallest element. Before beginning the comparisons, the smallest so far is initialized to the first element in the array. In the next example, assume again that `list` from the previous example already contains data. Also, we keep track of the index of the minimum element rather than the element itself.

```
/* Example: Find the smallest element (minimum) of list */
int current = 0;  /* The index of smallest element so far */
/* Loop through the elements of list. */
for ( index = 1; index < SIZE; index++ )
  if ( list[ index ] < list[ current ] ) current = index;
printf( "Minimum is list[ %d ] = %d\n", current, list[ current ] );
```

Notice that the `for` loop begins counting at 1 because no comparison is needed for element 0.

To use the minimum-finding code in a sorting algorithm, we parameterize it so that the beginning and ending indices can vary rather than being fixed to start at zero and end at SIZE - 1. Additionally, we place the code in a function in order to simplify the sort code. The details of the function header will become clearer after reading the subsequent section on arrays as parameters; alternative headers are possible. Also, for this example only, comments are given before the function for documentation purposes.

```
/* Function FindMin                                        */
/* Returns: int                                            */
/* Parameters: list (int array, SIZE elements)             */
/*                array to be processed.                   */
/*              start (int) index to begin processing      */
/*              end (int) index to end processing          */
/* Purpose: Find the index of the smallest element of list */
/*          between indices start and end - 1.             */
int FindMin( int list[ SIZE ], int start, int end )
{ int current, index;  /* Same usage as above. */
  current = start;  /* Use start, not zero, as beginning index. */
  /* Loop runs from start+1 up to end. */
  for ( index = start + 1; index < end; index++ )
    if ( list[ index ] < list[ current ] ) current = index;
```

```
        /* current is the index of the minimum value. */
        return(current);
    } /* FindMin() */
```

There is no requirement that the array parameter be named identically to the argument passed; see the discussion in Chapter 4 and later in this chapter in the section on arrays as parameters.

To find the minimum of the entire array, the function would be called as

```
/* Example: call FindMin to find the minimum element. */
smallest = FindMin( list, 0, SIZE );
printf( "Minimum is list[ %d ] = %d\n", smallest, list[ smallest ] );
```

assuming `smallest` is declared an `int`; see Figure 7.2.

The following sorting algorithm, called *selection sort,* works like this:

1. First, find the smallest element.
2. Place the smallest element in position 0 by exchanging (recall the discussion of the three-way exchange in Chapter 4) the smallest with `list[ 0 ]`.
3. Now the problem is one step smaller, because we need only consider the array from position 1 to the end. Find the second smallest element and exchange it into position 1.
4. Next find the third smallest element, and so on until done.

Figure 7.3 illustrates the first few steps.

```
/* Example: selection sort */
/* Loop until all elements are processed. */
for ( index = 0; index < LIST - 1; index++ ) {
    /* Find smallest from position index to end of the array. */
    current = FindMin( list, index, LIST );
    /* Swap smallest to its correct position. */
    exchange( &list[ index ], &list[ current ] );
}
```

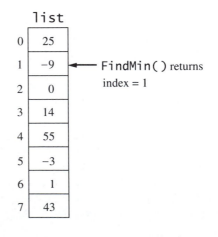

Figure 7.2   FindMin( ) returns the index of the smallest element

	list		list		list		list
0	-9	0	-9	0	-9	0	-9
1	25	1	-3	1	-3	1	-3
2	0	2	0	2	0	2	0
3	14	3	14	3	14	3	1
4	55	4	55	4	55	4	55
5	-3	5	25	5	25	5	25
6	1	6	1	6	1	6	14
7	43	7	43	7	43	7	43
(a)		(b)		(c)		(d)	

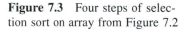

Figure 7.3 Four steps of selection sort on array from Figure 7.2

The second parameter to `FindMin` increases with each iteration, decreasing the number of array elements to be processed. The function `exchange` was discussed in Chapter 4. To put selection sort into a function, the header would be

```
void SelectionSort( int list[ SIZE ] )
```

Searching a Sorted One-Dimensional Array

Now that we can put the elements of a list into sorted order, let's return to the search problem. How can we take advantage of the ordering to speed up the search of an ordered array? Consider looking up a name in the telephone book. Would you start with the first name in the book, as we did with the previous search method? Probably not. You would more likely try to guess how far in the book the key would occur: If it started with *V*, you'd guess closer to the end of the book; if it started with *N*, you'd guess near the middle; and so on. Then you would check your guess. If you had gone too far, for example, you would only consider the pages in front of your guess and ignore the rest. This front section could now be treated in the same manner: Guess how far in your key is, check your guess, discard one section, and try again on the other section.

We will use a simplified version of this method, called *binary search,* in which we always guess in the middle of the current section rather than trying to construct a better guess (see Figure 7.4). Binary search uses an important feature of arrays. Their elements do not have to be accessed in sequential order—they can be processed in *random* order. In Chapter 10, where linked lists are discussed, we will see a structure similar to arrays but lacking the random access feature. (You might consider how to code the telephone book strategy, sometimes called *interpolation search,* a name that gives a hint about the implementation.)

The outline for binary search is

1. Compute the midpoint of the current section (initially the whole array).
2. Compare the search key to the midpoint element.
3. If equal, we are done; else if the search key is smaller than the midpoint, set the current section to the first half of the list; else reset it to the second half.
4. If we are not done, and the current section is not empty, return to step 1.

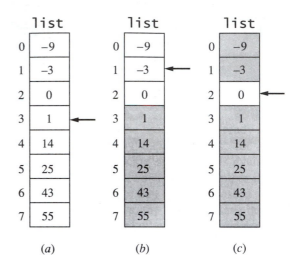

Figure 7.4 Binary search for element 0 rules out the middle element and one-half of the remaining array at each step

(a)   (b)   (c)

The current section is identified by its beginning and ending indices. To reset it to the first half, the ending index is set to 1 less than the midpoint. Setting the beginning index to 1 more than the midpoint resets the current section to the second half.

```
int BinSearch( int list[ SIZE ], int key ) {
int start, end, middle;   /* Index numbers used in the search   */
int found;                /* Flag for successful search         */
int KeyIndex;             /* Return value                       */
start = 0;
end   = LIST - 1;
found = FALSE;
/* Loop until found or start meets end. */
while (( start < end ) && ( !found )) {
  middle = ( start + end ) / 2;
  if ( key == list[ middle ] ) found = TRUE;
  else if ( key < list[ middle ] ) end = middle - 1;
  else start = middle + 1;
}
/* Check to see why the while loop ended. */
if ( found ) KeyIndex = middle;
else KeyIndex = -1;
return( KeyIndex );
}
```

The `while` loop condition has two parts. The first, (`start < end`), stops the search if the key is not in the list—if that happens, the current section will be narrowed down to just one element, then the indices will meet each other. The second, (`!found`), stops the search if the key is found; since the loop can terminate on either condition, we must check whether the search was successful in the last `if` statement. Inside the loop the midpoint index is computed in integer arithmetic. Because of truncation, the two "halves" of the list may not be of equal size. The nested `if` statements codify the plan discussed above.

Declaring New Types

In programs with functions that have arrays as parameters, often it is desirable to declare new data types for the arrays being used. This is done with the **typedef** statement. Like #define, the typedef statement usually comes in the preamble of a program or in a header (.h) file so that such definitions are global. For example, the point vector used previously could be defined as

```
#define SIZE    3
typedef double vector[ SIZE ];
```

Now there is a new type available for use: vector. Note that this is *not* a variable declaration. No memory is allocated for storage; only a symbolic name is declared. However, variables can now be declared to be of this type, as in

```
vector point;
```

which has the same result as the previous method of declaration of point. As before, references such as point[0] are valid.

Higher-Dimensional Arrays

As discussed at the beginning of the chapter, arrays of dimension 2 or greater can be visualized as tables (dimension 2), layers of tables (dimension 3), and so on, because C implements such arrays as arrays of arrays, arrays of arrays of arrays, and so on. For example, the syntax for declaring a two-dimensional array is

```
basetype ArrayName[ Size_1 ][ Size_2 ];
```

This means that ArrayName is a one-dimensional array of size Size_1, each of whose elements is an array of size Size_2 elements of basetype (see Figure 7.5a).

To illustrate this idea, consider the declarations

```
#define ROWS    3
#define COLUMNS 4
int table[ ROWS ][ COLUMNS ];
```

which allocates an array with three rows and four columns, twelve integers altogether. Row 0 of table has elements table[0][0], table[0][1], table[0][2], and table[0][3]. This row is itself a one-dimensional array, which can be referenced as table[0]. The other rows and individual elements can be accessed similarly, with the last entry in the array being table[2][3]. To access columns, we can refer only to the individual entries, not to the entire column. Column 2 has elements table[0][2], table[1][2], and table[2][2], but it cannot be referred to as table[2] (which is *row* 2) nor as table[ ][2].

The preceding discussion shows that C stores two-dimensional arrays in *row-major order*. Each row is treated as a one-dimensional array. The alternative would be *column-major*

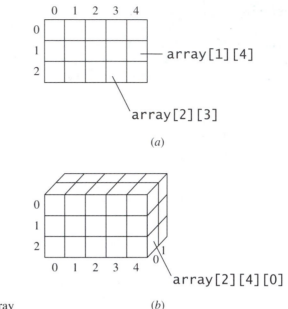

Figure 7.5   (*a*) 2-D array (*b*) 3-D array

order, in which each column is stored as an individual one-dimensional array. The FORTRAN language uses column-major order, but most other languages use row-major order. Another way of describing row-major order is that the rightmost array index (column number) varies faster than the index to its left (row number) as the array is traversed element by element in memory.

Arrays of higher dimension are treated in a similar way. In a three-dimensional array, the first index varies the slowest, the third the fastest, with the second in between (see Figure 7.5*b*). Specifics of storage usually are not worth thinking about in a high-level language, but the fact that a row can be treated as a unit has important consequences in manipulating arrays. This is discussed further in the section on arrays and pointers.

Examples

We present here a few examples dealing with two-dimensional arrays. Problems using higher dimensions are less common, but the methods shown in this section generalize easily from two dimensions to three and higher. See the problems at the end of this chapter for applications using three-dimensional arrays.

Matrix Inversion

Note: This section may be skipped without loss of continuity.

In linear algebra and other mathematical applications, a two-dimensional array is called a *matrix*. The numbers of rows and columns of a matrix depend on the specific application and need not be equal. A simple example is a 2×2 matrix, such as might arise from a system of two linear equations in two unknowns. For example, the system

$$3x + 4y = 1$$
$$x + 2y = 1$$

has matrix form

$$\begin{pmatrix} 3 & 4 \\ 1 & 2 \end{pmatrix}\begin{pmatrix} x \\ y \end{pmatrix} = \begin{pmatrix} 1 \\ 1 \end{pmatrix}$$

(Matrix multiplication is done by taking *rows* from the *left* matrix and multiplying them, element by element and summing, by *columns* of the *right* matrix. One row times one column produces one element of the product matrix. The identity matrix has ones as its diagonal elements and zeros elsewhere. As you can verify, if an identity matrix of the appropriate size is multiplied on the right or the left with any other matrix, that other matrix is the product.) The following code will represent the matrix storage part of this problem:

```
/* Example: Declare storage for a matrix. */
#define SIZE  2
double matrix[ SIZE ][ SIZE ];
matrix[ 0 ][ 0 ] = 3.0;
matrix[ 0 ][ 1 ] = 4.0;
matrix[ 1 ][ 0 ] = 1.0;
matrix[ 1 ][ 1 ] = 2.0;
```

The *inverse* of a square matrix is the matrix that, when multiplied with the original matrix, produces the identity matrix. Multiplying both sides of the matrix form of the system of linear equations with the inverse of the coefficient matrix solves the system:

$$\begin{pmatrix} 3 & 4 \\ 1 & 2 \end{pmatrix}^{-1}\begin{pmatrix} 3 & 4 \\ 1 & 2 \end{pmatrix}\begin{pmatrix} x \\ y \end{pmatrix} = \begin{pmatrix} 1 & 0 \\ 0 & 1 \end{pmatrix}\begin{pmatrix} x \\ y \end{pmatrix} = \begin{pmatrix} x \\ y \end{pmatrix} = \begin{pmatrix} 3 & 4 \\ 1 & 2 \end{pmatrix}^{-1}\begin{pmatrix} 1 \\ 1 \end{pmatrix}$$

Finding the inverse of a matrix is in general a difficult problem, but there is a simple method for finding the inverse of a 2 × 2 matrix:

1. Find the *determinant* of the matrix by multiplying the upper left element by the lower right element, subtracting the product of the upper right and lower left elements, as in

$$\det\begin{pmatrix} a & b \\ c & d \end{pmatrix} = ad - bc$$

   If this number is zero, stop. In that case the matrix has no inverse.
2. Swap the upper left and lower right elements.
3. Switch the sign on each of the upper right and lower left elements.
4. Finally, multiply each element by the reciprocal of the determinant.

Checking for a zero determinant is done using a tolerance value, as discussed in Chapter 3. The constant TOLERANCE in the following example can be defined according to the requirements of the application, or the system constant DBL_EPSILON (found in <float.h>) can be used. These steps can be coded as follows, using the new array newmatrix as the inverse:

```
/* Example: Compute the inverse of matrix */
double newmatrix[ SIZE ][ SIZE ];     /* Inverse of matrix.    */
double determinant,                   /* Determinant of matrix. */
       reciprocal;                    /* 1/determinant.         */
int    row, col;                      /* Row, column counters.  */
/* Compute the determinant */
determinant = matrix[ 0 ][ 0 ] * matrix[ 1 ][ 1 ]
            - matrix[ 0 ][ 1 ] * matrix[ 1 ][ 0 ];
```

```
/* Is the determinant nonzero? */
if ( fabs( determinant ) > TOLERANCE ) {
  /* Swap diagonal elements. */
  newmatrix[ 0 ][ 0 ] = matrix[ 1 ][ 1 ];
  newmatrix[ 1 ][ 1 ] = matrix[ 0 ][ 0 ];
  /* Switch signs of off-diagonal elements. */
  newmatrix[ 0 ][ 1 ] = -matrix[ 0 ][ 1 ];
  newmatrix[ 1 ][ 0 ] = -matrix[ 1 ][ 0 ];
  /* Multiply by reciprocal of the determinant. */
  reciprocal = 1.0 / determinant;
  for ( row = 0; row < SIZE; row++ )
    for ( col = 0; col < SIZE; col++ )
      newmatrix[ row ][ col ] = reciprocal * newmatrix[ row ][ col ];
} /* if */
```

Executing all of this code would produce `determinant` equal to 2, `reciprocal` equal to `0.5`, and `newmatrix` would be

$$\begin{pmatrix} 1 & -2 \\ -0.5 & 1.5 \end{pmatrix}$$

Multiplication of `matrix` times `newmatrix` yields the identity matrix. Several problems at the end of this chapter discuss more general matrix manipulation routines. For a complete discussion of computing matrix inverses, refer to [Anton] or [Burden and Faires].

Making the Grade

To keep track of test scores for a class of students, a two-dimensional array of `doubles` can be used, and each row of the array will represent one student's scores. Each column of the array will hold the scores from one test. We will make a few simplifying, but perhaps unrealistic, assumptions about this grade book application. The number of students in the class will equal the number of rows in the array, so all rows will be used. All columns will be used, too. In practice, of course, there may be fewer students enrolled than rows in the array, and we would have to keep track of the actual count. (Too many students would necessitate changes in the program.) A more versatile version of this algorithm would allow reference to a subarray of selected rows and selected columns (for example, those tests given up to a certain date), and would keep track of additional information regarding students and tests. These extensions to the problem are best handled with `structs`, discussed in Chapter 9, or with parallel arrays (see the problems at the end of this chapter).

With these simplifications and using `typedef` to define an array structure, our declarations are

```
#define NUMSTUDENTS 20
#define NUMTESTS     5
typedef double booktype[ NUMSTUDENTS ][ NUMTESTS ];
booktype gradebook;
```

and we can now write a set of functions that operate on `booktype` variables.

Function `InitBook` initializes the grade book to all zeros. (The next section discusses another way of initializing arrays.) Notice that `InitBook` traverses the array row by row.

```
void InitBook( booktype gradebook )
{ int row, col;  /* Counters for rows and columns. */
  /* Loop over all rows. */
  for ( row = 0; row < NUMSTUDENTS; row++ )
    /* Loop over all columns. */
    for ( col = 0; col < NUMTESTS; col++ )
      /* Set each grade to zero. */
      gradebook[ row ][ col ] = 0.0;
} /* InitBook() */
```

Note the nested `for` loop construction—the basic method for accessing every member of a two-dimensional array. Each row is processed successively; the elements of each row are accessed by varying the column number. The `for` loops could be reversed, processing the array column by column rather than row by row. A call to `InitBook` would be written

```
InitBook( gradebook );
```

because there is no return value.

The function `StudentGrade` finds the total grade for one student on all tests:

```
double StudentGrade( booktype gradebook, int student )
{ int   col;          /* Counter for columns.        */
  double sum = 0.0;   /* Accumulator of test scores. */
  /* Loop over one row. */
  for ( col = 0; col < NUMTESTS; col++ )
    /* Add in next test score. */
    sum += gradebook[ student ][ col ];
  return( sum );
} /* StudentGrade() */
```

Because `StudentGrade` traverses one row of the gradebook, only one `for` loop is used, and the loop varies the column number.

The following function, `TestSum`, computes the sum of all students' scores on one test:

```
double TestSum( booktype gradebook, int whichtest )
{ int   row;          /* Counter for rows      */
  double sum = 0.0;   /* Accumulator for tests */
  /* Loop over one column. */
  for ( row = 0; row < NUMSTUDENTS; row++ )
    /* Add in next student's score. */
    sum += gradebook[ row ][ whichtest ];
  return( sum );
} /* TestSum() */
```

This time, one column is traversed, so the `for` loop varies the row number.

The functions `StudentGrade` and `TestSum` can be used to compute more sophisticated reports and statistics. For example, the function `GenerateReport` prints the current total score of each student:

```
void GenerateReport( booktype gradebook )
{ int   row;        /* Row counter           */
  double total;    /* One student's grade */
  /* Loop over all students. */
  for ( row = 0; row < NUMSTUDENTS; row++ ) {
    /* Compute this student's grade and report it. */
    total = StudentGrade( gradebook, row );
    printf( "Student[ %d ]'s grade = %lf\n", row, total );
  } /* for */
} /* GenerateReport() */
```

Because the `for` loop in `GenerateReport` traverses all rows and the `for` loop in `StudentGrade` traverses all columns for a given row, every element of the array is accessed. The nested `for` loop structure is hidden by the function call rather than being explicit as it was in `InitBook`.

Initializing Arrays

In the function `InitBook` in the preceding section, we saw a way to initialize the elements of a two-dimensional array to a starting value. Similar functions can be written for arrays of any dimension and size and for any starting value. These functions can be called to set array values at any place in a program. Recall from Chapter 4 that variables of storage class `auto` are not guaranteed to be initialized to zero (although some compilers do such initialization). Arrays of class `auto` and other classes need to be initialized, although not necessarily to zero. A shortcut initialization method exists for doing this.

The shortcut method is similar to the initialization shown in Chapter 2 for simple variables at the time of their declaration. The starting value is placed after the variable declaration statement. For arrays, a list of values must be given, enclosed in braces or, for multidimensional arrays, nested braces.

Recall the array `score`, an array of five `double`s. The following statement initializes `score`:

```
double score[ NUMSCORES ] = { 50.0, 62.5, 77.0, 82.1, 98.0 };
```

Another shortcut will initialize an array's elements each to zero. Simply place that zero by itself inside braces, as

```
double score[ NUMSCORES ] = { 0.0 };
```

In fact, if the list in braces has fewer elements than the array, the elements not specified are initialized to zero by default, as

```
double score[ NUMSCORES ] = { 50.0, 62.5, 77.0 };
```

which would set `score[ 3 ]` and `score[ 4 ]` to 0.0. This default rule does not apply if *no* values are given for `auto` arrays, as already noted.

As another example, recall the array `table` used in the grade book functions, with three rows and four columns. It is initialized as

```
int table[ ROWS ][ COLUMNS ] = { { 50, 28, 78, 90 },   /* Row 0 */
                                 { 56, 40, 67, 88 },   /* Row 1 */
                                 { 38, 45, 88, 75 } }; /* Row 2 */
```

It is legal to omit the inner braces and use one long list of initial values, but this is not wise, because it creates confusion. If values are omitted, zero is substituted, as in one-dimensional arrays. The following will fill `table` with zeros:

```
int table[ ROWS ][ COLUMNS ] = { 0 };
```

Missing values at the end of a row are handled the same way. The following are equivalent initializations, but the first is much clearer:

```
int table[ ROWS ][ COLUMNS ] = { { 50, 28,  0, 0 },     /* Row 0 */
                                 { 56, 40, 67, 0 },     /* Row 1 */
                                 { 38,  0,  0, 0 } };   /* Row 2 */
```

or

```
int table[ ROWS ][ COLUMNS ] = { { 50, 28 },            /* Row 0 */
                                 { 56, 40, 67 },        /* Row 1 */
                                 { 38 } };              /* Row 2 */
```

If a row is to have zeros at the left but nonzero values at the right, the latter shortcut cannot be used.

Here is a final initialization example that shows how much better it is to use type definitions and array initializations. The simple statement

```
booktype gradebook = { 0.0 };
```

can replace the function `InitBook`.

Arrays, Parameters, and Pointers

Pass-by-address parameters to functions were discussed in Chapter 4. Recall that the arguments to such parameters were not variables but the addresses of the variables and were obtained by the & operator. The corresponding parameter's declaration used the pointer operator *, which was also used in the function body to dereference the pointer. With arrays, the syntax is somewhat different, as discussed in the next section.

Arrays as Parameters

An array, when referenced solely by its name, without brackets and an index number, is actually an address; that is, the array name is the address of the memory location of the starting point of the array. Recall the declarations

```
#define SIZE 10
int      list[ SIZE ];
```

The variable list is interpreted as the memory address where this array is stored. It is equivalent to the expression &list[0], which uses the address operator on the zeroth element of list.

As a result of this convention, arrays are always passed to functions by address and never by value. The calling statement will use the name of the array as the argument, and the parameter will use the array declaration syntax. Dereferencing the array parameter is done with brackets rather than the * operator.

We have already seen an example of this call and reference protocol in the FindMin function. It was called, with list as a parameter, as

```
smallest = FindMin( list, 0, SIZE );
```

Here the array name list was actually referring to the address of list, whatever that might be—and we do not need to know the actual address. This call corresponded to the definition of FindMin, which was

```
int FindMin( int list[ SIZE ], int start, int end )
```

By declaring list as an array of ints, we are automatically saying that FindMin is expecting a pointer (a single address) to an int. When list is referred to in the function's body, as in

```
if ( list[ index ] < list[ current ] ) current = index;
```

the array is dereferenced by [index] and [current], and no * is needed.

We note again that there is no requirement to name the parameter identically to the argument, so an alternate function definition is

```
int FindMin( int vector[ SIZE ], int start, int end )
```

and references in FindMin's body must be changed to use vector. There is an alternate way to call FindMin, using the other method mentioned above to get the address of list's starting position. It is

```
smallest = FindMin( &list[ 0 ], 0, SIZE );
```

In the example dealing with a teacher's grade book, we saw how to use a `typedef` statement to declare an array type and then use that type both for a variable declaration and for a function parameter. The resulting function declaration was

```
void InitBook( booktype gradebook );
```

which is simpler than the alternative

```
void InitBook( double gradebook[ NUMSTUDENTS ][ NUMTESTS ] );
```

And the call to `InitBook` used the array name

```
InitBook( gradebook );
```

which is simpler than

```
InitBook( &gradebook[ 0 ][ 0 ] );
```

even though this latter syntax would be a legal alternative. We see again that the use of `typedef` leads to a simpler and better-structured program.

Pointer Arithmetic on Arrays

The address calculation that is made when a particular element of an array is accessed is (and probably should remain) invisible to the user. However, C allows the user to manipulate addresses directly using *pointer arithmetic*. The idea behind allowing such a low-level operation in an otherwise high-level programming language is to provide flexibility in operations on arrays, specifically on array parameters in functions. A simple example will illustrate the method.

Once again, recall the example `list`, an array of `int`s. Whether in a main program or in a function, a reference to `list[ 2 ]` must be translated in the following way. Since `list` is the address of element `list[ 0 ]`, we need to move two places beyond `list` to find the desired element. "Places" here depends on the base type of the array—in this case, `int`. That is, the address of `list[ 2 ]` is equivalent to `list + 2 * sizeof( int )`. For example, if `list[ 0 ]` is stored at address 1000 and `int`s are four bytes, then `list[ 2 ]` is stored at address 1008.

Using pointer arithmetic, the same memory location can be accessed by the expression `*( list + 2 )`. That is, add 2 to the address in `list`, then dereference the address. The `sizeof` applied to the base type `int` is implicit here. As a further example, consider accessing every element of `list` to print out the values. This would normally be done with a `for` loop using the loop variable as the array index. Using pointer arithmetic, it is

```
/* Pointer arithmetic on a one-dimensional array. */
for ( i = 0; i < LIST; i++ )
  printf( "list[ %d ] = %d\n", i, *( list + i ));
```

Note that the actual address is not computed. Note also that a reference to `*( list + i * sizeof( int ))` is incorrect, because the `sizeof` operator is already automatically used.

For example, if `int`s were four bytes long, this incorrect reference would produce a memory reference equivalent to `list[ 4 * i ]`.

Similar arithmetic can be done on higher-dimensional arrays. Keep in mind that such arrays are conceptually arrays of smaller-dimension arrays. Reference must be made to the proper piece of the array. Also, surround pointer expressions with parentheses to ensure that the `*` operator associates correctly. Consider as an example the previously defined array `gradebook`, a 20 × 5 array of `double`s. One can write expressions such as

```
/* Pointer arithmetic on a two-dimensional example. */
*( gradebook[ 3 ] + 2 ) = 62.5;
printf( "%lf\n", *(( *( gradebook + 10 )) + 3 ));
```

The first reference is equivalent to `gradebook[ 3 ][ 2 ]`, while the second is the same as `gradebook[ 10 ][ 3 ]`.

The fact that pointer arithmetic *can* be done does not imply that it *should* be done. Code written using pointer arithmetic is harder to comprehend than code using the usual referencing method, and using it is therefore a bad idea. We mention it here because you may see this method elsewhere, and also because it reinforces what pointers and addressing are all about. When pointers are encountered again in Chapter 10 in the context of linked lists, pointer manipulation (although not pointer arithmetic) will be needed.

Recall that functions cannot return arrays; that is, the type of a function may not be an array. However, because arrays are pointers, a function may return a pointer to, say, an `int`, as in `int *function( parameters )`. This could mean that `function` returns the address of a one-dimensional array of `int`s, or just the address of a single `int`. This style is ambiguous and should also be avoided.

Arrays as Parameters, Again

As seen in the previous discussion of one-dimensional arrays and pointer arithmetic, the size of an array need not be known when referencing array elements. Only the starting address, the base type size, and the index are needed. This fact can be used to implement a version of *conformant* arrays: arrays whose size need not be known at compile time but can be decided at run time.

For example, a function that processes the array `list` could be defined as

```
void NewFunction( int list[], int ArraySize );
```

where the actual size of `list` is passed in the parameter `ArraySize` but is not directly associated with `list`. References such as `list[ 3 ]` are legal, but the burden of ensuring that out-of-bounds references are avoided is entirely up to the programmer. `ArraySize` is a parameter for that reason. A `for` loop inside `NewFunction` might look like

```
for ( i = 0; i < ArraySize; i++ )
  /* ... process list[ i ] ...*/
```

Calls to `NewFunction()` can then be made with *any* one-dimensional array of `int`s, as long as the actual size (or something smaller) is passed as the argument to `ArraySize`.

A weaker alternative is to declare a global constant, say SIZE, use it as the check on array bounds, and not pass the array size as a parameter. Then the for loop would be

```
for ( i = 0; i < SIZE; i++ )
  /* ... process list[ i ] ...*/
```

and only arrays with SIZE elements can be arguments.

Also, the declaration of the array parameter can be of the form int *list, as in

```
void NewFunction( int *list, int ArraySize );
```

which still permits references using square brackets. When writing prototypes for functions that accept array parameters, either style may be used. Each of the following is correct:

```
void NewFunction( int [], int );  /* Bracket method. */
void NewFunction( int *, int );     /* Pointer method. */
```

When higher-dimensional arrays are parameters to functions, the sizes of all but the first dimension must be declared in order to permit address computation. For example, the StudentGrade function (discussed earlier in the chapter) could be declared as either of

```
double StudentGrade(
  double gradebook[][ NUMTESTS ], int NumRows, int student );
double StudentGrade(
  double ( *gradebook )[ NUMTESTS ], int NumRows, int student );
```

The number of rows is irrelevant to computing element addresses, but the number of columns must be known. Any array with NUMTESTS columns could be an argument, provided the actual number of rows is passed in NumRows. Similarly, three-dimensional array parameters are required to specify the last (rightmost) two sizes, but not the first.

An alternative method to achieve conformant arrays, used in the problems at the end of the chapter, is to declare a very large array but use only part of it. The size of the used part is passed as a parameter to functions, as in the foregoing examples. The array parameter is declared the same size as the argument in the calling function. This method wastes some space because of the overlarge size used, but it has the advantage of exact typing, which is useful for debugging (even if the compiler may ignore the declared size of the parameter).

Advanced vi

In the following sections, we continue the discussion of the vi editor. Advanced editing techniques are presented to increase your efficiency in using vi. Most of the commands discussed in this section, including substitution and : commands, require that the return (or enter) key be pressed after them. Those that do not require a carriage return include the commands r, m, y, p, and '.

Movement

Besides advancing by single lines and characters and by page jumps, you can change the current position by several other commands. To move forward or backward by one word, the commands are w and b. To jump to the end of a line, use $; to jump to the beginning of a line, the command is 0 (zero).

Lines in a file are numbered. Either of the commands :f or control-G print the current line number and file name on the status line. Two commands to move to line *num* are :*num* and *num*G. For example, :34 changes the current line to number 34, whereas 1G moves to the first line in the file. The former method has the advantage of being echoed on the status line. Finally, G moves to the last line in the file.

Searching

The vi editor provides a method of searching for text strings within a file. The complementary commands /*pattern*/ and ?*pattern*? search forward and backward, respectively, for the text string *pattern*, making the line containing the first occurrence of the pattern the new current line. The final slash (or question mark) may be omitted. The command /dog/ searches forward for the first occurrence of the string dog. If the end of the file is reached, the search continues at the beginning of the file. If dog is not found, a message to that effect appears on the status line.

The pattern itself can include special matching characters or *metacharacters* (also known as "wild cards" or "magic characters") (see Figure 7.6 for a listing). Note that we will omit the slashes and question marks in what follows:

- The character . matches any single character, so the pattern a.b would match aab, a3b, and a+b, among others.
- The $ matches the end of a line, provided it is the last character of the pattern; for example, dog$ will match the string dog only if it is the last word on a line.
- Similarly, ∧ at the beginning of a string matches the beginning of a line.

Metacharacters

$	matches end of line
∧	matches start of line, or not in a set (only when used in [])
–	range of characters
[]	set of characters
*	matches 0 or more of preceding
.	matches any single character
\	treat next character as non-magic

Figure 7.6   Metacharacters for string matching

To indicate a set of characters, one of which may occur at a particular position, enclose them inside brackets. Character lists need no intervening space, but if separated by a dash, they indicate a range of characters. For example, [09] matches 0 and 9, while [0-9] matches any single digit. If the caret character ∧ is the first character inside brackets, the group matches anything *not* in it. For example, [∧0-9] matches any single nondigit character. The wild card * expands what precedes it to zero or more occurrences. Thus, a* matches a, aa, aaa, and so on. An identifier in the C language can be expressed as [a-zA-Z][a-zA-Z0-9_]*; that is, it starts with a letter and is followed by zero or more alphanumeric characters or an underscore.

When a metacharacter (such as ., $, ∧, *) must be included in a pattern as a regular character, it must be preceded by a backslash. For example, dog* matches the string dog*, but not the string dogg.

The special command % is available to match the grouping characters: parentheses, brackets, and braces. For example, when positioned on a left (or right) parenthesis, typing this command will find the matching right (respectively left) parenthesis. A beep will sound if no matching parenthesis is found.

Replacement

For replacing text, several simple commands are available. The r command replaces the current character (the one the cursor is on) with the next character typed. For example, positioning the cursor over the character x and typing ry will change it to y. The command R enters replacement mode, which is similar to insert mode in that all characters typed are inserted, but they replace the existing characters, and the escape key ends replacement mode. The special tilde command ˜ reverses case when over an alphabetic character. Tilde has no effect on other characters.

More sophisticated replacement is done with the substitute command

:*range* s/*pattern*/*newpattern*/*options*

to replace a pattern with a new pattern. The optional *range* specifies a pair of line numbers separated by commas; the substitution will occur on this range of lines. The code . indicates the current line (which is the default for both line numbers if no range is specified), and $ stands for the last line in the file. Numbers indicate absolute line numbers, but preceding a number with a + indicates a relative count from the current position. Thus, the range 1, 10 is the first 10 lines of the file; ., 100 means the lines from the current line to line 100; and ., +20 means the next 20 lines. One of the *options* is c, which will ask you to confirm each replacement by typing y and the enter key. (This process can be interrupted with the control-C key.) Another option is g, which will replace all occurrences of the pattern on each line (the default is to replace only the first occurrence on each line). For example, :.,$ s/life/death/ will search for the first occurrence of the string life on each line from the current line to the end of the file, replacing each with the string death, whereas :s/old/new/cg will replace all occurrences of old with new, but only on the current line and provided that you type y when prompted.

Cut and Paste

In vi there are *text buffers,* both numbered (1 through 9) and lettered (a through z), to which lines of text may be *yanked* (stored). To yank lines of text to a lettered buffer, construct the command " (double quote character), followed by the name of the buffer, followed by an optional line count, and finally followed by y. For example, the command "b3y will yank three lines to buffer b. The original lines are copied, not deleted.

Deletion can be done by substituting dd for y in the above. This is closer to the cut process than yanking is. For example, "g10dd will delete ten lines starting at the current cursor position and place them in buffer g.

Once text is in a buffer, it can be retrieved by a similar command. Substituting the *put* command p for the y and omitting the line count, as in "gp, will put (insert) buffer g's text at the current cursor position. This works regardless of which method was used to store the text in the buffer. When lines of text are deleted using the normal line deletion command dd, they are automatically stored in the numbered buffers 1, 2, and so on, and so can be recovered in case of accidental deletion. As new lines are deleted, the contents of the buffers are shifted up one number. Thus, "1p will always put the most recently deleted line of text at the current cursor position.

The m command, followed by a letter, will *mark* the current line with the letter as its *label*. For example, ma will mark the current line with label a. Once marked, a line may be referenced by other commands. To go directly to a marked line, type command ' followed by the label, as in 'a. If two lines have labels a and b, the text from the first line to the second can be written out to a file myfile by the command :'a,'b w myfile. Like yanking, writing does not delete the text; unlike yanking, it is not stored in a buffer. If the file already exists, you will be prompted to try again, substituting w! for w to overwrite the file. An existing file may be read in at the current cursor position by the command :r filename.

Settings

There are a number of environment variables that control the way vi behaves. These variables may be set manually using the :set command. Alternatively, they may be set automatically by placing the commands (but without colons) in a file named .exrc, which must be located in your home directory.

For example, :set number, or its abbreviation :set nu, will enable line numbering—that is, the lines of the file you are editing will have their line numbers displayed at the left of the screen. As with most settable commands, this one can be "unset" by using the no prefix, as in :set nonu.

A useful option when typing C programs is autoindent, :set autoindent or :set ai. This enables vi to remember the amount of indentation used from one line to the next. Programs use hanging indentation for a grouping effect, so this option removes the need to count in spaces or use the tab key when starting a new line. If you do not want the new line to have this indentation, you can backspace over it, while still in insert mode, using control-D (rather than the usual control-H).

When text that will overrun the end of a line is typed, a new line can be generated automatically by :set wrapmargin=num or :set wm=num, where num is an integer. This integer is used to measure from the right margin; when a line reaches this number of characters from that margin, the new line is created from the beginning of the word being typed.

To see what settings are in effect, type :set all; this will display a listing of all current options at the bottom of the screen. Each option has a default value, so whether you have set an option or not, it shows up in this list.

Other Useful Commands

The vi editor can be started with variants of the basic command vi *filename*. For example, to use vi in read-only mode, type view *filename*. All vi commands, including insertions, work as usual in this mode. However, you will not be able to write the file with :w, and if you have made any changes in the text, you must quit using :q!.

To start vi at a particular line number rather than at the beginning of the file, use vi +*num filename*, where *num* is the line number. The command vi + *filename* will go to the end of the file.

If a UNIX system crashes while you are editing a file, a version of that file is usually saved automatically. When you log in after the system recovers, you will receive a mail message from the system telling you that the file was saved. It must be recovered manually with the command vi -r *filename*. This command must be run in the same current directory in use at the time of the crash.

After editing a file and before exiting vi, you can change to another file with the next-file command, :n *newfilename*. If you have made changes to the old file but have not saved it before doing this, a message will be printed to that effect (the command :e *newfilename* works in a similar manner), suggesting that if you really want to go on to the new file without saving the old, you should type :n! *newfilename*. The next-file command is useful when a series of files is being edited. For example, to edit all files whose names end in .c in the current directory, first type the command vi *.c. A status line message tells the number of files to be edited, and the first file ending in .c is loaded. After editing this file, typing the command :n will bring up the second file (again with the same effect as just described if the current file was modified but not saved), and this same command may be repeated until all .c files have been edited.

Typing :!*command*, where *command* is a UNIX command, will cause that command to be executed. For example, if you need to include in the file you are editing a list of the files in the parent directory of the current directory, the command :!ls .. will show that list. You will then be prompted to press the enter key to continue, after which the list is erased from the screen. This does not actually include the list, of course; you would need to remember what you saw and type it in. A more sophisticated method would be to include the listing directly into the file by the commands :!ls .. > *tempfile* followed by :r *tempfile*. Alternatively, the command :!!ls .. also inputs the listing into the file being edited.

References

Anton, Howard, *Elementary Linear Algebra,* 7th ed., Wiley, New York, 1994.
Burden, Richard L., and J. Douglas Faires, *Numerical Analysis,* 5th ed., PWS-KENT, Boston, 1993.

Chapter Summary

■ **C Commands**

```
#define ROWS 3
#define COLUMNS 4
```
(Constants to define the following array type)

`typedef double ArrayType[ ROWS ]` `    [ COLUMNS ];`	Define a template for arrays with room to store 12 `double` variables (total capacity of the array equals `ROWS * COLUMNS`)
`ArrayType table;`	Declare a variable whose name is `table` and whose type is `ArrayType`. For $0 \leq i \leq (\text{ROWS} - 1)$ and $0 \leq j \leq (\text{COLUMNS} - 1)$, `table[ i ][ j ]` accesses the same `double` as `*( table + i * COLUMNS + j )`
`table = { 0.0 };`	Set all values of `table` to zero
`table[ 0 ] = { 0.0 };`	Set all values to zero in the first row of `table`
`void FirstFn( double list [ ],` `    int ListSize )`	Header for a function that can access `list` as a one-dimensional conformant array of `double`s whose actual size is specified by the parameter `ListSize`

`void SecondFn(`
`    double table [ ] [ COLUMNS ],`
`    int TableSize )`
	Header for a function that can access `table` as a two-dimensional conformant array of `double`s whose actual size is specified by the parameter `TableSize`

■ vi **Commands**

Cursor Movement

`w` *(b)*	Move cursor forward to next *word* (backward to previous word)
`$` *(0)*	Move cursor forward to end of *line* (backward to beginning of line)
`:2` or `2G`	Move to line 2 of the file
`G`	Move to last line in the file
`f`	Display current line number on the status line

Search

`/` *pattern* `/` *($ pattern $)*	Search forward (backward) for first occurrence of *pattern*
`/\[ /`	Search forward for first occurrence of a left bracket followed by a space
`/x.z/`	Search forward for first occurrence of an x, followed by any character, followed by a z
`/[xy]\*[^a-z]/`	Search forward for first occurrence of an x or y, followed by a star, followed by any character other than a lower case letter
`/^for(/`	Search forward for first occurrence of `for(` at the beginning of a line
`/)$/`	Search forward for first occurrence of a right parenthesis at the end of a line
`/+ [0-9][0-9]*/`	Search forward for first occurrence of + followed by a space followed by one or more digits
`%`	Search for a matching parenthesis, bracket, or brace

Replacement

`:1,4 s/int/double/c`	Search lines 1 through 4 and offer to replace the first occurrence of `int` with `double`
`:1,. s/int/double/g`	Search from line 1 to the current line and replace all occurrences of `int` with `double`
`:1,. s/int/double/cg`	Search from line 1 to the current line and *offer* to replace all occurrences of `int` with `double`
`:1,$ s/</(/g`	Search all lines and replace all occurrences of `<` with `(`
`ra`	Replace current character with `a`
`Rabc<esc>`	Replace current and next two characters with `abc`
`~`	Replace current lower case character with corresponding upper case character, or vice versa

Cut and Paste

`"by`	Yank (copy) current line to buffer b
`"b3y`	Yank (copy) 3 lines to buffer b
`"13y`	Yank (copy) 3 lines to buffer 1
`"1dd`	Delete current line and store in buffer 1
`"b33dd`	Delete 33 lines and store in buffer b
`"133dd`	Delete 33 lines and store in buffer 1
`"1p`	Put (paste) contents of buffer 1 at current cursor position
`ma`	Mark current line with label a
`:'a,'b w CopyFile`	Store a copy of lines a through b in `CopyFile`

Other Commands

`:set number (:set nonumber)`	Set line numbering option on (off)
`:set autoindent (:set noautoindent)`	Set automatic indentation option on (off)
`view filename`	Start the `vi` editor in read-only mode and view `filename`
`:q!`	Quit viewing without saving changes
`vi filename`	Start the `vi` editor in normal command mode and view `filename`
`vi +50 filename`	Start the `vi` editor in normal command mode and view `filename` beginning at line 50
`vi + filename`	Start the `vi` editor in normal command mode and view the end of `filename`

```
vi -r filename                        Start vi and recover latest version of filename
                                      following system crash

:!ls                                  Interrupt vi and list working directory
```

Review Problems

1. Here are several array declarations. In each case, first identify the type, size, dimension and name; then count the number of rows, columns and layers; and then rewrite the declaration using `typedef` and defined constants.
   a) `int fonts[ 33 ];`
   b)

   ```
   #define DEVICES 4
   int channels[ DEVICES ];
   ```

   c) `double weeks[ 7 ][ 52 ][ 10 ];`
   d)

   ```
   #define PROCESSORS 4
   #define CELLS 256
   long int addresses[ PROCESSORS ][ CELLS ];
   ```

2. Use the `sizeof()` function to find the number of bytes needed to store an `int`, a `double`, and a `long int` on your system. Then estimate the number of bytes of memory needed for each array in the preceding problem.

3. A company maintains two parallel arrays that contain the identification numbers and the hourly wage rates of its employees. (Arrays are *parallel* if they have the same size and if index values have the same meaning within each array; in this example a specific index refers to the same employee in each array.) Write array declarations (using `typedef`) and a simple loop (no error trapping or editing) for inserting data into these arrays. Use a constant `NumEMPLOYEES` to specify the number of employees and define this constant using a number of your choice.

4. Write a function whose input is a wage rate array, such as described in the preceding problem, and whose output is the average hourly wage rate. Document the function to specify external definitions and declarations that are assumed by the function.

5. Suppose the natural index range for a particular list is from 100 to 200.
   a) Write a function to prompt the user for `begin` and `end` index values (with $100 \leq$ `begin` $\leq$ `end` ≤ 200), and then ask the user to input array values within the index range from `begin` to `end`. The header for this function should be

   ```
   int FindSubArray( ArrayType list )
   ```

   where `ArrayType` defines an integer array of size 101. Note that you must translate user indices to the proper range of array indices. Let the function return 0 if the user inputs suitable values for `begin` and `end` and otherwise return 1.
   b) Write a related function to output the maximum value from the integer sequence

   ```
   list[ first ], list[ first + 1 ], ..., list[ last ]
   ```

This function should return the maximum value (not an index) and should also find a value for the parameter `freq`, an integer that counts the *frequency* of the maximum value (that is, the number of times the maximum value occurs within the list). Use the header

```
int FindMax( ArrayType list, int first, int last, int *freq )
```

   c) Carefully describe the output if an array with only one element (in which `first` equals `last`) is used for input to the function `FindMax()`.

6. Recall the previously defined functions `FindMin()`, which finds the index of the minimum value in an unsorted array, and `BinSearch()`, which tries to find the index of a given key in a sorted array.

   a) Can `FindMin()` be applied to a sorted array? If so, describe `FindMin()` more precisely than at the beginning of this problem.

   b) Can `FindMin()` be applied to an array in which a minimum element occurs more than once? If so, again describe `FindMin()` more precisely than at the beginning of this problem.

   c) Can `BinSearch()` be applied to an array in which a key occurs more than once? If so, describe `BinSearch()` more precisely than at the beginning of this problem.

   d) How can the binary search algorithm be modified so that it tries to find the *smallest* index of a given key in a sorted array?

7. This problem concerns the matrix `Original`, a 2×2 matrix of `doubles`, and its inverse matrix `InverseOfOriginal`.

   a) Write appropriate declarations and assignments for defining `Original` so that its first row has the elements 2.0 and 4.0, and its second row has the elements 1.0 and 1.0.

   b) Explain why you can be certain that `Original` has an inverse, without calculating the inverse.

   c) Manually calculate the elements of `InverseOfOriginal`.

   d) Manually calculate the two product matrices `Original * InverseOfOriginal` and `InverseOfOriginal * Original`.

8. The *Fibonacci sequence* is defined by the initial values

$$f_1 = 1, \qquad f_2 = 1,$$

and the iterative relationship

$$f_n = f_{n-1} + f_{n-2}, \quad \text{for } n \geq 3.$$

Write a function and related declarations to compute the values of an array containing the first 100 terms of the Fibonacci sequence.

9. This problem concerns array initialization and assignment of values.

   a) Define a type suitable for storing `double` arrays as small as 2 by 3 and as large as 200 by 201, and declare an array that is of this type and is initialized with zeros.

   b) Write a function whose input parameters include a variable of the type defined in part a), two parameters (`RowSize` and `ColSize`) to specify the size of a subarray, and a parameter (`c`) to specify the index of a single column within the subarray. The function should return 0 if the values of `RowSize`, `ColSize`, and `c` are all proper, 1 if they are not. If the values are all proper, the function should prompt the user to enter values for the specified column.

10. Write a function, `PrintSequence()`, to print a one-dimensional integer array. Input should include a conformant array of integers, an integer to specify the array's size, and another integer to specify the number of values to be displayed on each output line.

11. In the context of the following definitions and declaration, give an alternative reference for each element using the array name and any necessary indices (for example, `table[ 1 ][ 1 ]`).

```
#define ROWS 5
#define COLUMNS 10
double table[ ROWS ][ COLUMNS ]
```

a) `&table[ 0 ][ 0 ]`
b) `*( table[ 0 ] + 5 )`
c) `*( table[ 0 ] + 15 )`

12. (vi Tutorial) Choose a rather long file to copy for the purpose of practicing advanced vi commands. You may need to modify your file to fit these instructions; for example, you may need to add text containing parentheses and arithmetic operators before executing some of the search commands.

a) Open the file for viewing only.

b) Move to end of file; mark last line b; move to first line; mark first line a.

c) After ensuring that the name of the file you are editing appears on several lines of the file, replace all occurrences of the name of the file with `tempcopy`; change the first occurrence of `tempcopy` to `tempCopy` using tilde (~); change `tempCopy` to `TempCopy` using r; change `TempCopy` to `Tempfile` using R; change `Tempfile` to `TempFile` using r or tilde.

d) Save this edited file (from line a to line b) in `TempFile`; quit viewing the original file.

e) Start vi and open `TempCopy` at line 20; turn on line numbering.

f) Move to the top line; yank the first three lines to buffer a; delete the current line and store in buffer b; insert buffer a.

g) Move to the bottom line; check current line number; move to the last word on the line; move to the next-to-last word on the line; move to the last word on the line; move to the first word on the line; move to the second word on the line; move to the first word on the line.

h) Delete the bottom line using dd; move to the top line; delete the top line using dd; insert buffer 1; move to the bottom line; insert buffer 2.

i) Search forward for the first occurrence of a right parenthesis at the end of a line; search for a matching parenthesis.

j) Replace all occurrences of a with Aa.

k) Search forward for the first occurrence of an upper case letter followed by a lower case letter; search backward for the first occurrence of an arithmetic operator; with prompting, search from there to the end of the file, replacing all instances of + with – (if there are many instances of +, you may wish to use Control-C to abort this process before making all the substitutions).

l) Without prompting, replace all occurrences of " (" with " (".

m) Search forward for the first occurrence of a lower case letter followed by anything followed by a lower case letter.

Programming Problems

1. (Time Series Smoothing) Suppose financial information has been collected for several consecutive days. One method of smoothing the data, and thereby removing random fluctuations, is to replace each data value by an average taken over several days leading up to and including the current day. For instance, suppose we have an input array named `ActualReceipts` that represents raw data values for days 1 through 30 (inclusive), and that we wish to calculate an output array named `AveReceipts` that contains averages over ten-day periods for days 10 through 30. The first ten-day period averages days 1, 2, ..., 10; the 21st period averages days 21, 22, ..., 30. Write a function that does this task and has the header

   ```
   void TenDayAve( RawData ActualReceipts, SmoothData AveReceipts )
   ```

   Test this function with an array of random `double`s rounded to the second decimal place. Print both raw and smoothed data.

2. (Insertion Sort) Insertion sort is an easy way of sorting randomly arranged arrays. Nevertheless, the time required is proportional to the square of the array size, and therefore an insertion sort should not be applied to large arrays.

The insertion sort algorithm inserts elements, one at a time, into a partially sorted subarray consisting of all elements up to and including the current one. To implement insertion sort, begin by inserting the second element into its proper position within the subarray consisting of the first and second elements; then continue by inserting each subsequent element into its corresponding subarray, always requiring that previous elements are properly sorted before a given element is inserted. To insert a particular element:

1. Find the proper index for the new element within the corresponding subarray.
2. If any previous elements are greater than the current element, move the current element to its proper position and increment the index of any previous element that is greater than the new element (be careful to copy an element before it is overwritten).

For example, the array {6, 5, 4, 8, 4, 3, 1, 2} would go through the following rearrangements as it is sorted by this method:

$$\{5, 6, 4, 8, 4, 3, 1, 2\}$$

$$\{4, 5, 6, 8, 4, 3, 1, 2\}$$

$$\{4, 5, 6, 8, 4, 3, 1, 2\}$$

$$\{4, 4, 5, 6, 8, 3, 1, 2\}$$

$$\{3, 4, 4, 5, 6, 8, 1, 2\}$$

$$\{1, 3, 4, 4, 5, 6, 8, 2\}$$

$$\{1, 2, 3, 4, 4, 5, 6, 8\}$$

Write a function that uses the insertion sort algorithm to sort an array of integers and has the header

```
int InsertionSort( int MyArray[ ], int first, int last )
```

Have your function return an error code of 0 if `first < last`, and an error code of 1 in all other cases.

3. (Intensity Ramp) In computer graphics, and elsewhere, it is useful to find a sequence of interpolating values between two given values. Write a function whose input is two `doubles` and whose output is an array of `doubles` that forms an arithmetic sequence of numbers (the difference between two consecutive numbers being constant) connecting the given values. For example, if the given values are 1.0 and 7.0, an intensity ramp with 4 steps would be given by the sequence `{ 1.0, 2.5, 4.0, 5.5, 7.0 }`. Let the user determine the number of steps interactively.

4. Write a function whose input is an array of `doubles` and whose output is an array of integers representing the indices of the array if its values are to be displayed in increasing order. For example, the input array of values { 2.2, 3.3, 1.1 } should generate the output array of indices { 2, 0, 1 }, since the elements of the input array having indices 2, 0, and 1 are 1.1, 2.2, and 3.3 respectively.

5. Write a program to estimate the definite integral, average value, and derivatives of the function $f(x) = \sin x$ over the interval $0 \leq x \leq 2\pi$. These calculations should be based upon a sequence of n evenly spaced values in the given interval, where n is specified interactively. Use the composite trapezoidal rule (for background, see a calculus or numerical analysis textbook),

$$\int_a^b f(x)\, dx \approx \frac{(b-a)}{2n}\left[f(a) + f(b) + 2\sum_{i=1}^{n-1} f(x_i) \right]$$

where

$$x_i = a + i\left(\frac{b-a}{n}\right) \quad \text{for } i = 0, 1, 2, \ldots, n$$

to estimate the integral. The average value of the function is estimated by dividing the integral by the length of the interval. Estimate derivatives by finding the slopes between consecutive points on the function curve and storing these values in an array. Write a program that is easily modified to accept other functions and intervals.

6. (Sample Statistics) A random sample is a sequence

$$x_1, x_2, \ldots, x_n$$

of data values. In the following functions, represent a random sample by a conformant array of `doubles`.

a) Write functions to calculate the *sample mean* ($\bar{x}$), *sample variance* (s^2), and *sample standard deviation(s)*, as defined by

$$\bar{x} = \frac{1}{n}\sum_{i=1}^{n} x_i$$

$$s^2 = \frac{1}{n-1}\left[\sum_{i=1}^{n} x_i^2 - \frac{1}{n}\left(\sum_{i=1}^{n} x_i\right)^2\right]$$

$$s = \sqrt{s^2}$$

b) Write a function to calculate the *median* and *range*. For these calculations, first sort the data into increasing order. If the sample size n is odd, the median is defined to be the middle value of the sorted data set; and if the sample size n is even, the median is defined to be the average of the two middle values of the sorted data set. The range is the difference between the largest and smallest values.

c) Write a function to calculate the sample variance by the alternative definition

$$s^2 = \frac{1}{n-1}\sum_{i=1}^{n}(x_i - \bar{x})^2.$$

d) With exact arithmetic the two variance formulas produce identical results; however, with floating-point arithmetic the second variance formula sometimes produces less accurate values. Carefully plan and execute several experimental runs to test this claim.

7. Write an interactive program to compute sums of the form

$$1^6 + 2^6 + \cdots + N^6$$

where N is a positive integer. Do this by creating an array of `floats` whose first element is 1^6, the second element is 2^6, and so forth. Sum the values of this array twice: from first to last and then from last to first. Observe that the two sums may not agree, even for moderately small values of N. Try to explain this discrepancy, and test your explanation by writing and executing an experimental program. (Note that `floats` are specified here to make it easier to observe how the order of summation can affect the final sum; the same principle can be observed using `doubles` or any other floating-point type.)

8. Write a function that accepts two parallel arrays (arrays of equal size) as input and, referring to these arrays as x and y, calculates the *correlation coefficient* for the paired arrays as given by the formula

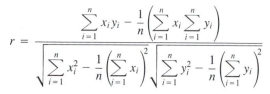

$$r = \frac{\displaystyle\sum_{i=1}^{n} x_i y_i - \frac{1}{n}\left(\sum_{i=1}^{n} x_i \sum_{i=1}^{n} y_i\right)}{\sqrt{\displaystyle\sum_{i=1}^{n} x_i^2 - \frac{1}{n}\left(\sum_{i=1}^{n} x_i\right)^2}\sqrt{\displaystyle\sum_{i=1}^{n} y_i^2 - \frac{1}{n}\left(\sum_{i=1}^{n} y_i\right)^2}}$$

Use an internal function to calculate the numerator as well as each radicand (expression inside a radical symbol).

9. (Matrix Editing) Write a collection of functions, as described in the following parts, to perform basic editing and manipulation on matrices of size at most 5×5. First define a data structure named ArrayType for two-dimensional arrays of doubles with five rows and five columns. This definition sets a maximum size for the matrices, each matrix being represented by a subarray of an ArrayType variable. For example, a 2×3 matrix uses rows 0 and 1 and columns 0, 1, and 2 of an ArrayType variable, as in:

{ 1.0, 2.0, 3.0, 0.0, 0.0 }

{ 1.0, 2.0, 3.0, 0.0, 0.0 }

{ 0.0, 0.0, 0.0, 0.0, 0.0 }

{ 0.0, 0.0, 0.0, 0.0, 0.0 }

{ 0.0, 0.0, 0.0, 0.0, 0.0 }

where all of the unused array values are set to 0.0. Any matrix having at most 5 rows and at most 5 columns can be represented in this manner.

a) Write a function EditMatrix() to edit a matrix of doubles. Input parameters are an array A and integers r and c (the number of rows and columns of A that contain the particular matrix). The function should return an error code of 0 (no error) or 1 (number of rows or columns not positive). If there is no input error, display the matrix, using exponential form for each entry, and allow the user to change as many matrix values as desired. This editing function should allow the user to change an individual value, change an entire row, change an entire column, or quit the function.

b) Write a function InputMatrix() to read a matrix of doubles from the keyboard into internal memory. Input parameters are an array A and integers r and c (the number of rows and columns of A that contain the particular matrix). The function should return an error code of 0 (no error) or 1 (number of rows or columns not positive). If there is no input error, fill the matrix with zeros and use the EditMatrix() function from part a) to allow the user to specify the desired matrix values.

c) Write a function SaveMatrix() to write a matrix of doubles to an external text file. Input values are an array A, integers r and c (the number of rows and columns of A that contain the particular matrix), and a file name for the external file; the function should return an error code of 0 (no error), 1 (number of rows or columns not positive), or 2 (unable to open or close file). If there is no input error, the function writes r+1 lines to the external file. The first line is of the form r c \n where r and c represent the number of rows and columns respectively. Each subsequent line contains c doubles and is terminated by \n.

d) Write a function ReadMatrix() to read a matrix of doubles from an external text file to internal memory. A file name must be input, and if there is no error, the function returns a positive integer r (the number of rows), a positive integer c (the number of columns), and a pointer to A (the array in which the matrix has been stored in memory). Assume that the first line of the text file is of the form r c \n, where r and c represent the number of rows and columns respectively. Assume that each subsequent line of data represents one row of the matrix. Pad the matrix with DBL_MAX (defined in <float.h>) to replace any missing values. Ignore any superfluous values contained in the text file. Use five error codes: 0 (no error), 1 (number of rows or columns not positive), 2 (insufficient data), 3 (extra data), or 4 (unable to open or close file). After a matrix has successfully been read into memory, display it on the screen, using exponential form for each entry.

10. (Jacobi Method) Suppose a two-dimensional array of doubles represents initial temperatures within a rectangular plate, with the row and column indices corresponding to a grid of points in the rectangle and with the array values indicating temperatures. If the temperatures along the rectangle's boundary are held constant, the internal temperatures eventually approach equilibrium.

One can apply the *Jacobi method* to estimate these equilibrium temperatures. The algorithm scans the interior points of the rectangle and computes an updated value for each point by averaging the temperature at the given point with the temperatures at the four neighbors that are due north, east, south, and west. Write a program to implement this algorithm iteratively. Calculate all of the averages before updating any temperatures. Continue updating temperatures until the maximum temperature change at any point is less than some specified constant.

11. (Image Processing by Neighbor Averaging) This is a variation on the preceding problem. Let the array values represent light intensities rather than temperatures. One iteration of the Jacobi algorithm described in the preceding problem can be used to reduce random noise within the picture by incorporating the following modifications: Use a weighted average, where each point intensity is weighted more heavily than the intensity at any of the neighbors; find an average for border points as well as interior points; and average over eight neighbors (additionally considering northeast, southeast, southwest, and northwest neighbors) whenever possible. Let the user specify a weighting factor for each point (call the weighting factor w and require $0.15 < w < 0.85$), and then find weighted averages using the following formula to update the intensity at the current point:

w * (intensity at current point) + (1 - w) * (average intensity at neighboring points)

12. (Double Integrals) Write a program to estimate a volume that is below a surface of the form $z = f(x, y)$, where f is an internally defined function, and above a specified rectangle in the plane. For simplicity, consider only functions whose values are nonnegative over the given rectangle. To estimate such a volume, subdivide the rectangle by a grid of squares. Evaluate the function at the midpoint of each small square (this approximates the surface height above the square), and multiply that height approximation by the square's area. Each such product estimates the volume above one square, and the sum of such products approximates the total volume between the rectangle and the surface.

For example, consider the volume that is under the surface $z = x + y$ and above the rectangle $0 \leq x \leq 2, 0 \leq y \leq 1$. If the rectangle is subdivided into eight squares, as shown in Figure 7.7, the midpoint of the square in the lower left corner has coordinates $(0.25, 0.25)$, the function value at this midpoint is $0.25 + 0.25 = 0.50$, and the volume above the square is approximately $0.50 \times 0.25 \times 0.25 = 0.03125$ (cubic units). The given grid produces a total volume estimate of 0.75 cubic units. *Note:* This particular grid produces a rather crude estimate; the exact volume is actually 3 cubic units.

Figure 7.7 A grid of eight squares subdividing the given rectangle in Programming Problem 12

13. (Tic-Tac-Toe) Write an interactive program to play the following variations on the game of tic-tac-toe:
    a) Two persons
    b) One person against the computer, with the computer making random choices
    c) One person against the computer, with the computer making strategic choices
    Hint: Represent the game board as a 3×3 array of integers with array values of 1 and 2 to designate marks by the two players, and a value of 0 to designate an unused position.

14. (Game of Life) The mathematician J. H. Conway invented the simulation game called Life, which is described as follows. The *world* is a two-dimensional array of cells, where each cell is either *alive* (inhabited by an organism) or *dead* (not inhabited). The cells live or die over time depending on relative population densities. We observe this world periodically, and the world changes over time according to the following rules:

    1. If at the last observation a cell was alive and had fewer than two living neighbors, it dies of loneliness.
    2. If at the last observation a cell was alive and had four or more living neighbors, it dies of overcrowding.
    3. If at the last observation a cell was alive and had two or three living neighbors, it survives.
    4. If at the last observation a cell was dead and had exactly three living neighbors, it springs to life.
    5. All other cells remain dead.

    Write a program to simulate the game of Life with a grid of 15 cells by 15 cells. Prompt the user for the number of observations, allowing a maximum of 15 transitions (for a total of 16 observations, including the initial grid). Have the user specify an initial grid by entering pairs of integers to indicate the grid coordinates of cells that are alive at the beginning. Let a pair of negative coordinates flag the end of this data.

    Display the world indicated by the initial grid and then display the updated grids for the specified number of transitions. Let a symbol such as * denote a living cell, use a space between cells, and print a border around the grid.

    Use a function to calculate the number of living neighbors of a given cell; this function should *not* have eight separate statements that look at each neighbor individually. Use two arrays, one to indicate the current status of each cell, and the other to count the number of live neighbors of each cell. At each transition, completely update the live neighbor array before updating the status array.

15. (Three-Dimensional Expense Ledger) Represent an expense ledger by an array whose ten rows represent expense categories; whose three columns represent "Budgeted Amount", "Actual Amount of Expense", and "Difference between Budget and Actual"; and whose four layers represent quarters of the year. Write a function whose input is data for the first two columns. The function should calculate values for the third column ("Difference between Budget and Actual"), and should print a table showing complete data for each quarter and for the entire year. Each table should also show column totals. Carefully plan for and accommodate missing data.

16. (Pascal's Triangle) Blaise Pascal is widely known not so much for having written a programming language (because he didn't) as for having devised a triangular array of numbers defined by the relation

$$x_{i,1} = x_{i,i} = 1 \quad \text{for } 1 \leq i,$$
$$x_{i,j} = x_{i-1,j} + x_{i-1,j-1} \quad \text{for } 3 \leq i \text{ and } 2 \leq j \leq (i-1)$$

The first five rows of Pascal's triangle are

```
      1
    1   1
   1  2   1
  1  3   3  1
 1  4   6  4  1
```

Each row begins and ends with 1; and, beginning with the third row, each entry between the first and last entry on a given row is the sum of the entry immediately above and the entry that is above and one column to the left.

a) Write a function that asks the user for a positive integer n and then calculates and displays an array (actually, a subarray) containing the first n rows of Pascal's triangle.

b) Write a function that asks the user for a positive integer n and then calculates and displays row n of Pascal's triangle. Use a one-dimensional array to represent just one row of the triangle. Start by putting row one into the array, and update this array $(n - 1)$ times so as to represent row 2, row 3, ..., row n in succession.

17. (Battleships Game) Write a computer version of the pencil-and-paper game known as Battleships. Use a three-dimensional data structure whose rows and columns represent positions on a grid and whose two layers represent the grids for players A and B. The values at a given grid position should be 0 (an empty cell), 1 (part of a patrol boat), 2 (part of a submarine), 3 (part of a cruiser), 4 (part of a battleship), or 5 (part of an aircraft carrier).

Chapter 8

Strings

A string is simply a sequence of characters. Strings are usually treated as units, but the individual characters can also be manipulated. Continuing the discussion begun in earlier chapters, this chapter covers string operations and standard string functions. The UNIX topics for this chapter include the following methods of finding string patterns in files: the `grep` family of commands, the `vi` text editor, and the `sed` stream editor.

String Variables

To the user, a string is a sequence of characters, such as

```
"this string contains four spaces"
```

which is a string of 32 characters. The four space characters are part of the string; the double quotation marks that mark the beginning and end are *not* considered as part of the string.

The C program regards each string as a subarray of characters whose beginning is position 0 in the array and whose end is marked by the special terminator character, `'\0'`, which must follow the last character of the string. For example, Figure 8.1 shows an eight-character string `"Jane Doe"` stored in a nine-character subarray at the beginning of an array of size 20. The compiler has responsibility for placing and finding the terminator character in each string, but the user must be careful to declare and assign string values while taking the terminator into account.

The declaration of a string variable must describe a one-dimensional array. The array size is an integer that is at least 1 more than the size of the largest string to be stored in the variable, and the array type is `char`. For example,

```
char name[ 20 ];
```

declares a 20-character array called name. Strings stored in name can have at most 19 characters in order to allow room for the terminator character. Most string functions use this character to avoid accessing memory beyond the end of the string. Failure to leave room for '\0' leads to program crashes, as does the more general error of not declaring an array size large enough for the entire string.

It is a good idea to use a typedef statement and a #define to define a string variable. The previous example could be accomplished by first declaring a new type with

```
#define NAMELENGTH 20
typedef char NameType[ NAMELENGTH ];
```

followed by the actual variable definition

```
NameType name;
```

The variable name is the same in both examples. Strings may be initialized within the declaration statement, as in

```
NameType name = "Jane Doe";
```

Unfortunately, this simple initialization using = is not possible after the declaration. For example, the fragment

```
NameType name;
name = "Jane Doe";    /* This line is incorrect! */
```

will cause an error when compiled. The string function **strcpy()** must be used in this case:

```
NameType name;
strcpy( name, "Jane Doe" );
```

This and other string functions are discussed in a subsequent section.

Input and Output of Strings

To read and write strings, use the input and output functions of Chapter 5. Recall that scanf() and fscanf() use the format control sequence %s. This format treats spaces as

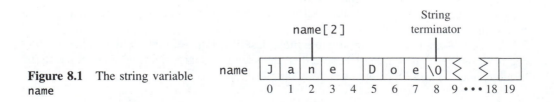

Figure 8.1 The string variable name

terminators, so that, if `name` were declared as above, the statement `scanf( "%s", name );` would not read all of the input `Jane Doe` typed on the keyboard. Instead, only `Jane` would be stored in `name`. When spaces are to be read, use the functions `gets()` and `fgets()`, which read all characters until `'\n'` is reached. For example, `gets( name );` will correctly read the input string `Jane Doe`.

String output is not constrained by spaces. The `printf()` and `fprintf()` functions write characters from a string to the screen or to a file until the character `'\0'` is encountered.

Thus the statement

```
printf( "%s \n", name );
```

will print either `Jane` or `Jane Doe`, depending on which value is stored in `name`. Other string output functions, as discussed in Chapter 5, are `puts()` and `fputs()`.

Individual characters within a string variable may be assigned or processed. A single character is accessed, like any array element, by using square brackets with an index number. For example, if `name` currently holds the string `Jane Doe`, the assignment `name [ 2 ] = 'k'` changes `name` to `Jake Doe`. There are input and output functions to handle single characters; see Chapter 5 for a full discussion of these functions, which include `getc()`, `getchar()`, `fgetc()`, and `fgetchar()` for input, and `putc()`, `putchar()`, `fputc()`, and `fputchar()` for output.

Like other types of arrays, strings are handled as pointers. Thus `name`, as previously declared, is a pointer to a `char`; that is, `name` is a variable of type `char *`. Individual characters, though, are not pointers. For example, `name[ 2 ]` is not a pointer, but `&name[ 2 ]` is. Strings are passed by address to functions, as already indicated by the `scanf( "%s", name );` example. Note, however, that since the actual type of such parameters is really `char *`, *any* string argument matches the parameter in type, regardless of the length of the string argument. A function can also return a pointer to a string as its return value, in which case it would be prototyped as `char *fn( some parameters );`

Arrays of Strings

An array of strings is a two-dimensional array of characters. Although each element of this character matrix can be referenced, each row is a string, and operations are usually done on rows. Either a single `typedef` statement or a sequence of two `typedef`s are used to define an array of strings. For example, suppose that we want to define a menu type, where each string of an array is used to hold one menu entry. We could define the string array with

```
#define ENTRYLENGTH 80    /* Maximum length of one menu entry is 79 */
#define MENULENGTH  3      /* Maximum number of menu entries is 3    */

typedef char MenuType[ MENULENGTH ][ ENTRYLENGTH ];
```

or we could first define a type for a single entry, then define the array, as in

```
typedef char EntryType[ ENTRYLENGTH ];
typedef EntryType MenuType[ MENULENGTH ];
```

Functionally, both are the same, although the latter emphasizes that the rows of `MenuType` are strings. Access to the rows is done by the usual array referencing. If we declare `MenuType menu;` using either definition, then `menu[ 0 ]` refers to the first row, `menu[ 1 ]` refers to the second row, and so on. Individual characters need a second reference, as in `menu[ 0 ][ 4 ]`, which is the fifth character of the first row. Again, note the difference between character pointers and characters, the former corresponding here to rows. For example, we could write `scanf( "%s", menu[ 0 ] );` to read entry 1 in without spaces, or `gets( menu[ 0 ] );` to read entry 1 in including blanks, since `menu[ 0 ]` is a character pointer.

To assign values to a string array at declaration time, string constants are enclosed in braces. For example, we could define a menu given the foregoing definitions by writing

```
MenuType menu = { "Menu Title", "1. Option one", "2. Option two" };
```

These entries are printed by the following code:

```
int count;

for (count = 0; count < MENULENGTH; count++ )
  printf( "%s\n", menu[ count ] );
```

When a string array is intended to hold constants, as a menu might, an alternative method of declaration is possible. The code

```
char *ptr[ MENULENGTH ] = { "Menu Title", "1. Option one", "2. Option two" };
```

defines a string array that holds the same strings as `menu` did but does not waste the unused characters at the end of each row, as `menu` did. Each row of `ptr` is allocated exactly enough room to hold the string constant given in the declaration, including the terminator `'\0'` for each. Thus the storage needed for `menu` is $3 \times 80 = 240$ bytes, whereas `ptr` uses $11 + 14 + 14$ bytes for the characters (including `'\0'`) plus room for three pointers (addresses), which is $3 \times 4 = 12$ bytes on a machine with 32-bit addresses, for a total of 51 bytes. Such an array is sometimes called a *ragged array*. A danger associated with ragged arrays is created by the fact that each row has a different size. Lacking a single constant defining the row length, new assignments may inadvertently overrun the end of a string.

String Functions

The string library contains several useful string functions. Use the statement `#include <string.h>` to include the header file containing the function prototypes. We now examine some of these functions and their usage. We will use "string" interchangeably with "character pointer" when discussing parameters and return values.

Basic Functions

The function `strcpy()`, as we know from previous examples, is used to copy one string to another. Its prototype is

```
char *strcpy( char *destination, char *source );
```

where `source` is the string being copied, and `destination` will hold the new copy. No length checking is done on `destination` to ensure that it is long enough to hold all the characters from `source`, nor is `source` checked for legal termination by `'\0'`. Finally, the function returns `source`, a redundancy shared by several other string functions. Suppose we use the previous `typedef` to declare

```
NameType myname, yourname;
```

Then the statements `strcpy( myname, "Boris" );` followed by `strcpy( yourname, myname );` result in both strings containing the value `Boris` (see Figure 8.2).

To concatenate two strings, the function **strcat()** may be used. Its prototype,

```
char *strcat( char *destination, char *source );
```

indicates that its use is similar to that of `strcpy()`: The `source` string is appended to `destination`. The original terminator character of `destination` is overwritten and a new one placed at the end of the longer string. For example, the fragment

```
strcpy( myname, "Boris" );
strcat( myname, " Badenov" );
```

puts the string `Boris Badenov` into `myname`, with the `'\0'` moved from position 5 to position 13.

To compare strings, use the function **strcmp()**. Its prototype

```
int strcmp( const char *first, const char *second );
```

shows that an integer is returned. If this value is zero, the two strings are identical. If the value is less than zero, then `first` is less than `second`, whereas if the value is greater than zero, `first` is greater than `second`. Here, "less than" and "greater than" refer to ordering based on the ASCII collating set. For example, suppose we make the declarations

```
NameType myname = "Natasha", yourname = "Boris";
```

Then `strcmp( myname, yourname )` would return a positive integer, while `strcmp( myname, "boris" )` would return a negative integer, since N precedes b in the ASCII set.

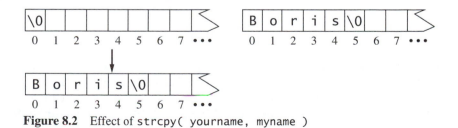

Figure 8.2   Effect of `strcpy( yourname, myname )`

Note that the function `toupper()` could be used to convert the characters of strings being compared to upper case before calling `strcmp()`.

To determine the number of characters in a string, the function **strlen()** is available. Its prototype is

```
int strlen( const char *str );
```

where `str`'s length is the return value. As usual, legally terminated strings are expected. The code

```
strcpy( myname, "Natasha" );
length = strlen( myname );
```

results in `length` equal to 7, assuming `length` is an `int` variable.

Other String Functions

Three of the functions discussed in the preceding section have variants that use an integer parameter to limit the action taken. For example, **strncpy()** has the prototype

```
char *strncpy( char *destination, char *source, size_t size );
```

where the last parameter indicates that at most `size` characters be copied into `destination`. The type `size_t` is another name for `unsigned int`. If `source` has `size` or more characters, `destination` may not be terminated by `'\0'`, because the `'\0'` terminator of `source` will not be copied. If `source` has fewer than `size` characters, then `destination` will be legally terminated and, in fact, padded with additional `'\0'` characters. As an example, consider this code:

```
NameType myname = "Bob", yourname = "Billy";
strncpy( myname, yourname, 2 );
printf( "%s\n", myname );
myname[ 2 ] = '\0';          /* Set the terminator manually. */
printf( "%s\n", myname );
```

This will print `Bib` first, since `myname`'s original terminator remains in character 3, and `Bi` second, after a terminator is placed manually at position 2.

The following two function prototypes have similar formats:

```
char *strncat( char *destination, char *source, size_t size );
int strncmp( const char *first, const char *second, size_t size );
```

The first function, **strncat()**, concatenates at most `size` characters from `source` onto `destination` and then appends `'\0'`. The second function, **strncmp()**, compares at most `size` characters of the strings `first` and `second`, returning the same integer codes as `strcmp()`: zero if equal, a negative value if `first` is lexically less than `second`, and a positive value otherwise. The example

```
NameType myname = "Bob", yourname = "Billy";

strncat( myname, yourname, 2 );
printf( "%s\n", myname );
printf( "%d\n", strncmp( myname, yourname, 1 ) );
```

will print the string BobBi and the integer zero, since the two strings agree in the first character.

It is sometimes necessary to search a string for a character or a substring. The prototypes

```
char *strchr( const char *target, int ch );
char *strstr( const char *target, const char *substr );
```

describe functions for these purposes. Note that both return char *, whose value points to the character in target containing ch or the first character of substr, if found, or NULL if not found. Note that these functions might better return the index of the matching character in target, but pointers are used instead. Consider the following example:

```
NameType yourname = "Billy";
char *ptr;

ptr = strchr( yourname, 'l' );
printf( "%s\n", ptr );

ptr = strstr( yourname, "il" );
printf( "%s\n", ptr );
```

The output of this code is lly and illy.

Formatted String Copy

There are two functions that manipulate strings in useful ways and whose prototypes appear in <stdio.h>. They are **sprintf()** and **sscanf()**, and they are related to printf() and scanf(), as their names indicate. Their prototypes are

```
int sprintf( char *target, const char *control, optional expressions );
int sscanf( char *target, const char *control, optional expressions );
```

where control is a series of format control characters as described in Chapter 5, and the optional expressions are most often variables. The target parameter is a string where output is sent by sprintf(), or input is obtained by sscanf(), matching the format control characters to the expression values. For example, the code fragment

```
char str[ 40 ];
int i = 23;

sprintf( str, "The value of i = %d\n", i );
```

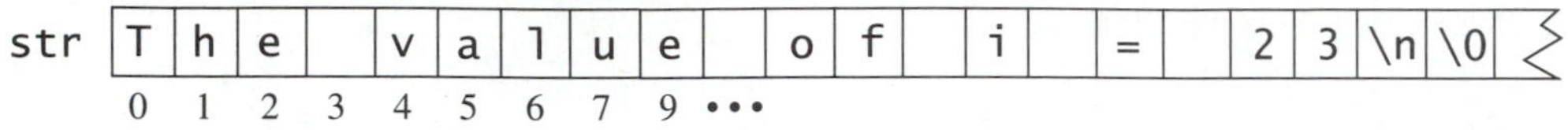

| str | T | h | e | | v | a | l | u | e | | o | f | | i | | = | | 2 | 3 | \n | \0 |

0   1   2   3   4   5   6   7   9 •••

Figure 8.3   Effect of `sprintf()` on `str`

stores the string `"The value of i = 23\n"` in `str` (see Figure 8.3). Similarly, the code

```
char str[ 40 ] = "23 4.2 Bob";
int i;
double x;
NameType myname;

sscanf( str, "%d%lf%s", &i, &x, myname );
```

will assign `i` as 23, `x` as 4.2, and `myname` as `"Bob"`. As another example, consider the code

```
NameType myname = "Bob", yourname;

sprintf( yourname, "%s", myname );
```

This results in copying the contents of `myname` into `yourname`, the equivalent of using `strcpy()`.

Searching a String Array

As seen with arrays of other types in Chapter 7, two common operations on string arrays are searching for a particular string (a key value) and sorting the array. The following example illustrates the search operation. Sorting string arrays follows the same logic as sorting numeric arrays, using the `strcmp()` function in place of >, ==, and <.

Recall that searching an array depends on whether the array is sorted or not; we assume an unordered array. Let us start by defining a string array and assigning values to it. In practice, assignment might be done by reading strings from a file or by input from the user. We also define some useful constants.

```
#define FALSE 0
#define TRUE  1
#define STRLENGTH 20
#define SIZE      10

typedef char string[ STRLENGTH ];
typedef string array[ SIZE ];

array list = { "dog", "Bob", "Boris", "Natasha", "6083",
               "grep", "grok", "Larry", "Life is good", "The End" };
```

The following code has the same pattern as the search code discussed in Chapter 7 but uses string comparison. The index number of the key's position, if found, is returned.

```
/* Example: Search an unordered array of string's */

string key,    /* Search key                        */
int index,     /* Array index                       */
    found;     /* Flag to tell when to quit searching */

/* Get the search key from the user. */
printf( "Enter the key to be found: " );
scanf( "%s", key );
```

Then the search is made:

```
/* Initialize the index and the flag. */
index = 0;
found = FALSE;

/* Search until found or end of array is reached. */
while (( index < SIZE ) && ( !found ))
  if ( strcmp( list[ index ], key ) = = 0 ) found = TRUE;
  else index ++;

/* Was it found? */
if ( found ) printf( "%s was found at position %d\n", key, index );
else printf( "%s was not found\n", key );
```

The while loop checks for two conditions: whether key was found and whether the end of the array was reached. To implement this code as a function, the string array might be declared more generically, as char *list[], for example, to allow searching other string array types besides array. In this case, the size of the array should be passed as a parameter to enable the end-of-array check.

Command Line Arguments

Many UNIX commands accept optional arguments, either to modify the actions they carry out, as with flags, or to indicate file names or other input data. Similarly, C programs can accept command line arguments if the main() function is set up to handle them. This requires that main() declare parameters in a special format.

To handle command line arguments, the parameters int argc and char *argv[] must be listed in the definition of main(), as in

```
main( int argc, char *argv[] )
```

The names of these parameters are system-defined. The first parameter, argc, tells how many command line arguments exist; it is at least 1, because the name of the C program's executable file is always counted as the first argument. The second parameter, argv[], holds the command line arguments. It is a ragged string array allocated at run time. The executable file name is stored in argv[0], and any other arguments are stored in argv[1], argv[2], . . . , each terminated by '\0' (see Figure 8.4).

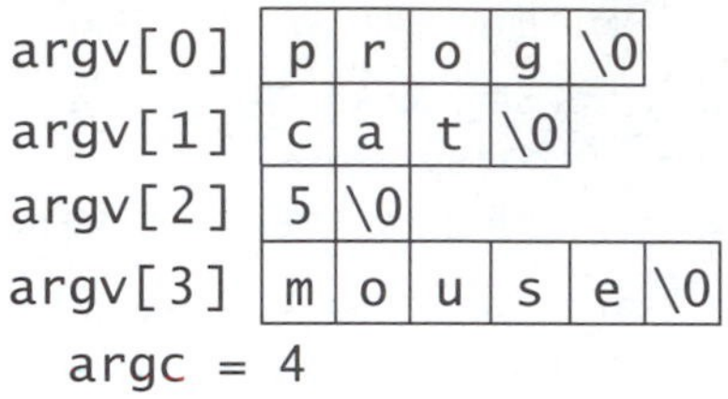

Figure 8.4 Command line arguments: prog cat 5 mouse

```
argv[0]   p  r  o  g  \0
argv[1]   c  a  t  \0
argv[2]   5  \0
argv[3]   m  o  u  s  e  \0
          argc = 4
```

In code to access command line arguments, argc should be used to run if statements or for loops so that nonexistent members of argv[] are not accessed. It is common to check for too many command line arguments as well as too few.

For example, suppose that a program needs the name of a file containing input data. To allow the file name to be passed on the command line, we could write the following code.

```
typedef char NameType[ 20 ];

main( int argc, char *argv[] ) {
  NameType filename;

  /* Check for file name on the command line */
  if ( argc > 1 )
    /* Use the second argument */
    strcpy( filename, argv[ 1 ] );
  else {
    /* No second argument, so prompt for the file name */
    printf( "Enter the input file name: " );
    scanf( "%s", filename );
    printf( "\n" );
  }/* else */
}/* main() */
```

The if statement checks whether there is more than one argument. If so, the second argument is copied into filename. Otherwise, the user is prompted to enter a file name. Either way, the variable filename would be used as an argument to fopen() to open the input file. For example, if this code were in the main module of a program named prog, a typical program call would be prog special_file if the user wished to open the file named special_file.

Pattern Matching in UNIX

In Chapter 4 the grep command was introduced to search for strings in files. The string arguments did not allow for much flexibility, because an exact match was sought. Chapter 7 contained a discussion of pattern matching with the vi editor. The following section continues that discussion as it describes general methods of searching files for patterns. Chapter 12 contains a discussion of lex, a UNIX utility for identifying string patterns, for use in applications such as parsing a language. The lex program uses the same patterns discussed here.

A *regular expression* is a string pattern that can include special characters, which we called metacharacters in Chapter 7, that match variable patterns according to the rules described in the list that follows. Ordinary characters are matched literally, but metacharacters may expand to match many patterns or to match strings that occur in certain situations. For example, a period in a pattern is a metacharacter that matches any single character. The pattern q. matches any two-character string beginning with q, such as qa, q7, qX, and q (that is, q and a space). These matches may actually be substrings inside another string, as in disquiet, where the qu matches the q. pattern.

Metacharacters, with examples, include the following:

- .: Matches any single character. Example: q. matches q, q , qa, and so on.
- *: Matches zero or more occurrences of the preceding character. Example: q* matches q, qq, qqq, and so on.
- .*: Matches zero or more occurrences of any character. Example: q.* matches q, qq, qqq, qa, q7, and any string beginning with q.
- []: Used to hold strings of single matching characters. Example: q[ab]r matches qar and qbr. This may be used with the *, for example, as in q[ab]*r, which matches qr, qar, qaar, qbr, qbbr, qabr, among others.
- [^]: Matches characters not in the brackets. Example: q[^ab]r matches qcr, q3r, and so on, but does not match qar or qbr.
- -: Used to indicate ranges of characters. Example: [a-z] matches any lower case letter. A ^ in front of a range is again treated as "not this set," as in [^0-9], which matches any non-digit character.
- $: Matches the end of a line. Example: dog$ matches occurrences of dog that are at the end of a line.
- ^: Matches the beginning of a line. Example: ^dog matches occurrences of dog that start a line. Note the possible confusion with the other meaning of ^.
- \: Forces literal interpretation of special characters. Example: q\. matches q. only.

Patterns in grep and vi

The grep command searches for the general patterns constructed from normal characters and metacharacters described in the previous section. Recall that grep may also take the name of a file to be searched for the pattern, or it may be used as a filter by accepting input from another command. When metacharacters or spaces are used in a grep expression, the string argument should be surrounded by single quotes to prevent the metacharacters or spaces from being interpreted by the shell.

For example, the command grep 'q*' mydata searches the file mydata for lines that contain matches to q*, that is, lines containing q, qq, qqq, and so on. If the string lacks the quotes, then the shell will expand q* to all file names in the current directory that begin with the letter q and pass those names to grep as the patterns for searching; that is not what was intended. As another example, consider grep '^[0-9]*\.[0-9]*' mydata. This matches any decimal number that begins a line in mydata.

As a filter, grep may be used to accept output from or send input to other commands or files using pipes, redirection, or both. The command sort mydata | grep '^q' > outfile will sort the input file mydata, then pass each line to grep, which will search for lines starting with q, and write such lines into the output file outfile.

The same patterns used in grep may also be used in vi to search for strings. Searching in vi has already been discussed in Chapter 7. Recall that the two methods for searching

More Metacharacters

+	Matches one or more of previous
?	Matches 0 or 1 of previous
()	Grouping
|	ORing strings

Figure 8.5   Extensions accepted by `egrep`

for a string are */string/* and *?string?*, where *string* may use any of the metacharacters just discussed. String matching is also used with the substitution commands in `vi`; the format is

`:`*range* `s`/*pattern*/*newpattern*/*options*

where *pattern* is a regular expression.

Using `egrep` and `fgrep`

There are two variants of the `grep` command. The **egrep** (which stands for *extended* `grep`) command allows other special characters and methods for constructing regular expressions. **fgrep**, which stands for *fast* `grep`, accepts only fixed strings (that is, it does not expand metacharacters). Both variants allow patterns to be placed in a file with use of the `-f` *filename* option; that allows editing of complicated patterns, as opposed to `grep`'s command line typing of patterns. We discuss only `egrep` below, because `fgrep` does not require further explanation.

The extensions allowed in `egrep` include +, ?, (), and | (see Figure 8.5; also, refer back to Figure 7.6 for the basic set of metacharacters). The character + is similar to *; it matches *one* or more (as opposed to zero or more) occurrences of the preceding character. For example, qq+ matches qq, qqq, qqqq, and so on, but not q. Similarly, ? matches exactly zero or one occurrence cf the preceding character. Parentheses are used to enclose expressions, to which the *, +, and ? operators may be applied. For example, (qq)+ matches one or more occurrences of the string qq. Regular expressions may be concatenated by writing them sequentially, as in (qq)(ab), or combined by the "or" operator, |, as in (qq) | (ab).

Suppose the file named `patterns` contains the following lines:

```
(qq)(ab)
(qq)|(ab)+
```

Then the command `egrep -f patterns mydata` searches for any strings that contain qqab in sequence, or contain qq, or contain one or more occurrences of ab.

Using `sed` to Make String Substitutions

We have already seen that `vi`, the text editor, has a substitution command to change string patterns into new patterns. The *stream editor* **sed** can also do this without `vi`'s overhead of screen output. The `sed` program is a UNIX filter. There are other commands for `sed` not discussed here; the substitution command is the one most commonly used.

The format for a `sed` substitution command is

`sed`'*commands*'*filenames*

where '*commands*' is a list of substitution commands (which include those pertaining to `vi` as discussed previously) and *filenames* are the file(s) to be edited. Output is sent to the screen by default, so `sed` is often used with redirection. Note that all lines of the edited files are sent to the output, not just those that were affected by a command. This can be overcome with the `-n` flag, which prints only lines affected by the `p` command (described subsequently). The `-f comfile` option allows commands to be stored in a file rather than typed on the command line.

Any command may be preceded by a range of lines on which to carry out the command. If no range is given, the whole file is processed. Ranges are given in the form `startlinenumber, endlinenumber`, where the latter may be `$` to indicate the end of the file.

The substitution command, `s`, uses the format `s`/*pattern*/*newpattern*/*options*. The *pattern* is a regular expression, as is *newpattern*. Valid options include `g`, for global change of all occurrences of *pattern* (the default is the first one found on a line); `p`, to print any lines processed by `s`; and `w outfile`, which prints any lines processed by `s` to the file `outfile`. For example, the command

```
sed 's/3\.14/pi/g' mydata
```

substitutes `pi` for all occurrences of `3.14` in the file `mydata`, displaying all lines on the screen. The command

```
sed 's/qq*/xxx/gw newfile' mydata
```

substitutes `xxx` for substrings containing one or more `q`'s, writing any affected lines to the file `newfile`, and displays all lines of output on the screen.

Substitution may be limited to a range of lines or to lines matching a pattern. Ranges, which precede the `s` command, are given in the form *location1*, *location2*, where each location is either a line number, a dollar sign `$` to indicate the last line, or a regular expression inside slashes. For example,

```
sed '28,/dog/s/3\.14/pi/g' mydata
```

substitutes `pi` for all occurrences of `3.14` in the file `mydata` from line number 28 to the next subsequent line containing the pattern `dog`.

The format for the `sed` deletion command is *location1*, *location2*d, which deletes lines from *location1* to *location2*. Each location may be specified as described in the preceding paragraph. For example, `sed '1,5d' mydata` deletes the first five lines of `mydata`, while `sed '1,/3\.14/d' mydata` deletes from the first line to the first occurrence of `3.14`, and `sed '/dog/,/cat/d' mydata` deletes lines from the first occurrence of `dog` to the first occurrence of `cat`.

The append command's format is *location*a*text*, which appends *text* after *location*, using \\ to indicate that more lines of text are expected, and ending with a line lacking the \\. It is easier to use a file to hold the commands in this case, so suppose that the file `comfile` contains these lines:

```
2a\
New text\
to be\
appended.
```

then the command `sed -f comfile mydata` will append the three lines of text in `comfile` after line 2 of `mydata`.

The insert command `i` and the change command `c` are used in a manner similar to the append command. Text to be inserted is placed before the indicated line rather than after that line. For example,

```
2i\
New text\
to be\
inserted.
```

will insert three new lines before line 2. The change command changes the indicated line or range of lines. For example,

```
2c\
New text\
to be\
inserted.
```

will remove the existing second line, replacing it with three new lines, whereas

```
2,8c\
New text\
to be\
inserted.
```

will remove lines 2 through 8, replacing them with three new lines.

Chapter Summary

■ **C Commands**

Declarations of String Variables

```
#define ITEMS 3
char *ptr_menu[ ITEMS ] =
  {"1st Choice",
   "2nd Choice",
   "3rd Choice" };
```

Declare and assign three menu strings to `ptr_menu`, a ragged array of 33 characters

`#define MAXSIZE 20` `typedef char ItemType[ MAXSIZE ];`	A template with room for a string of length at most 19 characters
`typedef ItemType MenuType[ ITEMS ];`	A template with room for 3 strings

`MenuType menu = { "1st Choice",`
`   "2nd Choice",`
`   "3rd Choice" };`
	Declare and assign three menu strings to a two-dimensional array

`char Astr[ MAXSIZE ],` `    Bstr[ MAXSIZE ];`	Declare two untyped string arrays with room for at most 19 characters in each

String Functions in *<string.h>*

`strlen( Bstr );`	Return the number of characters in `Bstr`
`strcpy( Astr, Bstr );`	Assign `Bstr` to the string variable `Astr`
`strncpy( Astr, Bstr, 4 );`	Assign at most 4 characters of `Bstr` to `Astr`
`strcat( Astr, Bstr );`	Concatenate the string `Bstr` at the end of `Astr`
`strncat( Astr, Bstr, 4 );`	Concatenate at most 4 characters of `Bstr` to `Astr`
`strcmp( Astr, Bstr );`	Compare (show lexical relation of) `Astr` and `Bstr`
`strncmp( Astr, Bstr, 4 );`	Compare at most 4 characters of `Astr` and `Bstr`
`strchr( Astr, ch );`	Return pointer to first occurrence of `ch` in `Astr`, or return NULL if `ch` is not in `Astr`
`strstr( Astr, Bstr );`	Return pointer to first occurrence of `Bstr` in `Astr`, or return NULL if `Bstr` is not in `Astr`

String Input/Output Functions in *<stdio.h>*

`scanf( "%s", Astr );`	Read `Astr` from standard input, stop at white space
`fscanf( f_ptr, "%s", Astr );`	Read `Astr` from file to which `f_ptr` is pointing
`sscanf( Astr, "%d", &i );`	Read the integer `i` from the string `Astr`
`gets( Astr );`	Read `Astr` from standard input, stop at `'\n'`
`fgets( Astr, n, f_ptr );`	Read into `Astr` at most `n` characters from the file to which `f_ptr` is pointing
`printf( "%s", Astr );`	Write the string `Astr` to standard output stream
`fprintf( f_ptr, "%s", Astr );`	Write `Astr` to file to which `f_ptr` is pointing
`sprintf( Astr, "%d", i );`	Write the integer `i` to the string `Astr`
`puts( Astr );`	Write `Astr` and `'\n'` to the standard output
`fputs( Astr, f_ptr );`	Write `Astr` to the file to which `f_ptr` is pointing

Command Line Arguments

`main( int argc, char *argv[ ] )`	Header for the main function of a program using command line arguments

■ UNIX Commands

Command Line Arguments

`a.out my_file`   Run the executable program `a.out` with `argv[ 0 ] = "a.out"` and `argv[ 1 ] = "my_file"`

Pattern Matching

`fgrep exit my_file`	Search `my_file` for lines containing the substring `exit`
`fgrep -f patterns my_file`	Search `my_file` for *fixed strings* listed (without quotes and separated by `'\n'`) in `patterns`
`grep exit my_file`	Search `my_file` for lines containing the substring `exit`
`grep '^exit' my_file`	Search `my_file` for lines beginning with `exit`
`grep '^e' my_file`	Search `my_file` for lines beginning with `'e'`
`grep '^[a-z]' my_file`	Search `my_file` for lines beginning with a lower case alphabetic character
`grep '^.[ab]' my_file`	Search `my_file` for lines whose second character is `'a'` or `'b'`
`grep '\.$' my_file`	Search `my_file` for lines whose last character is `'.'`
`grep ';$' my_file`	Search `my_file` for lines ending with `';'`
`grep ';;*$' my_file`	Search `my_file` for lines ending with one or more occurrences of `';'`
`grep ')[^;]$' my_file`	Search `my_file` for lines ending with `')'` followed by any character other than `';'`
`grep '(.*)' my_file`	Search `my_file` for lines containing expressions (possibly empty) enclosed in parentheses
`egrep ';+' my_file`	Search `my_file` for lines containing one or more occurrences of `';'`
`egrep 'my(_)?word' my_file`	Search `my_file` for lines containing `myword` or `my_word`
`egrep '(myword)	(my_word)' my_file`	Search `my_file` for lines containing `myword` or `my_word`
`egrep -f patterns my_file`	Search `my_file` for *expressions* listed (without quotes and separated by `'\n'`) in `patterns`

String Substitutions

`sed 's/myword/my_word/' file1`	Substitute `my_word` for the first occurrence (per line) of `myword` in `file1`
`sed '1,4s/myword/my_word/' file1`	Substitute `my_word` for the first occurrence (per line) of `myword` on lines 1 to 4 of `file1`

```
sed 's/myword/my_word/g' file1 file2
```
Substitute `my_word` for all occurrences of myword in `file1` and `file2`

```
sed 's/myword/my_word/gw changes' file1
```
Substitute `my_word` for all occurrences of myword in `file1`; append revised lines to the file `changes`

```
sed 's/myword/my_word/g' file1 >> file2
```
Substitute `my_word` for all occurrences of myword in `file1`; append the entire revision to `file2`

```
sed '3,5d' file1
```
Delete lines 3 through 5 of `file1`

```
sed '3,5d' file1 >> file2
```
Delete lines 3 through 5 of `file1`; append the entire revision to `file2`

```
sed '/start/,/stop/d' file1
```
Delete lines from first `start` to next `stop` in `file1`

```
sed '/\{/,/\}/d' file1
```
Delete lines from first '`{`' to next '`}`' in `file1`

```
sed '1,/spot/d' file1
```
Delete lines from first line to next `spot` in `file1`

```
sed '/\./,$d' file1
```
Delete lines from first '`.`' to the end of `file1`

```
sed -f comfile my_file
```
Make substitutions in `my_file` according to the instructions contained in the command file `comfile`

```
10a\
printf( "OK" );
```
A command file that will append the line `printf( "OK" );` after the tenth line

```
1i\
/* filename: MyFile */
```
A command file to insert the following line `/* filename: MyFile */` before the first line

```
1i\
/* filename: MyFile */\
/* date: __/__/__ */
```
A command file to insert two lines before the first line

```
1c\
/* filename: MyFile */
```
A command file to change the first line to `/* filename: MyFile */`

Review Problems

1. Explain the input and output of the following function.

```c
#include <stdio.h>
#include <string.h>

main( )
{ int index = 0,
  length;
  char in_str[ 11 ],
  out_str[ 6 ] = "";
```

```
       printf( "Enter a string having at most 10 characters: " );
       gets( in_str );
       length = strlen( in_str );
       while ( index < length ) {
         if ( index == 0 )
           strncpy( out_str, in_str, 1 );
         else
           strncat( out_str, ( in_str + index ), 1 );
         index += 2;
     }
     printf( "The output string is \"%s\".", out_str );
   }
```

2. Write a function to search a given file and print all words that contain a given string. Return a negative integer if the function is unable to open the given file; otherwise, return the number of words found.

3. Write a function `StringToDouble()` to convert strings containing numerical expressions into floating point values. The function should accept a character string for input and should return a `double`. Assume that the input string is of one the following types:

   1. A decimal point with one or more digits before the decimal point and one or more digits after the decimal point
   2. A division operator (/) with an integer expression before the slash and a nonzero integer expression after the slash

4. (`egrep` Tutorial) In this tutorial you will place the text from the man page for `grep` into a temporary file and then use `egrep` to search that file for various strings. Try to answer each part on your own before executing the appropriate UNIX command.
   a) Copy the man page for `grep` to a file named `grepstuff`.
   b) Use `egrep` to find information on flags by searching for the string "-".
   c) Redo part b) and pipe the output to `more` so that you can read all of the output.
   d) Note that the previous search finds hyphenated words as well as references to flags. Look again for flag information by searching for strings consisting of a space, a hyphen, a lower case letter, and then a space.
   e) Search for hyphenated words and expressions where there is a nonspace character both before and after the hyphen.
   f) Search for all occurrences of the phrase "regular expression" in all lower case or all upper case letters.
   g) Write a one-line pattern file, `patterns1`, to perform the searches in parts d) through f).
   h) What UNIX command executes the `egrep` searches of `patterns1` and appends the output to an existing file named `searches`?
   i) Write a four-line pattern file, `patterns2`, to perform the searches in parts d) through f).
   j) What UNIX command executes the `egrep` searches of `patterns2` and appends the output to an existing file named `searches`?

5. (`sed` Tutorial) In this tutorial you will place the text from the man page for `grep` into a temporary file and then use `sed` to modify various strings in that file. Try to answer each part on your own before executing the appropriate UNIX command.
   a) Copy the man page for `grep` to a file named `grepstuff`.
   b) Use `sed` to replace `grep` by GREP in all instances occurring in the first ten lines of `grepstuff`.
   c) Replace all occurrences of ∧ by ∧(shift-6) and send the revised lines to the existing file `changes`.

d) Delete the first ten lines of `grepstuff`.

e) Write a file, `comfile`, containing commands to insert four lines at the beginning of `grepstuff`. Each inserted line should contain a line number only.

f) What UNIX command executes the insertions of `comfile` and appends the revised file to an existing file named `changes`?

6. Describe the output resulting from the UNIX command `man grep | grep '*'`.

7. Write the proper UNIX command to print all lines containing comments (such as `/* this is a comment */`) in the file `my_prog`.

Programming Problems

1. (String Parsing) Write a function that asks the user to input a telephone number as a string containing a three-digit area code, followed by a seven-digit number. Also write an accompanying test program. The function should scan the input string, reading only the first 10 numeric digits (ignoring all other characters in the string), and should report the telephone number in the form `123/456-7890`. Note that the user may choose the input format, yet the program maintains a consistent output format.

2. (String Sorting) Write a program that asks a user to input a sequence of strings and then reports back the shortest and longest strings and prints the strings in alphabetical order.

3. (Database Management) Write a program to manage a small database that is stored in a text file with one record per line. Each record has last name, first name, birth month, and day of birth. Open the text file and present a menu that offers to insert a record, delete a record, edit one or more records, display all records, sort the records by name, or stop the program. Check for a command line argument specifying the name of the database file. A typical record would be

```
Hoover John 1 1
```

If you wish a more realistic database, add fields for middle name and birth year, as in

```
Hoover John Edgar 1 1 1895
```

4. (Stream Editor) Write a filter program, `Substitute`, similar to the `sed` command `'s/target/substitution/'`, to perform string substitutions for words whose spelling matches that of the target string in the manner to be described. The user should specify a target string and a substitution string on the command line. If these strings are not properly specified, terminate program execution with an error message. Otherwise, echo the input stream to the output stream, changing only those words that have all lower case characters and match the spelling of the specified target string or have all upper case characters and match the spelling of the target string; that is, if the target string is `bean`, substitute for the words `bean` and `BEAN`, but not for words such as `Bean`. Each substitution should be with the corresponding lower case or upper case spelling of the substitution string.

    For example, if the user enters the two lines

```
Substitute old new
The program replaces old and OLD but neither Old nor bold.^D
```

(in which ^D indicates the end-of-file character, control-D), the corresponding output should be the single line

```
The program replaces new and NEW but neither Old nor bold.
```

Assume that there is no white space in either the target string or the substitution string. As shown in the example, substitute only for words surrounded by white space; do not substitute for strings embedded in longer words. Echo white space and nonmatching words exactly as they appear in the input stream. Since this is a filter program, redirection and piping should be usable for input and output.

5. (Substitution Cipher) Write a program to encode and decode alphabetic messages using a substitution cipher, where each character is shifted by a fixed integer and printed in upper case. Additionally, reformat the output so that spaces occur after each five characters and nowhere else; also, ignore newline characters from the input and print each output line with five blocks of five characters. For example, if the shift is +1, then the string `My name is HAL` should be enciphered as `NZOBN FJTIB MBDCP MLFWC LLNOQ`, where the last 14 characters were randomly generated in order to pad the message and complete the final blocks of characters. Note also that both `z` and `Z` are replaced by `A` when the shift is +1.

Have the user specify the shift integer by giving a code word (also known as a key word), then sum the integer values of the characters in this code word and let the shift integer be the remainder when the sum is divided by 26. Write this as a filter program using the command line to specify the code word and using standard input for the plaintext (uncoded message) and standard output for the ciphertext (coded message).

6. (Insertion Sort) Write a program, based on the insertion sort algorithm described in the problem section of Chapter 7, to sort a ragged array of strings. Here is an example of an input array and the stages of rearrangement as the algorithm sorts the array:

```
{"Carol", "Bob", "alice", "Ted"}
{"Bob", "Carol", "alice", "Ted"}
{"Bob", "Carol", "alice", "Ted"}
{"Bob", "Carol", "Ted", "alice"}
```

7. (UNIX Session Log) Write a filter program that reads a sequence of UNIX commands and produces a file containing both the commands and the associated output. Let `STOP` mark the end of the UNIX command sequence.

Here is a sample session where the user entered

```
ls -l prog
wc prog
STOP
```

and the program produced a file with the following contents:

```
BEGINNING OF LOG FILE.
UNIX Command: ls -l prog
-rwxr-xr-x  1 w44           24576 May 16 10:57 prog
UNIX Command: wc prog
    121    330   24576 prog
END OF LOG FILE.
```

8. (File Management) Write an interactive C program that allows the user to list the working directory, view a file in the working directory, change a filename in the working directory, or delete a file in the working directory. All of this should be done with menus and prompts that do not require the user to know any UNIX commands.

Chapter 9

Structures

The ability to group common elements allows programmers to build components made of smaller parts. By hiding the details of the parts, the larger components become the focus of activity, leading to "chunks" of knowledge units. Such chunking is a common method for handling complexity both in everyday life and in programming. Earlier chapters have examined other methods for grouping. Functions group together common activities into one code unit, and arrays group data elements of a common type. This chapter discusses the **struct** type, used to group heterogeneous data elements into logical records. The **struct** is also the basis for discussing binary files. The UNIX topics for this chapter include methods for customizing your working environment.

The struct Type

A *logical record*, in database terminology, is a data unit constructed from several data fields. The **struct** in C is the data type used to represent records. Unlike arrays, records are not required to consist of identical parts. The fields of a **struct** can be and usually are of different types.

A record represents a physical object. Information about an employee is an example of a record. Such a record might comprise an employee's name, address, salary, and company id number. As an example from mathematics, a complex number could also be represented as a record; the real and imaginary parts of the complex number would be the fields. Because each part would be stored as a floating-point number, an array of two **double** elements might seem a better choice. A record, however, would emphasize that the two fields are quite different in use, despite the common base type.

Syntax

Since a **struct** is a user-defined type, we will adhere to the convention of defining each **struct** using a **typedef**. The syntax to define a **struct** is

```
typedef struct {
    typename1 fieldname1 ;
    typename2 fieldname2 ;
    typename3 fieldname3 ;
    /* and so on */
} RecordName ;
```

where each *typename* has been previously defined (either standard type or user-defined), each *fieldname* is the name of a field, and the *RecordName* is the name of the new record type being defined. No storage is declared by this `typedef`; it is only a template. Usually, this `typedef` information needs to be global, so `struct` declarations are often placed before `main()` or in `.h` files that are included by the source files that need them. Variables are declared by writing

```
RecordName variable1, variable2;   /* and so on */
```

For example, to define the employee record just discussed, we first make some preliminary definitions:

```
#define NAMESIZE  40
#define ADDRSIZE  80
typedef char NameType[ NAMESIZE ];
typedef char AddrType[ ADDRSIZE ];
```

Using these definitions, we now write

```
typedef struct {          /* Employee information: */
    NameType name;        /*    name               */
    AddrType address;     /*    address            */
    double   salary;      /*    salary             */
    unsigned int id;      /*    company id number  */
} EmpRecType;
```

This new data type can now be used to declare a variable:

```
EmpRecType employee;      /* Employee record variable */
```

Each `struct` field can store a value, just as a separate variable of that field's type can store a value; see Figure 9.1. Assignment of fields can be done at the time of definition, using syntax similar to array initialization. Each field value is listed, separated by commas, inside braces. To assign values to the variable `employee`, we could write

```
EmpRecType employee = { "John Dough", "123 Main St.",  18000.0, 1 };
```

To access the fields, the name of the `struct` and the name of the field are both used, separated by a period. In our employee example, the following references show the syntax

employee

name:	John Dough
address:	123 Main St.
salary:	18000.0
id:	1

Figure 9.1 The struct variable
employee of type EmpRecType

for accessing fields:

```
employee.salary = 25000.0;
strcpy( employee.name, "Jane Doe" );
printf( "Employee Identification number: %d\n", employee.id );
gets( employee.address );
```

Each field can be used any place a variable of that type is used in statements. For example, employee.salary is a double variable, and may occur in any statement in which any other double variable would occur—on either side in assignment statements, as an argument to printf(), and so on.

structs and Functions

A function may accept struct parameters, and a function may return a struct as its return type. Unlike array types, a struct is not inherently a pointer, so to pass a struct by address requires the & address operator. As will be illustrated later in this section, a new syntax rule is required to access fields of pass-by-address struct parameters.

Passing a struct by value is similar to passing any data type. The name of the struct type is used in the parameter list, and references to fields of the parameter use the period notation. For example, the function prototype

```
void DisplayRec( EmpRecType emp );
```

shows a pass-by-value parameter of EmpRecType as defined in the previous section. The body of the function might be as follows:

```
void DisplayRec( EmpRecType emp ) {
   printf( "Employee Number %d\n", emp.id );
   printf( "\t Name    : %s\n", emp.name );
   printf( "\t Address : %s\n", emp.address );
   printf( "\t Salary  : %8.2lf\n", emp.salary );
}  /* DisplayRec() */
```

From main(), this function would be called with the statements

```
EmpRecType employee;
/* Code to fill employee's fields goes here ...  */
DisplayRec( employee );
```

Since `emp` is a pass-by-value parameter, the fields of `employee` would not be changed if the corresponding fields of emp in `DisplayRec()` were altered.

To return a `struct`, a function is declared to be of that type, and a local variable is used to hold the data to be returned. For example, to read an EmpRecType record, we could write

```
EmpRecType GetRec( void ) {
    EmpRecType emp;
    printf( "Employee information entry\n\n" );
    printf( "Enter employee name: " );
    gets( emp.name );
    printf( "Enter employee address: " );
    gets( emp.address );
    printf( "Enter employee salary: " );
    scanf( "%lf", &emp.salary );
    printf( "Enter employee id #: " );
    scanf( "%d", &emp.id );
    return( emp );
}  /* GetRec() */
```

The call to this function from `main()` would be `employee = GetRec();`.

To pass a `struct` by address, a parameter must be declared with the * notation, and the argument matched with the parameter is preceded by & when the function is called. Inside the function, the fields of the parameter are accessed by using a new dereferencing operator, -> (that is, a minus sign followed by a greater-than sign, intended to look like an arrow). For example, we could write a different version of the previous input function as follows:

```
void ReadRec( EmpRecType *emp )
{
  printf( "Employee information entry\n\n" );
  printf( "Enter employee name: " );
  gets( emp->name );
  printf( "Enter employee address: " );
  gets( emp->address );
  printf( "Enter employee salary: " );
  scanf( "%lf", &emp->salary );
  printf( "Enter employee id #: " );
  scanf( "%d", &emp->id );
} /* ReadRec */
```

The statement `gets( emp->name );` shows the use of the arrow dereference symbol. The argument to `gets()` is a string. Similarly, `emp->salary` is a `double` variable, and `&emp->salary` is the address of that `double`, needed when the field is passed as a parameter to `scanf()`. The parameter `emp` itself is a pointer to a variable of type `EmpRecType` (see Figure 9.2).

The parameter `emp` could be dereferenced using the *, but expressions such as `(*emp).salary`, though legal, are rarely used. The call to this function from `main()` would be `ReadRec( &employee )`; assuming that the corresponding declaration is `EmpRecType employee;`.

Other Declaration Methods

For the sake of completeness, this section discusses alternate methods for declaring `struct` types. We prefer the method of the previous sections, but because these other methods are sometimes used, it is useful to know about them also.

The `struct` syntax allows for an optional *tagname* between the word `struct` and the left brace. A `struct` declared without the use of `typedef` must be referred to by `struct` *tagname*. For example, to declare a complex number type, we could write

```
struct complex {
  double real;
  double imaginary;
}
```

where `complex` is the tagname. The tagname can also be used to declare variables directly, as in

```
struct complex {
  double real;
  double imaginary;
} myvar;
```

However, this is not recommended, because type declarations are usually global but variables are not. Therefore, the usual way to declare a variable using a `struct` defined this way is by using both `struct` and the tagname, as in

```
struct complex myvar;
```

The variable `myvar` is a `struct`, and references such as `myvar.real` are correct.

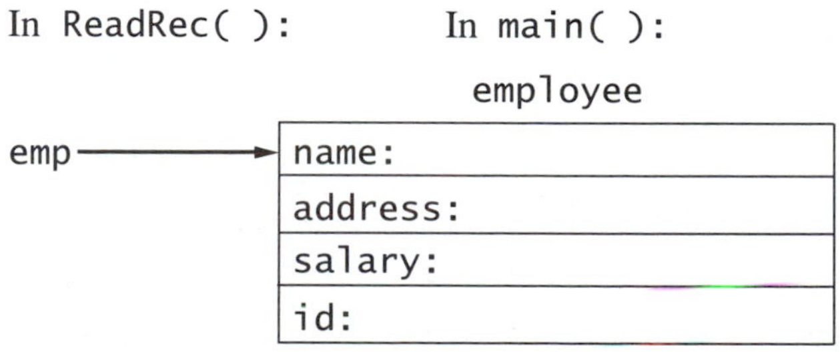

In `ReadRec( )`:   In `main( )`:

employee

emp ────────────▶ name:
                  address:
                  salary:
                  id:

Figure 9.2 Pass-by-address `struct` parameter

Because using two words to declare variables and parameters is somewhat cumbersome, a `typedef` can be used, as in

```
typedef struct complex ComplexType;
```

Following that line, we can use `ComplexType myvar;` to declare a variable.

Some programmers use the tagname as the type name, which appears odd in the `typedef` statement but is legal. For example,

```
typedef struct complex complex;
```

declares a new type name, `complex`. Now `complex myvar;` would declare a variable of this type.

When a `struct` is needed only temporarily (perhaps as a local definition inside a function), both the tagname and a type definition can be elided. The variables must be declared at the same time, however, because there is no way to reference the `struct` definition again. For example,

```
struct {
  double real;
  double imaginary;
} myvar;
```

declares `myvar` in the same way as before. It is not possible to pass a parameter of this type, because the `struct` is unnamed.

Nested Records

Once a `struct` has been defined, it can be used like any other available type, including as a field in another `struct`. Such nesting of records is valuable in constructing more complex structures to model real-world data more accurately.

Accessing nested fields, however, is a bit more complicated. For example, recall the employee record defined earlier. One of its fields was a string representing the employee's name. It might be better to allocate separate fields for first name, last name, and middle initial. Each would also be a string type. We could simply declare these new fields inside `EmpRecType`, or we could first declare a new `struct` to hold name records. Such a `struct` would be declared as

```
#define INITSIZE 2
typedef char InitType[ INITSIZE ];
typedef struct {         /* Name information: */
  NameType firstname;    /*    first name     */
  NameType lastname;     /*    family name    */
  InitType init;         /*    middle initial */
} NameRecType;
```

To use this `struct` as a field of `EmpRecType`, we would write

```
typedef struct {                /* Employee information: */
    NameRecType  namerec;       /*    name               */
    AddrType     address;       /*    address            */
    double       salary;        /*    salary             */
    unsigned int id;            /*    company id number  */
} EmpRecType;
```

and a variable would be declared by EmpRecType employee; as before. Accessing the various name fields is now a two-step process. For example, employee.namerec.firstname is the string for the employee's first name. Note the double usage of the period notation. The NameRecType field, namerec, is a field of employee, and it has a field itself, firstname, as shown in Figure 9.3.

When using a struct with a nested struct as a pass-by-address parameter, the arrow dereferencing is used only in the first part. For example, recall our function ReadRec(). To enter the first name of the employee, the statement gets(emp->namerec.firstname); would be used, and similarly for the other fields. Also, note that since the field namerec is itself a struct, it can be passed to functions that accept NameRecType parameters, either by value or by address. For example, we might write a function to handle name entry only:

```
void NameRecRead( NameRecType *thisname ) {
    printf( "Employee name entry\n\n" );
    printf( "Enter first name: " );
    gets( thisname->firstname );
    printf( "Enter last name: " );
    gets( thisname->lastname );
    printf( "Enter middle initial: " );
    gets( thisname->init );
} /* NameRecRead() */
```

Figure 9.3   Nested record

Now this function can be called from within `ReadRec()` to handle the name input details:

```
void ReadRec( EmpRecType *emp )
{
  /* Read the employee name record */
  NameReadRec( &emp->namerec );
  /* Get the other information */
  printf( "Enter employee address: " );
  gets( emp->address );
  /* ... and so on as before */
}
```

More than one nested record can be used at a time. In our employee example the address information is also a candidate for a `struct` of its own. Nesting can occur to many levels, too: records inside records inside records, and so on. The next sections discuss arrays of records and records containing arrays. With these combinations, complicated records can be built from the bottom up by constructing basic components first.

Design of Tables

As mentioned at the beginning of this chapter, records are the basis for most databases. In a relational database, records are organized into tables, where the columns are the fields of the record type and the rows are the individual records. To model this arrangement in C, there are two options. The table can be stored in a file, and the use of binary files for this purpose is discussed in a later section. In main memory, however, a table is represented as an array of records, which we now examine more closely.

In previous sections we noted that once a `struct` is defined, it can be used like any other variable type, such as in the declaration of array types. For example, suppose a company needs to keep track of many employees. Using the declaration of `EmpRecType` from earlier examples, we now define a type for a table of employee information as

```
#define MAXEMPS 100
typedef EmpRecType EmpTableType[ MAXEMPS ];
```

and a variable of this type as

```
EmpTableType EmpTable;
```

The variable `EmpTable` stores 100 copies of employee records. To process one of those records, both array syntax and `struct` syntax must be used. For example, to assign an id number of 5512 to the employee stored in record 38, we would write

```
EmpTable[ 38 ].id = 5512;
```

Similarly, because each of the entries of the array is a record of `EmpRecType`, each can be treated as a separate unit. Thus, to fill a record of the array, the function `GetRec()` is available:

```
EmpTable[ 14 ] = GetRec();   /* Fills record number 14, for example */
```

To fill the entire array, we could write

```
int i;
for ( i = 0; i < MAXEMPS; i++ )
  ReadRec( &EmpTable[ i ] );
```

This fragment uses the other input function `ReadRec()` developed earlier. Note that the `&` notation is needed since the `[]` dereference makes `EmpTable[ i ]` a single `EmpRecType`, but the function `ReadRec()` requires the address of such a record.

Encapsulation

When a table of records is used, the size of the array representing the table must be chosen large enough to handle the expected number of records. The actual number of records used in the program might be less than the maximum. While there are methods to minimize the space wasted by such a scheme, here we only discuss the problem of keeping track of the actual number of records used.

It would be simple enough to keep a separate `count` variable that holds the number of records used, and there is nothing wrong with this approach. However, a common method of controlling information is to *encapsulate* all the needed data in one unit. Encapsulation is related to both modularity and information hiding. One named object containing related data is defined, and this object is the unit of transaction among functions.

For example, the table of employees, defined as an array of employee records, is a candidate for encapsulation. At a minimum, the actual number of employees in the table and the table itself are possible fields:

```
typedef struct {            /* Employee table record:            */
  EmpTableType EmpTable;    /*    Table of employee information */
  int count;                /*    Number of employees           */
} EmpTableRecType;
```

A variable of this type is declared as `EmpTableRecType TableRec;` (see Figure 9.4). We say "at a minimum," because there may be other candidate fields, depending on the application. For example, a company might have component divisions, each of which requires a variable of `EmpTableRecType`. In this situation, a division name, address, manager, and so on, could also be fields in the table record. As we noted with nested records previously, accessing fields becomes more tedious when interior data must be referenced. For example, to assign an id number to employee number 38, as before, we would write

```
TableRec.EmpTable[ 38 ].id = 5512;
```

since the `EmpTable` field is now nested inside `TableRec`.

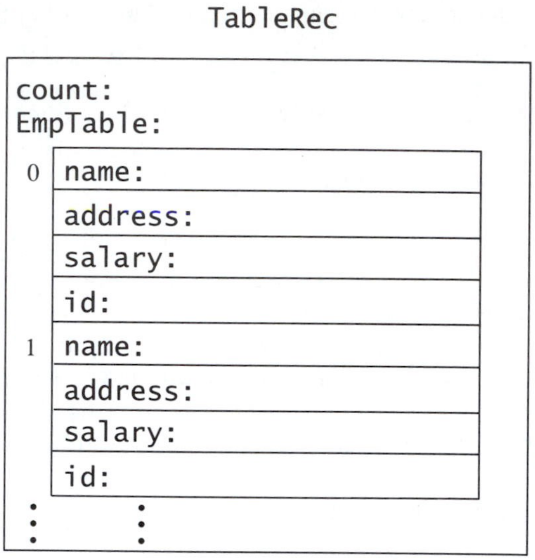

TableRec

```
count:
EmpTable:
  0 | name:
    | address:
    | salary:
    | id:
  1 | name:
    | address:
    | salary:
    | id:
```

Figure 9.4 Encapsulated employee table

To fill the table with some number of employees, the function `FillTable()` is given:

```c
void FillTable( EmpTableRecType *thistable ) {
  int empcount = 0;
  char answer[ 2 ];
  printf( "\n    Employee Table Entry \n\n" );
  printf( "Enter another record? y/n:" );
  scanf( "%s", answer );
  while (( toupper( answer[ 0 ] ) == 'Y') && ( empcount < MAXEMPS )) {
    thistable->EmpTable[ empcount ] = GetRec();
    empcount++;
    if ( empcount >= MAXEMPS )
      printf( "The employee table is now full.\n" );
    else {
      printf( "Enter another record? y/n:" );
      scanf( "%s", answer );
    } /* else */
  } /* while */
  thistable->count = empcount;
} /* FillTable() */
```

Note that `thistable` is passed by address, because the function fills the fields of this record. The call to this function is `FillTable( &TableRec );` assuming the proper variable declaration. The function `ReadRec()` could have been used in place of `GetRec()`, as in the function call `ReadRec( &thistable->EmpTable[ empcount ] );`

The code to display active employee records would now use the field `TableRec.count` to run a `for` loop, calling the function `DisplayRec()`, coded earlier, to print the records on the screen:

```c
for ( i = 0; i < TableRec.count; i++ )
  DisplayRec( TableRec.EmpTable[ i ] );
```

The union Type

Consider the following situation. Employees in our company example are offered the option of joining a standard health insurance plan or joining a health plan of their own choosing. If they join the standard plan, an identification number and the number of dependents covered by the plan must be known. If they opt for another plan, the name and address of the company and the employee's group number must be known.

Since the amount of information about health plans is fairly small for each employee, we could keep all the data about both options in one health record nested inside an employee record. This wastes space, because each employee record uses only some of these fields and not the others, and the wasted space will be multiplied by the size of the table. We would prefer to store *either* the standard plan's information *or* the optional plan's information, but not both, for each employee. This is the purpose of the **union** type, the C construct for declaring a *variant record*—the database term for storing alternate information in one record type.

A union is similar in syntax to a struct, differing only by interchanging these terms. As a simple example before we write the health insurance code, consider the definition

```
typedef union {
  int firstfield;
  char secondfield[ 10 ];
} MyUnionType;
MyUnionType myvar;
```

The two fields of myvar are accessed as in a struct: both myvar.firstfield and myvar.secondfield are correct syntactically. The logical difference between a union and a struct is that only one of these fields is active at a time. Which one is used is up to the programmer, but myvar stores only an int or a string, not both. A union can have any number of fields, not just two, and again, only one of them is active at a time.

The following fragment shows the usage of these fields (see Figure 9.5):

```
/* Use the integer field first */
myvar.firstfield = 17;
printf( "firstfield = %d\n", myvar.firstfield );

/* Now use the string */
printf( "Enter a string: " );
scanf( "%s", myvar.secondfield );
printf( "secondfield = %s\n", myvar.secondfield );

/* Now use the integer again??? */
myvar.firstfield ++;
printf( "firstfield = %d\n", myvar.firstfield );
```

The first section uses the int field, and the printf() will print 17, as expected. The second section uses the string field, and the printf() will print the string entered at the keyboard. The third section, however, is not correct. The original value of 17 is no longer stored in firstfield, although *something* is stored there. Only one field is active at a time, and the

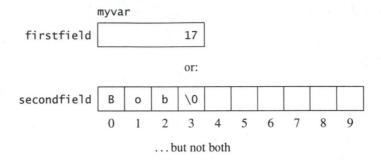

Figure 9.5 Simple union type

last assignment was to `secondfield`, so a reference to `firstfield` is incorrect except to assign a new value.

The reason that the previous paragraph said that "something" is stored in `firstfield` reflects the fact that the two fields actually share memory. The size of a `union` is the size of its largest field. How the memory is being used depends, as noted before, on the programmer. It is the programmer's job to keep straight which of the fields is active. To manage this, another variable is needed to use as a flag; if a `union` is nested in a `struct`, an extra field can be kept for this purpose. Such a variable or field is sometimes called a *discriminator* and uses a code, either `char` or `int`, to indicate the active field of the `union`, as is illustrated in the next example.

Returning to the health insurance information, let us declare a `struct` for each type of insurance option. Based on the previous description, we might write the following (some types were declared earlier in the chapter).

```
#define IDSIZE    20
#define GROUPSIZE 20
typedef char IdType[ IDSIZE ];          /* Id number string             */
typedef char GroupType[ GROUPSIZE ];    /* Group number string          */
typedef struct {                        /* Standard health plan record: */
  IdType id;                            /*    id number                 */
  int    numdependents;                 /*    number of dependents      */
} StandardType;
typedef struct {                        /* Optional health plan record: */
  NameType  company;                    /*    company name              */
  AddrType  address;                    /*    company address           */
  GroupType group;                      /*    group id                  */
} OptionalType;
```

Now, we define a `union` to hold these two records:

```
typedef union {          /* Insurance information variant record: */
  StandardType standard; /*    standard policy                    */
  OptionalType optional; /*    optional policy                    */
} InsInfoType;
```

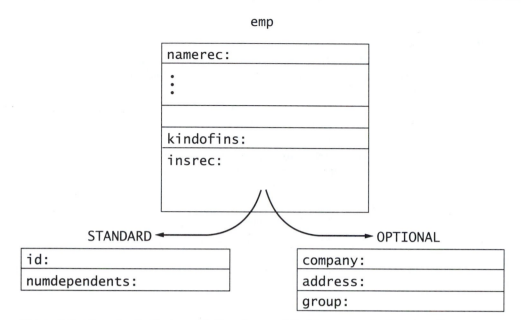

Figure 9.6   Use of a discriminator field; only one of STANDARD or OPTIONAL is valid

Finally, we redefine the EmpRecType to hold this new information:

```
typedef struct {          /* Employee information: */
  NameRecType  namerec;   /*    name             */
  AddrType     address;   /*    address          */
  double       salary;    /*    salary           */
  unsigned int id;        /*    company id number */
  int          kindofins; /*    discriminator    */
  InsInfoType  insrec;    /*    insurance info    */
} EmpRecType;
```

The field kindofins will hold a flag value to indicate which type of insurance the employee has chosen. We will use #define statements to declare the flag values:

```
#define STANDARD 0   /* Flag denoting standard insurance policy */
#define OPTIONAL 1   /* Flag denoting optional insurance policy */
```

This field is set when the employee's insurance option is learned, and it is used to control access to the insrec variant record as shown in Figure 9.6.

To illustrate the use of the insurance union, we rewrite the code that displays an employee record—the DisplayRec() function. The function DisplayNameRec(), used to display the first name, middle initial, and last name, is left to the reader.

```
void DisplayRec( EmpRecType emp ) {
  /* Display the common fields first */
  printf( "\nEmployee Number %d\n", emp.id );
```

```
         DisplayNameRec( emp.namerec );
         printf( "\t Address : %s\n", emp.address );
         printf( "\t Salary  : %8.2lf\n", emp.salary );
         /* Now choose among the insurance types using discriminator */
         switch ( kindofins ) {
           /* Standard plan */
           case STANDARD: printf( "Identification number : %s\n",
                                  emp.insrec.standard.id );
                          printf( "Number of dependents  : %d\n",
                                  emp.insrec.standard.numdependents );
                          break;
           /* Optional plan */
           case OPTIONAL: printf( "Insurance company   : %s\n",
                                  emp.insrec.optional.company );
                          printf( "          Address   : %s\n",
                                  emp.insrec.optional.address );
                          printf( "Group identification: %s\n",
                                  emp.insrec.optional.group );
                          break;
           /* No plan - error! */
           default:       printf( "Error: Insurance type not defined.\n");
         }   /* switch kindofins */
       } /* DisplayRec */
```

The gain of encapsulating the insurance records inside the `union` is offset by the difficulty in referencing the necessary fields. The phrase `emp.insrec.optional.company` shows how a reference must "burrow" into the innermost record: `emp` is the original `EmpRecType` record, `emp.insrec` is the `union` of type `InsInfoType`, `emp.insrec.optional` is the `struct` of type `OptionalType`, and finally `emp.insrec.optional.company` is the string containing the company name.

Binary Files

In Chapter 5 several commands were introduced to read and write text files. This section discusses the use of *binary* files. A binary file contains data that was written in the same format used to store data internally in main memory. For example, the `int` value 25 is stored as four bytes internally on the authors' machine and would be stored as four bytes in a binary file, not as the three-byte string `"25\0"`, as it would be in a text file. The larger integer 2566270 would still use four bytes in binary format but would use eight characters in text mode. The fact that a numeric value is a standard length makes binary files easier to handle. No special string-to-numeric conversions are necessary.

More often than not, binary files are used to store records, rather than values of the standard types. Thus, a C `struct` is the typical unit used for reading and writing binary files. The file functions discussed in Chapter 5 for reading and writing text files are not appropriate for binary files. Instead, a new set of functions is used to handle chunks of bytes as input and output. Additionally, a binary file must be opened in binary mode for proper access to occur.

Opening and Closing Binary Files

Recall that the `fopen()` function takes a mode string as its second parameter. To access a binary file, this mode string must contain the letter b. For example, to open a file for writing in binary mode, the statement

```
fptr = fopen( "myfile.bin", "wb" );
```

works, if the definition `FILE *fptr;` has been made. As before, the file name may be contained in a string variable, and the contents of `fptr` should be checked for equality with `NULL`, which indicates a problem in opening the file.

Each of the modes discussed in Chapter 5 has a corresponding binary mode. The `wb` mode creates a new file if the file does not yet exist; if the file does exist, its contents are erased. The `rb` mode opens an existing file for read access; if the file does not exist, `NULL` is returned. The `ab` mode creates a new file if necessary but does not erase an existing file. The dual modes are also available in binary format: `w+b` for write and read access (overwriting an existing file), `r+b` for read and write access (without overwriting an existing file), and `a+b` for append and read access (without overwriting an existing file, but setting the file position pointer to the end of the file). Note that the `w+b` creates a file if it does not exist and it overwrites an existing file, whereas `r+b` fails if the file does not exist and it does not overwrite an existing file.

When a binary file is created, there is no external indication that it is in fact binary. No special naming conventions are used except those you define yourself. For example, the extension `.bin` might be used, as in `myfile.bin`.

To close a binary file, the `fclose()` function is used in the same manner as with text files. The statement `fclose( fptr );` closes the file that was opened in the example shown.

Reading and Writing

The functions for reading from and writing to binary files take as a parameter, among others, a *generic pointer* (a pointer of type `void *`) to the section of memory being used. Since binary files usually contain records, this means that a pointer to a `struct` must be cast to a generic pointer. This syntax makes the function calls somewhat unwieldy.

The functions **fread()** and **fwrite()** are used for binary file access. They have similar syntax, as illustrated by their prototypes:

```
size_t fread( void *ptr, size_t size, size_t numItems, FILE *fptr );
size_t fwrite( void *ptr, size_t size, size_t numItems, FILE *fptr );
```

The first parameter of each is the generic pointer just mentioned. The second parameter, `size`, is the number of bytes per item to be read or written; the `sizeof()` function should be used here for safety. The third parameter, `numItems`, tells how many items to read or write. Many applications read or write one record at a time, so `numItems` is usually 1. An array of items may be accessed, though, in which case this parameter is greater than 1. The final parameter is the non-NULL file pointer returned by `fopen()`.

To illustrate the use of these functions, recall the definition of the employee records used previously (see Figure 9.7):

```
typedef struct {              /* Employee information: */
    NameRecType  namerec;     /*    name               */
    AddrType     address;     /*    address            */
    double       salary;      /*    salary             */
    unsigned int id;          /*    company id number  */
} EmpRecType;
```

Suppose a variable of this type has been declared by `EmpRecType employee;` and its fields filled by `employee = GetRec();`. To write this record to a file opened with wb access and having file pointer `fptr`, the statement

```
fwrite( (void *) &employee, sizeof( EmpRecType ), 1, fptr );
```

does the job. The latter three arguments should be obvious, although we note again the use of `sizeof()` to determine the number of bytes in a record of this type rather than guessing the size. The first argument is constructed to match the parameter type for this slot. The record `employee` contains the information to be written to the file, `&employee` is its memory address, and the prefix `(void *)` is used to cast an `EmpRecType` pointer to a generic pointer.

If the file in this example were successfully closed, it could be reopened with rb access, and the record could be read by the statement

```
fread ( (void *) &employee, sizeof( EmpRecType ), 1, fptr );
```

A call to `DisplayRec()` would show the information now stored in `employee`.

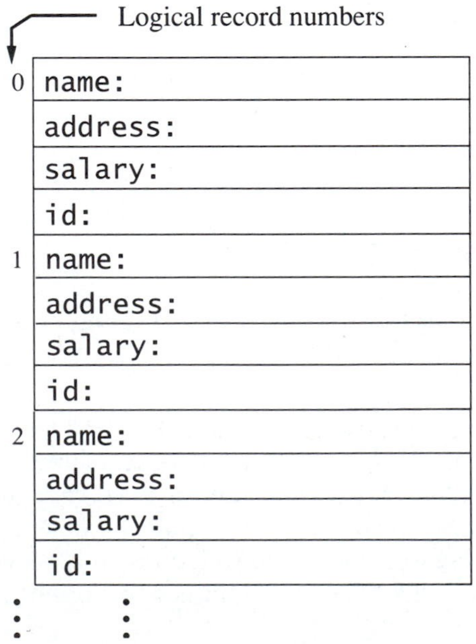

Figure 9.7 A binary file is similar to an array of `struct`s; multiply logical record number by size of the record to get the physical byte number

Both `fread()` and `fwrite()` return integers. The value returned should match the number sent in the third parameter: the number of records requested to be read or written. If the return value is less than the number requested, an error has occurred. For `fread()`, this is an indication that the end of the file has been reached.

Positioning the File Pointer

Many applications use binary files in a manner similar to arrays of records. Each can be accessed sequentially, one element at a time, but each can also be accessed at random, processing elements in any order. In an array, the index number of an element is used for this purpose. The record number in a binary file serves the same purpose, but this number must be translated to a byte number or *offset* into the file. Furthermore, special commands are needed to set the *file position* (also called the file pointer, not to be confused with the FILE * variable used with `fopen()`) before reading or writing.

The function **fseek()** is the basic command for setting the file position. Its prototype is

```
int fseek( FILE *fptr, long offset, int fromwhere );
```

The first argument is the return value from `fopen()`. The second parameter is the number of bytes to move the file position, counting from zero. Notice that this parameter is of type `long`, not `int`. The `offset` argument may be positive, negative, or zero, depending on the desired movement. The third parameter is a flag value indicating from where in the file to compute the offset. Only three values are valid in this slot: the constant SEEK_SET (which is defined as zero in `<stdio.h>`), the beginning of the file; SEEK_CUR (one), the current position; and SEEK_END (two), the end of the file. If successful, `fseek()` returns zero.

The `fread()` and `fwrite()` functions have the side effect of changing the file position, leaving it set to the first byte after the last record read or written. When a program is both reading a record from and writing it to a binary file, a call to `fseek()` *must be used* between the calls to `fread()` and `fwrite()`. A call to `rewind()` or `fflush()` (described subsequently) may be substituted for this mandatory call to `fseek()`.

For example, to write a record of type EmpRecType to a binary file, then read it back, we could use the following code:

```
fptr = fopen( "empfile.bin", "w+b" );
if ( fptr == NULL ) {
  printf( "Error opening empfile.bin\n" );
  exit( 0 );
}
/* Fill the fields of employee, then write the record */
fwrite( (void *) &employee, sizeof( EmpRecType ), 1, fptr );
/* Set the file position back to the beginning of the file */
fseek( fptr, 0, SEEK_SET );
/* Read the record */
fread( (void *) &employee, sizeof( EmpRecType ), 1, fptr );
/* Close the file */
fclose( fptr );
```

The function **rewind()** is used to reset the file position to the beginning of the file. Its prototype,

```
void rewind( FILE *fptr );
```

shows that it takes only the file pointer variable as a parameter. A call to rewind() is equivalent to the call fseek(fptr, 0, SEEK_SET).

To find out where the file position is set, the function **ftell()** is used. It returns a long value equal to the byte number offset from the beginning of the file, or -1 on an error. Its only parameter is the file pointer value. For example,

```
long position;
position = ftell( fptr );
printf( "Position = %ld\n", position );
```

would display the current file position.

Reading and writing are buffered by the operating system. This means that data being read from or written to files is temporarily stored by the operating system before it is transferred to a program. Thus, calls to fread() and fwrite() may not receive or send data directly from or to the file. To remove data from the buffer, a call to the function **fflush()** may be used. Its only parameter is the file pointer (FILE *) variable, and it returns an int, zero if successful. Normally, fflush() is used only when a file is being accessed by two different programs simultaneously, one reading from the file and one writing to the file. When writing occurs, fflush() ensures that data stored in a buffer is moved to the file, so that subsequent reading will access the updated information.

Searching a Binary File

If a file of records is sorted according to one of the fields, then searching the file for a particular record can be accomplished most efficiently using a binary search. If a file is unsorted (or is sorted on a field other than the one being searched), a sequential search must be used. Since any record in a binary file may be directly accessed by using fseek() before reading or writing, a binary file is logically equivalent to an array of records. The same methods used in Chapter 7 for searching arrays, sorted or unsorted, may be applied here.

Searches are usually conducted using one field of a record. Recall that the value being searched for is called the key. By definition, a key is a value that uniquely identifies the record to which it belongs; that is, no duplicates are allowed in the key field. Nevertheless, searches may be done on fields that allow duplicates, in which case either the first record matching the key value is sought, or all records with the key value are produced. A search need not focus on a single field, either. For example, a set of field values may be the search target (key or not). For simplicity, the following examples assume that the id field is a key for the struct of type EmpRecType.

Searching an Unordered File

To search an unordered file, each record of the file is examined for a match with the key value. The search terminates when a match is found or the end of the file is encountered. Because each record is accessed in turn, there is no need to use the fseek() function.

The following function `EmpSearch()` has three parameters: `id`, the key value to be found; `emprec`, a pointer to a `struct` of `EmpRecType`, which is used to return the desired record; and `fptr`, a file pointer. The function assumes that the key value is legal and that the file has been opened successfully for reading. It returns an integer value denoting where the record was found in the file for a successful search, or `-1` for an unsuccessful search. Note that this is the *record* number, not the byte number. If the record needs to be retrieved again, a call to `fseek()` will have to be made using this number multiplied by the `struct` size.

```
int EmpSearch( unsigned int id, EmpRecType *emprec, FILE *fptr ) {
  int found,              /* Flag to tell when to quit searching */
    count,                /* Record counter                      */
    size;                 /* Size of one struct                  */
  found = FALSE;                 /* Initialize the flag          */
  count = -1;                    /* Initialize record counter    */
  size  = sizeof( EmpRecType ); /* Set the struct size          */
  rewind( fptr );                /* Start at record 0            */
  /* Search until id is found or end of file is reached */
  while (( !found ) && ( fread( (void *) emprec, size, 1, fptr ) == 1 )) {
    if ( emprec->id == id )
      found = TRUE;
    count++;
  }   /*   while   */
  /* Check if found */
  if ( !found )
    count = -1;
  return( count );
} /*  EmpSearch() */
```

Other styles are possible for the function interface. For example, a pointer to a `struct` of `EmpRecType` could be returned instead, using `NULL` as a flag that the key was not found.

Searching an Ordered File

Chapter 7 discussed the concept of a binary search on a sorted array. The same principle is used here: Choose the middle record in the file, then check it for the key value. If it is a match, we're done; otherwise, we need to search the first half of the file or the second half, depending on whether the key value is less than or greater than the key field of the middle record. Each step of the search decreases the number of records to be searched by one-half. For arrays, the number of elements to be searched was usually the size of the array; the alternative was to keep track of the number of active elements in the array. For a file of records, the number of records is not fixed. We must either keep track of the number of records explicitly or compute it from the file size.

The following function computes the number of records in a file, given the file pointer `fptr` and the record size `size`.

```
int fsize( int size, FILE *fptr ) {
  int number;
  long last;
```

```
      /* Check for zero record size */
      if ( size == 0 )
        number = 0;
      else {
        /* Seek to the last byte */
        fseek( fptr, 0, SEEK_END );
        /* Get the number of the last byte and divide by the size */
        last = ftell( fptr );
        number = last/size;
      } /* else */
      return( number );
    }  /* fsize() */
```

The file corresponding to `fptr` is assumed to be open; an alternative would be to have `fsize()` open the file. The example below shows how to use `fsize()`.

The following binary search function corresponds to the code from Chapter 7 for searching an array. Note the use of `fseek()` to position the file pointer to the middle record. Since `fseek()` uses byte offsets rather than record numbers, the offset must be computed. Parameter `id` is the search key, and `emprec` is used both to read a file record and to pass back the record containing `id`, if found. The return value is the logical record number if `id` is found and `-1` otherwise.

```
int EmpBinSearch( unsigned int id, EmpRecType *emprec, FILE *fptr ) {
   int start, end, middle; /* Record numbers used in the search */
   int found;              /* Flag for successful search         */
   int KeyIndex;           /* Return value                       */
   int size;               /* Record size in bytes               */
   /* Initialize record numbers and flag */
   size  = sizeof( EmpRecType );
   start = 0;
   end   = fsize( size, fptr ) - 1;
   found = FALSE;
   /* Loop until found or start meets end */
   while (( !found ) && ( start <= end )) {
      middle = ( start + end ) /2;
      fseek( fptr, middle * size, SEEK_SET );
      fread( (void *) emprec, size, 1, fptr );
      if ( id == emprec->id ) found = TRUE;
      else if ( id < emprec->id ) end = middle - 1;
      else start = middle + 1;
   } /* while */
   if ( found )
      KeyIndex = middle;
   else
      KeyIndex = -1;
   return( KeyIndex );
}   /* EmpBinSearch() */
```

This code illustrates the difference between logical record numbers (such as start, middle, and end) and physical record numbers (such as middle * size). Our EmpRecType records are the units we would prefer to work in, but the fseek() function requires physical byte numbers. It is important to remember which unit of measurement is being used.

Sorting a Binary File

The sorting methods discussed in Chapter 7 for arrays can be used for files of records, because, as we have seen, the fseek() function allows random access to the records in a file. Small files of records that can be read into an array can be sorted by, say, selection sort (see Chapter 7), then written to a new file. For performance reasons, these earlier methods are usually restricted to main-memory arrays rather than applied directly to the files. This is a consequence of the many read and write operations needed (recall the exchange() function needed for sorting). Larger files, especially, require other methods because main memory may not hold the entire file. These come under the heading of *external* sorting algorithms (as opposed to the *internal* methods for sorting arrays).

One common external sort is *sort merge*. A two-way sort merge, as the name implies, merges two sorted files into one final file. This was illustrated in Chapter 5 using simple integer data. Recall that the method worked by comparing the current smallest integer of each input file, writing the smaller of these two elements to the output file, and replacing it by a new integer from the affected file. One input file is finished being processed before the other, the remainder of which must then be copied to the output file. For records, the process is the same, using the key field for comparisons. This is actually the second phase of sort merge and is called the *merge phase*.

The first part of sort merge produces the sorted files. In general, a large file must be broken into manageable pieces. Each piece is read into an array, sorted using an internal method, then written out to a new subfile. These subfiles are the input to the merge phase. If there are more than two sorted subfiles, a two-way merge phase must make several passes. Each pass merges pairs of subfiles into new subfiles. The final pass merges one pair of subfiles into the final sorted file.

A *k*-way sort merge merges several subfiles on each pass of the merge phase. The comparison operation must consider the current smallest elements from *k* files, where *k* is greater than or equal to 2 and chosen for convenience. Finding the minimum element in the list of current smallest elements was also discussed in Chapter 5, although a selection tree, similar to a tennis tournament match structure, is often used. Again, if the file is large, several merge passes may be needed to produce the final file.

Hash Files

As a last example, we examine a strategy for storing records that allows them to be found more quickly, on average, than either a sequential search on an unsorted file or a binary search on a sorted file does. This method is known as *hashing*. The main idea is to store a record at a position that is easily computable from information in the record itself. This computation is done using a *hash function*, which accepts all or part of the record as a parameter and returns an integer in the range from zero to the size (in logical records, not bytes) of the file minus 1. This hash value is the probable position of the record in the file. It is not required that the hash function return a unique integer for each record; duplicates are possible. Thus, two or more records may hash to the same position, as shown in Figure 9.8.

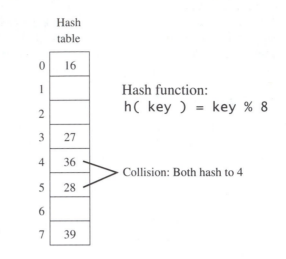

Figure 9.8 A hash table on integer values

The hash file is initially empty. To store a record, its hash value is computed, and the record is written at the position indicated by the hash value, provided that spot is empty. If the spot is already taken by a previously stored record with the same hash value, then another position must be found. The various algorithms available for this task are called *collision resolution* schemes. We will examine the simplest method, called *linear hashing*. Linear hashing resolves conflicts among hash positions by looking one position at a time further in the file until an empty spot is found. If the end of the file is reached, the file pointer is set to the start of the file, and the search for an empty position continues.

There are several implications of the linear hashing strategy:

1. Empty records must be distinguishable from stored records in the file. Either an extra field is used as a flag for this purpose, or a special value is stored in an existing field. In either case, the other fields of an empty record position are invalid. The problem of empty records is related to the deletion of records from a hash file. Deleting a record may cause a break in a chain of records that collided on insertion. Marking a record as "deleted," rather than as "empty," is a safer strategy.
2. Because the file is accessed in a circular manner, there must be a stopping condition when searching for an empty record. This can be accomplished by requiring that the file always have at least one empty record or simply by keeping count of the number of records accessed.
3. When a hash file is to be searched for a particular record, there must be a way to tell when to quit searching; this is related to the previous point. The search continues until either the desired record is found, an empty position is found, or the entire file has been searched.

The speed of a hash algorithm depends on the number of collisions. If a record is found near its hash value, the algorithm is quite fast, requiring only a few read operations or even just one. As more records are stored, more collisions occur, and many read operations may be needed—perhaps as many as in a sequential search. The allure of hashing schemes is the fast search performance when conditions are right.

The hash function, as already noted, must produce an integer value in the range $0 \ldots$ MAXREC-1, where MAXREC is the size of the file in records. This can be achieved using integer division by MAXREC. The number to be divided by MAXREC should be easy to compute. Assuming that a single field of a record is used for this purpose, there are many possible hash functions. If the field is an integer, for example, then the absolute value of the field can be used. However, it is possible that this field's values and MAXREC can interact in troublesome ways, producing many collisions among records. Consider an employee number in which the last three digits are used as a city location code. Dividing by 1000 will produce the same hash value for all employees in a given city. Such pathological cases can be constructed for most hash functions. It is usually best if the hash function spreads values uniformly over the entire range $0 \ldots$ MAXREC-1. The employee number could be squared, for example, or its digits summed, before dividing by MAXREC. For string fields, the ASCII values of the characters are often summed or multiplied before division.

In the following example the hash function divides the id field of a record whose type is EmpRecType, defined earlier in this section, by MAXREC. Linear hashing is used to resolve collisions. We assume that the function InitializeFile(), which writes empty records to the file, has been called to mark each record as empty by storing -1 in each id field. Three functions are provided: hash(), the hash function; StoreEmpRec(), which stores records in the hash file; and HashSearch(), which searches for a record in the file. The latter two functions include parameters for binary files; these are assumed to be open in binary mode.

```
int hash( unsigned int key ) {
  /* Return the value of h( key ) */
  return( key % MAXREC );
} /* hash() */
```

The function StoreEmpRec() stores the value of the parameter emprec in the file referenced by fptr using a linear hashing scheme.

```
void StoreEmpRec( EmpRecType emprec, FILE *fptr ) {
  int  spot,    /* Hash value of emprec.id */
       count,   /* Record count            */
       size;    /* EmpRecType size         */
  long where;   /* Byte number in file     */
  EmpRecType candidate; /* Record in hash file */
  /* Initializations */
  count = 0;
  size = sizeof( EmpRecType );
  /* Compute the hash value and set the file pointer */
  spot  = hash( emprec.id );
  where = spot * size;
  fseek( fptr, where, SEEK_SET );
  /* Loop until an empty record is found */
  /* or the entire file is read */
  fread( (void *) &candidate, size, 1, fptr );
  while (( candidate.id != -1 ) && ( count < MAXREC )) {
    /* Move up one logical record and count it. */
    spot++;
    count++;
    /* Wrap to the beginning of the file if necessary */
    if ( spot == MAXREC ) {
      rewind( fptr );
```

```
        spot = 0;
    } /* if spot */
    fread( (void *) &candidate, size, 1, fptr );
  } /* while */
  /* Check for full file */
  if ( count == MAXREC )
    printf( "Error: file is full.\n" );
  else {
    /* Position the file pointer and write the new record */
    where = spot * size;
    fseek( fptr, where, 0 );
    fwrite( (void *) &emprec, size, 1, fptr );
  } /* else */
} /* StoreEmpRec() */
```

The function HashSearch() uses the parameter id to hash into the file referenced by fptr. If the record containing id is found using linear hashing, emprec is used to pass this record back and the logical record number is returned; otherwise, −1 is returned to indicate "not found."

```
int HashSearch( unsigned int id, EmpRecType *emprec, FILE *fptr ) {
  int  spot,    /* Hash value of id */
       count,   /* Record count     */
       size;    /* EmpRecType size  */
  long where;  /* Byte number       */
  /* Initializations */
  count = 0;
  size = sizeof( EmpRecType );
  /* Compute the hash value and set the file pointer */
  spot  = hash( id );
  where = spot * size;
  fseek( fptr, where, SEEK_SET );
  /* Loop until id is found, or empty record is found, */
  /* or entire file is read                            */
  fread( (void *) emprec, size, 1, fptr );
  while (( emprec->id != id ) && ( emprec->id != -1 ) && ( count < MAXREC )) {
    /* Move up one logical record and count it. */
    spot++;
    count++;
    /* Wrap to the beginning of the file if necessary */
    if ( spot == MAXREC ) {
      rewind( fptr );
      spot = 0;
    } /* if spot */
    fread( (void *) emprec, size, 1, fptr );
  } /* while */
  /* Why did the loop stop? */
```

```
    if (( count == MAXREC ) || ( emprec->id != id ))
      spot = -1;
    return( spot );
  } /* HashSearch() */
```

As a general rule, hashing schemes work best when the file is 50 to 80 percent full. A file less than 50 percent full wastes too much space on empty records, and one over 80 percent full requires too much time on collision resolution. Linear hashing, although simple to implement, is the least efficient of collision resolution schemes. For other algorithms, see [Sedgewick]. Since random access makes hashing work, hashing can also be used to store data in arrays.

The UNIX Environment

Previous chapters have noted that the UNIX environment can be modified in certain ways. This section discusses several other useful ways that a UNIX session can be made more convenient, including how to create customized commands and how to recall previous commands.

C Shell Environment

In Chapter 4 some of the differences between the C shell (`csh`) and the Bourne shell (`sh`) were described. Other shells, including the Korn shell (`ksh`) and the enhanced C shell (`tcsh`), are available on many systems. Which shell a particular user begins running at login is set by the system administrator, but the other shells can be run by typing their respective commands. Some special commands for the C shell are described subsequently. For details about the other shells, either see their manual pages or consult [Abrahams and Larson].

Chapter 4 discussed the C shell's predefined variables. Recall that these included `term`, the terminal type you are using; `path`, the directories searched for commands; and `home`, your home directory. There are several others, known as *environment variables*. These are like C global variables in that their values are passed on to *child* processes of the current shell (Chapter 10 discusses this further). Some examples are PATH and HOME, which are updated when `path` and `home` are changed but can be given values independently. The commands to assign values to shell variables are `set` and `setenv`; the latter is used for environment variables only. Their syntax is slightly different: `set term = vt100` and `setenv HOME /usr/home/jones` show the variations.

New shell variables may be created and used using `set`. The command `set myvar = "Hello, world"`, for example, creates the variable `myvar` and assigns it the given string value. Such variables are usually needed only in *shell scripts*, which are discussed in Chapter 10. Finally, recall that the `echo` command is used to display values, as in `echo $path` or `echo $myvar`.

The effects of both `set` and `setenv` may be undone by using `unset` and `unsetenv`, respectively. For example, `unset myvar` would make `myvar` undefined, and entering `echo $myvar` after the `unset` would give the message `myvar: Undefined variable.` or the like. Beware using these commands on shell and environment variables, because unintended effects may result.

File Name Completion

It is possible to refer to files without typing their entire names. When a file name contains one of the wildcard characters *, ?, or ~, the wildcard is replaced by any string, any single character, or the user's home directory, respectively. We have used the * wildcard character before. For example, in the command `ls *.c`, the argument to `ls` expands to any file ending in `.c`, matching, for example, `prog1.c` and `myfile.c`, if they exist in the current directory. Similarly, in the command `ls prog?.c`, the argument to `ls` expands to `prog1.c` and `prog2.c` but not to `prog10.c`, since the expansion can contain only one character.

We have already seen the use of the tilde character as a shorthand notation for pathnames. For example, `cd ~jones` will change the current working directory to user `jones`'s home directory.

The effect of wildcard characters may be turned off using the shell variable `noglob`. If we type `set noglob`, the wildcard characters are treated as regular characters. For example, the sequence

```
% set noglob
% ls *.c
```

lists only the file `*.c`, if it exists. The command `unset noglob` returns wildcards to their special status.

Another C shell variable, `filec`, turns on and off the *file completion* feature of the shell, which is used to reduce the need for retyping file names. It is used in conjunction with the escape key and control-D, as illustrated in the following example.

```
% set filec
% ls
prog1.c  prog1.o todolist
```

Suppose we now type `more tod<esc>` (that is, we press the escape key after typing the last letter d). The command line will now be changed to `more todolist`, which can be executed by pressing the enter key. In other words, the current directory is searched for a file name that matches the typed characters `tod`. If there is more than one match, as much of the file name as can be matched unambiguously is displayed, and the terminal beeps. For example, if we type `cp pro<esc>`, the command line will now change to `cp prog1.`, with the cursor positioned after the period, because there are two matches to the prefix `pro` and both names are identical as far as the period. At this point, we must decide either to complete the name ourselves, or we can type control-D. The latter causes all matches to be displayed, and the command line will be redisplayed. Consider the entire scenario as follows:

```
% cp pro<esc>      (The line changes to:)
% cp prog1.        (and the terminal beeps; we now type control-D)
prog1.c prog1.o
% cp prog1.c newprog.c
```

where, in the last line, we complete the command and press the enter key. The command `set filec` is often placed in the `.cshrc` file. As expected, the command `unset filec` turns off the file completion feature.

New Command Names

There are ways that the C shell environment can be made easier to live with. The **alias** command, for example, allows new names to be given to commands. The syntax is `alias` *newcmd string*, where *newcmd* is the new name, and *string* holds the command(s) to be executed when *newcmd* is typed. For example, to produce a command that gives a long directory listing, we could write `alias dir ls -l`. Running the command `dir` would now be the same as running the command `ls -l`. The string may be placed in single or double quotes, as in `alias dir 'ls -l'`.

A common practice is to make aliases for regularly used commands. For example, recall that the `rm` command, without flags, does not double-check whether the target file should be deleted, but the command `rm -i` does. For safety's sake, we could write `alias rm rm -i`, which causes any later use of `rm` to be invoked with the interactive option. Similarly, `alias m more` makes the use of `more` a bit easier. Users who are familiar with another operating system can alias commands from that system to UNIX commands, decreasing the number of UNIX commands they need to remember. The `dir` alias with which we began is such an example, since `dir` is a command in MS-DOS. Aliasing is particularly useful with long or hard-to-remember commands. For example, to change the current directory to a specific directory containing, say, a particular project's code, we might write `alias work cd ~userid/project/code/module1`. Another common practice is to anticipate misspelled commands. For example, the command `alias logotu logout` handles misspelling the `logout` command. Multiple commands may be contained in an `alias`, provided the commands are separated by semicolons. For example, `alias myhome 'cd; ls -l'` combines a return to one's home directory with the listing of that directory.

Alias commands may be typed at the command line, but it is more useful to place them in the `.cshrc` file in the home directory, which is read when the C shell is started. Any alias command contained there will then become part of the working environment. If new commands are added to the `.cshrc` file using `vi` or some other editor, they do not become active until the shell is activated again, which is normally at login time; on systems using a windowed environment, however, the modifications become active when a new window is created, but only for that window. To make additions to `.cshrc` become active immediately, use the command `source .cshrc`, which causes the `.cshrc` file to be reread.

One can overdo aliasing, in which case the new commands are as hard to remember as the regular UNIX commands. If the command `alias` is entered with no arguments, a list of all alias commands and replacement strings is displayed. Also, alias commands may be revoked using the **unalias** command. For example, the statement `unalias logotu` removes the previously defined alias of `logotu` as `logout`.

Old Command Retrieval

The C shell has a built-in facility for keeping track of the commands recently typed. This is known as the **history** facility. Commands are kept in a numbered list, which can be seen by typing `history`. Only the most recent commands are kept around, but the user can control the size of the list. The command `set history = 40` limits the list to the 40 most recent commands, for example. Such a command would normally be placed in the `.cshrc` file. (Note that `history` is used both as a command and as a C shell variable.) Thus, if the first three commands executed after logging in were `ls`, `cat .cshrc`, and `cd work`, the command `history` would produce the output

```
1 ls
2 cat .cshrc
3 cd work
4 history
```

The list is normally discarded at logout, but another variable, `savehist`, sets the number of commands saved for the next login session, as in `set savehist = 20`.

The `history` list may be used to reexecute previous commands using the syntax $!< commandnumber >$, where $< commandnumber >$ is the number of a command in the `history` list. For example, using the previous example of four commands, the command `!2` causes the `cat .cshrc` command to be executed again. The usefulness of reexecution, as with `alias`, increases with command length and complexity.

There are several variants on the exclamation point syntax. Two exclamation points, `!!`, reexecutes the most recent command in the `history` list, that is, the previous command. If a string is given after the exclamation point instead of a command number, the list is searched for the most recent occurrence of that string; if a match is found, that command is reexecuted. For example, `!c`, using the foregoing list, is equivalent to `!3`, and `!ca` is equivalent to `!2`. Substitutions can be made in previous commands using the syntax `!<command>:s/oldstring/newstring`, according to the substitution commands discussed in Chapter 7. For example, either `!2:s/cshrc/login` or `!ca:s/cshrc/login` is equivalent to `cat .login`.

Directory Retrieval

Previously accessed directories, like old commands, can be retrieved and made the current working directory. But unlike the `history` utility, this process is not automatic; it uses the special commands **pushd**, **popd**, and **dirs**.

The C shell keeps track of a list of directories in the form of a stack. Directory names are added and deleted only from the front of this list, and the first (top) entry on the stack is the current working directory. When the command `pushd dirname` is executed, the effect is to push (add) the directory `dirname` onto this stack, then to change the current working directory to `dirname`; the latter part is equivalent to using `cd dirname`. The contents of the stack are also displayed. To return to the previous directory, the command `popd` is given with no arguments; `popd` pops (deletes) the top directory from the stack and executes a `cd` to the next directory. At any time, the `dirs` command shows the entire contents of the directory stack, which is never quite empty: it always contains the initial current working directory. So typing `dirs` before any `pushd` or `popd` commands has the same effect as `pwd`.

For example, suppose user `jones` is in his home directory `/usr/home/jones`, where directory `~jones` has subdirectories `project1`, `project2`, and `mymail`. If we type `pushd project1`, the line

```
~/project1 ~
```

is displayed, indicating the new working directory and the old one, and then the current working directory changes to `project1`. Now suppose we type `pushd ~smith`, where `smith` is the home directory of user `smith`. The line

```
/usr/home/smith ~/project1 ~
```

is displayed showing the directory stack (three directories), and the new working directory is `/usr/home/smith`. The command `dirs` at this point shows the same information:

```
/usr/home/smith ~/project1 ~
```

If we now type `popd`, the line

```
~/project1 ~
```

is displayed, and the new current working directory is again `project1`, the subdirectory of `jones`. Typing `popd` again makes the initial directory, `~jones`, the current directory.

When the `pushd` command is given without an argument, the resulting action depends on the contents of the directory stack. If it contains only the initial working directory, an error message is given, because there is no directory argument to push. If there are at least two directories on the stack, the result is to reverse the top two entries and change directories to the new top entry. For example, consider the following sequence of commands and results.

```
% pwd
/usr/home/jones
% pushd project1
~/project1 ~
% pwd
/usr/home/jones/project1
% pushd ../mymail
~/mymail ~/project1 ~
% pwd
/usr/home/jones/mymail
% pushd
~/project1 ~/mymail ~
% pwd
/usr/home/jones/project1
```

The last `pushd`, which has no arguments, switches the entries ~/mymail and ~/project1 on the stack.

The entries of the directory stack may be referenced by number, where the first entry is 0, the next is 1, and so on. If an integer preceded by a plus sign is used as an argument to `pushd`, that directory is moved to the front of the list. The sequence

```
% dirs
~/project1 ~/mymail ~
% pushd +2
~ ~/project1 ~/mymail
```

illustrates this variation. The `popd` command also allows for integer arguments. The effect is to remove the corresponding directory from the stack, as in

```
% dirs
~ ~/project1 ~/mymail
% popd +1
~ ~/mymail
```

where entry 1, `~/project1`, is removed.

References

Abrahams, Paul W. and Bruce R. Larson, *UNIX for the Impatient,* Addison-Wesley, Reading, MA, 1992.

Sedgewick, Robert, *Algorithms in C,* Addison-Wesley, Reading, MA, 1990.

Chapter Summary

■ C Commands

Declarations and Assignments of Structure Variables

```
typedef struct {
   double my_real;
   int my_integer;
   char *my_string;
} MyRecordType;
```
Define a `struct` template with room for:
   one `double`, *and*
   one `int`, *and*
   one (untyped) string

```
MyRecordType Item1;
```
Declare a `struct` variable whose type is `MyRecordType`

```
MyRecordType Item1 = { 1.0, 1, "one" };
```
Declare and assign fields of a variable of type `MyRecordType`

```
Item1.my_real = 2.0;
```
Assign a value to the first field of `Item1`

```
MyRecordType *Item2;
```
Declare `Item2`, a pointer to a variable whose type is `MyRecordType`

```
&Item2->my_real = 2.0;
```
Assign a value to the first field of `Item2`

```
typedef union {
   double my_real;
   int my_integer;
   char *my_string;
} MyUnionType;
```
Define a `union` template with room for:
   one `double`, *or*
   one `int`, *or*
   one (untyped) string

```
MyUnionType Item3;
```
Declare a `union` variable whose type is `MyUnionType`

```
Item3.my_real = 1.0;
```
Erase any currently active field of `Item3` and assign a value to the field `my_real`

```
typedef struct {
  char ch;
  MyUnionType Item;
} ImprovedUnionType;
```
Define a data structure that allows the use of ch as a discriminator variable to indicate the currently active field of Item

Binary Files

`FILE *fptr`

`fptr = fopen( "file1.bin", "rb" );`
Open the binary file for reading; return a pointer to file1.bin if opening is successful, otherwise return NULL

`fptr = fopen( "file1.bin", "wb" );`
Create (overwrite if necessary) a binary file, open the file for writing

`fptr = fopen( "file1.bin", "ab" );`
Open the binary file for writing, set file position pointer at the end of the file

`fptr = fopen( "file1.bin", "r+b" );`
Open the binary file for reading and writing; return a pointer to file1.bin if opening is successful, otherwise return NULL

`fptr = fopen( "file1.bin", "w+b" );`
Create (overwrite if necessary) a binary file, open the file for writing and reading

`fptr = fopen( "file1.bin", "a+b" );`
Open the binary file for writing and reading, set file position pointer at the end of the file

```
fread( (void *) &Item1,
  sizeof( MyRecordType ),
  1, fptr );
```
Read one item from the file to which fptr is pointing and store it in Item1 (declared in the previous subsection)

```
fwrite( (void *) &Item1,
  sizeof( MyRecordType ),
  1, fptr );
```
Write the contents of Item1 as one item in the file to which fptr is pointing

`rewind( fptr );`
Set the file position pointer to the beginning of the file to which fptr is pointing

`fseek( fptr, 0, SEEK_SET );`
Equivalent to rewind(fptr);

`fseek( fptr, 0, SEEK_END );`
Set the file position pointer to the end of the file to which fptr is pointing

```
fseek( fptr, -sizeof( MyRecordType ),
  SEEK_CUR );
```
Set the file position pointer to the record prior to the current record

`fflush( fptr );`
Send any remaining buffered data to the output stream (file) to which fptr is pointing

`fclose( fptr );`
Close the binary file to which fptr is pointing

■ **C Shell Commands**

System and Environment Controls

`set`
Display current values of all shell variables

`setenv`
Display current values of all environment variables

`ls ~/subdir1`	List files in `subdir1`, a subdirectory of the home directory
`ls *.out`	List files ending with the suffix `.out`
`ls *.?`	List files ending with a period followed by a single character
`set noglob`	Turn off recognition of file name wildcard characters
`unset noglob`	Turn on recognition of file name wildcard characters
`set filec`	Turn on the file name completion feature
`unset filec`	Turn off the file name completion feature
`alias workdir cd ~userid/dir1/dir2`	Define an alias for changing the directory to the subdirectory given by the indicated pathname
`unalias workdir`	Discard the alias `workdir`
`set history = 40`	Keep the 40 most recent commands; discard this list at the end of the current session
`set savehist = 40`	Keep the 40 most recent commands; save this list at the end of the current session
`history`	Display recent commands
`!1`	Execute command number 1 on the `history` list
`!ca`	Execute the most recent command beginning with the string `ca`
`!ca:s/old/new/`	Execute the most recent command beginning with the string `ca`, and substitute `new` in place of `old` in the command
`dirs`	Display the directory stack
`pushd dir1`	Push `dir1` onto the top of the directory stack and change the working directory to `dir1`
`popd`	Pop the top directory from the directory stack, and change the working directory to that directory

Review Problems

1. a) Define a data structure `MyNumberType` to store a number either as an integer or as a floating-point number.
   b) Write a code fragment to store a number x in the variable `stored_number`, a variable of type `MyNumberType`. If the distance from x to the nearest integer is within 0.001, assign the nearest integer to `stored_number`; otherwise store x in `stored_number`.

2. Consider the following type definitions, which are each designed to store an item's name and length.

```
#define NAMEMAX 20
typedef struct {
  char name[ NAMEMAX ];  /* Item name                    */
```

```
    int feet,inches;       /* Item length, e.g., 3 ft, 2 in */
} FirstItemType;
typedef struct {
    char name[ NAMEMAX ];   /* Item name                    */
    double centimeters;     /* Item length, e.g., 96.52 cm  */
} SecondItemType;
```

a) Write a function to read an item's name and length and then return these values in a variable of type FirstItemType.

b) Write a function to read an item's name and length and store these values in a SecondItemType variable whose address is passed to the function.

c) Design a data structure to store an item's name and length in either of the two formats just defined.

d) Write a function to display the values stored in a variable of the type defined in part c).

3. a) Write an expression for the number of bytes used to store a variable of the following type:

```
typedef struct {
    char flag;
    int i;
    double x;
} MyStructType;
```

   b) Write an expression for the number of bytes used to store individually one char, one int, and one double.

4. Write a function to open a binary file of doubles. If there is an error in opening the file, simply return the integer 1. Otherwise, write the file's contents in reverse order, report the name and size of the file, and return the integer 0.

5. A database designer is planning the data structures for a large database. Each record is to be stored in a variable of type struct, and the designer must now decide whether to store the entire database in a binary file containing a) many individual struct variables or b) a single array of struct variables. Discuss the strengths and weaknesses of each choice.

6. Consider a file of employee records that is to be arranged and searched using one of the following hash functions: If rec is one employee record, hash function f(rec) returns the last three digits of the employee's social security number, g(rec) returns the *first* three digits of the employee's home telephone number, and h(rec) returns the *last* three digits of the employee's office telephone number.

   a) Which (if any) of these functions would be a good choice for a file containing at most a few hundred records? Explain your answer.

   b) Which (if any) of these functions would be a good choice for a file containing several thousand records? Explain your answer.

7. (UNIX C Shell Tutorial) Change to a new working directory and in that directory create four files named file1.temp, file2.temp, fileA.temp and another.temp. Then execute the indicated UNIX commands and observe the system response to each command.

   a) List all files ending with the suffix .temp.

   b) List all files whose names are of the form fileI.temp, where I is a single character.

   c) Turn off the file name wildcard recognition feature, and verify the corresponding change in the list of C shell variables.

   d) Using the appropriate wildcard character, attempt to list all files ending with the suffix .temp.

   e) Turn on the file name wildcard recognition feature and the file completion feature and verify the corresponding changes in the list of C shell variables.

f) What further specification (if any) is needed to complete the instruction cat f<esc> so as to view the contents of file1.temp?

g) What further specification (if any) is needed to complete the instruction cat fileA<esc> so as to view the contents of fileA.temp?

h) Turn off the file completion feature and verify the corresponding change in the list of C shell variables.

i) Remove all files ending with the suffix .temp.

8. (UNIX C Shell Tutorial) Create a new working directory tempdir and in that directory create two subdirectories named subdir1 and subdir2. Within the first subdirectory create two subsubdirectories named subsubdir1a and subsubdir1b. Return to tempdir and execute the indicated UNIX commands, observing the system response to each command.

a) Create an alias path_stack to show the current directory path and the directory stack.

b) Verify that you are in tempdir and show the directory stack.

c) Push subsubdir1a onto the directory stack and verify the directory and stack changes.

d) Return to tempdir and verify the directory and stack changes.

e) Using the history command, repeat the last commands of parts c) and d).

f) Discard the alias path_stack.

g) Locate the C shell resource file, .cshrc, in your home directory; then view its contents to see how your own personal environment is initialized.

Programming Problems

1. (Nutritional Information Table) Write a program to display, edit, store, and retrieve a summary of nutritional information such as is found on a cereal box. Store all information in a variable that has both string and integer components. Use the following display format:

```
Serving Size: 1 oz.
                                 With 1/2 cup
                     1 oz.        Skim Milk

==============================================
Calories             130          170
Protein                3 g          7 g
Carbohydrates         18 g         24 g
Fat                    6 g          6 g
Cholesterol            0 mg         0 mg
Sodium                15 mg        80 mg
Potassium            135 mg       340 mg
```

2. (Editing Binary Files) Write a program to view, insert, and delete items in a binary file of doubles. Allow command line arguments to specify the input file and the output file, where the output file may be the same as the input file, or may be a different file.

3. (Matrix Operations) This problem continues the matrix editing problem of Chapter 7.

a) Develop a data structure to store the name, dimensions, and data values of a matrix (a two-dimensional array of doubles).

b) Using the data structure of part a), rewrite the functions from the matrix editing problem of Chapter 7.

c) Using the data structures and routines of parts a) and b), write a function, MatrixMult(), to multiply two matrices.

4. (Database Management) Write a program to manage a small database containing names, addresses, and phone numbers. Each record should have fields for first name, middle name, last name, street address, city, state (both city and state names may contain multiple words, as in New York, New York), ZIP code (5 digits or 5 + 4 digits), and telephone (neither ZIP code, area code, nor exchange may begin with the digit 0). Display phone numbers using the format 202/395-3000. Store the database in a binary file. The program should offer a menu having options to insert a record, delete a record, edit one or more records, display all records, sort the records by name, or stop the program. Check for a command line argument specifying the name of the database file.

5. (Hash Sort) Write a program to manage a binary file of at most 100 employee records. Let each record have fields for last name, first name, and identification number (a four-digit integer). Offer options of creating a file of 100 empty records, adding a record, displaying a record, editing a record, and stopping the program.

6. (Game of Life) Write a program to play the game of Life, as described in the Programming Problems of Chapter 7. In this version of the program, rather than using two arrays of numbers, use a single array of `struct` records, with one record per cell. Let each record have two fields: one to indicate the current status of the cell and the other to count the number of live neighbors of that cell. At each transition, completely update the live-neighbor information before updating the current status information.

Chapter

10

Dynamic Memory Management

So far, we have discussed several methods of constructing data structures. These basic building blocks have included arrays, strings, records, and files. This chapter discusses the use of *dynamic memory* to create list-based data structures. Dynamic memory allocation is the ability, within a C program, to request new blocks or chunks of memory at run time rather than at compile time. These new blocks are often in the form of records that are linked together. The UNIX topic of this chapter is shell programming in the C shell, a method of creating command files in the C shell language.

Pointers and `malloc()`

The use of pointers has been discussed in several previous chapters. For example, parameters passed by address to functions are in fact pointers to memory locations. Also, when arrays are declared, the name of an array variable is actually a pointer to (address of) the first entry of the array. Chapter 7 discussed the use of pointer arithmetic in processing arrays, and this same idea was repeated in Chapter 8 in the context of strings.

In all these cases, the memory being referenced by a pointer is allocated when the program is compiled. All memory needed for the execution of a program containing only such variables is known before compilation, since each declared variable has a definite size. Pass-by-value parameters and local variables in functions are also of known size at compile time, but they are handled differently, because a function may be called many times during the execution of a program. Function variables—local variables, pass-by-value parameters, and other space needed by the function—are allocated from an area of memory, known as the *stack,* which is reserved for this purpose.

Dynamic memory, on the other hand, is allocated from an area of memory, known as the *heap,* which is simply a finite supply of memory that can be accessed using the methods we will discuss later. (The term *heap* has another use, referring to a certain kind of binary tree structure; the memory heap is, as its name implies, a "big" chunk of memory.) It is possible to use up all of the stack or heap, since both are of some definite size that is machine-dependent. A program uses stack memory when a function is called, and this memory is released when the function exits. Allocation and deallocation of stack memory is thus automatic. This is not the case for heap memory, and the programmer must carefully manage the allocation and deallocation of heap memory.

Allocating Memory

To use the memory allocation functions described here, <stdlib.h> must be included. To request memory from the heap, the **malloc()** function is used. Its prototype is

```
void *malloc( size_t size );
```

which indicates that a generic pointer is returned to a chunk of memory containing size bytes. Note that the generic pointer value must be typecast to the needed type. The value NULL is returned if the heap is exhausted. For example, the fragment

```
#include <stdlib.h>
    int *ptr;
    ptr = (int *) malloc( sizeof( int ));
```

asks that space for one int value be allocated and that the address of this space be placed in ptr, which is not an int variable but a pointer—that is, an address—to an int. Note the use of the sizeof() function to avoid guessing the number of bytes needed. Before the call to malloc() the statement *ptr = 43; would not be legal, because no space had been allocated yet, but it is legal after the call. The first use of *ptr must be to assign it a value, because the memory allocated by malloc() is not initialized.

It is very important to note the difference between what ptr stores and what it points to. Its value is an address; such physical address values are not important to know, and they change from machine to machine and from execution to execution. The address belongs to an integer; that is, ptr points to another memory location where the integer is stored. Thus, ptr stores the address where the integer is stored.

The related function **calloc()** can also be used for memory allocation. Its prototype is

```
void *calloc( size_t num, size_t size );
```

which asks that num consecutive copies of size bytes be allocated, returning the address of the first copy. The memory allocated by calloc() is initialized to zeros. Thus, the call

```
ptr = (int *) calloc( num, sizeof( int ));
```

is equivalent to

```
ptr = (int *) malloc( num * sizeof( int ));
```

in the amount of space allocated but not in its contents, since `calloc()` places a zero in each allocated memory location. Typically, the `calloc()` function is used to allocate arrays. Like `malloc()`, `calloc()` returns NULL as an error flag.

The function **realloc()** is used to increase or decrease the size of a chunk of memory previously allocated. Its prototype is

```
void *realloc( void *ptr, size_t size );
```

where `ptr` is the address of the old memory chunk (and may be NULL; if so, `realloc()` is the same as a call to `malloc()`) and `size` is the new number of bytes requested. The contents of the old chunk of memory are unchanged. If the new `size` is greater than the size of the existing chunk, the new portion is not initialized. NULL is returned on error. As an example, consider the following fragment:

```
char *str1, *str2;
str1 = (char *) malloc( 4 );
strcpy( str1, "dog" );
str2 = (char *) realloc( str1, 7 );
strcpy( str2, "bigdog" );
```

The second character pointer will now point to the string `"bigdog"`. The first character pointer will probably point to the same string, but if rearrangement of the heap was necessary, this may not be true.

Memory that has been allocated from the heap can be returned to the heap for reuse by using the **free()** function. Its prototype is

```
void free( void *genericptr );
```

where the `genericptr` variable must be of the `void *` type or cast to this type. For example, `free( (void *) ptr );` using the previous definition of `ptr` offers the memory pointed to by `ptr` back to the system.

The functions described in this section are handled in a slightly different manner in Kernighan and Ritchie C, where generic pointers are typed as `char *`. Each allocation function thus returns a pointer to a character. Other details are the same.

Using Pointers

The previous examples have shown some of the usage of pointer variables. The essence is similar to pass-by-address function parameters. Pointers are declared and dereferenced using an asterisk; the variable itself without the asterisk refers to the actual address.

Consider the following fragment, which uses both regular `int` variables and pointers to `int`s:

```
int i,      /* Regular integer        */
    *ptr1,  /* Pointer to an integer */
```

```
  *ptr2;    /* Pointer to an integer */
i = 11;
/* Get space for one integer and assign a value */
ptr1 = (int *) malloc( sizeof( int ));
*ptr1 = 43;
/* Use already allocated space */
ptr2 = &i;
printf( "i, *ptr1, and *ptr2 = %d, %d, %d\n", i, *ptr1, *ptr2 );
```

The output of this fragment is

```
i, *ptr1, and *ptr2 = 11, 43, 11
```

since `ptr1` is directly assigned a value and `ptr2` uses the address of `i` (see Figure 10.1*a*).

What happens if we now write `*ptr2 = -78;`? Because `ptr2` does not refer to a memory location of its own but to `i`'s, there is only one value that changes. The `printf()` statement would now produce

```
i, *ptr1, and *ptr2 = -78, 43, -78
```

As noted earlier, variables such as `ptr1` and `ptr2` store addresses, not integers (See Figure 10.1*b*).

You might be wondering about the utility of this feature. Setting pointers to regular variables is not in itself all that useful, but the same concept, when applied to linked records, is the basis for the linked-list structures discussed in the next sections.

Linked Lists

A *linked list* is a dynamic data structure consisting of records (called list *nodes*) that contain data and are linked to each other by some method. The linking method most often used is pointers (addresses), so each record contains the address of the next node on the list in addition to its regular data. A pointer to the first node in a list, called the *head* of the list, is used as the list's identifier. A linked list grows and shrinks as data (nodes) are added and deleted, allowing the list to accommodate an arbitrary number of elements (see Figure 10.2).

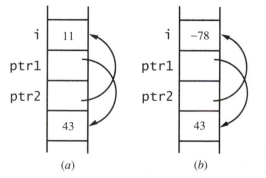

(a)   (b)

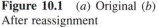

Figure 10.1   (*a*) Original (*b*) After reassignment

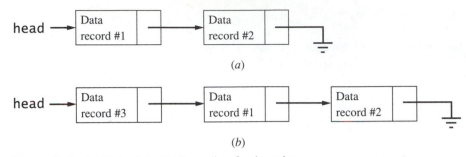

Figure 10.2 (*a*) Linked list (*b*) Same list after insertion

A linked list is a linear data structure. All operations on the list must begin by accessing the first node on the list, then the second node, and so on. Compared to arrays of records, this sequential access is a significant performance drawback. Array elements can be accessed randomly—recall the binary search algorithm, for example. A linked-list element can be accessed only after all preceding nodes have been accessed; this results in slower searching algorithms.

The main advantage of linked lists is their dynamic nature. Using dynamic memory allocation, a list can grow to arbitrary size. New nodes can be added in between existing nodes with a few simple pointer manipulations, and deletions are also easy. Recall that adding a new element to an array or deleting an existing element could cause significant movement of other elements. An array also suffers from being static in size; it is declared, once and for all, to have a maximum number of elements. Even if more elements need to be stored, an array's size cannot be adjusted. Using a linked list, any number of elements can be inserted, as long as the heap has not been exhausted. Thus, linked lists offer a viable alternative to arrays for many applications.

The conceptual view of a linked list is shown in Figure 10.3. Each box represents one list node, containing the appropriate data for the given application. Arrows represent the links, which will be implemented as pointers. The head of the list is itself a pointer to a node. The last node on the list must contain some sort of flag to indicate that there are no other nodes on the list; the diagram uses the "ground" symbol for this.

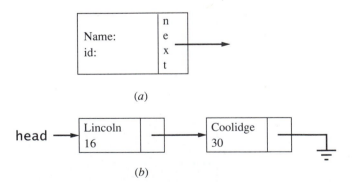

Figure 10.3 (*a*) One node (*b*) Head and list

The operations on linked lists, discussed subsequently in this section, include the following:

- Initialize a list
- Search a list for a node containing a key value
- Create a new node (used when inserting a new node)
- Insert a new node into a list
- Delete an existing node from a list
- Traverse a list (visit each node)

A list may be unsorted, or it may be sorted on a key value; this affects the search operation's implementation. It is a good practice to sketch the conceptual view of each operation even before planning the implementation. Several figures are provided for this purpose.

Once the mechanics of linked lists are mastered, many other related data structures can be designed. Stacks, queues, and a variety of trees are straightforward extensions of linked lists, and some of these are discussed later in this chapter.

Design of Nodes

The data to be stored in a linked-list node depends on the application. A `struct` is used to package the data, as discussed in Chapter 9. In addition, a pointer is needed for each node to link it to its successor. This requires a slightly different approach in defining the list's `struct`. As in most of Chapter 9's examples, we will use a `typedef` to define the record type for a node, but keep in mind that other variations are possible.

Recall that a `struct` definition can include a tagname, which Chapter 9's records did not need. To implement pointers to nodes, however, we need a tagname in order to have a record definition refer to itself. As an example, suppose that we wish to create a linked list of employee last names and integer identification numbers, using these definitions:

```
#define NAMELEN  20                    /* Maximum size of employee last names */
typedef char NameString[ NAMELEN ];  /* String to hold employee last name   */
```

Three fields are needed: the name, the id, and the link field, which we call `next`. (While this is the most common name for the link field, any other name, such as `link` or `successor`, could be used.) The definition

```
typedef struct node {  /* Employee node record:    */
  NameString   name;   /*    last name string      */
  int          id;     /*    identification number */
  struct node *next;   /*    link to next node      */
} EmpRecType;
```

includes these fields. Note the tagname `node` and the way it is used to define the `next` field. The `next` field has to be a pointer to the same type of record in which it occurs. It might seem straightforward to use `EmpRecType` directly, as in `EmpRecType *next;`, but this style is not possible in C, because when `next` is declared, the definition of `EmpRecType` has not yet been completed—the compiler has not even encountered the name yet. Fortunately, when the tagname node is used, struct node is another name for EmpRecType, and the compiler does "know" about it. Thus, struct node * defines next as a pointer to a node of EmpRecType.

If we now declare a variable of this type, as in

```
EmpRecType emprec;
```

storage for one record (including the link field) is created. Recall, though, that the linked list itself is identified by the head of the list, which is a pointer to the first node. The definition

```
EmpRecType *head;    /* Linked-list head pointer */
```

declares such a pointer. Because head is a pointer to a node rather than a node itself, and since we will need other pointer variables, we will use the following style when declaring linked-list node types:

```
typedef struct node {  /* Employee node record:   */
  NameString   name;    /*     last name string    */
  int          id;      /*     identification number */
  struct node *next;    /*     link to next node    */
} EmpRecType, *EmpRecPtr;
```

The type EmpRecPtr is defined here as a pointer to an EmpRecType. The same effect could be achieved by a separate typedef statement, as in

```
typedef EmpRecType *EmpRecPtr;
```

but we will always declare both at once. The declaration of head then becomes

```
EmpRecPtr head;    /* Linked-list head pointer */
```

which has the same effect as the previous version.

Operations on Linked Lists

Each of the operations on linked lists uses the employee node defined in the previous section. Note that there are other useful utility operations on nodes, such as displaying the data stored in a node (excluding the pointer field) and asking a user to fill in the data fields. We will assume that such utility functions exist.

Node Allocation

List nodes are created on demand. When data needs to be inserted, a new list node must be created to hold it. The malloc() function presented earlier is the basis for this allocation. The essential statement is

```
newptr = (EmpRecPtr) malloc( sizeof( EmpRecType ));
```

where `newptr` is of type `EmpRecPtr`. Note the uses of the two types previously defined. `EmpRecPtr` is used to cast the `void *` pointer returned by `malloc()` to the appropriate type, and `EmpRecType` is used as the argument to `sizeof()` to request the number of bytes needed for one list node. A common mistake is to write `sizeof( EmpRecPtr )`, which asks for enough bytes to store a pointer, not an actual node. Provided that `malloc()` does not return NULL, we can now fill the fields of the record pointed to by `newptr`. For example, `newptr->id = 1;` puts the constant 1 into the `id` field of the list node. Typically, a utility function would fill in the data fields.

Even though the foregoing single statement is all that is needed for node allocation, we will package it inside a function call with an error check. The code is

```
EmpRecPtr allocate( void )
{
  EmpRecPtr ptr;    /* Temporary local node pointer */
  /* Request memory from the heap */
  ptr = (EmpRecPtr) malloc( sizeof( EmpRecType ));
  /* Check for error condition */
  if ( ptr == NULL )
    printf( "Error: cannot allocate a new node.\n" );
  return( ptr );
}  /* allocate() */
```

The `allocate()` function checks whether `malloc()` returned NULL to indicate that the heap is empty. The value stored in `ptr`, possibly NULL, is then returned. (Note that an alternative to returning a null pointer would be simply to exit the program.) This function would be called by a sequence such as

```
EmpRecPtr myptr;
myptr = allocate();
```

after which we could again check the value of `myptr` for the NULL value. If non-NULL, the data fields of the list node could now be filled.

Initialization

Since list nodes are created only as needed, the list is initially empty. Initialization of a linked list is simple: Assign the value NULL to the head of the list. This only needs to be done once, and can be done when the head is declared, as in

```
EmpRecPtr head = NULL;
```

or it can be implemented as a function:

```
void initialize( EmpRecPtr *ptr )
{
  *ptr = NULL;
} /* initialize() */
```

which would be called as `initialize( &head )`.

This is the first instance, but not the last, of a sometimes confusing idea. The parameter to `initialize()` is not simply a pointer to an employee node, but is a pointer to the *address* of an employee node. Because of the conventions of pass-by-address parameters, we need to tell `initialize()` where to store the NULL value, and so must pass the address of `head`. The variable `head` *has* an address (where it is stored) and *stores* an address (eventually, the address of the first list node when one is created). Thus, the call `initialize( &head )`; sends &head, a pointer to a pointer, as the argument. A pointer to a pointer is sometimes called a *handle*.

Easy Insertion (Unsorted List)

Recall that a list may be kept in sorted order based on some data field. In that case, inserting a new node requires finding the correct position. This is discussed in a later section. Here, we cover the easier case: insertion into an unsorted list. For an array, such an insertion would be done at the end of the used part of the array, to avoid moving existing elements. Although this could be done for a list, it would require finding the last node, because only the next to the last node "knows" where the last node is (that is, contains a pointer to it); and only the second from the last node knows where the next-to-last node is; and so on. On the other hand, the head of the list points to the first node, so a new node can be inserted at the *front* of the list without any extra work.

In order to insert a node at the beginning of a list, the following steps are performed. A new node is allocated; its data fields are filled; the new node's `next` field is set to point to the first node on the existing list; and the head of the list is reset to point to the new node. The following function, `insert()`, implements these steps.

```
void insert( EmpRecPtr *head, EmpRecType rec ) {
  EmpRecPtr newptr;    /* Pointer to a new node */
  /* Get a new node to store the data */
  newptr = allocate();
  if ( newptr == NULL ) {
    printf( "Error in insert: no node allocated.\n" );
    return;
  } /* if */
  /* Fill the node with data */
  strcpy( newptr->name, rec.name );
  newptr->id = rec.id;
  /* Insert at the front of the list */
  newptr->next = *head;
  *head = newptr;
} /* insert() */
```

Note that because the head of the list is receiving a new value, it is a pass-by-address parameter. The data for the new node is being passed inside `rec`, which is assumed to be filled by the calling function. Figure 10.4*a* shows the list's state after a new node has been allocated and filled with data. Figure 10.4*b* shows the state after `newptr->next` has been assigned the value `head`; that is, both pointers reference the same node. Figure 10.4*c* shows the final state; both `head` and `newptr` now point to the (new) first node of the list.

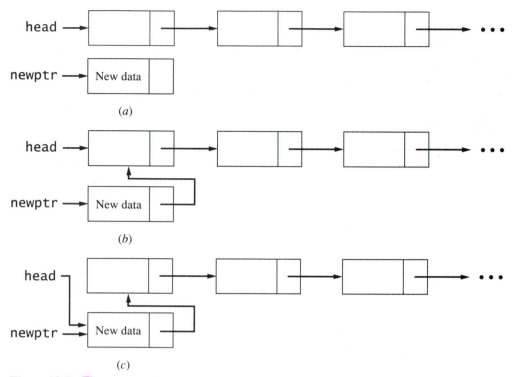

Figure 10.4 Three steps to insert a new node at the front of the list

Two potential problems need to be addressed concerning insert(). First, what if the two pointer assignment statements are interchanged? If *head is reset before its value is copied into newptr->next, we lose any reference to what had been the first node on the list, and therefore to the entire previous list. Only head pointed to this first node, and if we do not copy head before resetting it, it is overwritten. Second, does the function work if the list is empty? This case is often overlooked when writing linked-list code. If the value of *head is NULL, that value is written into newptr->next. This is correct, because we want the list to be NULL-terminated, and the new node is actually the first (and last) node. Also, a new value is correctly written into *head, overwriting the NULL value.

As an example of the usage of insert(), consider the following driver fragment.

```
EmpRecPtr   head;
EmpRecType  rec;
int         flag;
initialize( &head );
flag = ReadRec( &rec );
while ( flag ) {
  insert( &head, rec );
  flag = ReadRec( &rec );
} /* while */
```

We assume that the function ReadRec() either fills rec with data, in which case it returns

true (1), or else it returns false (0) if there is no more data to insert. This data is passed on to
`insert()`, where it is copied into a new node and inserted into the list.

Suppose the fragment above were executed using "`Jones`", 1 and "`Miller`", 2 as input. `head`, after being initialized as NULL, would first point to a node containing "`Jones`", 1 (which would contain NULL in its `next` field), then would point to a node containing "`Miller`", 2, which in turn would point to "`Jones`"'s node; see Figure 10.5.

Traversal

The traversal operation visits each node of a list, processing the data in each node in some way. For simplicity, we will only display the data. The traversal algorithm will use a temporary pointer, which is initialized to point to the first node on the list. After a node is processed, this pointer is reset to point to the next node on the list. This is continued until the end of the list is reached.

```
void traverse( EmpRecPtr head )
{
  EmpRecPtr current;
  /* Initialize to front of list */
  current = head;
  /*  Loop until done */
  while ( current != NULL ) {
    DisplayRec( *current );
    /* Reset current to its successor */
    current = current->next;
  } /* while */
} /*traverse() */
```

The function `DisplayRec()` is assumed to exist and handle the details of displaying the values stored in one node. The statement that resets `current` to point to its successor uses the value stored in `current->next`. Thus, `current` begins by pointing to the list's first node, then to the second node, and so on, "walking" from one node to the next (see

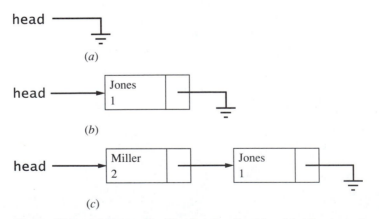

Figure 10.5 (*a*) Empty list (*b*) After first insertion (*c*) After second insertion

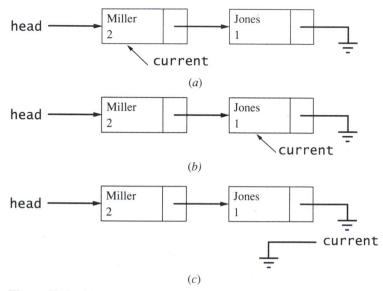

Figure 10.6   (*a*) `current` at head (*b*) `current` moves (*c*) Done

Figure 10.6). The `while` loop quits when NULL is encountered; that is, the list must be properly terminated with a NULL value. If the list is empty, `head` will be NULL, and the loop will not execute at all.

To use this function, we simply call it as `traverse( head )`. For example, this statement could be added to the previous driver fragment, immediately after the `while ( flag )` loop, to inspect the list created by that loop.

Search

The search operation attempts to find the node containing particular data, often one field of the data record, usually the key field (a unique identifier of the record). A search function should then accept as parameters the head of the list and the value being sought. The return value may be either a pointer to the node—assuming that the calling function will use this pointer (possibly NULL if the search was unsuccessful) to access the record—or the data record itself. Also, a list may be unsorted, in which case an unsuccessful search terminates at the end of the list, or sorted, in which case an unsuccessful search on the sort field can stop when the search value's correct position has been passed. The next two sections show functions for searching an unsorted list and a sorted list. The latter is used in a subsequent section on insertion into sorted lists.

Unsorted-List Search

The function `search()`, shown after this paragraph, accepts two parameters: the head of the linked list and the key value to be found. We will use the `id` field for the second parameter. No assumption is made about the ordering of the nodes; the list might as well be unsorted. Searching on the `name` field, however, would require writing another function using string comparisons. `search()` returns a pointer to the node containing `key` if found and NULL otherwise. The code is quite similar to the `traverse()` function, with `current` being advanced one node at a time (see Figure 10.7).

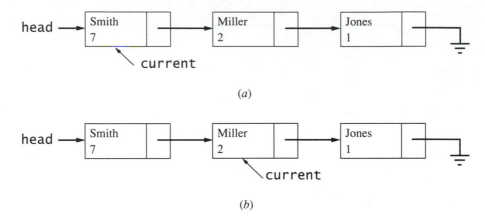

Figure 10.7   (*a*) Search for Smith (*b*) Search for Miller

```
EmpRecPtr   search( EmpRecPtr head, int key ) {
  EmpRecPtr current;
  int       found;
  /*  Start at the beginning of the list, not yet found */
  current = head;
  found   = FALSE;
  /* Loop until found or no more nodes */
  while (( !found ) && ( current != NULL ))
    /* Check current node's id against key */
    if ( current->id == key )
      /* Quit if found */
      found = TRUE;
    else
      /* Move pointer to successor */
      current = current->next;
  /* Return pointer */
  return( current );
}  /* search() */
```

Note that `current` may be NULL at the `return` statement, indicating an unsuccessful search. If the parameter `head` is NULL, so is `current`; the `while` loop's body is not executed, and NULL is returned. The statements

```
myptr = search( head, 2 );
if ( myptr == NULL )
  printf( "Key not found.\n" );
else
  DisplayRec( *myptr );
```

search the list pointed to by **head** for the identification number 2. If found, the node's data is displayed; otherwise, an error message is printed.

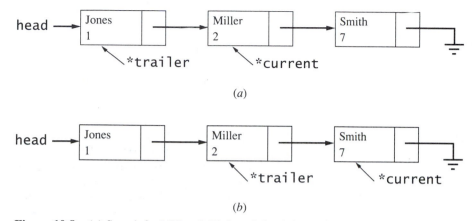

(a)

(b)

Figure 10.8   (a) Search for Miller, 2 (b) Search for Adams, 5

Sorted-List Search

A sorted list is built by repeated insertion. Rather than inserting all nodes and then calling a sort routine, as was done with arrays, each new node is inserted in its proper place. To implement this idea, a function is needed to find that proper place for a given record. The function `bracket()`, given in this section, searches a sorted list for a key value. Unlike `search()`, it returns an `int` used as a flag to indicate the search's result: true if found and false if not. Instead of returning a pointer to a node, two pass-by-address parameters are returned; these point to the node containing the search key and the node directly in front of it in the list, its predecessor. For a successful search, this second pointer is unnecessary. For an unsuccessful search, however, this predecessor pointer is exactly what is needed to find the proper place for the search key. The two returned pointers *bracket* the correct position for insertion of the search key (see Figure 10.8). The additional work needed to implement this search pays off in the simpler insertion function given in the next section.

The two pointer parameters traverse the list, one in front of the other. As nodes are checked for the search key, the trailing pointer is advanced, then the current pointer is advanced. Special consideration is needed at the end of the list traversal to determine why the loop terminated. Also note the use of < in the comparison statement that controls the `while` loop. By using < rather than >, we are assuming the list is kept in ascending order.

```
int bracket( EmpRecPtr head, EmpRecPtr *trailer, EmpRecPtr *current, int key )
{
    /* Note: TRUE and FALSE are assumed to be defined elsewhere */
    int found;  /* Returned flag */
    /* Initialize the trailing pointer to NULL and the current pointer to head */
    *trailer = NULL;
    *current = head;
    /* Loop until end of list or gone too far */
    while (( *current != NULL ) && (( *current )->id < key )){
        /* Advance the pointers */
        *trailer = *current;
        *current = ( *current )->next;
    } /* while */
```

```
      /* Why did the loop quit? */
      if ( *current == NULL ) found = FALSE;
      else if (( *current )->id != key ) found = FALSE;
      else found = TRUE;
      return( found );
} /* bracket() */
```

Note again the use of pass-by-address parameters, where the base type is already a pointer. Care is needed in referencing the nodes pointed to by these pointers; for example, (*current)->id is used to ensure that the dereferencing operator * is evaluated before the arrow operator. The while loop can terminate on two conditions: either the end of the list is found (when *current is NULL), or the position of key has been passed (when the current id is greater than or equal to key). In the latter case, the key may have been found (equal) or not (greater than). These three states are checked after the loop to determine the correct value to return in found. If head is initially NULL, *current will be too, and the loop terminates immediately. The reader should verify that two other special cases (called *boundary conditions*) are handled correctly: first, if key is smaller than any id value in the list, and second, when key is larger than any list value.

The calling function must declare two pointers to be used as arguments matching trailer and current. For example, the fragment

```
EmpRecPtr predecessor, ptr;
int       found;
found = bracket( head, &predecessor, &ptr, 7 );
if ( !found )
  printf( "Key not found\n" );
else
  DisplayRec( *ptr );
```

declares two pointer arguments that match the parameters trailer and current in bracket(). If found is true, the value of predecessor is ignored, but ptr points to the node containing 7. If found is false, note that the values stored in predecessor and ptr may tell where 7 should be stored. Recall that false is returned if, for example, the list is empty, in which case the value of ptr is NULL. Attempting to access node information in such a case is a common source of errors.

Sorted Insertion

As already noted, a sorted linked list is built by inserting new nodes in their correct position. The function bracket() in the previous section was designed for that purpose. When a new key is to be added to the list, bracket() will return the address of the two nodes between which the new key should be inserted. A new node is then created and linked to the preceding and following nodes. Two points must be noted. First, if the new key belongs at the front of the list, the head pointer for the list must be changed. This is also true if the list is initially empty. Second, a policy on duplicate keys must be decided. Since we have assumed previously that "key" means a unique identifier for a record, we do not allow duplicates. The code in this section can be changed easily to accommodate duplicates.

The function SortedInsert() has a prototype similar to the insert() function used earlier for insertions at the front of a linked list. The information to be inserted is stored in rec

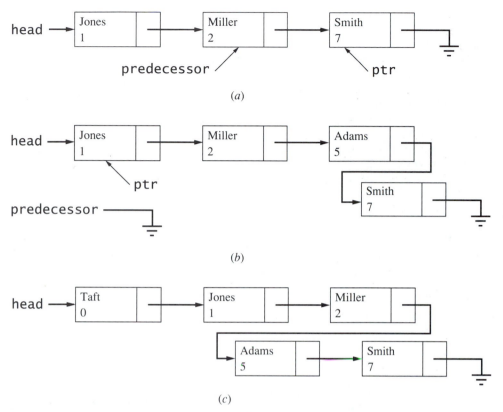

Figure 10.9   (*a*) Insert Adams, 5 (*b*) Insert Taft, 0 (*c*) Final list

and must be copied into a new node. The pointer to the first node, **head**, is passed by address, because its value may be updated. The **bracket()** function does most of the work, traversing the list to find the correct position. The value of **predecessor** returned from **bracket()**, if NULL, indicates that the new information belongs at the front of the list; see Figure 10.9.

```
void SortedInsert( EmpRecPtr *head, EmpRecType rec ) {
  EmpRecPtr newptr;             /* Pointer to a new node  */
  EmpRecPtr predecessor, ptr;   /* Needed for the search  */
  int       found;              /* Flag for search        */
  /* Search for the key */
  found = bracket( *head, &predecessor, &ptr, rec.id );
  /* Check for duplicate key */
  if ( found )
    printf( "Error: duplicate key.\n" );
  else {
    /* Get a new node to store the data */
    newptr = allocate();
    if ( newptr == NULL ) {
      printf( "Error in insert: no node allocated.\n" );
      return;
    } /* if */
```

```
/* Fill the node with data */
strcpy( newptr->name, rec.name );
newptr->id = rec.id;
/* Check whether the insertion is at the front of the list */
if ( predecessor == NULL ) {
  newptr->next = *head;
  *head = newptr;
} /* if predecessor is NULL */
else {
  predecessor->next = newptr;
  newptr->next = ptr;
}  /* else predecessor is not NULL */
} /* else not found */
}  /* SortedInsert() */
```

In comparing `SortedInsert()` with the `insert()` function discussed earlier, note that the last `if` clause inserts the new node at the front of the list as was the case in `insert()`. The last `else` clause handles insertion in the middle or at the end of the list. The reader should verify that the code is correct in the case of a key that belongs at the end of the list. To call `SortedInsert()`, the fragment that illustrated the use of `insert()` can be modified to call `SortedInsert()` instead of `insert()`.

Deletion

The problem of deleting a node with a given key, like inserting a new node, involves two steps: finding the node, then changing pointers in the list to skip the node. Additionally, the deleted node's memory can be given back to the system using the `free()` function. If the list is sorted, we can use the `bracket()` function, since we need not only a pointer to the node to be deleted but also a pointer to the preceding node. These are needed to accomplish the pointer reassignment (see Figure 10.10). If the list is not sorted, then a function similar

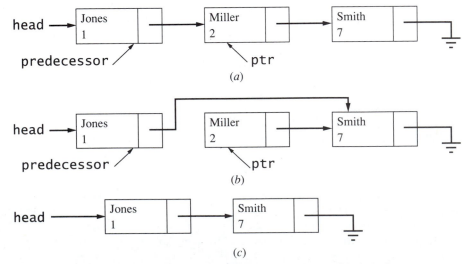

Figure 10.10   (a) Find Miller, 2 (b) Delete Miller, 2 (c) Free Miller's node

to `bracket()` is needed to search the unsorted list and return both necessary pointers. We show only the sorted version here.

In the following `SortedDelete()` function, note the check on the flag returned by `bracket()`; false here indicates an error. Also, a special case is used to handle deleting the first node on the list.

```
void SortedDelete( EmpRecPtr *head, EmpRecType rec ) {
  EmpRecPtr predecessor, ptr;  /* Needed for the search */
  int       found;             /* Flag for search       */
  /* Search for the key */
  found = bracket( *head, &predecessor, &ptr, rec.id );
  /* Check if found */
  if ( !found )
    printf( "Error: key not found, cannot delete.\n" );
  else {
    /* Check if the deletion is at the front of the list */
    if ( predecessor == NULL )
      *head = ptr->next;
    else
      predecessor->next = ptr->next;
    /* Give the node back to the system */
    free( (void *) ptr );
  } /* else not found */
}/*   SortedDelete() */
```

If the first node is deleted, the head of the list must be reset; thus, the list's head is a pass-by-address parameter. The following fragment illustrates a call to `SortedDelete()`.

```
EmpRecType rec;
flag = ReadRec( &rec );
if ( flag )
  SortedDelete( &head, rec );
```

The fragment assumes that `head` has been properly initialized.

An Example

To pull together the functions discussed in this chapter so far, the following outline of a driver program is provided. You can fill in the details as needed. The program allows a user to add, delete, modify, and find single employee records and to print the entire linked list of employees. The program uses the sorted versions of insert and delete.

```
/* Sketch of a driver program; many details are omitted. */
main() {
  EmpRecPtr  head;
  EmpRecPtr  predecessor, ptr;
  EmpRecType rec;
```

```
        int         key, choice,
                    found;
    initialize( &head );
    choice = getchoice();
    while ( choice != QUIT ) {
      /* Choose the appropriate action */
      switch ( choice ) {
        /* Get employee record from the user and insert it */
        case ADD:    ReadRec( &rec );
                     SortedInsert( &head, rec );
                     break;
        /* Get employee record from the user and delete it */
        case DELETE: ReadRec( &rec );
                     SortedDelete( &head, rec );
                     break;
        /* Get employee key from the user, find record, and display it */
        case FIND:   key = ReadKey();
                     found = bracket( head, &predecessor, &ptr, key );
                     if ( found )
                       DisplayRec( *ptr );
                     else
                       printf( "Key not found.\n" );
                     break;
        /* Show all employee records */
        case PRINT:  traverse( head );
                     break;
        /* Find record and change it */
        case MODIFY: /* Left to the reader */
                     break;
        default:     printf( "Incorrect choice, try again.\n" );
                     break;
      }   /* switch choice */
      choice = getchoice();
    }  /* while choice */
}/* main program */
```

Each **case** has one or more operations to perform, so a separate function for each would be more appropriate. For the MODIFY option, one possible sequence of operations is

- Ask for a key.
- Find the node.
- Display the record.
- Ask the user for modification.
- If there are no changes, quit, else delete the old node and insert the new (modified) node.

Deletion followed by reinsertion allows the key field id to be changed, and this affects the placement of the modified node in the sorted list.

Array Implementation

The linked lists discussed so far have used the heap for space to allocate new nodes. It is possible to implement linked lists by simulating the heap with a user-declared array. To do this, an address is interpreted as an array index, and management of the free and used nodes is done manually. This section briefly discusses the implementation of linked lists using arrays and provides good practice.

The following record declaration is needed before the declaration of the linked-list array.

```
typedef struct {        /* Employee record:         */
  NameString   name;    /*    last name string      */
  int          id;      /*    identification number */
  int          next;    /*    link to next node     */
} EmpRecType;
```

The `next` field is of type `int`, because it references another array position. The declaration of the linked-list type is

```
#define MAXSIZE 100                 /* List array size */
typedef EmpRecType listtype[ MAXSIZE ];   /* List array type */
listtype list;                      /* List array      */
int head;                           /* List head       */
```

The variable `head` stores the index of the first list node. It is initialized to a null value, as in

```
#define MYNULL -1
head = MYNULL;
```

The constant `NULL` cannot be used here because its value is zero, which is a valid array index.

Nodes on the list may be referred to by index number, but they must be dereferenced using array notation rather than `->` notation. For example, if `head` is not equal to `MYNULL`, then `list[ head ].name` and `list[ head ].id` are the two data fields of the first list node.

The operations on linked lists can now be implemented. For example, allocation of new nodes involves finding an unused spot in the array. Insertion at the front of the list is very similar to the pointer version of this operation. The essential step (see Figure 10.11),

```
list[ newptr ].next = *head;
*head = newptr;
```

links the new node to the list and assumes that `head` is passed by address. Other operations must be adjusted in a similar manner.

Using Linked Lists

Once the basic linked-list operations have been implemented, lists can be used to build other logical data structures. We outline two such structures: stacks and queues.

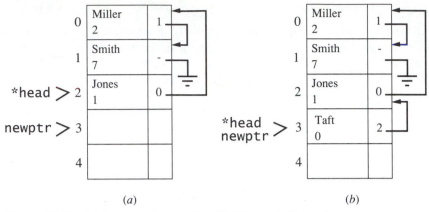

(a) (b)

Figure 10.11   (*a*) Array implementation (*b*) New node inserted

Stacks

A *stack* is sometimes called a last-in, first-out list. When an item is inserted on a stack (called the *push* operation), it is placed at the front of the list. To delete an item (called the *pop* operation), the first node is removed from the list. A stack is useful when trying to remember what path was taken to get to some point.

For example, consider the problem of evaluating a postfix numeric expression. In postfix expressions, the operator follows its operands, as in 4 5 * 3 +. This expression is equivalent to the infix expression 4 * 5 + 3, which equals 23. A simple algorithm using a stack of operands to evaluate postfix expressions is this: When an operand is encountered, it is pushed on the stack. When an operator is evaluated, two operands are popped from the stack, the operator is applied to them, and the result is pushed on the stack. At the end, the final answer is popped from the stack. For the postfix expression given here, the following sequence would occur:

- Push 4.
- Push 5.
- Pop 5 and pop 4, multiply them, and push 20.
- Push 3.
- Pop 3 and pop 20, add them, and push 23.
- Pop the final answer, 23.

See Figure 10.12.

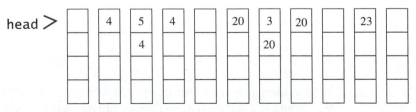

Figure 10.12   Results of stack `push` and `pop` operations

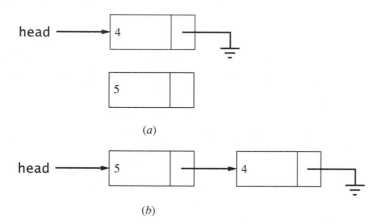

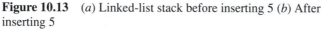

Figure 10.13   (*a*) Linked-list stack before inserting 5 (*b*) After inserting 5

To implement this, we define the following linked-list node type.

```
typedef struct node {     /* Nodes for postfix evaluation: */
  int operand;            /* Only integers for simplicity  */
  struct node *next;      /* Link field                    */
} PostfixRec, *PostfixPtr;
```

The definition of the stack is given by

```
PostfixPtr head;
```

We will assume that the linked-list functions developed for employee records have been modified to accept `PostfixRec` and `PostfixPtr` types. The push operation can then be implemented as

```
void push( PostfixPtr *head, int op )
{
  insert( head, op );
}   /* push() */
```

which is the version that inserts at the front of a list. Figure 10.13 illustrates the push operation.

The pop operation is next:

```
int pop( PostfixPtr *head )
{
  int value = 0;
  if ( isempty( head ))
    printf( "Error: stack is empty.\n" );
  else {
    value = ( *head )->operand;
    *head = ( *head )->next;
  } /* else not empty */
```

```
    return( value );
}   /* pop() */
```

Incorrect postfix expressions may cause the stack to become empty when it should contain an operand; thus the need for the isempty() check, which can be implemented as

```
int isempty( PostfixPtr head )
{
  int value = 0;   /* Return value; default is false */
  /* Check if list is empty */
  if ( head == NULL )
    value = 1;
  return( value );
}   /* isempty() */
```

This function returns true if the list's head is NULL and false otherwise.

Given these definitions of push and pop, we leave it to you to construct the complete postfix evaluation program.

Queues

A *queue,* sometimes called a first-in, first-out list, is fair in the way items are processed. Insertion of a new item is done at the end of the list, but deletion is done at the front, thus simulating a waiting line at a bank: The first item in line gets serviced first.

As an example, suppose we need to keep a queue of employees who have requested use of the university condo, which is shared on a first-come, first-served basis. The definition of the queue type and declaration of an associated variable are shown next:

```
typedef struct {     /* Employee record queue:      */
  EmpRecPtr head,     /* Points to first queue node */
            tail;     /* Points to last queue node  */
  int       count;    /* Number of queued nodes      */
} QueueType, *QueuePtr;
QueueType queue;       /* Queue declaration */
```

The head field is the pointer to the first node of the linked list, while tail points to the last node. When the queue is empty, both of these are NULL. For convenience, the count field is used to keep track of the number of waiting employees. Figure 10.14 shows a queue containing several employee nodes.

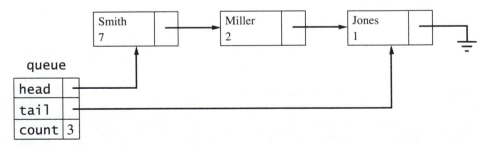
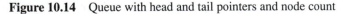

Figure 10.14   Queue with head and tail pointers and node count

Inserting a node on a queue is done as follows. Insertion is always done at the end of the list, which is pointed to by `tail`:

```
void enqueue( QueuePtr queue, EmpRecType rec )
{
  EmpRecPtr newnode;
  /* Allocate space and fill it */
  newnode = allocate();
  strcpy( newnode->name, rec.name );
  newnode->id = rec.id;
  /* If the queue is empty, the head pointer must be set */
  if ( queue->head == NULL )
    queue->head = newnode;
  else
    /* Else link the last node to the new node */
    queue->tail->next = newnode;
  /* Tail pointer points to new node */
  queue->tail = newnode;  /* There are now two pointers to newnode */
  /* Update the count */
  queue->count++;
} /* enqueue() */
```

The `enqueue()` function assumes that the three fields of `queue` have been properly initialized. An example call is

```
EmpRecType rec;
ReadRec( &rec );
enqueue( &queue, rec );
```

The complementary function `dequeue()` returns a pointer to an employee record or `NULL`; its prototype is

```
EmpRecPtr dequeue( QueuePtr queue );
```

which is called as

```
ptr = dequeue( &queue );
```

Another useful function is `numqueue()`, which returns the number of nodes on the queue. These functions are left to the reader.

Other Dynamic Structures

There are many variations on the linked-list theme. Two are discussed in the following sections: doubly linked lists and binary search trees. Each one keeps two pointer fields per node. Doubly linked lists use the extra pointer to link to the predecessor node, whereas a binary tree node uses its pointers to link to two successor nodes.

Doubly Linked Lists

As the name implies, a *doubly linked list* has two sets of links: one pointing forward and the other backward. In this way, traversals in either direction are possible from any starting point. While some extra processing is needed to maintain the new links, insertions and deletions are easier to code.

The definition of a node for a doubly linked list is

```
typedef struct node {  /* Employee node record:    */
   NameString   name;    /*     last name string       */
   int          id;      /*     identification number */
   struct node *next,    /*     link to next node      */
               *prev;    /*     link to previous node */
} EmpRecType, *EmpRecPtr;
```

The only change from the previous definition of `EmpRecType` is the addition of the `prev` field. This is set to `NULL` for the first node on the list, just like the last node's `next` field.

Operations on doubly linked lists are quite similar to those on singly linked lists, but the `prev` field must additionally be maintained. For example, to insert a new node, four pointers, rather than two, must be changed (see Figure 10.15). For a sorted doubly linked list, finding the place to do an insertion or deletion is simpler than the `bracket()` function used earlier. A search function need only return one pointer; the `next` and `prev` fields of that node point to the needed neighbors.

Trees

A *tree* is a hierarchical data structure. The *root* node acts like the head of a linked list. A binary tree allows for two *child* nodes of each *parent*. A parent may point to zero, one, or two child nodes, which in turn may act like parent nodes and point to their own children. As shown in Figure 10.16, the terminating nodes, called *leaf* nodes, contain two `NULL` pointers.

The nodes of a tree may be organized according to various rules applied to the data they store. For example, the *heap* rule requires that a parent's key value be greater than that of either child's key value. (Note that this usage of the term *heap* is different from our previous usage.) Applied to all tree nodes, the resulting heap's root node contains the largest key in the tree.

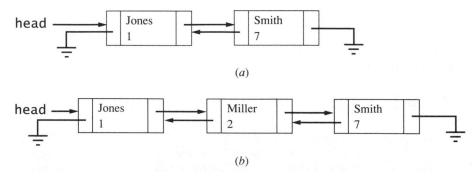

Figure 10.15   (*a*) Doubly linked list (*b*) After inserting Miller, 2

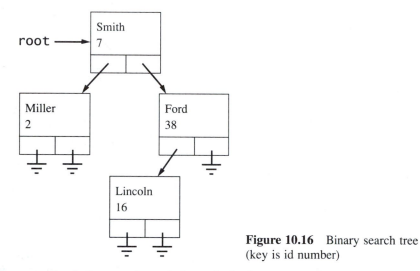

root

Figure 10.16   Binary search tree
(key is id number)

The examples below use the ordering rule for *binary search* trees: The key value of the left child is smaller than the parent's key, and the key value of the right child is greater than the parent's key (as in the tree of Figure 10.16). This rule results in the smallest key in the leftmost leaf. More importantly, it provides a fast search strategy: To find a key, compare it to the current node, starting with the root. If equal, the search is successful; if the key is smaller than the current node's key, make the left child the current node, else make the right child the current node. Unsuccessful searches terminate at a NULL pointer.

The definition of a tree node using employee information is

```
typedef struct node {  /* Tree node record:          */
   NameString    name;  /*    last name string         */
   int           id;    /*    identification number    */
   struct node   *left, /*    link to left child       */
                 *right; /*   link to right child       */
} TreeNode, *TreePtr
```

and the root pointer is declared as `TreePtr root;` and set to NULL initially. Insertions are always done at the bottom of the tree, and both `left` and `right` of a new node are set to NULL.

The search function applies the less-than-left, greater-than-right rule and assumes no duplicates.

```
TreePtr search( TreePtr root, TreeNode rec ) {
   TreePtr current; /* Needed for traversal */
   int     found;   /* Search flag          */
   /* Initialization */
   found = FALSE;
   current = root;
   /* Search until found or NULL is encountered */
   while (( current != NULL ) && ( !found )) {
      if ( rec.id == current->id )
         /* Found: set flag to quit loop */
         found = TRUE;
```

```
      else if ( rec.id < current->id )
        /* Move to the left child */
        current = current->left;
      else
        /* Move to the right child */
        current = current->right;
    }  /* while */
    /* Return either NULL or pointer to correct node */
    return( current );
  }  /* search() */
```

This function is called as

```
ptr = search( head, rec );
```

assuming that the proper declarations have been made.

Searching for a key in a binary search tree is very similar to a binary search of a sorted array. At each step, the `current` pointer is moved to the left or right child, depending on the comparison of the search key and the current node's key. This rules out about half of the remaining nodes from consideration. However, "about half" is not a guarantee of half at each step, which a binary search of an array *does* guarantee. If the tree is unbalanced, then significantly less than half of the remaining nodes may be eliminated. In fact, in the worst case, a binary search tree can degenerate into a linked list, which occurs when the keys to be inserted are already in sorted order. Only if the root is the median of the keys will the left half and the right half of the tree be balanced. Applying this rule recursively to each node ensures a completely balanced tree. Keys are usually encountered and inserted in random order, so binary search trees are rarely balanced.

Insertions are done at the bottom of the tree, either under a leaf node (with two NULL pointers) or a node with just one NULL pointer. Note that an unsuccessful search returns NULL. This is not helpful when searching for the correct node under which to insert a new node. A different algorithm, similar to the `bracket()` function for linked lists, is needed to return a pointer to the correct node, which will be the parent of the new node. The following `insert()` function implements this specialized search (see Figure 10.17):

```
void insert( TreePtr *root, TreeNode rec ) {
  TreePtr current,  /* Search pointer to traverse tree    */
          prev,     /* Pointer to trail the search pointer */
          newnode;  /* New tree node                       */
  /* Allocate new tree node and fill its fields */
  newnode = allocate();   /* This function must be defined externally */
  strcpy( newnode->name, rec.name );
  newnode->id    = rec.id;
  newnode->left  = NULL;
  newnode->right = NULL;
  /* Is this the first node? */
  if ( *root == NULL )
    /* If yes, make the new node the root */
    root = newnode;
```

```
else {
  /* Otherwise, search for the key to bottom of tree */
  /* Initialize the search and trailing pointers.    */
  current = root;
  prev    = NULL;
  /* Loop until leaf node is found */
  while ( current != NULL ) {
    /* Move the trailer up to the current position */
    prev = current;
    /* Use search rule to decide which way to move */
    if ( rec.id < current->id )
      current = current->left;
    else
      current = current->right;
  } /* while current != NULL */
  /* On which side should the new node be inserted? */
  if ( rec.id < prev->id )
    /* If new key is less than prev key, insert as left child */
    prev->left = newnode;
  else
    /* Otherwise, insert as right child */
    prev->right = newnode;
} /* else root not null */
} /* insert() */
```

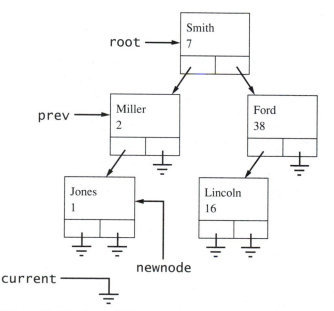

Figure 10.17   Tree of Figure 10.16 after inserting Jones, 1.
Note that current is NULL, whereas prev points to the parent
of the new node

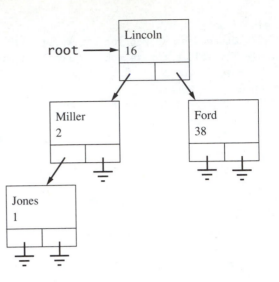

Figure 10.18 Tree of Figure 10.17 after deleting Smith, 7 and promoting Lincoln, 16

The `allocate()` function, not shown, uses `malloc()` to get the address of a tree node–sized memory chunk. As previously noted, there is no guarantee that multiple insertions will leave the tree balanced. There exist variants of binary search trees, such as AVL trees, that maintain balance at the price of extra tree maintenance; see [Sedgewick] for further details.

Deleting a tree node is easy if the node is a leaf node, because only one pointer (the leaf's parent) needs to be changed. For an internal node, things are made simpler by the following observation: The successor of any given key is located by moving to the right child, then following left pointers as far as possible. When the successor is a leaf, the successor key can be copied into the given key's node, and the leaf can be deleted. When the successor is not a leaf, the situation is more complicated; the reader should think through a solution for this case; see Figure 10.18.

Tree traversal can be done according to any of several visitation strategies. For example, a *breadth-first* traversal visits the nodes level by level: the root first, then all of the root's children, then the root's grandchildren, and so on. The most common traversal for a binary search tree is the *inorder* traversal, which visits the nodes in sorted order on the key values. This is most easily accomplished (although not necessarily in the most efficient manner) by using a recursive strategy: For each node, visit (display) its left child first, visit the current node, then visit the right child. (Chapter 13 covers recursion in more detail and discusses other kinds of tree traversals.)

The following function implements the inorder traversal strategy as a recursive function.

```
void inorder( TreePtr ptr ) {
    /* Base case: do nothing if null */
    if ( ptr == NULL ) return;
    else {
        /* Visit the left child first */
        inorder( ptr->left );
        /* Visit the current node */
        DisplayRec( *ptr );
        /* Visit the right child last */
```

```
      inorder( ptr->right );
      return;
   } /* else not NULL */
} /* inorder() */
```

Note that the two `return` statements have been added for clarity; a shorter implementation is achieved by changing the first line to `if ( ptr != NULL )` and omitting both `return` statements. The function is called as `inorder( head );` and works correctly even if `head` is NULL. The inefficiency results in the many calls to `inorder()` using new values of the parameter `ptr`. Figure 10.19 shows a small example of `inorder()` operation.

Shell Scripts

Shell scripts are the batch programs of UNIX. A script contains shell commands, some of which have been discussed in earlier chapters, and other commands that implement control constructs similar to those of a programming language. Scripts are not compiled, however. A script is executed line by line by the shell. A script is usually stored in a file (which must be executable) but can be a series of commands typed at the command prompt. A script is used in place of a C program in order to make the use of UNIX commands easier, to help improve the user interface (in the same style as `alias` commands do), and to write small, quick programs to decrease development time.

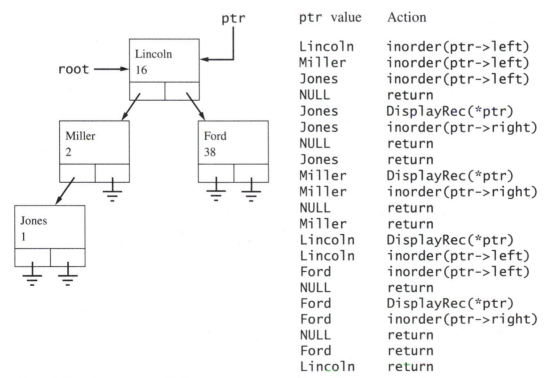

ptr value	Action
Lincoln	inorder(ptr->left)
Miller	inorder(ptr->left)
Jones	inorder(ptr->left)
NULL	return
Jones	DisplayRec(*ptr)
Jones	inorder(ptr->right)
NULL	return
Jones	return
Miller	DisplayRec(*ptr)
Miller	inorder(ptr->right)
NULL	return
Miller	return
Lincoln	DisplayRec(*ptr)
Lincoln	inorder(ptr->left)
Ford	inorder(ptr->left)
NULL	return
Ford	DisplayRec(*ptr)
Ford	inorder(ptr->right)
NULL	return
Ford	return
Lincoln	return

Figure 10.19   Inorder traversal, showing recursive function calls and parameter values

Script files are created with an editor. They must be executable, which means that their permissions must be changed manually. The command `chmod +x` *filename* adds permission to execute *filename* for the user, group, and world, for example, while `chmod u+x` *filename* adds execution privileges only for the owner (user). A script is executed by typing *filename,* perhaps with command line parameters.

C Shell, Bourne Shell, Korn Shell

Recall that there are several shells in use on UNIX systems. We have focused on the C shell and will continue to do so. The shell commands for the Bourne shell are different in syntax from the C sheil, but in general every C shell command has an analog in the Bourne shell. Since the Korn shell was designed to combine the best of the Bourne and C shells, scripts for the Korn shell have similarities to both. For more details on the other shells, see [Abrahams and Larson].

The following sections describe the basic elements of C shell scripts. While some of the C shell commands from earlier chapters are explained here, it is assumed that the reader can recall the usage of the others.

C Shell Script Format

A C shell script *must* begin with the line

```
#!/bin/csh
```

to signal that its contents are to be interpreted by the shell. By default, the shell reads your `.cshrc` file before executing the commands in the file. If the optional `-f` flag appears on that first line, the `.cshrc` file is not read. The symbol # normally signals the start of a comment; comments are terminated by the end of the line. Blank lines are allowed for spacing. Semicolons are not needed to terminate lines, but may be used to separate two commands placed on the same line. There is no begin-end pairing needed to enclose a script (although some control statements use such enclosures).

Any C shell command may be used in a script. For example, suppose the script

```
#!/bin/csh -f
ls -l
```

was stored in `myfile` (we will use this file name for our script examples and assume it has execution permission). Typing `myfile` on the command line has the same effect as typing `ls -l` alone. A simple script like this one is better implemented by the `alias` command, but shell scripts can be used like an `alias` for complex commands. A script is a better choice than an `alias` when input is needed, either from the command line or from a file, or when some programming is involved.

Scripts can be difficult to debug. It is a good idea to write scripts incrementally. During development, the `-v` (for verbose mode, which displays each line before execution) and `-x` (for expanded mode, which displays each line with variables' values before execution) flags can be used. The first script line is then

```
#!/bin/csh -vx
```

In addition, liberal use of `echo` statements (see the following discussion) to print the values of variables is encouraged. Error messages during script execution are cryptic and not always helpful.

Variables, Assignment, and Retrieval

Shell variables are arrays of strings. They are given values with the **set** command, as in `set mydir = '~user1'`. Recall that shell variable values are extracted using the dollar sign operator, as in `set mydir = $HOME`. Note the space on each side of the equal sign. While it is legal to omit both spaces, it is not legal to omit only one. There are other places where a space is required, so our `set` expressions will use the extra spaces. If the string value contains blanks, the words that constitute the string may be referenced individually. For example, the command `set myvar = '~user1 ~user2 ~user3'` stores `~user1` in `myvar[1]` (note the lack of spaces around 1), `~user2` in `myvar[2]`, and `~user3` in `myvar[3]`. Parentheses are used to concatenate strings, so a similar effect is achieved by either of the statements `set myvar = ('~user1' '~user2' '~user3')` or `set var1 = '~user1'; set myvar = ($var1 '~user2' '~user3')`.

Without array syntax, a variable references the entire string; `myvar` holds all of `~user1 ~user2 ~user3`, for example. Also, ranges may be specified, as in `myvar[2-3]`, which has the value `~user2 ~user3`. The expression `$#myvar` (note the use of the # here) holds the number of elements of the string array.

Command line arguments are stored in the system variable **argv**. The name of the script is stored in `argv[0]`, which cannot be accessed (but see below). The first command line parameter is stored in `argv[1]`, the second in `argv[2]`, and so on, and `$#argv` stores the number of command line arguments. For example,

```
myfile first second third
```

would result in `first` stored in `argv[1]`, `second` in `argv[2]`, `third` in `argv[3]`, and 3 in `#argv` (the count excludes the script name). The shortcut variables `$1`, `$2`, ... are equivalent to `$argv[1]`, `$argv[2]`, and so on. Additionally, the variable `$0` contains the script name and can be accessed, unlike `$argv[0]`.

Integer constant values may be assigned to variables using the @ sign in place of `set`. For example, `@ x = 2` stores the value 2 into x. The space after @ is required. Integer values contained in other variables are assigned using `set`, however, as in

```
@ x = 2
set y = x
```

Furthermore, to apply a numeric operator to a variable's value, the @ symbol is used in conjunction with any C language numeric operator. For example, the statement `@ x++` increments x to 3. However, note that the * symbol is treated as a metacharacter, and that / is used for integer division.

Input and Output

Input from the keyboard may be captured by the `$<` command. For example, `set myvar = $<` waits for a line of user input. Of course, user keyboard input should be prompted. The **echo** command displays information on the screen. Thus, the fragment

```
echo Enter a filename:
set myvar = $<
echo Your filename is $myvar
```

displays a prompt, waits for input, then displays the string entered by the user. Note the use of the dollar sign to retrieve the contents of the variable `myvar`. Without it, the word `myvar` would be printed literally. The use of quotes is optional but desirable. The prompt could be written `echo 'Enter a filename:'` or `echo "Enter a filename:"`. Single quotes prevent the shell from evaluating any metacharacters inside the string; double quotes only group the characters as a string but provide no metacharacter protection. Consider the fragment

```
set myvar = 'prog1.c'
echo 'myvar = ' $myvar
echo 'myvar = $myvar'
echo "myvar = $myvar"
```

The output produced by this fragment is

```
myvar =  prog1.c
myvar = $myvar
myvar = prog1.c
```

since the first `echo` does not include `$myvar` in the literal string, the second does (and protects the dollar sign from evaluation), and the third does (but does not protect the dollar sign).

To produce a blank line of output, use the command `echo ''`. The `echo` command may take the `-n` flag, which prevents a newline. Thus,

```
echo -n 'Enter a filename: '
set myvar = $<
```

would show the prompt and leave the cursor on the same line to await input.

Input and output may be redirected using the <, >, and >> symbols. For example, the command

```
echo 'Your filename is ' $myvar >  outfile
```

prints to the file `outfile` rather than the screen.

The output of UNIX or C shell commands may be captured in a variable using back quotes (grave accents on some screens), illustrated by this example: `set myvar = 'date'`. After this command, the contents of `myvar` would be the date string normally displayed on the screen by `date`.

Control Flow

The flow of execution through a C shell script is controlled by two branching constructs, `if` and `switch`, and two looping constructs, `while` and **foreach**. These constructs are patterned on their C language counterparts but conform to a different set of syntax rules.

Boolean conditions are tested by the C operators. The value 0 stands for false and 1 for true. Comparisons are done using ==, !=, >, and so on. Compound conditions are constructed using &&, | |, and ! operators.

The `if` and `switch` Statements

The `if` statement has three formats, each of which tests a boolean condition:

1. A simple `if` does not use the word `then` and allows only one command after it. For example, the statement

```
if ($#argv == 1) exit
```

   shows the usage of simple `if`. The **exit** statement, similar to the C `exit()` function, is executed only if there is only one command line argument.
2. In the second variation, which executes more than one command when the condition is true, `then` and **endif** must enclose the commands. For example,

```
if ($#argv == 1) then
  echo 'Error on the command line'
  exit
endif
```

   displays an error message before exiting. Indentation is optional but suggested for readability.
3. An `else` clause, the third variation, allows for multiple commands to be executed when the condition is false. For example,

```
if ($#argv == 1) then
  echo 'Error on the command line'
  exit
else
  set filename = $argv[1]
  echo 'Processing file' $argv[1]
endif
```

   shows the usage of the `else` clause. Note that only one `endif` is needed. Multiple `if`—`then`—`else` statements may be nested to handle several cases, provided each `if` statement is paired with an `endif`.

The `switch` statement is logically equivalent to multiple `if` statements. Unlike its C counterpart, the shell's `switch` may be matched to any string constants and variables, not merely to integers and single characters, in the various `case` categories. Each `case` may contain several commands, with each section terminated by the statement **breaksw**. One `default` statement is allowed, also ended by `breaksw`. An unusual syntax requirement is that the `case` and `default` statements themselves must be on separate lines. The entire `switch` is terminated by **endsw**. The following example, which implements a simple form of command aliasing, illustrates the syntax:

```
echo -n 'Enter a command:'
set cmd = $<
switch ( $cmd )
```

```
        case dir:
                ls -l | more
                echo ''
                breaksw
        case where:
                pwd
                echo ''
                breaksw
        case self:
                whoami | finger
                echo ''
                breaksw
        default:
                echo ''
                echo 'No alias for command ' $cmd
                breaksw
    endsw
```

Note that each command group begins on a new line after the `case` command. Each `case` argument is a string and could be enclosed in either single or double quotes, as in `case 'dir':`.

The `while` and `for` Loops

The `while` loop is a general-purpose looping construct. The format is `while` (*condition*) *commands end*, where the commands are executed as long as *condition* is true. For example, suppose that a script expects arguments to be entered on the command line. The following code outline shows how to process those arguments one at a time:

```
#!/bin/csh
set numargs = $#argv
@ num = 1
while ( $num <= $numargs )
  switch ( $argv[$num] )
    case x:
            (some code here)
            breaksw
    case y:
            (some code here)
            breaksw
    case z:
            (and so on)
            breaksw
    default:
            breaksw
  endsw
  @ num++
end
```

This fragment uses a counter variable, num, to count from 1 to the number of command line arguments, which is stored in numargs for convenience. As with C language while loops, the loop condition must have the chance to change within the loop body to avoid infinite looping.

The foreach is not usually used for counting, but it is used to step through arrays and lists of values. Its syntax is foreach *variable* (*list of values*) *commands end*, where the *variable* takes on each of the values in the list, one at a time, and the *commands* in the loop body are executed. The number of repetitions depends on the size of the list, which is often a string array.

For example, consider the following script:

```csh
#!/bin/csh
set filelist = 'ls'
foreach filename ( $filelist )
  echo $filename
  more $filename
  echo ''
end
```

The string filelist captures the listing of the current directory. The loop variable filename is set in turn to each file in the current directory. The loop body displays the filename and the contents of each file. If the current directory contains the files prog.c and prog.h, then filelist contains both names, and filename is set to each of these names in succession. Literal lists are possible, as in foreach name (Biff Moe Boopsy)..., where name is assigned the literal Biff first, Moe second, and so on. Note that commas are not used to separate the literals.

Other C Shell Commands

There are many other commands in the C shell language. This section describes a few other useful commands.

The exit command has already been used in the preceding section. Its execution causes the script to end. An optional parameter may be used with exit, as in exit 0. Recall that the C function exit() takes an integer parameter. In both cases, this parameter is copied into the standard shell variable **status**, which holds the exit value of the last program that executed. Thus, exit 1 sets status to 1.

Both the **goto** and **onintr** commands cause a jump to a labeled line. The statement goto mylabel must have an associated labeled line, mylabel:. Execution of the goto statement sends control to the labeled line. Most often, this is used in an if statement, as in if (condition) goto mylabel. (Use of goto statements is less desirable than use of the previously discussed control constructs.) For example, the fragment

```
if ( $myvar == 3 ) goto mylabel
...   some other code, skipped when the condition is false ...
mylabel:   # jump here when the condition is true
...   some more code ...
```

shows a common usage of goto. The `onintr` (on interrupt) statement uses the same syntax but responds to the user pressing the control-C (interrupt) keys. For example, the fragment

```
onintr mylabel
while ( 1 )
   echo Hello there
end


mylabel:
echo All done
```

will display the string Hello there until control-C is pressed.

The **shift** command moves the contents of a string array one position forward, discarding the first element and decrementing the count of array elements. For example, suppose the variable str is filled using the command set str = (dog cat horse). Then the statements

```
echo $str[1]
shift str
echo $str[1]
shift str
echo $str[1]
```

display

```
dog
cat
horse
```

as each substring is moved successively into the first position. Note that $#str is decremented by each shift.

There are several ways to gather information about files. The following commands, which have the appearance of command line flags, are used for this purpose, and evaluate to true or false. The command -e $filename tests for the existence of the file stored in $filename; the command -f $filename tests whether filename is a file and not a directory; and -d $filename tests whether filename is a directory and not a file. For example, consider the following script:

```
#!/bin/csh
if ( $#argv == 1 ) then
   if ( -e $argv[1] ) then
      if ( -f $argv[1] ) then
         more $argv[1]
      else
         ls -l $argv[1]
      endif
```

```
   else
      echo $argv[1] ' does not exist'
   endif
endif
```

After checking for a command line argument, UNIX searches the current directory for an entry by that name. An existing entry, if a file, is displayed using more, and if a directory, has its contents listed using ls -l.

Example

As a final example, the following script is presented. It uses many of the C shell commands discussed in previous sections. When executed, it displays a menu of options, prompting for an integer choice. Each option is implemented in a controlled manner, clearing the screen beforehand and holding the screen before displaying the menu again. Execution continues until the user decides to quit.

```
#!/bin/csh -f
# Simple menu of commands
# Set the menu string and default choice
set menu = ("Directory listing" "File contents" "Current directory"
   "User information" "Quit")
set answer = 1
# Loop until done
while ( $answer != 5 )
   # Clear the screen, present the options, and get the choice
   clear
   @ i=1
   echo " "
   while ($i <= $#menu)
     echo "      " $i." " $menu[$i]
     @ i++
   end
   echo " "
   echo -n "Enter your choice (by number): "
   set answer = $<
   # Choose among the options
   switch ($answer)
     # ls option
     case 1 :
       clear
       echo " "
       echo " "
       ls | more
       echo " "
       echo -n "    --- Press enter to continue ---"
       set x = $<
       breaksw
```

```
# more option
case 2:
  clear
  echo " "
  echo -n "Enter filename: "
  set filename = $<
  if (-f $filename) then
      clear
      more $filename
  else
      echo $filename " does not exist."
  endif
  echo " "
  echo -n "   --- Press enter to continue ---"
  set x = $<
  breaksw
 # pwd option
case 3:
  clear
  echo " "
  echo " "
  pwd
  echo " "
  echo -n "   --- Press enter to continue ---"
  set x = $<
  breaksw
# finger option
case 4:
  clear
  echo " "
  echo -n "Enter userid: "
  set name = $<
  clear
  echo " "
  finger $name
  echo " "
  echo -n "   --- Press enter to continue ---"
  set x = $<
  breaksw
# quit option
case 5:
  echo "Exiting"
  breaksw
# default option
```

```
    default:
      clear
      echo "Error on input, try again"
      echo " "
      echo -n "    --- Press enter to continue ---"
      set x = $<
      breaksw
  endsw
end
```

The reader is encouraged to suggest changes to this script to improve readability and reliability.

References

Abrahams, Paul W., and Bruce R. Larson, *UNIX for the Impatient,* Addison-Wesley, Reading, MA, 1992.

Sedgewick, Robert, *Algorithms in C,* Addison-Wesley, Reading, MA, 1990.

Chapter Summary

■   **C Commands**

Managing Dynamic Memory

```
#include <stdlib.h>
```

```
double *ptr1, *ptr2, *ptr3;
```

`ptr1 = (double *) malloc(` `sizeof( double ));`	Allocate heap space for one `double`
`ptr2 = (double *) calloc(` `2, sizeof( double ));`	Allocate heap space for two consecutive `doubles` initialized to zero
`ptr3 = (double *) realloc( ptr2, 4 );`	Allocate heap space for four consecutive `doubles`, the first two of which have starting addresses given by `ptr2`
`free( (void *) ptr2 );`	Release the heap memory whose starting address is `ptr2`, making it available for further allocation

Linked Lists

The stack and queue linked lists, which use one link per node, are shown in Figure 10.20. The doubly linked list and binary search tree, which use two links per node, are shown in Figure 10.21.

Stack:

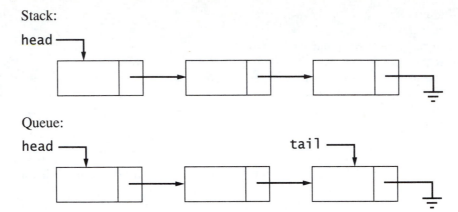

Queue:

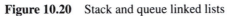

Figure 10.20 Stack and queue linked lists

Doubly Linked List:

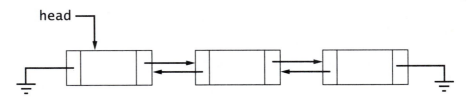

Binary Search Tree:

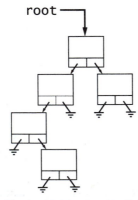

Figure 10.21 Doubly linked list and binary search tree

■ C Shell Commands

Shell Scripts

```
#!/bin/csh
```
Begin a shell script

```
#!/bin/csh -f
```
Begin a shell script but do not read `.cshrc`

`#!/bin/csh -vx`	Begin a shell script; use verbose mode (-v) to echo each shell command, and (-x) to echo each command with its variables expanded
`echo 'myvar = ' $myvar`	Print the string `'myvar = '` followed by the value of the variable `myvar`
`echo "myvar = $myvar"`	Print the given string but recognize the $ as a shell script operator and print the value of `myvar` after the equals sign
`echo -n 'Enter a filename: '` `set mystr = $<`	On one line, prompt the user and await input of a string value for the variable `mystr`
`set mystr = 'myfilename'`	Assign the string `myfilename` to `mystr`
`set mystr = 'whoami'`	Execute the shell command `whoami` and store the resulting string in the variable `mystr`
`set mystr = ($str1 $str2)`	Concatenate `str1` and `str2`; assign the new string to `mystr`
`shift mystr`	Discard `$mystr[1]` and shift succeeding elements toward the front of `mystr`
`@ mynum = $<`	Await input of an integer value for `mynum`
`@ mynum = 2001`	Assign an integer constant to `mynum`

```
#comment: make an assignment
if ( $#argv == 0 ) then
  filename = 'default_file'
  exit
else
  set filename = $argv[1]
  exit
endif
#comment: make a report
echo "filename has been set to $filename"
```

A fragment to assign either `default_file` or the first command line argument to the (string) variable `filename`

```
switch ( $variable )
  case value1:
          echo case 1, line 1
          echo case 1, line 2
          breaksw
  case value2:

  case value3:
          echo case 2 or 3
          breaksw
  default:
          echo default case
          breaksw
endsw
```

A fragment illustrating the `switch` statement

```
@ count = 1
while ( $count <= 5 )
  echo $count
  @ count++
end
```
A loop to print five positive integers, one per line

```
foreach number( 1 2 3 4 5 )
  echo number
end
```
A loop to print five positive integers, one per line

```
onintr TerminationLabel
while ( 1 )
  echo Press Control-C to stop program
TerminationLabel:
echo program is stopping
exit
```
A fragment allowing user to stop the program

```
echo Press S to stop program
echo Press any other key to continue
set response = $<
if ( $response == S )
  echo Program is stopping.
  exit
endif
echo Program is continuing.
```
A fragment allowing user to stop the program

Review Problems

1. Consider the functions `calloc()` and `malloc()`:
   a) How are these functions similar?
   b) How do they differ?
   c) What might cause either of these functions to return NULL?
2. Consider the function `traverse()`, discussed in the section on traversing a linked list. Describe the result of executing the function call

   ```
   traverse( head->next );
   ```

3. In the function `search()`, discussed in the section on searching an unsorted linked list, the node pointer is incremented by the instruction

   ```
   current = current->next;
   ```

   What error would be caused by replacing this instruction with the following?

   ```
   current++;
   ```

4. Describe the flow of control in the function `bracket()`, discussed in the section on searching a sorted linked list, for the following boundary conditions.
   a) The parameter `key` is smaller than every `id` value in the list.
   b) The parameter `key` is larger than every `id` value in the list.

5. Describe the flow of control in the function `SortedInsert()`, discussed in the section on inserting nodes into a sorted linked list, for the case where the key belongs at the end of the list.
6. Modify the function `SortedInsert()`, discussed in the section on inserting nodes into a sorted linked list, to accommodate duplicate keys.
7. Write a function, `UNSortedDelete()`, to delete a node from an unsorted linked list of employee records as described in this chapter.
8. Describe the flow of control in the function `insert()`, discussed in the section on binary trees, if the value of `rec.id` is the same as the `id` field in one of the existing nodes.
9. For each of the following situations decide whether a linked list, a stack, a queue, or a binary tree is the most appropriate data structure.
   a) We wish to maintain a large list of names, with the capability of inserting and deleting names and with the capability of printing the list in alphabetical order.
   b) We wish to maintain a list of invoice numbers, with new numbers always being greater than previous numbers, with old numbers being deleted as bills are paid, and with the capability of printing the list in numerical order.
   c) We wish to store a list of customers who have requested service calls, with the capability of identifying and removing the customer who has been on the list for the longest time.
   d) We wish to maintain a list of subdirectories indicating the path from the root directory to the current working directory, and to update the list as we change directories.
10. Create a binary search tree by inserting the given keys, one at a time and in the specified order:
    a) 0, 2, 4, 1
    b) 1, 2, 3, 4
    c) 4, 3, 2, 1
    d) 3, 2, 1, 0, 4, 5, 6
    e) 2, 6, 5, 3, 7
11. Consider the binary search tree shown in Figure 10.22.
    a) In what sequence were the keys inserted into this tree?
    b) Draw a picture of this tree after deleting the node whose key is 1.
    c) Draw a picture of the tree after also deleting the node whose key is 4.
12. Consider the binary search tree shown in Figure 10.23. Draw pictures of the binary trees obtained by deleting the root node and then continuing to delete the root node of each new tree until you obtain a tree with only one node.

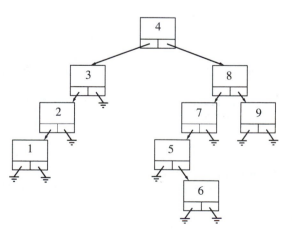

Figure 10.22 A binary search tree for Review Problem 11

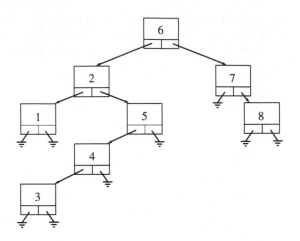

Figure 10.23 A binary search tree for Review Problem 12

13. Write a C shell script to report information about persons whose user ids are given on the command line when the script is executed.

14. Write a C shell script to execute a program whose name is given on the command line when the script is executed. If the program allows a command line argument for a file that the program will process, also allow for that data file to be specified on the script command line.

15. Write a C shell script to echo all command line arguments given when the script is executed. Use the shift command to access successive command line arguments. Echo each argument on a separate line.

Programming Problems

1. Write the functions dequeue() and numqueue(), as described in the section on queues.

2. Write a C shell script, my_calc, to perform simple calculator arithmetic according to an expression given on the command line. The expression should be a sequence of integers, with an *integer* operator (+, -, X, /) between each pair of integers. Use a strict left-to-right order of preference for the operators. For example, the command

```
my_calc 2 - 1 / 2 X 7
```

should be evaluated as $((2 - 1)/2) \times 7 = (1/2) \times 7 = 0 \times 7$, and should thus produce

```
2 - 1 / 2 X 7 = 0
```

on the next line. Note: Do not use the star symbol for the multiplication operator, because the shell interprets * as a metacharacter.

3. Write a C program to scan text expressions of a specified form and evaluate the corresponding numerical expression. The specified form of an expression is

```
(operand1 operator operand2)
```

where the operator is +, -, *, or /, where each operand is either a floating-point number or is a nested expression having the same specified form, and where each expression must be enclosed in parentheses. For example the expression

```
( ( ( 2.2 - 1 ) / 2 ) * 7 )
```

should result in output such as

```
( ( ( 2.2 - 1 ) / 2 ) * 7 ) = 4.200 .
```

Permit extra blank spaces in the input, but provide uniform spacing in the output.

4. Write a program to read a list of integers from a binary file, temporarily store the input as a linked list, sort the linked list into numerical order, and then write the sorted list back to the original file. Allow repeated integers in the list.

5. Write a program to test the function `SortedInsert()`, given in the section on Sorted Insertion. Read input from a binary file of employee records, displaying the records as they are read and storing them in a sorted linked list. Also display the sorted linked list.

6. Write a driver program, based on the example program sketched in the text, to manage a sorted linked list of employee records.

7. Write an interactive program to manage linked lists of characters, implemented using an array that simulates the heap. Include options to create a new list, to insert or delete a character from an existing list, and to display or sort an existing list. Clearly document whether or not the list may contain repeated characters.

8. Write a program to maintain an itinerary of cities using a doubly linked list. Allow return visits to any city and allow city names to contain white space.

9. Write a program to manage a binary tree of strings. Include options to create a new tree, insert a string, delete a string, and search for all strings beginning with a specified character regardless of case (e.g., in searching for strings beginning with m, the search should identify both `Mary` and `mother`). Clearly document whether or not the tree may contain duplicate strings.

10. Write a C shell script to offer a menu with options of listing the current working directory, viewing the contents of any file in the current directory, removing a file from the current directory, or changing the current directory. Do not trap for input errors such as naming a nonexistent directory.

Chapter 11

Data Structure Design

In Chapter 6 we discussed methods for designing programs. The emphasis there was on creating modular programs, that is, designing functions and modules (groups of functions) based on a logical decomposition of the general problem. Chapters 7 through 10 covered several basic data structures available in C. This chapter discusses the design of data structures in general and also returns to data flow design, one of the design methods described in Chapter 6. The UNIX topics of this chapter include communication, file utilities, and typesetting.

Data Structures

It is useful to distinguish between *physical* data structures, such as arrays or records, and *logical* or *conceptual* data structures, such as queues or trees. To see the difference, consider the conceptual view of a stack. Recall that a stack is defined by the operations permitted on it (*push, pop, isempty,* and *isfull*) and the results of applying these operations to data items. For example, if we push item *A* on a stack and then push item *B*, popping items should yield first *B*, then *A*. This is the logical view of the stack data structure: The *push* and *pop* operations store and retrieve data in a well-defined manner. The stack and its operations constitute an *abstract data type* that can be used to solve a problem without worrying about the details of how the operations are implemented.

The physical view of a data structure, on the other hand, is concerned precisely with the implementation details. For example, a stack can be implemented in several ways. If the stack is implemented as a linked list, the stack's *push* operation is an insertion of a node at the head of the list. Thus, pushing item *A* requires creating a new node to hold *A*, linking the current first node of the list to it, and making the new node the first node on the list. If the stack is implemented as an array, then the *push* operation increments a counter, and item *A* is copied into an array position (provided the array is not full). In other words, the physical view deals with the many details of making an operation work correctly. The logical view deals only with the results of the operation and assumes that the operation does work correctly. The physical implementation is (or at least should be) independent of the logical view of the data structure.

The following basic physical data structures were discussed in previous chapters:

- Arrays of various dimensions provide efficient access to a table of data items.
- Strings are arrays used to store characters.
- Records are `struct` variables used to group related data.
- Linked lists, like arrays, store sequential sets of data items, but unlike arrays, they cannot be accessed in random fashion.

From these basic building blocks, many logical data structures can be constructed. Some, such as stacks, queues, hash tables, and binary search trees, have been discussed previously.

As a general rule, the high-level portion of the design phase deals with the logical view of a data structure, and the detailed design handles the physical view. Choosing which logical data structure to use in a program clarifies how the parts of the program communicate with each other. If, for example, a reservation system needs to enqueue a pending request, the reservation module might pass the request to the queue module via a call to the enqueue operation. Dequeuing a request causes the queue module to return a request to the reservation module. The high-level design specifies these operations but is not concerned with the details of how the operations are carried out. The detailed design specifies how various modules modify the queue data structure via function calls and how those functions will be coded.

On the other hand, the details of a particular structure may influence a design, because some programming details—when, where, and how a data structure is modified—need to be worked out to ensure that the right data gets to the right modules. The general rule stated in the preceding paragraph is not absolute. The two parts of the design phase are not always mutually exclusive. Logical data structures have an obvious influence on physical structures, but programming limitations and other physical constraints can affect logical design. Recall that the iterated waterfall model of software development accounts for such feedback, but here the feedback is between parts of one phase, not between phases.

Choosing Data Structures

The choice to use one or more data structures in a program depends on several main concerns:

1. What kind of data needs to be stored? Although many of the examples in this book assume either a basic C type (`int`, `double`, and so on) or a record (a C `struct`), there are many varieties of data, such as raw bit strings for encoded messages, graphical data to describe engineering drawings or printed page layouts, and audio data for voice or music applications.
2. What operations need to be done on the data? This includes the fairly simple operations discussed in previous chapters, such as sorting an array or searching a linked list for a particular data item, but as with the data itself, there are a variety of operations, too. For example, various signal-processing operations may be required for audio data. Also, old operations take on new meanings, as in sorting graphical data, which has an expanded meaning for two- or three-dimensional objects.

3. What performance constraints must be considered? For many applications it is not enough to specify data items and a set of operations on them. The operations may need to be performed with special efficiency in time of access or in space used.

The study of *algorithms* (the step-by-step procedures that implement operations on a data structure) attempts to measure the time it takes to perform each operation on a data structure. The measurement is often stated in terms of a function of the number of data items in the structure. A linear-time algorithm, for example, is one whose operation count is a scalar multiple of the number of data items, whereas a quadratic-time algorithm is a scalar multiple of the square of the number of data items. Operation counts must state *what* operation is being counted (such as comparisons of floating-point numbers) and whether they are long-term averages (which we will assume here), worst-case performance, or best-case performance. A shorthand notation, called *big-Oh* notation, is used to classify and compare algorithms. The notation $O(n)$, for example, signifies linear-time performance (where n represents the number of items in the structure), whereas $O(n^2)$ denotes quadratic-time performance. In big-Oh notation, only the most significant term of the function that estimates the number of operations is reported. For a full discussion of algorithm analysis and big-Oh notation, see [Sedgewick].

For example, recall the algorithm used to sort an array of integers in Chapter 7. The method used there, selection sort, repeatedly finds the smallest element out of the remaining elements and moves it to its correct position. The first step of selection sort sets the first array element as the candidate for the minimum, then compares each of the other elements to the candidate; if an element is smaller than the current candidate, it becomes the new candidate (see Figure 11.1). In all, $n - 1$ comparisons are needed on this first pass. On the second pass, $n - 2$ comparisons are needed, because the same process is applied to the array elements, less the minimum found in the first step. The succeeding steps require $n - 3$ comparisons, $n - 4$ comparisons, and so on, down to one comparison at the last step. Thus the sum of all the steps takes $(n - 1) + (n - 2) + (n - 3) + \cdots + 2 + 1 = n(n - 1)/2$

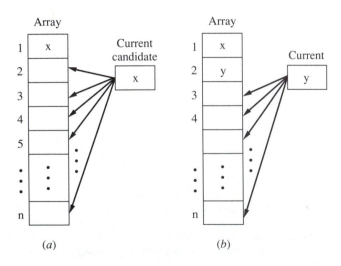

Figure 11.1 Selection sort: two steps

(a)   (b)

comparisons. This is a quadratic function of n, so selection sort is classified as $O(n^2)$: Selection sort is a quadratic-time algorithm.

An important question in the study of algorithms, and one that consequently affects the choice of a data structure, is this: What is a good algorithm to do some operation on a data structure? We ask for a *good* one rather than the *optimal* one because, in general, the difficulty of discovering and implementing optimal algorithms offsets their usefulness, and "pretty good" algorithms usually suffice in noncritical applications. For example, what is a good way to sort an array of integers? In particular, is selection sort's performance sufficient, or are there other algorithms that work better? In this case, there are several reasonable sorting algorithms that work in $O(n \lg n)$ time, where the notation ($\lg n$) represents the *base-two logarithm* of n, or $\log_2 n$. Base-two logarithmic functions result when a halving process is used; for example, the binary search algorithm for sorted arrays, discussed in Chapter 7, is $O(\lg n)$; see Figure 11.2.

These three critical factors—data type, operations, and performance—as well as the space requirements of the expected number of data items and the flexibility of the structure with respect to insertions, deletions, and modifications of the data must be considered when choosing a data structure. Some data structures, such as linked lists, easily handle insertions and deletions, whereas others, such as sorted arrays, do not. The faster search time of a sorted array must be balanced against the difficulty of maintaining sorted order when new items are inserted. (The examples in the next section examine similar trade-offs.) Knowledge of data structures and algorithms is thus quite valuable to a programmer or analyst. References such as [Korsh], [Knuth], and [Sedgewick] should be consulted when in doubt, and commercial or in-house libraries of functions and data structures are also useful. Textbook or library software is rarely an exact fit for a given application, however, so be creative and learn from your experiences.

Examples

In this section, we look at examples of several data structures. In each case, suggested uses of each structure and physical implementations are outlined. This is not meant as a

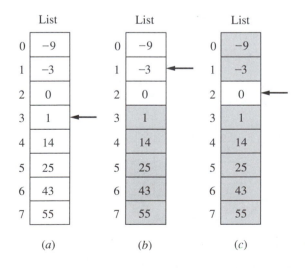

Figure 11.2   Binary search: three steps

survey of data structures or algorithms—see the previously mentioned references for that—but simply as a quick look at some useful structures to help illustrate the ideas just discussed.

Tables

Sometimes an application area may require a specific type of structure. A relational database, for example, uses a *table* (also called a *relation*) as its basic logical data structure. In fact, the definition of a relational database (as opposed to, say, a network database or a hierarchical database) is based on tables (whereas a network database uses graphs and a hierarchical database uses trees). Logically, a table is a set of parallel arrays whose rows represent records (also called *tuples*) and columns represent fields (also called *attributes*). This allows discussion of a particular record (or row), a set of field values (column), and a particular attribute value (one row's entry in some column). For example, suppose a relation called `student` has attributes `name`, `idnumber`, and `address`. The record (`Jones, 47, 123 Main Street`) would occupy one row. This tuple's `idnumber` attribute value is 47. See Figure 11.3a.

	name	idnumber	address
0	Jones	47	123 Main Street
1	Smith	85	456 Elm Street
2	Miller	12	789 Oak Street
3	Jones	38	112 Fir Street
.	.	.	.

(a)

Jones	47	123 Main Street
Jones	38	112 Fir Street

(b)

name	idnumber
Jones	47
Smith	85
Miller	12
Jones	38

(c)

Figure 11.3   (*a*) Table `student`
(*b*) Selection (*c*) Projection

	course	idnumber	letter_grade
0	English	47	A
1	Math	47	C
2	English	12	D
•	•	•	•
•	•	•	•
•	•	•	•

(*d*)

	name	idnumber	address	course	letter_grade
0	Jones	47	123 Main Street	English	A
1	Jones	47	123 Main Street	Math	C
2	Miller	12	789 Oak Street	English	D
•	•	•	•	•	•
•	•	•	•	•	•
•	•	•	•	•	•

(*e*)

Figure 11.3   (continued) (*d*) Table grades (*e*) Join of student and grades

Operations on tables include the following. *Selection* takes row subsets based on one or more attribute values. The operation "select from student where name = Jones" produces a table with (name, idnumber, address) records that all have Jones in the name field (see Figure 11.3*b*). *Projection* forms column subsets. For example, "project name, idnumber from student" produces a table with attributes (name, idnumber) (see Figure 11.3*c*). Selection and projection are often combined, as in "project name, idnumber from (select student where name = Jones)," which produces a table with attributes (name, idnumber) such that all the records have Jones in the name field. *Join* merges two tables with one or more common columns based on equality (or some other operator) of values in the common columns. Using table grades with attributes (course, idnumber, letter_grade) (see Figure 11.3*d*), the operation "join student and grades where student.idnumber = grades.idnumber" produces a table with attributes (name, idnumber, address, course, letter_grade) and with records that match on idnumber (see Figure 11.3*e*). If Jones received an A in English and a C in Basketweaving, then the join would produce two tuples for Jones, one for each course, containing the combined information from student and grades. Other operations include insertion, deletion, and modification of tuples. (For more details, see [Date].)

Keep in mind that the logical data structure is independent of its physical implementation. The implementation of a table could be as parallel one-dimensional arrays of different base types, as a one-dimensional array of structs with fields of different types, as a file of structs, as a binary file of characters that must be cast to the correct types, and so on. Each choice would have corresponding implementations of the necessary operations. "Select from student where name = Jones," for example, might be implemented as a binary search of an array of strings for Jones, or as a sequential search of a file of structs for Jones, and so on.

Commercial relational database programs use generic file storage and implement index structures for efficient searching. That is, files are stored as character strings that are interpreted (cast) according to information kept in the database's catalogs, which store the attribute size and type data for all relations. Typically, an application program requests data from the database via a *query* in a standard language such as SQL. The database program handles the messy file access details, and the application program handles the (presumably) easier task of data processing.

Stacks and Queues

We have already seen both stacks and queues in Chapter 10. A stack handles data on a last-in, first-out basis. Its defining operations are *push, pop, isempty,* and (if necessary) *isfull.* Items pushed onto a stack are popped off in reverse order. A queue, on the other hand, handles data on a first-in, first-out basis. Its defining operations are *enqueue, dequeue, isempty,* and (again, if necessary) *isfull.* Items enqueued are dequeued in the same order; that is, a queue treats items fairly according to arrival time.

As with most data structures, stacks and queues can be created for any specific data type. In Chapter 14, we will consider how C handles structures for generic data. Whatever the data type, the logical view of a stack or queue relies on the meaning of their operations.

Typical stack applications need to "remember" what data items have been encountered so that a back-up (push, then pop) can be accomplished. For example, consider checking for matching parentheses in an algebraic statement. As the statement is processed from left to right, each opening (left) parenthesis is pushed on a stack; as each closing (right) parenthesis is encountered, the stack is popped. (See Figure 11.4.) An empty stack at the end signifies a legal set of parentheses. This example is similar in spirit to the postfix evaluation problem discussed in Chapter 10. In both cases, evaluation of a symbol is delayed until the correct course of action is known.

A similar example lies in certain graph-processing algorithms. A common goal of graph algorithms is to find a path from one node of the graph to another according to some criteria (number of edges traversed, perhaps, or the cost of following the path). Because many paths are possible in a graph, finding a good path often takes the form of trying a path, deciding it is not correct, then backing up to a previous node and trying another direction. The steps of the path can be saved by pushing them onto a stack, then popping each as a path is retraced.

Most queue applications involve waiting in line, as the name implies. Waiters are handled fairly, so that items are dequeued in the same order they were originally enqueued.

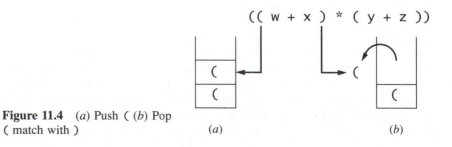

Figure 11.4   (*a*) Push ((*b*) Pop
(match with)

(*a*)

(*b*)

This makes a queue the structure to use in applications handling requests for service (perhaps from computer devices such as printers or communications requests, for example), but more generally for processing service requests (such as requests in a network database or in event-driven programming). (Many graphics applications work in *event-driven* mode, where events are keystrokes, mouse movement, or mouse button presses.) In these examples, a request must be saved until the program can process it, and processing should be according to the first-in, first-out principle.

A common variation on queues is the priority queue, used when items stored in the queue are assigned a priority value to indicate their importance relative to other items. A priority queue can be thought of as a series of queues, one for each priority value. Many realtime system applications need such an arrangement in order to ensure prompt processing of time-critical events.

As Chapter 10 explained, dynamic-memory linked lists are a common basis of implementation for both stacks and queues. For a stack, the push and pop operations are equivalent to insertion and deletion of a node at the head of a linked list, respectively. However, other implementations are possible. An array-based stack uses an integer index to indicate the top of the stack. Similarly, an array-based queue uses two integer indexes to indicate the head and tail items of the queue. Care is needed to prevent array overflow and underflow in both cases. The array-based queue must also provide for circular access to the array, because the used positions are between the head and tail indexes (which are moved on dequeue and enqueue operations, respectively), not between 0 and the head.

String Space

Many applications store large amounts of character data arranged as strings. Chapter 8 discussed strings and string functions. Recall that a C string is a character array in which the last stored character is followed by the string termination character \0.

A compiler is one application that needs to keep track of strings of varying length. A compiler's job is to read a source program and translate it into some other form, such as assembly language or machine code. As words and other *tokens* are encountered by a compiler reading a source program, the existing set of strings is searched for each token. New tokens are stored for later reference. Special tokens, such as reserved words and arithmetic symbols, are sometimes kept in a separate set, since these are all known beforehand. *String space* is the term used for the data structure that stores the tokens.

Text analysis programs use a string space in a similar manner. A text analysis program stores words from documents or speech transcriptions. After all words have been stored, statistical analysis (counting word frequencies, for example) or searches for particular words can be performed.

Conceptually, each of these applications deals with strings as units, but each also needs to store many strings of arbitrary length in the string space. Operations on the string space include the following. The space can be searched for a string. A new string can be inserted in or deleted from the space. Duplicates are not usually entered separately; a text analyzer, however, counts occurrences of duplicates. Besides storing this counter, other attributes of the strings may be stored, such as token categories and values of constants. We ignore these other attributes in the discussion that follows.

The simplest implementation of a string space is an array of standard fixed-length C strings. (See Figure 11.5a.) This implementation has several disadvantages. Maximum sizes

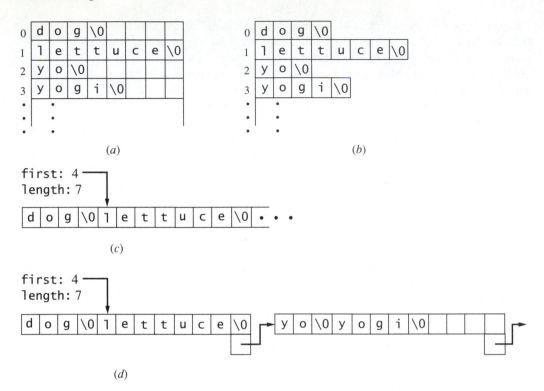

Figure 11.5   String space variations: (*a*) Array of fixed-length strings (*b*) Ragged array (*c*) Single `struct` with indexes (*d*) Linked list of `struct`s with indexes

must be chosen for both the individual strings and for the array that holds them. These guesses may not be large enough, causing a failure when attempting to process longer strings or more strings than anticipated. Most strings will be shorter, however, and the fixed-length string variables will waste space, possibly a considerable amount.

A second method is a ragged array. Each individual string would be declared as a character pointer. (See Figure 11.5*b*.) At run time, a string of the exact size needed is dynamically allocated using `malloc()` (the same function used to create linked-list nodes). This eliminates the wasted space of fixed-length strings, because each string's size is determined by the data to be stored. More time is used by this method, however, because of the calls to `malloc()` for each string.

A third method is to allocate one very large string to hold all the characters that will be processed. The individual strings are then represented by a `struct` containing two integers: `first`, the index number of the first character of the string, and `length`, the string's length (see Figure 11.5*c*). In this way, all of the string space is allocated at once, and the strings are packed together with no waste between strings. Of course, there may be wasted space at the end of the string space, because a guess must be made of the total size.

Yet another method combines dynamic allocation and packed strings. A linked list of medium-length strings is used, and individual strings are again `struct`s containing (`first`, `length`) integer pairs. The first medium-length string is packed with strings, and when it is filled, a new node is created and linked to it (see Figure 11.5*d*). Because multiple medium-length strings are eventually used, an individual string's `first` index must be handled with respect to `SIZE`, the maximum size of the medium-length strings. The value of `first / SIZE` indicates how many links must be traversed to get to the correct node, and `first % SIZE` is the true starting index in that node's string space. If an individual string does not fit at the end of one medium-length string, it can either be divided among the current node and the newly allocated node or be placed entirely in the new node, wasting some space at the end of the current node.

The first two methods each used an array of strings, but the strings could be arranged in some other way. Arrays of strings may be kept in sorted order for faster searching, but insertion and deletion become more difficult. In other organizations, such as trees or hash tables, searches are more efficient and insertions are easier. Similarly, in the latter two implementations, the `struct`s that hold the (`first`, `length`) pairs may be organized into any suitable structure. The string space itself is the raw character storage, independent of the way the strings are organized.

Search Trees

Chapter 10 discussed the use of binary search trees. Recall that there are two defining rules for these trees: each node has a maximum of two child nodes, and the keys are ordered so that a left child's key is smaller than its parent's key and a right child's key is larger than its parent's key. Provided that the tree is not too unbalanced, the search algorithm is approximately the same as a binary search of a sorted array. This performance is $O(\lg n)$. The reason for this is as follows (refer to Figure 11.6): If n is of the form $2^k - 1$, then a k-level tree can hold all the items. If n is not of that form, then we can find k such that $2^{k-1} - 1 < n \leq 2^k - 1$, and the k-level tree is sufficient to hold all items. In either case, k is the longest possible search path, and k is $O(\lg n)$. If the tree becomes unbalanced, then searches are more like linked-list searches, and the performance degenerates to linear, $O(n)$, time.

Since an ordinary binary search tree may be unbalanced, other kinds of trees have been developed. For example, the *AVL tree* (named after its discoverers, G. M. Adelson-Velskii and E. M. Landis) is designed to maintain approximate balance by requiring that any two paths from the root node to a leaf differ by at most one level (see Figure 11.7). An AVL tree achieves this balance by keeping track, for each node, of the difference in length between the longest path to a leaf via the left child and that via the right child. This difference may only be 0, 1, or -1. When an insertion or deletion causes a greater difference, the tree is rebalanced by *rotating*, an operation that rearranges the affected parts of the tree. The modified tree still obeys the binary search tree ordering rule, but some of the keys shift position. (See [Korsh] for details.)

Similarly, the *B-tree* data structure maintains balance to ensure fast search times. A B-tree achieves this by allowing a variable number of keys, rather than just one, in each node; this number must be between the minimum and maximum capacity of a node. The variability in the actual node capacity entails a slightly more complicated search algorithm. However, having node capacity greater than one key allows more keys to be stored in fewer levels, making B-tree searches faster on average than binary tree searches. The insertion and deletion algorithms are tricky to code and sometimes involve key rearrangement. Finally,

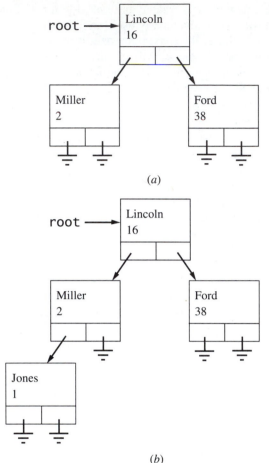

Figure 11.6 (*a*) $n = 3 = 2^2 - 1$ nodes; $k = 2$ levels (*b*) $n = 4$ nodes, $2^2 - 1 = 3 < 4 < 7 = 2^3 - 1$ nodes; $k = 3$ levels

B-trees are not usually built in main memory. Instead, they are built on disk, where a "node" is interpreted as a file block. (See [Korsh] for more information.)

In binary search trees, AVL trees, and B-trees the same main operations—search, insert, and delete—are used by the application. The details of implementation, though, are quite different. This is a case in which the performance requirements of the application must be examined to see whether the more efficient structures are needed and whether they are worth the price in coding and maintenance. Note also that sorted-order retrieval is another operation on trees. Inorder traversals are not very efficient for these trees, especially compared to a sorted array. A *threaded* tree, which uses the NULL pointers in nodes at the bottom of a binary search tree to link nodes in sequential order, allows sorted-order retrieval in linear time at the price of extra maintenance.

The type of data stored in these trees is, of course, dependent on the application. Tree nodes may store entire records, or they may store only the keys of records plus an index number (or pointer) to the associated record. For the string space discussed in the previous section, the nodes could contain the strings of fixed length, or character pointers, or the (first, length) integer pairs that refer to large or medium character arrays. In the latter two cases,

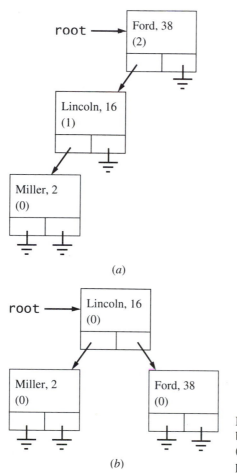

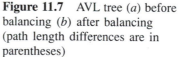

Figure 11.7 AVL tree (*a*) before balancing (*b*) after balancing (path length differences are in parentheses)

the raw storage of packed strings is separate from the logical arrangement of the strings in a tree. This allows the tree nodes to be operated on without affecting the actual string storage area.

Hash Tables

Recall from Chapter 9 that a hash table uses a mathematical function to compute an index number from a key value, then looks up the key and its associated record in the hash table at the position indicated by the index. If the key and record are found there (or at least nearby), then hashing is an $O(1)$ (constant-time) algorithm. This is significantly faster than linear or even logarithmic performance. To ensure this speed, the number of collisions (keys that should be stored in the same place) in the table must be small.

Operations on a hash table are similar to those for trees: insert, delete, and search. It is not feasible to extract items from a hash table in sorted order, because the keys are stored in hash order. Insertion and search rely on the collision resolution method used. Deletion is more difficult to implement and is sometimes ignored. If a table fills to near capacity, a larger

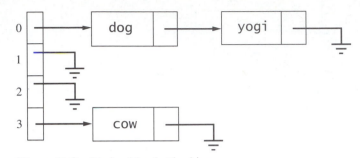

Figure 11.8   Chained-bucket hashing

table should be allocated and the data items rehashed into the new table. This maintenance operation is expensive.

If constant-time performance were guaranteed for hash tables without difficulties arising, every application that needed to search for keys would use them. The difficulties that do arise in practice come from the increase in collisions as the number of items stored in the hash table increases. Several collision resolution schemes exist to try to minimize collision frequency. However, as a table fills up, collisions are inevitable despite the scheme chosen; these collisions degrade performance.

Chapter 9 described the simplest form of collision resolution, *linear hashing*. To insert, the index value computed from the new key is used to access the hash table. If this table position is already occupied, the next available position is sought by incrementing the index by one, wrapping back to the first position if necessary. Although Chapter 9's example used a binary file of records as the hash table, a main memory array of data items could be used.

Another form of collision resolution is called *chained-bucket hashing*. In this method, a hash table entry is not a data item but instead is the head of a linked list of nodes (called *buckets* here), containing data items (see Figure 11.8). To find or insert an item, the index value computed from the key is used to find the appropriate linked-list head. This list must be accessed sequentially for the correct node or position. The data items in the linked list are usually kept in sorted order.

Data Flow Design

The function-oriented design method was discussed in Chapter 6. It uses top-down design to break up larger problems into smaller, more manageable pieces. The emphasis is on functions, and flow of control is more important than the data being used. By comparison, the data flow design method concentrates on a program's data, how it moves through a program, and especially how it is transformed at the various stages of the program. Data flow design is often called *structured analysis and design*. We present a simplified version of data flow design here; for a more detailed description, see [Sommerville].

Recall that the data flow design method models each part of a program as a process that accepts input data, processes the data in some way, and produces output data. Processes are connected to each other by data flow paths, so that a program is modeled as a graph (network) of process nodes and directed edges representing data flow. The kind of data moving between process nodes depends on the processes' needs. Additionally, data *sources* (such as data files and user input) and data *sinks* (such as output files and user displays) are represented. Identifying the kind of data on each edge not only indicates flow, but also begins to clarify the data structures needed in the program.

A data flow diagram (DFD) is a graphical representation of a data flow design. Circles (bubbles) represent processes, and arrows represent data flow edges. DFDs are hierarchical. A top-level diagram shows the large-scale processes of the program. Each process is decomposed into components at each lower level of the DFD. Thus, top-down design is utilized in the context of data flow. Identifying the nature of processes (how each transforms its input data into output data), plus the hierarchical nature of the diagramming process, shows the nature of the overall program design.

Structured design also considers the flow of control through a program as distinct from data flow. User choices, branches, and repetition are often modeled using a separate set of diagrams. We will show only DFDs here.

The data that flows between processes is often thought of as *record-oriented*. The advantage of thinking in terms of records is that the operations performed by the process nodes are usually stated as external requirements—what the user wants—rather than internal requirements—what the program will use. On the other hand, data structures—how records or other component data pieces are organized—are usually chosen for performance or algorithmic needs that are only indirectly related to user needs. As discussed earlier in this chapter, these data structure choices are often part of the detailed design activities.

As an illustration of the data flow design method, consider again the CICOS example from Chapter 6. Briefly, recall that CICOS is an automated hotel check-in/check-out system that checks occupants in, looks up occupant information, prepares itemized bills at check-out, creates statistical reports on hotel occupancy, and keeps a transaction history of recent occupants. The following examples look at only parts of this system, not the entire system, to show how data flow design works.

Each major task of the program is modeled as a process and shown in a DFD as a circle. Check-in, check-out, show occupancy information, and so on would each be a process. Connecting these processes are edges that represent occupant information, room information, floor information, billing data, and so on. A first pass over the problem shows these basic processes and data paths.

Consider the check-out process, shown in Figure 11.9. Its input consists of both an occupant record and a room record, and its output is a billing record. The occupant record might

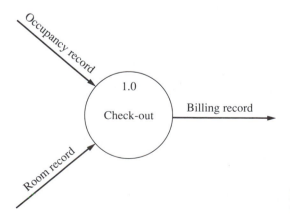

Figure 11.9 Data flow diagram for the check-out process

contain information about a customer: name, address, automobile registration, check-in date, room assignment, and so on. The room record for this occupant might include size of the room, accoutrements (whirlpool bath, massage attachment, and so on), and the room rate. The billing record is a merger of these records so that an itemized bill can be printed, and it contains the charges incurred by the occupant. Each record's contents are determined by what the process needs to accomplish. The check-out process's job, then, is to compute the occupant's charges and to construct the billing record. The occupant record and the room record are provided by (that is, are the output of) some other process. Similarly, the billing record is the input to another process, the display module, for example. (The larger context of the check-out process has not been shown here.)

Constructing a high-level DFD such as Figure 11.9 often takes several tries. Neither the processes nor the data flow edges are necessarily obvious. As with many formal methodologies, it helps to have software tools for creating and editing DFDs. Also note that DFDs are often used at the requirements specification phase rather than the design phase. Our use of DFDs here is to focus on the records and other data passed between processes.

Figure 11.10 shows a refinement of the check-out process. Each component process of check-out helps in the overall job. For example, the room charge calculation computes the occupant's charges based on the check-in date and the room rate. (We ignore other charges, such as a phone bill, for simplicity.) Note that while there are new edges representing data flow internally for the check-out process, the input and output of the entire process remains the same as the previous level: namely, the occupant, room, and billing records. There are automated tools to check DFDs for this consistency.

Figure 11.11 shows one more refinement of the room charge calculation process. The component parts are to compute the number of days stayed, to compute the base room charge, and to compute taxes on the base charge. Again, the input and output for this lower level are the same as the process being refined, but internally, different data items are communicated.

Stepwise refinement is being applied to the processes to achieve smaller, easier-to-handle (both to design and to program) processes. Recall that Chapter 6 broke the design phase into two parts: high-level and low-level design. High-level design proceeds until the designer is satisfied that each process can be coded as a function, at least approximately. The ensuing low-level design lays out the necessary steps for each function.

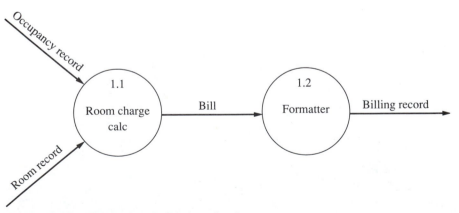

Figure 11.10   Check-out, expanded one level

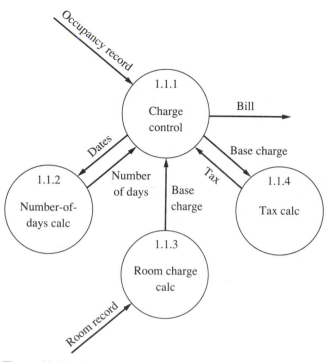

Figure 11.11   Room charge calc, expanded

Module Design

Once the DFD has been fully decomposed, the structure of the program is much clearer. Two important considerations remain: how processes are represented as functions and organized into modules, and what form the data structures take. This section discusses module design considerations.

Function design is straightforward, for the most part. At the lowest level of decomposition, each process bubble is a candidate to be a function. However, depending on the degree of decomposition, a process may be too large or too small to be a function. Too large implies either further DFD decomposition or designing a set of cooperating functions that accomplish the process's tasks. Too small simply means that the decomposition has gone lower than it needed for design purposes (although not necessarily too far for the sake of clarity). In this case, several related processes should be designed as one function. Those functions that constitute a part of the decomposition hierarchy should be the ones that are grouped together in a single module.

Module design also should mirror the DFD hierarchy. Recall the discussion in Chapter 6 of module cohesion. Using the decomposition hierarchy to group functions into modules will yield modules with high or functional cohesion, because each function is a subtask of a larger job, by definition of the decomposition. Also notice, however, that the job of data flow is accomplished in the working program through function calls and parameter passing. One function calling another implies that the calling function is acting like a master and the called function is the slave (or, to use more up-to-date terminology, the caller is the *client* and the callee is the *server*). In the case of a hierarchy of functions (derived from process nodes), this is obvious: The parent function calls its children in succession, and this rule is applied recursively through the hierarchy.

This design strategy is eased when a controller function is used. That is, the parent function may not do any work except to call the child functions. The parent acts like a traffic cop, handling the details of parameter passing among the function calls and repackaging data if necessary to match argument lists. For example, consider Figure 11.11 again. The process labeled 1.1.1, room record control, is an example of a controller function, with three child functions.

This simple parent-child structure may not cover all situations, however. Especially at higher levels of the DFD, but possibly at any level, processes may act as peers rather than parents and children. In this case, it is not necessarily obvious which function should be the caller and which should be the callee. For example, suppose that process A and process B are connected by a data edge, where A passes record AB to B. Also, suppose a similar relationship holds between processes B, C, and record BC (see Figure 11.12). Imagine for a moment that this graph is physical—that the nodes are paper circles connected by string edges. Holding the graph by A causes B to dangle under A and C to dangle under B. Using A as the parent (caller) function requires that it call B, sending the necessary data as parameters. Similarly, B as a parent calls C. The structure of A is then

```
While not done do
    Get some input
    Process the input into AB record
    Call B (send AB record)
```

Since B is the parent of C, it calls C after processing the AB record into a BC record. Process C is in charge of the output details. Note that we are assuming that a single AB record meets B's requirements. In reality, some number of such records may be needed, and may be passed to B in a larger structure.

Another possible arrangement results from holding the physical model at B. In this case, B is the parent to both A and C, implying that B calls A and C. The structure of B is then

```
While not done do
    Call A (receive AB record)
    Process AB into BC
    Call C (send BC)
```

Process A handles the input, and process C handles the output.

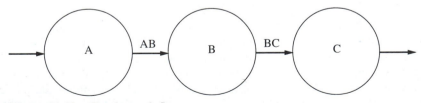

Figure 11.12   Simple graph flow

Holding the model at C yields the third possible arrangement, with C as the parent of B, which is in turn the parent of A. C's structure is then

```
While not done do
    Call B (receive BC record)
    Process  BC
    Output  data
```

Process B calls A in turn. See, for example, [van Vliet] for a discussion of this technique.

Finally, in the CICOS example of Figure 11.11, we could have decomposed the room charge calculation process without using a controller. Figure 11.13 shows a linear sequence of processes in which each process passes on its data to the next process. Any of the three processes could be chosen as the master.

Data Structure Design Using DFDs

The preceding discussion of data flow design assumed that the data flow was record-oriented. This is easier to conceptualize at the high-level design phase than when thinking about how the records themselves are organized. The input and output for each high-level process can be decided early on, simply because recognizing the processes means recognizing what is needed to accomplish some task and what the results will be.

Records of a type indicated at this stage may not be the appropriate type for efficient storage. In addition, the big-picture view of high-level design deliberately ignores the lower-level details. As the operations on the data become more refined through decompositions, candidate data structures present themselves. Operations and algorithm requirements, as discussed in previous sections, lead to one or more possible structures from which a good choice can be made.

Returning to our previous example, recall the check-out process shown in Figure 11.10. Each room record contains information about one hotel room. Each occupant record contains information pertinent to one hotel patron. The room records are static; that is, they are created for the hotel once and for all (barring redecorating or building an addition). These records could be stored in a file and read into a main memory structure at the beginning of the program. The kind of structure used depends on what operations are needed. For check-out, rooms are looked up based on room number, so a two-dimensional array will work, where the first index is the floor number and the second index is the remainder (as in $301 = 3, 01$) (see Figure 11.14a.) Other processes in the program may need different operations. Check-in, for example, might need to look up rooms based on room features, such as rate or number of beds.

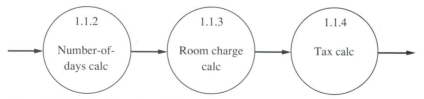

Figure 11.13   Another view of Room charge calc

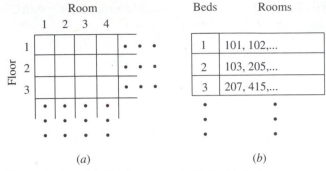

Figure 11.14   (*a*) Hotel room array (*b*) Bed index

An auxiliary structure could be used to ensure fast lookup on one or more of these features (see Figure 11.14*b*).

Occupant records, on the other hand, are dynamic, because they keep track of the current guests. The check-out process probably requires looking up guests based on last name. A fast main-memory lookup structure, such a sorted array or hash table, can be used. The transaction history stores these records (and other information) in a data file. This information provides a log of previous transactions, and fast lookup does not seem required, because of the probable low frequency of lookups. New records are stored often, however, so a simple heap file in binary form can be used.

UNIX Tools

In the next sections, we discuss several useful UNIX tools for communicating with others, including electronic mail, file utility programs, and typesetting facilities.

Electronic Mail

If your UNIX system is connected to a computer network (and most are), then you probably have access to electronic mail. The details of *e-mail,* as it is usually called, vary from site to site. The following discussion describes the basics of the `mail` command.

Typing the command `mail` with no parameters tells the system to check for incoming e-mail messages for you. If there are none, the message "No mail for <*your user id*>" appears. If there are messages, then the `mail` program is started. After some general information is displayed, a numbered list of headers is shown, one header per e-mail message. A header shows, among other things, the sender, its size, and the date and time the message was received. A mail prompt symbol, usually an ampersand, follows the headers.

For example, the following information might be displayed by `mail`:

```
Mail version 2.3.1, Oct. 1994.  Type ? for help.
>N 1 jjr3@node2      Wed Nov 16  8:40  10 / 133  What's shaking?
 N 2 bob             Thu Nov 17 10:16   9 / 89   Re: Requirements specs
&
```

There are two headers, 1 and 2, indicating messages from jjr3 and bob. The N at the beginning of each header stands for "new," and the comment at the end of each line is the subject of the message.

Various commands can be performed on the messages; a full list of the options is displayed by entering ? at the prompt. The most commonly used options are p to print (display) a message; s to save a message in a file; r to send a reply to the sender; d to delete a message; h to redisplay the header list; m to send mail to a user; and either q or x to quit. The first four commands use the header number to specify a message, the s command also requires a file name, and the m command needs a user id.

Using the previous example, consider this sequence of commands: One might type p 2 to display the second message. After reading it, a reply to user bob may be in order; this is accomplished by r 2. This is followed by a prompt for a subject (which is optional), and then typing the message body, terminated by control-D. If user nancy needs to be informed of bob's message, a message can be sent with m nancy and entering the message. If bob's note can now be discarded, d 2 does it. After all this, the header list is probably no longer visible; h redisplays it. To save the first message in a file, s 1 jjr3.note creates a file called jjr3.note. Finally, q quits the mail program. Any messages that were not displayed or saved will reappear the next time mail is run; any messages that were displayed but not deleted are saved in the file mbox (created if necessary in your home directory). To see them again, the command mail -f mbox must be used. If x is used to quit instead, changes to the message list are not carried out, so that bob's message is not deleted and will still be in the mail list the next time mail is run.

Mail messages can be sent by another method besides the m command. If mail is run with a user id as a command line parameter, then a message to that user can be entered immediately. For example, mail bob prompts for the subject, then allows a message to be typed. The message is terminated by either control-D or a period (.) at the beginning of the last, empty line, or aborted using the sequence control-C control-C. Input to this version can be redirected from a file, which is useful when the message is long or needs to be carefully composed and edited. For example, suppose the file bob.letter was created using vi and contains a message intended for bob. The command mail bob < bob.letter sends the message. The -s flag may be used to add a subject line when using this style, as in the command

```
mail bob -s 'Your pay raise' < bob.letter
```

A simple command, from, checks your current mail from the command line, without invoking the mail program. The from command simply displays the headers of current messages.

As indicated in the foregoing example header list, user ids may be appended with host information. The designation jjr3@node2 means that user jjr3's mailbox is on machine node2. Because most UNIX machines are attached to a local area network, this style of addressing may be necessary. If access to the Internet is available, mail can be sent to users outside your organization, and to do so a full network address is required. Full network addresses have the form userid@machine.part1.part2.part3, where the machine name is followed by one or more network domain names. For example, the sample address bob@moogie.psu.edu shows that bob receives mail on machine moogie, which is on the psu domain, which is a subdomain of the edu (educational institutions) domain.

Other Commands

Two other commands for communicating with other users are `write` and `talk`, each of which takes the user id of a currently logged-on user as a parameter. The `write` command allows short messages to be sent to another user. These messages will be displayed (usually at the bottom of his or her screen) along with who sent the message. To reply, that person must use `write` with the first person's id as an argument. For example, to send a message to bob, one would type `write bob`, then type the message, ending with control-D.

The `talk` command requires a confirmation by the receiver before messages can be sent. For example, if `nancy` types `talk bob`, then user bob receives a message on screen that `nancy` is trying to open a `talk` connection. If bob wants to take part, typing `talk nancy` establishes the two-way connection. Once this happens, each user's screen is divided into an upper area, where a user writes text, and a lower area, where text is received. Messages are not terminated by control-D. Instead, the screen acts like a chalkboard, and the users simply type their messages. When either area of a user's screen becomes full, new text is written starting at the top of that area. A session ends when either user types control-C.

While these commands are useful for quick communication with other users, it is sometimes annoying to receive unwanted messages in the middle of a work session. The command `mesg` turns message receipt permission on and off. Typing `mesg n` causes messages to be refused, and typing `mesg y` allows messages to be received (the default state).

File Utilities

The next few subsections describe some useful file utility commands. These include programs that combine files for storage on tape or diskette, compress files to save disk space, or encrypt files for security.

Saving to Tape or Diskette

The tape archive program, `tar`, is used to place files and directories, usually for storage, on either tape or floppy diskettes. An *archive* is a package consisting of files and directories; often, an archive is used for backup purposes. Note that a tape or diskette must be formatted before use; details depend on the device and system. One device is usually designated as the default for `tar` reading or writing; to use another device, see the f flag discussed subsequently. Of course, not all UNIX systems have these devices, although they may be available through network access at your site. In addition, `tar` can also be used to store or unpack a group of files as one file, either before transmittal over a network (via `mail` or `ftp`, the file transfer program) or after retrieval of such a file.

The options for `tar` come in two groups. First, only one action option may be chosen from the following list: c, r, u, x, and t. The c option is used to create a new archive, overwriting any existing files. The r option appends files after any existing files. Thus c is used to start an archive file, and r is used to add to it. The u command checks for the existence of a file within the archive (a process that may be slow) and appends the file if it was not found. The x option extracts an archive or files from an archive, whereas t displays a listing (similar to what `ls` produces for disk files) of the files in an archive.

The second group includes the following options, of which more than one may be chosen at a time: v, w, and f. The v option means verbose mode, causing file names to be displayed as they are archived or extracted; when this option is used with t, a listing similar to `ls -l` is displayed. The w option asks for confirmation before reading or writing. The f option, followed by a file name, indicates that a file is the target of the archive. (Recall that `tar` may be used to create file packages for network transfer.) Since UNIX treats devices by giving them file names, though, this option is also used to specify that `tar` use a device other than the default. If the file name is a hyphen (-), then standard input or output is used instead of tape, disk, or file; this makes `tar` usable as a filter for piping input or output. (See the section on file compression for an example.)

For example, suppose that the directory `/usr/home/bob` contains the files `myfile.c` and `myfile.data`. To write these files to the default device, either the command `tar -cv /usr/home/bob` or `tar -cv bob` will work. Both commands use verbose mode so that `tar`'s actions can be monitored. The latter command is used when the current working directory is `/usr/home`. The choice of a relative directory name, such as `bob`, over an absolute name, such as `/usr/home/bob`, is useful if the files will be extracted to a new directory, as is often the case. That is, writing using an absolute name forces the extraction to occur exactly that way, which may not be desired (or even possible, if the extraction is done on another UNIX machine).

A listing of the files is obtained by `tar -tv`, which displays the long listing for `myfile.c` and `myfile.data`. The command `tar xv` extracts the files. If the first of the formats in the preceding paragraph was used to write the files, then `tar` will attempt to place the files in the same directory, `/usr/home/bob`. If the second format was used, then the files are written in the current working directory.

Suppose that there is a floppy disk drive associated with the file `/dev/rdiskette`. To write the same files on a floppy (again assuming that it has been formatted), the command is `tar -cvf /dev/rdiskette bob`. Similarly, to create a file named `package` containing those files, the command is `tar -cvf package bob`, which creates a file named `package` in the current working directory. Such `tarred` files may themselves be written onto floppy disks or onto tapes, may be copied to another part of the file system, or transferred to another machine.

Compressing Files

In order to reduce the amount of disk space used by a file, the UNIX utility **compress** may be used. This program uses a file-compression algorithm to encode the characters of the file into a more compact form. The new file is generally unreadable by normal means such as `cat` or `vi`, but the original file can be restored using the complementary program **uncompress**. The amount of compression achieved depends on the kind of data stored in the file. For example, text files may not compact as much as graphics files (such as bitmaps and other digital images), which can often be compressed by a factor of 2 or more.

The command `compress myfile` creates a new file `myfile.Z`, which replaces the original; thus, the decision to compress a file should be made only when the file will not be needed for some period of time. The flag `-v` reports the percentage of compression achieved. To restore the file, the command is `uncompress myfile`, which replaces `myfile.Z` with `myfile` (note that the `.Z` extension in the argument to `uncompress` is optional).

Compression is often used in conjunction with `tar`. Usually a collection of files is packaged using `tar` first, and then the resulting `tar` file is compressed. For example, the files in the directory `~bob` can be packaged and compressed using the sequence

```
tar -cvf package bob
compress package
```

where the first command creates `package` and the second creates the file `package.Z`. The files from **bob** can be restored using either of the two equivalent commands

```
uncompress < package | tar -xvf -
cat package.Z | uncompress | tar -xvf -
```

Recall that the minus sign in place of the file name when using `tar`'s `f` option alerts `tar` to use standard input as the extraction file. The alternative command **zcat** also uncompresses files and `cat`s them to the standard output. Thus, the foregoing command could be written

```
zcat package | tar -xvf -.
```

Encryption

The **crypt** command provides minimal security for files by encrypting them using an encryption key. Stronger encryption methods are available via both commercial and free-ware sources. The `crypt` utility is used for both encryption and decryption. The command has the form `crypt key < infile > outfile`, where the `key` is chosen by the user, and the other parameters are the files to be encrypted and decrypted (or vice versa when decrypting).

For example, given the file `myfile.dat`, the command

```
crypt orangutan < myfile.dat >  newfile
```

encrypts `myfile.dat` using the key `orangutan`, creating the encrypted file `newfile`. To decrypt the resulting file,

```
crypt orangutan < newfile >  outfile
```

is the command. Note that the user is charged with remembering the key. Also note that because the key is given on the command line, it is not very secret, since another user executing `w` (the "what" command) at the same time is able to see it. A safer alternative is to use `crypt < newfile > outfile`, which will prompt for the key. Finally, the `crypt` command does not remove the cleartext file, so the user may want to delete it (perhaps saving it on a floppy first).

Typesetting

While a text editor such as `vi` can format text to some degree, typesetting programs offer much more control over output. Rather than describing typesetting in full, this section merely mentions the existence of two UNIX typesetting programs: `nroff` and `troff`. Our justification for this brief overview is that learning any typesetting program entails a large amount of work. Committed users of one typesetter swear by their program, while advocates of another might simply swear. As with programming languages, there is no accounting for taste in typesetting. The `nroff` system has been the typesetting language of choice in many UNIX environments, as evidenced by the fact that man pages are formatted with it.

Other typesetting programs (such as TEX) and, more recently, word processing programs (such as Word Perfect) that provide what-you-see-is-what-you-get environments, are available for UNIX systems. This gives users options other than learning `nroff` commands. Check with your system administrator to see what is available on your system.

Commands for `nroff` and `troff` are quite similar; the latter is intended for printed output and thus has greater flexibility in the choice of fonts, spacing, and so on (depending, of course, on the printer). To give the flavor of `nroff`, we give the following simple example, which would be created with `vi` or some other editor. It uses the `ms` macro package, one of several common packages that define new commands based on `nroff` primitive commands.

```
.RS
.TL
An
.I nroff
Example
.AU
Bob User
.NH
Expressions
.PP
.I nroff
is an
expression language for typesetting applications.  When used with the
.I ms
macro package, special expressions are interpreted as formatting commands.
.NH
Conclusion
.PP
The end.
```

Assuming that the foregoing is stored in the file `myfile.ms`, the command to format it is

```
nroff -ms myfile.ms | more
```

where the `ms` refers to the macro package, and the output is piped through `more` because an `nroff` page exceeds the usual length of video terminals. The output looks something like this:

An
nroff
Example
Bob User

1. Expressions
    nroff is an expression language for typesetting applications. When used with the *ms* macro package, special expressions are interpreted as formatting commands.
2. Conclusion
    The end.

The macros used in the example are as follows:

`.RS`: Shift the output 5 spaces to the right
`.TL`: Centered title
`.I`: Italicize the remainder of the line
`.AU`: Centered author
`.NH`: Numbered section header (continues until `.PP` is encountered)
`.PP`: Begin paragraph

Font changes, such as `.I`, typically affect one line, and are thus set off from the surrounding text. On a video display, `nroff` may only approximate font changes, often by underlining. Note that the title is printed on three lines and that a running count is kept for numbered section headers.

References

Date, C. J., *An Introduction to Database Systems,* 5th ed., Addison-Wesley, Reading, MA, 1990.

Gardner, Martin, *Wheels, Life and Other Mathematical Amusements,* Freeman, New York, 1983.

Knuth, Donald, *The Art of Computer Programming,* 2nd ed., *Volume 1, Fundamental Algorithms,* Addison-Wesley, Reading, MA, 1973.

Korsh, James F., and Leonard J. Garrett, *Data Structures, Algorithms and Program Style Using C,* PWS-Kent, Boston, 1988.

Sedgewick, Robert, *Algorithms in C,* Addison-Wesley, Reading, MA, 1990.

Sommerville, Ian, *Software Engineering,* 4th ed., Addison-Wesley, Reading, MA, 1992.

van Vliet, J. C., *Software Engineering, Principles and Practice,* Wiley, New York, 1993.

Chapter Summary

■ **Data Structures**

Basic Principles

- Distinguish between *logical data structures* and their physical implementations. For example, a stack is a logical data structure that may be implemented using either a linked list or an array as its *physical data structure.*
- Physical data structures include arrays, records, variant records, linked lists, text files, and binary files.
- Logical data structures include tables, stacks, queues, strings, string spaces, binary search trees, B-trees, and hash tables.
- Choice of a data structure depends on the data type(s) to be stored, the data operations to be performed, and the performance specifications.
- *Data flow diagrams* picture data flow using arrows for input and output data and circles (or ovals) for data operations. These diagrams can represent data flow both on a macro level, showing only primary data flows and operations, and on a micro level, showing detailed data flow and operations for one part of a data process.
- Data flow design must also consider how data flow is controlled; for example, it must distinguish between *parent processes,* which initiate requests for data flow and data operations, and *child processes,* which react to those requests.

■ **UNIX Commands**

Electronic Mail

`mail`	Report any incoming messages; if there are messages, display the header list and continue the mail program
`mail thw`	Mail a message to user `thw`; enter the message, terminated by control-D or a period at the start of the last line, or aborted using control-C control-C
`write thw`	Send an immediate message to `thw`, terminated as with `mail` (this works only if `thw` is logged on and is accepting such messages)
`talk dew`	Attempt to initiate interactive conversation with `dew`; use control-C to terminate the conversation
`mesg y`	Accept interactive messages
`mesg n`	Refuse to accept interactive messages
`mail thw < toms_letter`	Mail the file `toms_letter` to user `thw`; `thw` must be a valid userid on the same machine
`mail dew@email.psu.edu < urgent`	Mail the file `urgent` to user `dew` at the machine with Internet address `email.psu.edu`

Responses to the Mail Program Prompt (shown here as &)

`& ?`	Display a summary of `mail` commands
`& p 1`	Print the contents of the first message
`& s 1`	Save the contents of the first message
`& d 1`	Discard the first message
`& h`	Redisplay the header
`& r 1`	Reply to the sender of the first message; enter the response, terminated by control-D or a period at the start of the last line, or aborted using two control-C's
`& m thw`	Mail a message to user `thw`; enter the message, terminated by control-D or a period at the start of the last line, or aborted using two control-C's
`& q`	Quit the `mail` program, saving changes to mail list
`& x`	Exit the `mail` program without saving changes

Archiving Files

`tar -cvw mydir/file1 mydir/file2`	Create (c) a new archive file on the default device and write `mydir/file1` and `mydir/file2` onto the archive file (assuming that `mydir` is a subdirectory of the current working directory), using verbose instructions (v) and waiting (w) for confirmation

`tar -cvwf package mydir file1 file2`	Same as the preceding, but write to a new file `package` in the current working directory, instead of writing to the default device
`tar -cvw mydir`	Archive all files in `mydir`
`tar -rf package file3`	Append `file3` to the existing archive file `package`
`tar -uf package file4`	If `file4` has not previously been archived in `package`, do so now
`tar -tf package`	List all files archived in `package`
`tar -xf package file1`	Extract `file1` from `package`
`tar -xf package`	Extract all files from `package`
`tar -xf -`	Extract all files from standard input (used with piped input)

Compressing Files

`compress greedyfile`	Replace the file `greedyfile` by a compressed file `greedyfile.Z`
`uncompress frugalfile.Z`	Replace `frugalfile.Z` by an uncompressed file `frugalfile`

Encrypting Files

`crypt enigma < cleartext > mush`	Translate the file `cleartext` to an encoded file `mush`; use the coding key `enigma`
`crypt enigma < mush > cleartext`	Translate the file `mush` to a decoded file `cleartext`; use the coding key `enigma`

Review Problems

1. Logically, a table is described as a set of parallel arrays. Why would the physical implementation of a table usually be done with parallel arrays rather than a single multidimensional array?
2. Choose an appropriate physical implementation for each of the following types of matrix.
   a) A 5×5 matrix of real numbers
   b) A 5×5 matrix of complex numbers
   c) A 1000×1000 *diagonal* matrix of real numbers. *Note*: A diagonal matrix has the value zero in each position whose row and column indices are different.
   d) A 1000×2000 *sparse* matrix of real numbers. *Note*: A sparse matrix has relatively few nonzero values.
3. How can underflow occur with an array-based stack or queue?
4. Referring to the fourth string in Figure 11.5*d*, what are the values of `first`, `length`, SIZE, `first` / SIZE, and `first % SIZE`?
5. Note that a binary search tree with three nodes has a minimum of two levels and a maximum of three levels.
   a) What are the minimum number of levels in binary search trees having 7, 8, 9, 31, 32, and 33 nodes, respectively?
   b) What are the maximum number of levels in binary search trees having 7, 8, 9, 31, 32, and 33 nodes, respectively?

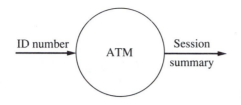

Figure 11.15 One session at an ATM

6. Consider a program that obtains two input strings, finds the longest substring common to both strings, and then prints a report. Rather than writing the full program, only write a preliminary version of the program with functions that assign test values to the input strings, the maximal substring(s), and all other data variables. Use a single data structure to store the two strings and the substring, and use a simple controller function for the main() module. Run the program to test program control and data flow.

7. Figure 11.15 shows a high-level data flow diagram for a single session at an automatic teller machine: An identification number is read from a magnetic strip, the session process is executed, and a session summary is produced.

   a) Represent the overall process by a data flow diagram built on the data flow diagrams given in Figure 11.16.

   b) Figure 11.17 shows a data flow diagram for the Report Balance process. Draw a similar diagram for the Withdrawal process.

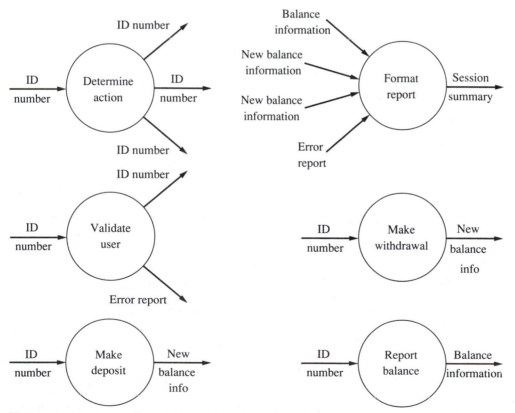

Figure 11.16 Subprocesses for an ATM session

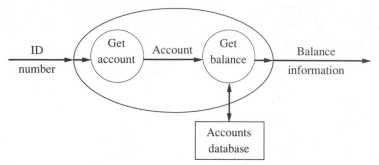

Figure 11.17   Flow diagram for the Report Balance process

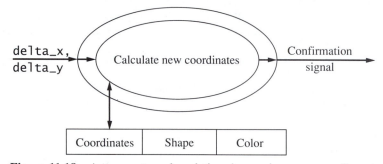

Figure 11.18   A process to make relative changes in screen coordinates

8. Figure 11.18 gives a data flow diagram for a process that updates the screen position of a cursor by making changes in the cursor's current x and y coordinates. For example, if the current screen coordinates are x = 100 and y = 200, and the input increments are delta_x = 10 and delta_y = −20, this process should update the database with new screen coordinates of 110 and 180. *Note:* the database could be in RAM, on disk, or elsewhere; the relative coordinate changes could originate with a mouse, a keyboard, a joystick, a program calculation, or elsewhere.
   a) Write the corresponding data flow diagram for a process that updates screen position using absolute coordinates (that is, taking input that gives the new coordinates without reference to the previous coordinates).
   b) Write a data flow diagram for a process whose input is a signal to draw a cursor using information from the database and whose output is a signal indicating completion of the task.
9. (UNIX Tutorial—Mail) Experiment with the UNIX mail command by answering the question and executing the given instructions:
   a) Can you send mail to yourself?
   b) Use the mail command to compose and mail a brief message.
   c) Use the mail command to mail a file that has been previously created.
10. (UNIX Tutorial—File Translations and Archiving) Experiment with the UNIX file commands by answering the following questions:
   a) Does tar -xf file1 actually remove the extracted file from the archive?
   b) When crypt encodes a file, does the coded file have the same size as the cleartext file?
   c) What is the result of executing the command crypt enigma < file1 | crypt enigma?
   d) Does the command compress file1 | compress file1.Z cause a double compression of file1?
11. Show that if $n = 2^k − 1$, then k is $O(\lg n)$, where $\lg n$ is the base-two logarithm of n; in other words, $2^{\lg n} = n$.

Programming Problems

1. (Set Operations) Write a program that allows a user to specify a universal set and several sets within that universe and then to construct additional sets using the operations of union, intersection, and complement. Use this program to demonstrate several instances of DeMorgan's law, which states that

$$\overline{X \cup Y} = \overline{X} \cap \overline{Y} \quad \text{and} \quad \overline{X \cap Y} = \overline{X} \cup \overline{Y} \quad \text{for all } X \text{ and all } Y$$

2. (Fuzzy Sets) *Fuzzy sets* and fuzzy set operations are the building blocks for *fuzzy logic,* which is used to control processes and make decisions in areas such as transportation, consumer electronics, and financial management. A fuzzy set is specified not by stating with certainty which elements of the given universal set are in the fuzzy set but rather by stating a *degree* of membership (similar to a probability of membership) for each of the universal set elements.

For example, if the universal set is $U = \{a, b, c, d\}$ and the degrees of membership for $a, b, c,$ and d are 0.1, 0.2, 0.3, and 0.4, respectively, then the fuzzy set X is described conveniently by the notation $X = [0.1, 0.2, 0.3, 0.4]$. Equivalently, the fuzzy set X is specified by a function f_X where

$$f_X(a) = 0.1, \quad f_X(b) = 0.2, \quad f_X(c) = 0.3, \quad \text{and} \quad f_X(d) = 0.4$$

The three elementary fuzzy set operations are *complement, union,* and *intersection.* $\overline{X}$, the complement of the fuzzy set X, is defined using the complementary function:

$$f_{\overline{X}}(i) = 1 - f_X(i), \quad \text{for each element } i \text{ of the universal set}$$

$X \cup Y$, the union of the fuzzy sets X and Y, is defined using the maximum function:

$$f_{X \cup Y}(i) = \max[f_X(i), f_Y(i)] \quad \text{for each element } i$$

Similarly, $X \cap Y$, the intersection of the fuzzy sets X and Y, is defined using the minimum function:

$$f_{X \cap Y}(i) = \min[f_X(i), f_Y(i)] \quad \text{for each element } i$$

For example, given the universal set $\{a, b, c, d\}$ and two fuzzy sets,

$$X = [0.1, 0.2, 0.3, 0.4] \quad \text{and} \quad Y = [0.2, 0.4, 0.3, 0.0]$$

some of the associated compound fuzzy sets obtained by applying these operations are

$$\overline{X} = [0.9, 0.8, 0.7, 0.6] \quad \overline{Y} = [0.8, 0.6, 0.7, 1.0]$$

$$X \cup Y = [0.2, 0.4, 0.3, 0.4] \quad \text{and} \quad X \cap Y = [0.1, 0.2, 0.3, 0.0]$$

Write a program that allows a user to specify a universal set and several fuzzy sets within that universe, and then to construct additional fuzzy sets using the three given operations. Use this program to demonstrate several instances of DeMorgan's law, which states that

$$\overline{X \cup Y} = \overline{X} \cap \overline{Y} \quad \text{and} \quad \overline{X \cap Y} = \overline{X} \cup \overline{Y} \quad \text{for all } X \text{ and all } Y$$

3. (Encryption) When the function `crypt` encodes a file, it first creates 128 pairs of ASCII characters and then writes the output file, replacing each character from the input file by the other character of its pair. For example, if the characters A and g are paired, then every input character A is replaced by g and every input character g is replaced by A. Write a program to test this claim.

4. (Game of Life—Bigger than Life) Write a program to play the following variation on the game of Life (previously described in the problems of Chapter 7). Use the largest possible square grid of cells (the size of this grid should be limited only by the requirement to address cells using integer labels), and allow the user to designate which cells are alive in the first generation. As in the previous game of Life, a living cell remains alive if and only if it currently has either two or

three living neighbors (except for cells on the border of the grid, each cell has eight neighbors); a dead cell comes to life if and only if it currently has exactly three living neighbors. Figure 11.19 shows the first two generations of one particular game; living cells are marked, and dead cells are empty. The shape in generation 1 is called a *glider*. Because of the large grid, the program must allow the user to pan left–right and up–down to view different regions of the grid.

5. (Game of Life—What Goes Around Comes Around) Write a program to play the following variation on the game of Life (previously described in the problems of Chapter 7). Use a 4 × 4 grid of cells, and allow the user to designate which cells are alive in the first generation. Let each cell have eight neighbors: the right-hand neighbors of cells on the right border are the corresponding cells of the left border, cells on the left border have left-hand neighbors on the right border, cells on the top have neighbors on the bottom, and cells on the bottom have neighbors on the top. Moreover, each corner cell also has a neighbor at the opposite corner.

For example, in Figure 11.20 the neighbors of cell 1 are cells 4, 16, 13, 14, 2, 6, 5, and 8, given in clockwise order starting to the immediate left of cell 1.

As in the original game of Life, a living cell remains alive if and only if it currently has either two or three living neighbors; a dead cell comes to life if and only if it currently has exactly three living neighbors. Figure 11.21 shows the first two generations of one particular game; living cells are marked, and dead cells are empty.

6. (A Cellular Automaton Game) The following game, similar to the game of Life described above, was discovered by Edward Fredkin. Consider a large two-dimensional array of cells. If, in the present generation, a cell has an even number of living neighbors among the four orthogonally adjacent cells (i.e., the four neighbors above, below, to the left, and to the right), this cell remains dead or

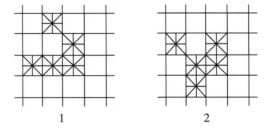

Figure 11.19 The first and second generations of one particular game of *Bigger than Life*

1   2

1	2	3	4
5	6	7	8
9	10	11	12
13	14	15	16

Figure 11.20 A grid of 16 cells

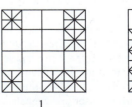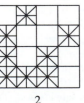

Figure 11.21 The first and second generations of one particular game of *What Goes Around Comes Around*

1   2

dies in the next generation. If, in the present generation, a cell has an odd number of living neighbors among the four orthogonally adjacent cells, this cell remains alive or springs to life in the next generation. Figure 11.22 shows the first two generations of one particular game; living cells are marked, and dead cells are empty. Write a program to play this game. In testing the program note the very interesting result that occurs in the fourth generation of the game begun in Figure 11.22. See [Gardner] for more information on this game and similar games.

7. (Cereal Box Puzzle) How many squares can be found in the grid of Figure 11.20? Note that there is one 4×4 square, there are sixteen 1×1 squares, and there are other squares also. Answer this puzzle by creating a data structure to represent an arbitrary grid of size $n \times n$ and a function to scan the grid and count squares of sizes 1×1 through $n \times n$. Include all of this in a program that asks the user to specify n and then finds the number of squares in an $n \times n$ grid. For output, produce a detailed report that shows more than just the total number of squares.

8. (ATM) Write a program to perform the operations of an automatic teller machine.

9. (Database of Address Labels—Version 1) Write a program for maintaining a database of mailing labels in the following manner. An individual label is a record whose fields are last name, first name, middle initial, street address, city, state, and postal code. The maximum allowable length for each name and for the city is 16 characters, the maximum length for the street address is 32 characters, the state is a two-character string, and the postal code is a five-digit number. Store the data base on disk as a binary file. For editing and printing, load the list into RAM as a linked list of records and maintain an array of pointers so that the records can be printed in order according to postal code (primary key) and name (secondary key). Add new records at the end of the linked list.

10. (Database of Address Labels—Version 2) Write a program for maintaining a database of mailing labels in the following manner. An individual label is a record whose fields are last name, first name, middle initial, street address, city, state, and postal code. The maximum allowable length for each name and for the city is 16 characters, the maximum length for the street address is 32 characters, the state is a two-character string, and the postal code is a five-digit number. Store the data base on disk as a binary file. For editing and printing, load the list into RAM using a hash table and chained-bucket hashing. Let the buckets correspond to postal codes; store the data for each bucket as a linked list that is sorted by name.

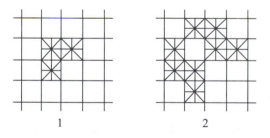

Figure 11.22   The first and second generations of one particular Cellular Automaton game

Chapter 12

Specialized Tools

In previous chapters, we examined ways to write readable C code. Documentation, good variable names, `#define`d constants, and modular programs—all are methods for making software more readable. In this chapter we discuss several specialized tools that help make C programs both more readable and more portable. These tools include constants, enumerated types, macros, and conditional compilation. The UNIX topics for this chapter examine `lex` and `yacc`, specialized tools for analyzing text.

The `const` Declaration

Recall that constants declared with the `#define` statement are handled by the precompiler, not the compiler. Each such constant is a *macro*, that is, an alias that the precompiler replaces with the macro's definition. An alternate method for defining constants is the **const** declaration. By placing the keyword `const` in front of a variable declaration, the variable is made read-only. Such a constant *must* be assigned a value at the time it is declared, and this value cannot be changed later. In other words, it has the same meaning as a constant defined using `#define`, except that the type of the constant is explicit rather than implicit, as is the case with `#define`.

For example, the following declarations show the usage of `const`:

```
const int flag = -1;
const double normal_temp = 98.6;
const char ch = 'A';
```

In addition, the `const` keyword may be applied to structured types, such as arrays and records, as in the following:

```
#define SIZE   3
typedef int list_type[ SIZE ];
const list_type list = { 5, 10, 15 };
typedef struct {
  int     id_number;
  double price;
} part_struct;
const part_struct widget = { 501, 14.2 };
```

Note that the `const` keyword is applied to the variable definition and not to the `typedef` for both the array and the record examples. This makes `list` and `widget` read-only, but other variables of types `list_type` and `part_struct` can be regular read/write variables by omitting the keyword `const`. It is legal to apply `const` to the `typedef` itself, but this restricts *all* variables of that type to being read-only. This alternative is shown next:

```
typedef const struct {
  int     id_number;
  double price;
} part_struct;
part_struct widget = { 501, 14.2 };
```

Here, `widget` is still read-only, and any other variables of type `part_struct` are also read-only.

Choosing between `const` and `#define` is partly a matter of style, but there are certain restrictions to keep in mind. First, because the precompiler substitutes the definition of `#defined` constants, they are global in nature. Constants declared with `const`, however, follow the same scoping rules as variables. Second, for similar reasons, the sizes of arrays and strings are usually declared using `#defined` constants. This was done in the foregoing definition of `list_type`. It is legal but unusual to use a `const`-declared constant for this purpose. Finally, not all compilers handle `const` definitions in the same way. Some compilers allow variables declared using `const` to be reassigned, although a warning is issued. You should test this on the compiler you are using.

The `const` keyword can also be used before a function's array parameter declarations to indicate that the array may not be changed—that is, for the purposes of the function, the array is a read-only variable. For example, consider the prototype of the function `strcpy()` from the header file `<string.h>`:

```
char *strcpy( char *, const char * );
```

The second parameter, which is the string (array of `char`) from which characters are being copied, is prefaced by `const`. The string's contents cannot be changed by `strcpy()`.

Enumerated Types

The *enumerated* type is useful when a set of constants, rather than just one, is needed. As its name implies, an enumerated type is a list of values explicitly defined by the programmer.

	When defined	*Number of values*	*Implemented as*
`#define`	Precompile	Single	Macro
`const`	Compile	Single	Variable
`enum`	Compile	Range	`int` variable

Figure 12.1 Relative characteristics of `#define`, `const`, `enum`

A variable declared of such a type can then assume any *one* of those values. Like constants defined using `const` or `#define` statements, these values are fixed values and can have meaningful names, which makes them useful in writing self-documenting code. The difference between **enum** values and `const` or `#define`d constants is thus one of style rather than substance. When an expression can take any one of a limited set of specific values, a rule of thumb is that when the numeric value is important to the application, use `#define` or `const`; if not, use an enumerated type (see Figure 12.1). This is not to say the enumerated types in C do not have numeric values; they do, as discussed subsequently.

The syntax for enumerated types is

```
typedef enum { myvalue1 , myvalue2 , ... , myvaluen } myname ;
```

where *myname* is the type's name and *myvalue1*, *myvalue2*, and so on are the list of constants. As with `struct` definitions, this method provides a single type name for later reference. For example, the definition

```
typedef enum { Sunday, Monday, Tuesday,
   Wednesday, Thursday, Friday, Saturday } days;
```

specifies an enumerated type for the days of the week. Then the statements

```
days today;
today = Thursday;
```

declare variable `today` of type `days` and assign it the value `Thursday`. There is no inherent meaning in the ordering of the enumerated values; ordering is up to the programmer. Thus, we could have exchanged `Tuesday` with `Saturday` in the foregoing definition or permuted the order in any way. Of course, some value sets have a natural ordering, as these do, but others do not. Also, some sets with a natural ordering may be cyclic in nature, as are the days of the week, so that any of the elements can have been placed first.

We mention an alternative but less desirable method for defining an enumerated type:

```
enum tagname { myvalue1 , myvalue2 , ... , myvaluen };
```

The drawback of this method is the need to mention both the keyword `enum` and the tagname in order to reference the type. For example, the statements

```
enum days { Sunday, Monday, Tuesday,
   Wednesday, Thursday, Friday, Saturday };
enum days today;
today = Thursday;
```

achieve the same effect as the previous example.

Values of Enumerated Types

Like the `char` type, an enumerated type is implemented as an integer by the compiler. Each constant in the enumerated list is assigned an integer value, by default starting at zero and increasing through the list. Consider the following example:

```
typedef enum { work, play, study, sleep, eat } activities;
```

The underlying value of `work` is 0, that of `play` is 1, and so on, with `eat` being 4.

We again note the style rule that `#defined` constants rather than enumerated types are used when the numeric value is important. In fact, the numbering scheme for `enum` types often has little relation to the real-world constants being represented. For instance, in the previous example, `sleep` is given the value 3, which is probably meaningless. On the other hand, in the earlier `days` definition, `Monday`, the first day of the work week, is given the value 1, which makes at least some sense. Nevertheless, the underlying numeric values may be used to good effect in some situations. In those cases where a constant should have a certain underlying value, the default values can be overridden using the syntax

```
typedef enum { value1  = integer1,
   value2  = integer2 , ... , valuen  = integern } myname ;
```

where `integer1`, `integer2`, and so on are the integer values to be associated with the enumerated constants. Each of these integer assignments is optional; if any are omitted, the underlying value of the affected constant is one greater than the previous constant's value (starting, if necessary, with zero at the beginning of the list). Thus, the definition

```
typedef enum { work, play = 11, study, sleep = 5, eat } activities;
```

assigns 0 to `work`, 11 to `play`, 12 to `study`, 5 to `sleep`, and 6 to `eat`. It is legal but probably not logical (due to the potential for confusion) to assign the same underlying value to more than one constant in an `enum` list. It is not legal, however, to repeat an enumerated constant within either the same or multiple `enum` types.

Using Enumerated Types

As noted above, enumerated types help make code self-documenting. The constant values make the code read more like English by avoiding the use of special numeric values. Common uses include array access, menu options, and discriminator fields for `unions`, each of which is discussed subsequently.

Suppose, for example, that an application keeps track of the number of units of a product sold on each day of the week. Consider the following definitions:

```
#define SIZE 7
typedef enum { Sunday, Monday, Tuesday,
   Wednesday, Thursday, Friday, Saturday } days;
typedef int product[ SIZE ];
product sales;
```

The array `sales` has slots for the number of units sold on each day of the week, and the enumerated type `days` matches the indexing scheme used to access the array. Thus, `sales[ Tuesday ] = 47;` and `scanf( "%d", &sales[ Friday ] );` access entries 2 and 5 of `sales`, respectively. Similarly, we could print out the contents of `sales` with the loop

```
for ( today = Sunday; today <= Saturday; today++ )
  printf( "sales[ %d ] = %d\n", today, sales[ today ] );
```

assuming that the `sales` array has been filled with data. The value of `today` begins with `Sunday` and increases by 1 on each loop iteration up to `Saturday` because of the statement `today++`. Thus Tuesday's sales figures appear in the output as

```
sales[ 2 ] = 47
```

and similarly for the other entries of `sales`.

There are several other things worth noting about this example. First, the values printed when %d is replaced by `today` are integers, not the strings `Sunday`, `Monday`, and so on. We must work a bit harder to print string values; a method for doing so is illustrated in a subsequent paragraph. Second, even though days of the week are cyclic in real life, type `days` is not. If the loop had been written as

```
for ( today = Wednesday; today <= Tuesday; today++ )
  printf( "sales[ %d ] = %d\n", today, sales[ today ] );
```

for example, the program does not produce any output, since the first value of `today`, namely `Wednesday`, already exceeds that of `Tuesday`, so the loop continuation condition would immediately fail. A common remedy for this situation is to write a function that computes the successor value for the enumerated type. In this case, the function has the prototype

```
days nextday( days );
```

and the key step in its implementation is to ensure that `nextday( Saturday )` returns `Sunday`. Then one might be tempted to rewrite the loop as

```
for ( today = Wednesday; today != Tuesday; today = nextday( today ))
  printf( "sales[ %d ] = %d\n", today, sales[ today ] );
```

although this does not quite do the trick. You are encouraged to determine the problem with this fragment, fix it, and also to code the nextday() function. Also note that when nonsequential values are used in an **enum** type, as was the case in the activities example, for loop array access is no longer feasible.

The task of printing the string equivalents of enumerated constants must be done manually. That is, a parallel list of string values must be declared independently of the enumerated type. It is entirely the programmer's job to maintain the logical connection between the two lists (see Figure 12.2). Using the code from the foregoing days example, the following declaration shows this idea:

```
#define STRSIZE 10
char daystrings[ SIZE ][ STRSIZE ] = {
   "Sunday", "Monday", "Tuesday", "Wednesday",
   "Thursday", "Friday", "Saturday" };
for ( today = Sunday; today <= Saturday; today++ )
   printf( "sales[ %-9s ] = %5d\n", daystrings[ today ], sales[ today ] );
```

Now the output shows day names in the index position of sales[], as in Tuesday's output:

```
sales[ Tuesday ] =    47
```

In previous chapters menu options used #defined constants, but an enumerated type can do the same job. For example, consider the following definition:

```
typedef enum { checkin, checkout, search, roomstats, quit } MenuChoices;
MenuChoices choice;
```

days			daystrings	
enum	*Value*		*Index*	*Value*
Sunday	0		0	"Sunday"
Monday	1		1	"Monday"
Tuesday	2		2	"Tuesday"
Wednesday	3		3	"Wednesday"
Thursday	4		4	"Thursday"
Friday	5		5	"Friday"
Saturday	6		6	"Saturday"

Figure 12.2 enum definition and parallel string array

The variable choice, after being assigned a value of type MenuChoices from a menu display function, can be used to guide a switch construct:

```
switch ( choice ) {
  case checkin  : /* some code here */
                  break;
  case checkout : /* some code here */
                  break;
  case search   : /* some code here */
                  break;
  case roomstats: /* some code here */
                  break;
  case quit     : /* some code here */
                  break;
  default       : /* some code here */
                  break;
} /* switch choice */
```

The case options are clearly stated in terms of the enumerated values.

Recall that the discriminator of a union is used to choose among the union's various fields. An enumerated type can be the discriminant, as shown in the next example:

```
/* Assume reasonable typedef's for nametype and addrtype. */
typedef enum { AUTO, HOME, LIFE } instype;  /* Kind of insurance */
typedef union {        /* Insurance information:                   */
  nametype model;      /*    automobile model (for AUTO insurance)  */
  addrtype address;    /*    building address (for HOME insurance)  */
  nametype spouse;     /*    spouse's name    (for LIFE insurance)  */
} insurance_info;
typedef struct {         /* Customer information: */
  nametype     name;     /*    insured's name    */
  addrtype     address;  /*    insured's address */
  instype      insurance;/*    kind of insurance */
  insurance_info  ins;   /*    insurance info    */
} customer_rec;
```

The instype enumerated type defines constants for three kinds of insurance. The discriminator inside the customer_rec record indicates which of the three fields of the insurance_info union field ins should be used: model, address, or spouse. A typical code fragment (assuming the declaration customer_rec cust;) is

```
if ( cust.insurance == LIFE )
  printf( "Spouse : %s\n", cust.ins.spouse );
/* and so on */
```

As in previous examples, an enumerated discriminator is less useful in input and output operations, because again the underlying values are integers, not strings. The value of cust.insurance in the foregoing fragment might be HOME, which is useful to the programmer, but displaying the underlying value, 1, would not help the user.

Macros

The #define mechanism has more utility than just defining constants. As noted earlier, a constant declared using #define is a form of macro or alias, whose definition is substituted by the precompiler. This section shows how more complicated macros can be constructed using #define. (*Note*: in Kernighan and Ritchie C a #define statement must begin in the leftmost column with no preceding spaces. In ANSI C this is not required.)

A common use for macros is to create a single word that stands for a phrase or command. In UNIX the alias command is used for this purpose. In a C program a macro is created by the syntax

```
#define macro macro-definition
```

For example, consider the following macro:

```
#define BLANKLINE printf( "\n" )
```

This allows the use of the macro BLANKLINE in place of the command printf("\n"), as in this fragment:

```
for ( i = 0; i < 5; i++ )
    BLANKLINE;
```

Note that the macro definition did not contain a semicolon, so one was needed at the end of the fragment that uses the macro. The definition could have included a semicolon and the fragment's semicolon could then be deleted, but it would make the code fragment confusing.

We could write a macro for the entire loop just shown:

```
#define FIVEBLANKLINES  for ( i = 0; i < 5; i++ ) printf( "\n" )
```

To use this new macro, the variable i must be declared separately:

```
int i;
FIVEBLANKLINES;
```

or else i must be declared within the macro, as in

```
#define FIVEBLANKLINES  { int i; for ( i = 0; i < 5; i++ ) printf( "\n" ) }
```

The braces define a new scope, so that i is local to this scope. (Recall the discussion of inner scopes in Chapter 4.) Note that this macro has more of the feel of a function call, and in fact, it would be simple to write a function that does the same job as the macro. Choosing one or the other is partly a matter of style (which is influenced by the readability of the resulting code) and partly a matter of efficiency of execution. Macros, by virtue of the precompiler's work, do not incur the penalty of extra execution time that function calls do. On the other hand, for simple functions this extra time will not be noticeable in most programs.

Functions, however, can accept parameters and return a value. A macro can also accept parameters, although without the type checking provided by functions, and can have the same effect as returning a value if so desired. Keep in mind that macro substitution by the precompiler is done literally. These differences make macros with parameters more dangerous than functions with parameters, as will be shown in a later example. To show the use of parameters, consider the definition

```
/* Note the lack of any white space between the macro and the left '(' */
#define BLANKLINES( num )   for ( i = 0; i < num; i++ ) printf( "\n" )
```

There must be *no spaces* between the end of the word BLANKLINES and the left parenthesis. The parameter to the macro, num, is used as the upper bound of the for loop—that is, an integer argument to BLANKLINES that tells how many blank lines are to be printed. The statement BLANKLINES(5); has the same effect as FIVEBLANKLINES; from the previous example. Macro parameters are untyped, so num need not be an integer for the substitution to take place. This can cause a problem at run time, as in the statement BLANKLINES("bob");. The precompiler will handle this obviously incorrect statement in the same way it handles BLANKLINES(5); but the resulting code is quite meaningless, because "bob" is not an integer.

Further trouble can result from literal substitution. Consider the macro and the statement using it in the following:

```
#define SubSeven( num ) num - 7
i = 2 * SubSeven( 9 );
```

The new value of i is not 4, as might be expected from the calculation 2 * (9 - 7). Instead, i is assigned 11, the value of the expression 2 * 9 - 7, because of the literal substitution of num - 7. The rule of thumb for macros using parameters is to use plenty of parentheses. Rewriting the foregoing macro as

```
#define SubSeven( num )   (( num ) - 7 )
```

will produce the desired result.

A common construction used in macros is the conditional phrase (*expression*) ? *value1* : *value2*, which we examined previously in Chapter 3's discussion of conditional assignment. To illustrate its use, consider the following definition:

```
#define min( first, second )
  ((( first ) < ( second )) ? ( first ) : ( second ))
```

This macro evaluates to the smaller of its two arguments by first evaluating the expression ((first) < (second)); if true, the macro's value is (first); otherwise, it is (second). The fragment

```
int i, j;
/* .... Assign some values to i and j .... */
printf( "The smaller of %d and %d is %d.\n", i, j, min( i, j ));
```

would print, if i = 7 and j = 2,

```
The smaller of 7 and 2 is 2.
```

while the statement

```
k = 2 * min( i - 6, j );
```

causes k to be assigned the value 2. Again, no type checking is provided on the arguments. The macro min() can take int, double, or other basic variable types as arguments.

There are several standard functions in various C libraries that are actually implemented as macros. The fact that they *are* macros rather than functions has little consequence to writing programs. Standard macros include getchar() and putchar() in the <stdio.h> file, and many of the functions defined in <ctype.h>, such as isalpha(), isdigit(), toupper(), and so on.

Conditional Compilation

Several other constructs are recognized by the precompiler. Their use allows flexibility in the way C programs are compiled, because they provide pathways of code, usually definitions or typedef statements, that can be either included or excluded based on conditions at compile time.

The first of these constructs is the **#if-#else-#endif** conditional statement. As with C's regular if-else construct, a boolean condition is tested. Unlike C, though, it is tested only once by the precompiler. If the boolean condition is true, the if clause, and not the second optional else clause, becomes part of the code. If false, the first part is ignored, and if present, the else clause is incorporated into the code. No evaluation of the condition is made at execution time, because the precompiler handles the details. Thus the boolean condition must be something that in fact *can* be evaluated by the precompiler, that is, it must be an expression using literal and #defined constants.

Suppose that we want a C program to be used on two different machines, with file blocks or sectors (the unit of storage on most disk systems) either of size 1024 bytes on the first machine or 4096 bytes on the second machine. The constant BUFFERSIZE declares a character buffer for reading and writing file blocks. In order for this constant to have the correct value, we place one of the following statements in the file model.h:

```
#define MODEL 1
```

or

```
#define MODEL 2
```

depending on which machine is being used. This file could be modified, for example, by the users according to the machine at their installation. The file prog.h, containing the usual definitions and prototypes for the program, contains the following fragment:

```
#include "model.h"    /* Contains the definition of MODEL */
#if ( MODEL == 1 )
  #define BUFFERSIZE 1024
#else
  #define BUFFERSIZE 4096
#endif
typedef char BufferType[ BUFFERSIZE ];
```

Depending on which value was assigned to MODEL, one of the two #defines for BUFFERSIZE is included in the code and the other is deleted by the precompiler. Thus, if MODEL is 1, then the type BufferType is a character string of 1024 bytes, but if MODEL is 2, then BufferType contains 4096 bytes. Thus, the site-specific file model.h simplifies the task of making the code fit the user's needs, since the user might find it confusing to search for occurrences of BUFFERSIZE and change them.

Another construct, **#elif**, is an abbreviation for **#else #if** (on separate lines) and allows more complicated statements to be created. Note that only one #endif was needed in the previous example because only one #if statement was used. Use of #elif does not require another #endif, but use of #else #if does. For example, consider these two equivalent fragments:

```
#if ( MODEL == 1 )
  #define BUFFERSIZE 1024
#else
  #if ( MODEL == 2 )
    #define BUFFERSIZE 4096
  #endif
#endif
```

The two #if statements in the first fragment call for two #endifs.

```
#if ( MODEL == 1 )
  #define BUFFERSIZE 1024
#elif ( MODEL == 2 )
  #define BUFFERSIZE 4096
#endif
```

Here, only one #if statement is used, requiring only one #endif statement.

Note that the value of the constant being tested in the previous examples is not really needed. When this is the case, an alternate construct can be used, **#ifdef**, which simply tests whether a constant has been defined at all. For example, suppose that for the first machine, the statement #define MODEL is placed in the file model.h. Note that no value is assigned to MODEL. If the second machine is used, nothing is placed in model.h. Now the fragment in prog.h becomes

```
#ifdef MODEL
   #define BUFFERSIZE 1024
#else
   #define BUFFERSIZE 4096
#endif
```

The first statement checks whether or not MODEL has already been defined. If so, 1024 is assigned to BUFFERSIZE; otherwise 4096 is used.

A similar construct, **#ifndef**, is useful for checking if a constant has been defined before attempting to define it. This construct asks the opposite question: "Has a constant *not* been defined?" For example, the constants TRUE and FALSE are commonly used but are not system-defined, so many programs define them. To ensure that duplicate definitions are not made, the fragment

```
#ifndef FALSE
   #define FALSE 0
#endif
#ifndef TRUE
   #define TRUE !FALSE
#endif
```

first checks for previous definitions of each constant before assigning a value.

When .h files are to be included, it is sometimes useful to check to ensure that a file is included only once. This can be accomplished using the #ifndef construct, as shown in the following example. Suppose that the file prog.h will be included by several .h and .c files. To prevent multiple definitions, prog.h's contents are given the following format:

```
#ifndef PROG
   #define PROG
   ...  rest of the prog.h file ...
#endif
```

For example, suppose that stuff.h and morestuff.h both contain the line #include "prog.h", and both are #included in the file prog.c. If stuff.h is processed first, then prog.h is included for the first time. PROG, not yet encountered, causes the #ifndef to evaluate as true, and PROG is defined. When morestuff.h is processed, PROG has a definition, so the body of prog.h is skipped. Thus, the definition of PROG occurs only once, and consequently prog.h's contents are included only once.

The preprocessor construct **#undef** causes constants to become undefined. For example, #undef TRUE makes the constant TRUE undefined (regardless of whether it has been defined or not), so that a later test, such as #ifdef TRUE, fails.

The **#error** construct performs a role for the precompiler similar to the one that exit() plays at execution time—that is, processing stops when such a statement is reached. Most often, #error is used to exit the precompilation process when some inconsistency is detected in #defined constants. A string argument may be used with this construct, as the following example shows.

```
#ifndef BUFFERSIZE
  #error "Buffer size is not declared"
#endif
```

If in fact BUFFERSIZE has not been defined, precompilation stops at the #error line, the string is displayed, and no further compilation is attempted.

Bit Operations

There are some applications in which it is necessary to manipulate the bit strings that represent the standard types. These applications deal with low-level control information, such as device drivers and communications protocols, and are highly specialized. This section may be omitted by readers who are not concerned with such applications.

Bit strings are the binary (base-two) representations of data. Like standard base-ten numbers, the digits (0 or 1 only) of a binary number have values associated with their position. The rightmost position is the ones' place, next is the twos' place (rather than the tens' place in base ten notation), next is the fours' place (using two squared rather than ten squared), and so on. The assignment char c = 'A';, for example, places the integer 65 in c. The one-byte (eight-bit) binary representation of 65 is 0100 0001 (written in groups of four bits for readability), since

$$65 = (1 \times 64) + (0 \times 32) + (0 \times 16) + (0 \times 8) + (0 \times 4) + (0 \times 2) + (1 \times 1)$$

See Figure 12.3.

If one is adept with binary numbers, simple arithmetic operations are enough to place any desired bit pattern in a variable. To assist this process, however, C provides bit operators. These operators come in two varieties: logical operators and shift operators. Both of these are discussed in the following sections.

Logical Operators

The logical operators are similar to the boolean operators used for testing conditions. Listed by symbol (and note the difference from the C boolean operators), they include the binary operators & (*and*), | (*or*), ∧ (*exclusive or*), and the unary operator ~ (*not*).

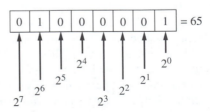

Figure 12.3 Binary number place values

The *and* operator compares its two operands *one bit at a time* using the standard logical *and* operation, treating 0 as false and 1 as true. Thus, 1 & 1 evaluates to 1, whereas other combinations evaluate to 0. Similarly, for the *or* operator, 0 | 0 evaluates to 0, whereas other combinations evaluate to 1. The *exclusive or* operator has no equivalent among the C boolean operators. Both 0 ∧ 1 and 1 ∧ 0 evaluate to 1, while 0 ∧ 0 and 1 ∧ 1 evaluate to 0. The *not* operator changes a bit from 0 to 1 or vice versa. These operators are summarized in Figure 12.4.

For example, consider the following declarations:

```
unsigned char first = 3, second = 5;
unsigned char third;
```

The bit pattern for `first` is 0000 0011, and the pattern for `second` is 0000 0101. The lower-order bits contain the four combinations of zeros and ones needed to illustrate the result of each of the operations. Thus, we can determine the following patterns:

```
third = first & second;    /* third now contains 0000 0001 */
third = first | second;    /* third now contains 0000 0111 */
third = first ^ second;    /* third now contains 0000 0110 */
third = ~first;            /* third now contains 1111 1100 */
```

Each operator may also be used in conjunction with the assignment operator, as in `first |= second;` which is equivalent to `first = first | second;`

The & operator is often used to *mask* out bits. A mask value is a bit pattern that, when &ed with a variable, zeroes out any bits that are not ones in the mask but leaves the remaining bits of the variable with their original value. For example, consider the definition `#define MASK 15`, which has the bit pattern 0000 1111. Now the fragment

```
unsigned char first = 92;    /* first contains 0101 1100 */
first &= MASK;               /* first contains 0000 1100 */
```

shows the application of the mask to `first`. The first four bits are now zero, since MASK's upper bits were all zeros. MASK's lower-order bits were all ones, so the lower bits of `first` remain unchanged.

a	b	a & b		a	b	a | b		a	b	a ∧ b		a	~a
0	0	0		0	0	0		0	0	0		0	1
0	1	0		0	1	1		0	1	1		1	0
1	0	0		1	0	1		1	0	1			
1	1	1		1	1	1		1	1	0			

Figure 12.4   Logical operators: *and, or, exclusive or, not*

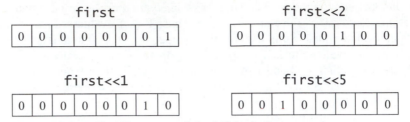

Figure 12.5   Left shift operator; right shift is similar

Similarly, a mask may be used with the | operator, which has the effect of turning bits on where the mask has ones and leaving the other bits unchanged. Applying the mask, we have

```
unsigned char first = 92;    /* first contains 0101 1100 */
first |= MASK;               /* first contains 0101 1111 */
```

where the upper bits of first are unchanged and the lower bits that were zeros are now ones.

Shift Operators

The shift operators move the bit pattern one or more positions to the left or right, depending on which operator is used. The shift is *not cyclic*. That is, bits moving out one end do not reenter on the other end; instead, zeros replace the bits emptied by the shift.

The two operators are << for shifting to the left and >> for shifting to the right. Each operates on a variable and takes an integer parameter indicating the number of bit positions to shift. For example, using the definition unsigned char first = 1; (bit pattern 0000 0001), then first << 1 indicates shifting first's bits to the left by one position, resulting in the bit pattern 0000 0010 (see Figure 12.5). This fragment does not affect first itself. The shift operators may be used with assignment, as in first = first << 1; or first <<= 1; either of which reassigns first to 0000 0010.

The right shift operates in the same way, as the following fragment shows:

```
unsigned char first = 49;    /* first contains 0011 0001 */
first >>= 4;                  /* first contains 0000 0011 */
```

Note that the 1 in the original ones' position was shifted out of first, while zeros were used to fill in the leftmost bit positions.

UNIX Parsing Tools

UNIX provides two tools to help process text. These tools, **lex** and **yacc**, are quite specialized and have a strong computer science flavor. This section only introduces the most basic facts of lex and yacc; further details may be found in [Levine et al.].

The lex Utility

When processing text, it is useful to break up the text into words or some other units. The lex program facilitates this task by generating C code based on a definition of what units should be used and what should be done with them as they are found in the input. The program compiled from the lex-generated source code will read characters from an input file and attempt to recognize specified tokens.

lex is short for *lexical analysis*, also known as *scanning,* which is the process of breaking input text into *tokens*, the units of text that are typically passed along to another program (like yacc) or function for further processing. Lexical analysis is the first of the several components that make up a compiler.

Tokens are defined in lex using regular expressions (see Chapter 8 for a discussion). Token definitions are placed in a special input file according to lex specifications. The file has three parts (each separated by a line containing %%): definitions, actions taken when tokens are recognized, and code, as shown in Figure 12.6. The code section may include main() for quick-and-dirty applications, or it may contain functions that are called from another source file, in which case a .h file may be used for common definitions and prototypes.

The actions specified in the middle section of a lex file are considered sequentially. Once an appropriate action is identified, later actions are ignored. No comments are permitted on action lines.

The lex utility provides one function and several variables that may be used within this code. The function is **yylex()**, which returns an int value that may be specified in the middle section of the specification file. If a given token does not have an assigned value, lex returns 0 for that token. The variables include the string **yytext**, which holds the token, and **yyleng**, the length of yytext.

Consider the following simple example. Suppose that the input text contains only unsigned integers, unsigned floating-point numbers, and white space. (Note that if arithmetic operators were added, this could form the basis for a desk calculator–like language.) The following file illustrates the lex specification file format and some of the special lex features.

Figure 12.6   lex input file format

```
/* lex specification file */
/* Constant declarations */
%{
#include <stdio.h>
                        /* Constants for yylex():  */
#define FLOAT 257    /* Floating-point number   */
#define INT   258    /* Integer number          */
%}
/* Token definitions */
digit   [0-9]                /* A digit is one character in the range 0 - 9 */
integer {digit}+             /* An integer is one or more consecutive digits */
float   {digit}+\.{digit}*   /* A float is an integer followed by a period   */
                             /*    and an optional decimal part              */
ws      [ \t\n]+             /* Three white space characters                 */
other   .                    /* Anything else                                */
%%
{float}   { return( FLOAT ); }
{ws}      { /* no action */; }
{integer} { return( INT ); }
%%
/* Code section */
main() {
  int tokentype;  /* Return value of yylex() */
  int ivalue;     /* Converted integer value */
  float fvalue;   /* Converted float value   */
  while ( !feof( stdin )) {     /* Until no more input */
    /* Call yylex() and check the token. */
    tokentype = yylex();
    /* Token must be an integer or float */
    if ( tokentype > 0 ) {
      /* Just print out the values - no processing */
      printf( "yylex returned %d\n", tokentype );
      printf( "yytext = %s\n", yytext );
      /* Token is an integer */
      if ( tokentype == INT ) {
        sscanf( yytext, "%d", &ivalue );
        printf( "value = %d\n", ivalue );
      /* Token is a float */
      } else {
        sscanf( yytext, "%f", &fvalue );
        printf( "value = %f\n", fvalue );
      } /* else */
    } /* if tokentype > 0 */
  } /* while */
} /* main() */
```

The first section contains `#include` and `#define` statements (surrounded by %{ and %}) in addition to token definitions. Note that `#defines` begin at 257, because the first 256 values are reserved by `lex`. The first section also defines tokens labeled `digit`, `integer`, `float`, `ws` (white space), and `other`. The second section contains tokens and the actions, if any, to be taken when tokens are found. In this example, `yylex()` returns `FLOAT` when it recognizes a float token, `INT` when it recognizes an integer, and 0 otherwise. The third section contains code; in this simple example it contains a main program.

The `main()` function calls `yylex()` to get the next token. The token type is returned as an integer and is displayed, along with the token string and converted value. Note that if `main()` were in another `.c` file, the token string and value would need to be copied from `yytext` into other variables or parameters or stored in a table. White space is ignored; so are other kinds of input, although a more reasonable action might be to produce an error message.

Suppose that the foregoing file is named `mylex`. Issuing the command `lex mylex` produces the file `lex.yy.c`, the standard name of the C source file output by `lex`. This file may now be compiled using the command `cc lex.yy.c -ll -o prog`, which asks that the `lex` library be linked (due to `-ll`) and produces the executable file `prog`. When `prog` is run, input lines are separated into numerical tokens, which are displayed twice, as strings and as numbers, to illustrate the use of `yytext` and its converted value. Other tokens are ignored. If the line

```
1    5.9     7.27
```

is stored in the file `prog.input`, then the command `prog < prog.input` produces the output

```
yylex returned 258
yytext = 1
value = 1
yylex returned 257
yytext = 5.9
value = 5.900000
yylex returned 257
yytext = 7.27
value = 7.270000
```

In a more useful version of `mylex`, of course, meaningful processing of the tokens would take place.

The `yacc` Utility

The `yacc` program's initials stand for "yet another compiler-compiler," which indicates its job: produce the C code for the parser section of a compiler so that programs written in some language (such as a desk calculator language or something more complicated, like Pascal) can be processed. It is beyond the scope of this book to discuss parsing, grammars, and compilation, but we do discuss in general how `yacc` operates.

Like `lex`, `yacc` uses a three-part setup file consisting of definitions, a grammar specification with actions, and user-provided code. The *grammar*—the rules that describe how correct statements are constructed in the language being *parsed* (analyzed for correct syntax)—must be written in a special format. The associated actions specify what operations must be performed to process the program. For a desk calculator language, for example, these actions would involve pushing operands onto a stack or popping them off and applying an operator.

The `yacc` program is usually used in conjunction with `lex`. Tokens are identified by `lex` and processed by `yacc`, partly by the grammar actions and partly by the user-provided code. To make this connection, common definitions must be placed in a `.h` file `#include`d by both specification files. Additionally, the `yylex()` function and the `yytext` variable may be used in the `yacc` code. A `yacc` file named `myyacc` is processed by the commands

```
yacc myyacc
cc y.tab.c -o prog2
```

where `y.tab.c` is the C source file generated by `yacc`. We assume here that `main()` is part of the user-provided code in `myyacc`, and we ignore the details of making the connection to `lex`-generated code.

Reference

Levine, John, Tony Mason, and Doug Brown, *lex and yacc,* 2nd ed., O'Reilly and Associates, Sebastopol, CA, 1992.

Chapter Summary

■ **C Commands**

Precompiler Macros

`#define MAX 99`	Replace MAX by 99 before compiling the program
`#define SamIAm system( "whoami" )`	Define SamIAm, a macro to report the current userid, assuming that `<stdlib.h>` has been included

`#define lg( x ) ((( x ) > 0 ) ? ( log( x ) / log( 2 )) : log( x ))`

A macro for the base-two logarithm function, assuming that `<math.h>` has been included

Precompiler Constructs for Conditional Compilation

```
#if ( VERSION > 1 )
  #define ARRAY_MAX 1024
#else
  #define ARRAY_MAX 256
#endif
```
Define ARRAY_MAX depending on the value of the VERSION at the time of precompilation; VERSION must already have an assigned value

```
#if ( VERSION == 2 )
  #define ARRAY_MAX 1024
#elif ( VERSION == 3 )
  #define ARRAY_MAX 2048
#endif
```
Define ARRAY_MAX depending on the value of the VERSION at the time of precompilation; but only if VERSION is 2 or 3

```
#ifdef VERSION
  #define ARRAY_MAX 2048
#else
  #define ARRAY_MAX 1024
#endif
```
If the constant `VERSION` has been defined, then define `ARRAY_MAX` to be 2048; otherwise, define `ARRAY_MAX` to be 1024

```
#ifndef FALSE
  #define FALSE 0
#endif
```
If `FALSE` has not yet been defined, at this time define `FALSE` to be 0

```
#ifndef TRUE
  #define TRUE !FALSE
#endif
```
If `TRUE` has not yet been defined, at this time define `TRUE` to be `!FALSE`

```
#ifndef MYMACROS
  #define MYMACROS
    #define TIME_LIMIT 20
    #define ERROR_LIMIT 3
#endif
```
Define macros included in the macro `MYMACROS` only if these definitions have not yet been made

```
#undef MYMACROS
```
Delete the definition of the macro `MYMACROS`

```
#error "Type 1 error has occurred"
```
Display an error message and stop precompilation

Compiler Constants

```
const int time_limit = 20;
```
Create a read-only variable `time_limit` and assign it the value 20

```
const char daychars[ 5 ] = { 'M', 'T', 'W', 'R', 'F' };
```
Define a constant array of characters to label the five days of a standard work week

Enumerated Types

```
typedef enum { M, T, W, R, F } daychars;
```
Define the type `daychars`; variables of this type can be assigned any of the five given constants, which have integer values from 0 to 4

Bit Operations

```
c = a & b;
```
Assign `c` the integer whose individual bits are 1 only when both corresponding bits of `a` and `b` are 1

```
c = a | b;
```
Assign `c` the integer whose individual bits are 0 only when both corresponding bits of `a` and `b` are 0

```
c = a ^ b;
```
Assign `c` the integer whose individual bits are 1 only when both corresponding bits of `a` and `b` are unequal

```
c = ~a;
```
Assign `c` the integer whose individual bits are 1 only when the corresponding bit of `a` is 0

```
#define MASK 127
```
In binary, `MASK` = 0111 1111

`c = a & MASK;`	Assign c the integer represented by the seven low bits of a
`c = a & ( ^MASK );`	Assign c the integer represented by the highest bit of a
`c = ( MASK >> 4 );`	Shift the bits of MASK four places to the right and assign this integer to c; in binary, c is 0000 0111 and MASK is still 0111 1111
`c = ( MASK << 4 );`	Shift the bits of MASK four places to the left and assign this integer to c; in binary, c is 1111 0000 and MASK is still 0111 1111

■ UNIX Commands

Lexical Analysis (lex)

```
/* Author: B&W   */
/* Title: Luthor */
/* This is a sample program file to be used as input for lex. */
/* The instructions in main() use text input from          */
/* standard input and send text output to standard output,  */
/* with certain tokens receiving special attention.         */

/* Constant definitions: */
%{
#include <stdio.h>
/* One constant for yylex(): */
#define OUR_HERO 257
%}
/* Token definitions: */
name1 Superman
name2 superman
other .
%%
{name1} { return( OUR_HERO ); }
{name2} { return( OUR_HERO ); }
%%
/* Code section: */
main() {
  int tokentype; /* Value returned by yylex() */
  while ( !feof( stdin )) {   /* Until no more input */
    /* Call yylex() and check the token */
    tokentype = yylex();
    if ( tokentype == OUR_HERO )
      printf( "\n%s (GOTCHA!!!)\n", yytext );
    else if ( tokentype > 0 )
      printf( "%s", yytext );
  } /* end of while loop */
}
```

Review Problems

1. Write a program to find out what your system does when an assignment is made to a variable that has been previously declared using a const construction.
2. In each of the following situations, would it be preferable to use const or #define to specify a constant value of MAX?
   a) MAX specifies the number of entries in an array type that is to be declared with a typedef construct.
   b) MAX is a global constant.
   c) MAX is a local constant used only within the scope of one function.
   d) MAX is a parameter named in a function header, and the value of MAX must not be changed.
3. Consider the following declarations:

   ```
   #define SIZE 7
   typedef enum { Su, Mo, Tu, We, Th, Fr, Sa } day;
   typedef int attendance[ SIZE ];
   attendance students;
   ```

   a) Write a function to find the successor for each day of the week; use the prototype

   ```
   day nextday( day today );
   ```

   b) What is wrong with the following loop, whose purpose is to print attendance figures for a week beginning on Wednesday and ending on Tuesday?

   ```
   for ( today = We; today != Tu; today = nextday( today ))
      printf( "students[ %d ] = %d\n", today, students[ today ] );
   ```

   c) Rewrite the fragment given in part b) so that it executes correctly.
4. Consider the macro

   ```
   #define lg( x ) ((( x ) > 0 ) ? ( log( x ) / log( 2 )) : log( x )).
   ```

   a) Verify the claim that this macro correctly defines the base-two logarithm function.
   b) Why is the inner set of parentheses needed in the expression ((x) > 0)?
   c) What is the advantage of using this macro rather than calling a user-defined function to evaluate lg x ?
5. Given the definition #define b 66 and the assignment two_b = (b << 1); evaluate the following expressions in both binary and decimal notation.
   a) b
   b) two_b
   c) two_b | (~two_b)
   d) two_b ^ (~two_b)
   e) two_b & (~two_b)
6. In each part, define an integer MASK and a suitable expression for b in order to produce the specified result.
   a) For any (eight-bit) integer a, b is the sixth bit (the bit whose place value is 32) of a.
   b) For any (eight-bit) integer a, b is the integer corresponding to the four low-order bits of a. For example, if a = 65 (in binary, a = 0100 0001) then b = 1.

7. Consider `Luthor`, the sample `lex` program file given in the Chapter Summary.
   a) What sequence of commands would be used to create an executable C file, `CatchHim`, to analyze text input according to the instructions given in the `main()` section of the `Luthor` file?
   b) Describe the effect of using `CatchHim` to analyze an input stream.

Programming Problems

1. (ISBN Check Digit) This book and most others have a 10-digit code, called the *International Standard Book Number* (ISBN), whose last digit is a check digit that can be used to validate correct codes and to catch errors when an ISBN is copied or reported. The check digit rule for an ISBN is that once the first nine digits $(d_1, d_2, \ldots, d_9)$ are specified, the tenth digit (d_{10}) is chosen so that the number

$$10d_1 + 9d_2 + 8d_3 + 7d_4 + 6d_5 + 5d_6 + 4d_7 + 3d_8 + 2d_9 + d_{10}$$

is a multiple of 11. When the check digit is 10, it is coded with the letter X; the first nine digits are ordinary decimal digits.

A better description of the check digit rule uses modular arithmetic with modulus 11, where the allowable digits are 0, 1, 2, 3, 4, 5, 6, 7, 8, 9, and X (X represents 10). When using modulus 11, modular addition, subtraction, multiplication, and division operations are defined to be the remainders of the corresponding base-ten operations after integer division by 11. For example, X + 9 "equals" 8, since 8 is the remainder of 19 divided by 11. This is usually written as

$$X + 9 \equiv 8 \ (\mathrm{mod}\ 11)$$

where the symbol $\equiv$ is usually read "is congruent to" or "is equivalent to." Using modular arithmetic, the ISBN check digit requirement is that d_{10} must be chosen so that

$$10d_1 + 9d_2 + 8d_3 + 7d_4 + 6d_5 + 5d_6 + 4d_7 + 3d_8 + 2d_9 + d_{10} \equiv 0 \ (\mathrm{mod}\ 11)$$

Write a program that can calculate the check digit for a new ISBN code and can also validate a given ISBN code. Do not use any of the operators +, -, *, /, % anywhere other than in macros that define the modular arithmetic operations. Allow the user to enter data either interactively or with command line arguments.

2. (Numerical Conversions) Write a program to display the binary, octal, and hexadecimal conversions of an integer expression. For input accept eight-character strings whose first character is +, -, or a digit, and whose remaining characters are all digits. When converting from base 10 to another base, do not use any arithmetic operators (+, -, *, /, %), and also do not use binary, octal, or hex conversion sequences to display the conversions. Allow the user to enter an expression either interactively or on the command line.

3. (Semi-Perpetual Calendar) Write a program to display the correct calendar for a given month or year between January 1800 A.D. and December 2200 A.D. Use enumerated types and macros wherever appropriate. Do not use the system function `cal`. *Hint*: Refer to the definitions of Gregorian calendar, leap year, and centesimal year, and note that only those centesimal years divisible by 400 are leap years.

4. (Information Coding) A weather service uses an array to code the five-day forecast for various cities. For example, the data array

```
{LAX, T, C, S, F, F, F}
```

indicates that the city is Los Angeles (each city has a three-letter code) and that the current data begins with the forecast for Tuesday and forecasts *C*loudy skies on Tuesday, *S*unny skies on Wednesday, and *F*air skies for Thursday through Saturday.

Write a program to create, edit, and display a file containing such information, but expanded to include low and high temperatures and probabilities of precipitation. Store the data for each city in a record. The display of weather information for a city should have a format similar to the following.

```
Seven-Day Forecast for Los Angeles:
    Day         Low    High    Weather     Precipitation Prob.
    Tuesday     50     79      Cloudy      0.20
    Wednesday   55     82      Sunny       0.00
```

and so forth.

5. (Calculator) Use `lex` to create an interactive program to scan and evaluate numerical expressions of the form

operand1 operator operand2

where *operator* indicates either addition, subtraction, multiplication, or division, and each *operand* is either a number or another expression enclosed in parentheses. Also allow the entire expression to be enclosed in parentheses. Terminate input with either an equal sign, to evaluate the expression, or control-D, to abort the program. Place user-defined types, function prototypes, and user-defined functions in the code section of the `lex` file. Here are some typical input and output lines:

```
1+(3.0- -3)= 7.000000.
((2.0/ 4) + (2.5 - 1.5) ) = 1.500000.
-2 + ( ( 1- 1) = CONTAINS AN INPUT ERROR.
```

6. (Preliminary Syntax Checker) Use `lex` to create a program to scan a program file and check for equal numbers of left and right parentheses as well as equal numbers of left and right brackets. Do not count parentheses or brackets occurring inside comments. Note that this program does not fully check parenthesis and bracket syntax, because it does not recognize the order of the notation. For example, the line

```
printf) "\n" (;
```

has incorrect C syntax but passes the check for equal numbers of left and right parentheses.

Chapter

13

Advanced Programming Topics

This chapter discusses several advanced topics in C programming, including the use of recursive functions, function pointers, and low-level file-processing commands. Advanced UNIX topics relating to process creation and management are also covered. The UNIX section also includes a discussion of C function calls for process manipulation from within C programs.

Recursion

Recursive functions were mentioned in Chapter 4 when functions were first introduced. A recursive function call was defined there as a function calling itself—that is, within a function's body there is a call to the same function. Thus, a recursive function causes another version of itself to be created when the self-call is made, with new parameters and local variables completely separate from any other versions of the function. Recursive functions provide a powerful tool for implementing many algorithms that might otherwise be more complicated.

At execution time, a recursive function acts somewhat like the body of a loop. A recursive function accepts parameters indicating the part of the problem or range of values it needs to process and returns a value to the calling function that is the result of or answer to the recursion at that level. Based on its input parameter values, the recursive function determines whether it needs to call itself again. For example, the recursive inorder tree traversal algorithm of Chapter 10 returns without calling itself again when passed a NULL pointer value. If the recursive function does call itself, return is delayed, of course, until all lower-level calls have finished.

Since the new "cloned" function can call itself again, care must be taken to prevent an infinite sequence of calls. If the input parameters indicate the *base case* (the last recursive call), then the recursion ends by passing a value back to the previous call. This check prevents an infinite recursion from occurring. Note that in practice only a finite number of recursive calls may occur, because each call requires a memory allocation; eventually, the program's memory allotment will be used up and the program will crash. It is the programmer's job to prevent this abnormal behavior; most errors in recursive programming result from incorrectly coding for this possibility.

The return value to the calling function provides an answer from the lower level up to the next level in the recursion. The run-time system must manage this sequence of calls by storing the calling parameters at each level until that level returns. In practical terms this shifts the bookkeeping from the programmer to the run-time system, resulting in a large overhead burden. In general, recursive algorithms require less code but are less efficient than straightforward solutions.

As an example, consider the problem of computing the factorial of a positive integer. The recursive definition of factorial, using the notation $n!$ for "n factorial" is

$$0! = 1$$
$$n! = n(n-1)!, \quad \text{for } n > 0$$

The base case is $0!$. The recursive step uses the definition of $(n-1)!$, that is, of the factorial of one less than n. Using this definition, one can compute in stages that $3! = 6$, since $3! = 3 \times 2! = 3 \times 2 \times 1! = 3 \times 2 \times 1 \times 0!$, where finally $0!$ is defined as 1, and the multiplication can proceed. Similarly, $5! = 120$, $8! = 40,320$, and both $-4!$ and $0.5!$ are undefined. Several notes are in order:

1. Factorial values grow very quickly as n gets larger; this growth can overwhelm `int` variables.
2. We ignore the more general mathematical definition of factorial that includes all real numbers.
3. Most important for implementation, a straightforward definition of factorial using a `for` loop rather than recursion is more efficient than the recursive code to be shown presently. You should code the `for` loop version for practice.

The following function is a recursive implementation of factorial.

```
int factorial( int n ) {
  if ( n == 0 ) {      /* Base case                     */
    return( 1 );
  } else {             /* Otherwise, make a recursive call */
    return( n * factorial( n - 1 ));
  }
}
```

After checking for the base case, which returns 1, the recursive call is made with `n - 1` as the argument. An alternative method, using the local variable `int i`, uses two steps to make the recursive call more obvious:

```
i = factorial( n - 1 );
return( i * n );
```

The following function call,

```
printf( "3! = %d\n", factorial( 3 ));
```

will display 3! = 6. The execution of `factorial( 3 )` follows the pattern just outlined (see Figure 13.1). First, `factorial( n )` is created with n = 3. Since this is not the base case, the `return` statement is delayed until `factorial( 2 )` returns a value. Second, `factorial( 2 )` is created; its `return` statement is delayed until `factorial( 1 )` is returned. Similarly, `factorial( 1 )` is created and awaits the return value from `factorial( 0 )`. In this instance of `factorial()`, the parameter is the base case, so 1 is returned to the waiting version `factorial( 1 )`, which now computes its return value, 1 * 1. This value is returned to the previous waiter, `factorial( 2 )`, which computes its return value 2 * 1, finally returned to `factorial( 3 )`, which computes 3 * 2 to be sent back to the original call. Both this description and the execution require more work than the `for` loop implementation.

This solution correctly checks for the base case, but it ignores two other potential problems already mentioned: negative arguments and the potential for overflow (integers too large to store in an `int` variable). Using the `unsigned` type does not quite correct the former problem, since, due to C's weak type checking, a negative argument would still be accepted by `factorial()`. Instead, an explicit check may be used as the first line in the function. For example,

```
if ( n < 0 ) return( 0 );
```

returns zero for negative arguments; alternatively, an error message could be printed. The overflow problem is only delayed by substituting either `long` or `double` for `int`, because each of these types overflows for large arguments, albeit larger ones than the `int` version can handle. To be safe, adding the line

```
if ( n > MAXFACTVALUE ) return( 0 );
```

protects against overflow for a suitably defined value of MAXFACTVALUE, which depends on the size of `int`s on the user's machine.

Designing with Recursion

There are many problems whose solution is best stated by a recursive algorithm. This is obviously true for those problems of a mathematical nature that are defined recursively, such as the factorial function. It is also true for operations on many data structures, such as linked lists and trees. Algorithms that work on the *divide-and-conquer* principle are candidates for recursion. Divide-and-conquer attempts to split a problem into several (often two) smaller parts, solve each part separately, then combine the separate solutions into the final answer. Each part, being a smaller version of the original, may also be solved by the same method. Recall, for example, the binary search algorithm on a sorted array from Chapter 7. Its strategy was to divide the array into two parts at the middle array element. Either the search key is equal to the element, or the search is continued in one of the two halves using the same strategy. This algorithm is coded in the next section as a recursive function. Also, recall that in Chapter 10 a recursive function was used to implement the inorder traversal operation for a binary tree. Binary trees are also a natural target for recursion, given the branching from the parent to children nodes.

We point out again the trade-off of execution performance versus ease of coding. Experience has shown that for some algorithms a recursive solution is easier to code than a

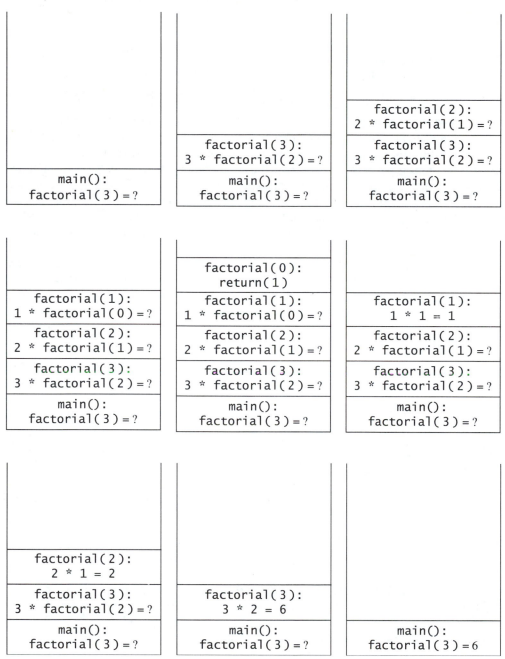

Figure 13.1 Call stack for factorial(3)

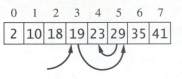

Figure 13.2   Binary search for 23. Successive midpoint values are 19, 29, and 23.

nonrecursive solution. The reason is that the nonrecursive code must keep track of a counter and, more importantly, the path taken through a data structure for possible backtracking. This explicit record keeping adds to the complexity of the code. Recursive algorithms, on the one hand, let the run-time environment keep track of some of this information, which is stored implicitly and thus is not of direct concern to the programmer. On the other hand, this implicit information contributes to the higher overhead of recursive schemes. Since the run-time system creates new function "clones" for recursive calls, there are unseen (by the programmer) penalties for using a recursive solution. In general, a rule of thumb is that recursive algorithms are faster to code but slower to execute, and conversely, nonrecursive algorithms take longer to code but run more efficiently.

If a recursive implementation is used, it may be converted to nonrecursive code by keeping track of the stack information explicitly. That is, a stack data structure must be maintained by the program to keep track of the path taken through the data structure. Conversion from recursive to nonrecursive code is, in general, time-consuming and messy.

Examples

We now examine several examples of recursive algorithms on data structures that have been discussed previously. These include sorted arrays, linked lists, and binary search trees.

Binary Search of Sorted Arrays

In Chapter 7 sorted arrays were used to store a fixed number of items sorted on a key. The problem of initially sorting the array was discussed in Chapter 7 using selection sort and will be discussed again in the next section using merge sort. Here, we reexamine the binary search algorithm for finding a key in a sorted array.

Recall that the binary search algorithm uses the divide-and-conquer method described in a previous section. Each step of the binary search performs three tasks:

1. Given the current endpoint indices, compute the new midpoint index.
2. Compare the middle element to the search key, and quit if equal.
3. Choose the correct half of the array to search next.

In addition, the search is halted when it can be determined that the key is not in the array. One way to do this is to stop if the current endpoint indices are not correctly ordered. This is the stopping condition for the recursion in the following function (see Figure 13.2). Both this example and the nonrecursive binary search code in Chapter 7 use an array of `int`s.

```
void BinSearch( int list[ SIZE ], int key, int low, int high ) {
  int middle;   /* Midpoint index */
  /* Stopping condition */
  if ( low > high ) printf( "Key not found.\n" );
  else {
  /* Compute the new midpoint index. */
```

```
        middle = ( low + high ) / 2;
        /* Compare the middle element and the search key for equality. */
        if ( key == list[ middle ] ) printf( "Found at index = %d\n", middle );
        /* Otherwise, recurse on the correct half of the array. */
        else if ( key < list[ middle ] ) BinSearch( list, key, low, middle - 1 );
        else BinSearch( list, key, middle + 1, high );
    }
}
```

A call to this function from `main()` takes the form

```
BinSearch( list, searchkey, 0, LIST - 1 );
```

Note that the argument matching the `high` parameter is the largest index, not the size of the array. Additional checks on `low` and `high` inside `BinSearch()` could be added to eliminate erroneous calls, such as

```
BinSearch( list, searchkey, -12, LIST - 1 );
```

which passes a negative index argument.

Merge Sort for Sorted Arrays

Merge sort uses the divide-and-conquer strategy to halve the array to be sorted, sort each half, then merge the two halves into one sorted list. Each half is sorted by the same method. Halving continues until the resulting subarrays are small enough to be sorted easily—down to one element, if taken to the furthest level, but in practice, down to a manageable size. Most of the work of merge sort comes in the merging phase, where elements are actually compared. In addition, merge sort requires that extra space be available for temporarily storing the results of the merge step (see Figure 13.3).

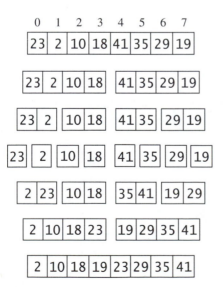

Figure 13.3 Splitting and merging steps of `MergeSort()`

The following function shows the recursive implementation of merge sort. The stopping condition checks for a list of size 1.

```
void MergeSort( int list[ SIZE ], int low, int high ) {
  int middle;   /* Midpoint index */
  /* Check stopping condition */
  if ( high > low ) {
    middle = ( low + high ) / 2;
    /* Sort the upper half */
    MergeSort( list, low, middle );
    /* Sort the lower half */
    MergeSort( list, middle + 1, high );
    /* Merge the two halves */
    merge( list, low, high );
  } /* if */
} /* MergeSort */
```

As with binary search, the middle index value is computed to divide the list into two halves. Each half is sorted by calling `MergeSort()` recursively. There is no reason the upper half (from index `middle + 1` to `high`) could not be sorted before the lower half by exchanging the recursive calls. The function `merge()` combines the two half-lists; its details are left to you.

Recursion for Linked Lists

The traversal procedure for linked lists is quite simple to code in a straightforward manner, but we include it here as a recursion example for illustration purposes. Recall that traversal visits every node on the list and processes the data contained in each one.

The following example uses a simple node type, containing only an integer data field and the `next` pointer field. Processing a node simply prints the data field. The node definition is

```
typedef struct node {  /* Linked list node: */
  int         data;   /*     Data field    */
  struct node *next;   /*     Pointer field */
} Node, *NodePtr;
```

The stopping condition for the recursion is the same as for the nonrecursive implementation: Quit when `NULL` is encountered. The traversal function is then

```
void traversal( NodePtr current ){
  /* Check the stopping condition */
  if ( current != NULL ) {
    /* Process this node's data */
    printf( "Data = %d\n", current->data );
    /* Recursive call */
    traversal( current->next );
  } /* if */
} /* traversal */
```

From `main()` the call `traverse( head )` prints the list pointed to by `head`, assuming the proper declaration and initiation of `head`. The placement of the recursive call relative to processing the data is critical. If the two are reversed, the list will be processed in reverse order. You are invited to show that this is true and to consider how to implement a nonrecursive function to process the list's nodes in reverse order.

Recursion for Trees

In Chapter 10 we coded an inorder binary search tree traversal using recursion. Recall that an inorder traversal processes the nodes in sorted order according to the key field of the tree nodes. The ordering of the steps in the function in Chapter 10 was, for each node, to make a recursive call to the left child, process the current node, then make a recursive call to the right child. Thus for each node, starting from the root, the left subtree is visited first, the current node is visited next, and the right subtree is visited last. By rearranging these steps, several other traversals can be achieved.

A *preorder* traversal of a binary tree visits the current node first, then visits the left subtree, and finally visits the right subtree. In a *postorder* traversal, the left subtree is visited first, followed by the right subtree, with the current node visited last. A *breadth-first* traversal (or level-order traversal) is a nonrecursive tree traversal that visits all the nodes on a given level before moving to the next level. The root node is visited first, then all of the children of the root are visited, then all of the root's grandchildren are visited, and so on. Since this method is not recursive, we will not consider it further.

To code preorder and postorder traversals, the inorder traversal code is simply rearranged. The stopping condition (checking for a NULL pointer) is the same for all three. The preorder traversal function is as follows. It assumes appropriate definitions for `TreePtr`, the corresponding tree node `TreeNode`, and the node processing function `ProcessNode` that accepts a parameter of type `TreeNode`. See Chapter 10 for the original example.

```
void preorder( TreePtr ptr )
{
  /* Base case: do nothing if null */
  if ( ptr == NULL ) return;
  else {
    /* Visit the current node */
    ProcessNode( *ptr );
    /* Visit the left child */
    preorder( ptr->left );
    /* Visit the right child last */
    preorder( ptr->right );
  } /* else not NULL */
} /* preorder */
```

Postorder traversal has a similar form, as shown next.

```
void postorder( TreePtr ptr )
{
  /* Base case: do nothing if null */
  if ( ptr == NULL ) return;
```

```
  else {
    /* Visit the left child first */
    postorder( ptr->left );
    /* Visit the right child next */
    postorder( ptr->right );
    /* Visit the current node */
    ProcessNode( *ptr );
  } /* else not NULL */
} /* postorder */
```

Neither preorder nor postorder traversal makes much sense for a binary search tree, where the data is stored for inorder retrieval. However, recall that there are rules for storing data in a tree other than the binary search rule ("smaller left, larger right"). For example, arithmetic expressions may be stored as trees in which leaf nodes contain operands and interior nodes contain binary arithmetic operators. The tree for the expression 2 * 3 + 4 is shown in Figure 13.4. Traversing this tree via inorder yields the original infix expression. (Note that, without using parentheses, we cannot distinguish between (2 * 3) + 4 and 2 * (3 + 4). That is, the latter expression's tree, though different from Figure 13.4, also produces the expression 2 * 3 + 4 on an inorder traversal.) Preorder traversal gives the expression + * 2 3 4, the prefix notation version of the expression. Postorder traversal yields 2 3 * 4 +, the expression's postfix notation version.

Function Pointers

To provide a more general method of processing data, C programs may use *function pointers*. Like a variable pointer, a function pointer is an address, but it is the address of a function. Typically used to pass a function as an argument to another function, function pointers delay the decision of which function to use for processing a set of data from compile time to run time.

The syntax for a function pointer is

typename (* *function name*)(*parameter list*)

where *typename* and *parameter list* use the usual function syntax. The difference to note is the placement of parentheses and * in (* *function name*). The parentheses are used to enforce correct binding of * to *function name* (rather than to *typename*, which would be the effect of *typename* * *function name*). In other words, the statement declares a pointer to a function that returns a value of *typename*. For example, the prototype

```
int (* fn)( int, double );
```

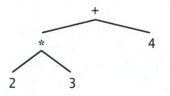

Figure 13.4 Tree for the infix expression 2 * 3 + 4

declares a pointer `fn` to a function `(* fn)()` that returns an `int` value and whose two parameters are an `int` and a `double`. As a function pointer, `(* fn)()` does not yet refer to any particular function. A function pointer can, however, be matched with any function that has its characteristics—in this case, a function that accepts an `int` and a `double` parameter, in that order, and returns an `int`.

Function pointer notation can be tricky. Consider the following prototypes:

```
char *fn1( char * );
char (* fn2)( char * );
char *(* fn3)( char * );
```

Each of the three functions accepts a character pointer as a parameter. The first prototype is similar to the string functions seen in previous chapters: The function `fn1()` returns a character pointer. The second is a function pointer; `(* fn2)()` returns a single character. The third example is also a function pointer, but `(* fn3)()` returns a character pointer.

In the following example the function pointer notation is shown in its most common usage: in the parameter list of another function.

```
void table( double (* func)( double ), double low, double high, int steps );
```

The function `table()`, whose code is shown in the next paragraph, prints a table of values of a mathematical function from `low` to `high`. The first parameter is a function pointer, `(* func)`, for a function that accepts a `double` parameter and also returns a `double`. The other parameters to `table()`—two `double`s and one `int`—are used in the usual way. The function pointer is used by sending an argument function that matches the parameter type; that is, the argument must be a function that accepts a `double` parameter and returns a `double` value.

Now consider the code for `table()`:

```
void table( double (* func)( double ), double low, double high, int steps ) {
    double xvalue,     /* Domain value           */
           yvalue,     /* Range value            */
           increment;  /* One step in the domain */
    int    count;      /* Loop counter           */
    /* Compute the x increment */
    increment = ( high - low ) / steps;
    /* Initialize x */
    xvalue    = low;
    /* Print the table header */
    printf( "    x    |    y\n" );
    printf( " ------------------\n" );
    for ( count = 0; count <= steps; count++ ) {
        yvalue = func( xvalue );
        printf( "%8.2lf | %8.2lf\n", xvalue, yvalue );
        xvalue += increment;
    } /* for */
} /* table() */
```

The parameters `low` and `high` determine the domain of `xvalue` and are used to compute `increment`, the amount that `xvalue` is incremented on each step. The `for` loop executes `steps + 1` times, printing one line of the table on each iteration. The `yvalue` corresponding to each `xvalue` is computed by calling the function `func()` with `xvalue` as a parameter.

An example call to `table()` is

```
table( sin, 0.0, 3.14, 6 );
```

where the argument `sin` is the sine function from the math library. The output of this call is a table of values of the sine function from `0.0` to `3.14`:

```
     x   |     y
-------------------
  0.00 |     0.00
  0.52 |     0.50
  1.05 |     0.87
  1.57 |     1.00
  2.09 |     0.87
  2.62 |     0.50
  3.14 |     0.00
```

Similarly, the call `table( cos, -3.14, 3.14, 20 );` produces a table of 21 cosine values. Again, any function fitting the prototype in the parameter list will do, so a user-defined function may be used as well. The next example shows such a function that computes one value of the quadratic polynomial $2x^2 - 3x$:

```
double myfunc( double x ){
  return( 2.0 * x * x - 3.0 * x );
} /* myfunc */
```

The following call to `table()`,

```
table( myfunc, -5.0, 5.0, 10 );
```

produces a table of 11 values of the given quadratic function.

The use of function pointers as parameters makes code more generic, because different arguments make the called function behave differently. This is a powerful tool for writing reusable code. One difficulty, however, is ensuring a proper match of parameter types. These points are illustrated in the next example.

Consider the following prototype from `<stdlib.h>`:

```
void qsort( void *, size_t, size_t, int (*)( const void *, const void * ));
```

The `qsort()` function is an implementation of quicksort, a sorting algorithm described more fully in this chapter's problem section. Recall that in a prototype it is legal to omit the names of the parameters, as done here, including the last parameter, which is a function pointer. This prototype specifies a function that returns an integer value and accepts two parameters of type `const void *`, or generic pointers. The argument matched to this parameter is intended to be a function that compares its two parameters and returns 0 if the parameters are equal, a negative integer if the first parameter is smaller than the second, and a positive integer otherwise. For example, the `strcmp()` function almost matches these specifications; however, its parameters are not of the correct type.

The `qsort()` function's other parameters are these: first, a generic pointer (intended as the name of an array); second, the number of elements in the array; and third, the size in bytes of one array element. For example, consider the following definitions:

```
#define SIZE   10    /* Number of strings */
#define LENGTH 80    /* Size of one string */
char array[ SIZE ][ LENGTH ];
```

Assuming that `array` has been filled with 10 legally terminated strings, the incorrect call

```
qsort( array, SIZE, LENGTH, strcmp );
```

fails because of `strcmp()`'s parameter specification. To overcome this, we must write an auxiliary function, shown next.

```
int  string_compare( const void *first, const void *second ){
  return( strcmp( (char *) first, (char *) second ));
} /* string_compare */
```

The function `string_compare()` simply casts its generic `void *` parameters to character pointers and calls `strcmp()` to do the actual comparison work. Now the call

```
qsort( (void *) array, SIZE, LENGTH, string_compare );
```

is correct (including a cast of `array`). The extra work of ensuring that the comparison function is correct is a small price to pay for using a built-in sort routine. See the problem section for exercises on using `qsort()` and on programming the quicksort algorithm.

Low-Level File Processing

In previous chapters two methods of file access were discussed. The first method uses `fscanf()` and `fprintf()` to process data in text files, using format conversion characters such as %d and %s. The second method uses `fread()` and `fwrite()` on binary files; these functions operate on records defined by `struct`s. These two methods use *buffered* input and output—that is, the operating system handles the details of data retrieval and storage; the system stores data temporarily (buffers it) in order to optimize file system access.

In this section we discuss low-level methods (sometimes called *bulk methods* because of the amount of data often handled) for file access. The primary functions, **read()** and **write()**, use byte strings for their operations. The term *unbuffered input/output* is used to describe these functions, since they are handled directly as system calls without buffering by the operating system. (Note that the actual details of I/O are more complicated than is suggested here.) The read() and write() functions are those most often used for interprocess communication, discussed in this chapter's UNIX section.

In order to use the low-level file functions, #include the header files <sys/types.h>, <sys/stat.h>, and <fcntl.h>.

Opening and Closing Files

Recall that a variable of type FILE * (a pointer to a file record) was associated with a file opened by the fopen() command. Low-level file operations use a *file descriptor*, a nonnegative integer assigned by the operating system, to identify a file. The file descriptor is the return value of the **open()** function, whose prototype is

```
int open( const *name, int flag [, mode_t mode ] );
```

An error is indicated if the return value is -1. The first parameter is the file name (optionally including a pathname). The optional mode parameter indicates the UNIX permissions assigned to a new file and is in fact required if a new file is being created.

The flag parameter is a combination of constants (see Figure 13.5) that indicates what will be done to the file's data. Only one of the following three constants may be used: O_RDONLY, read-only access; O_WRONLY, write-only access; O_RDWR, read/write access. Optionally, flag may be combined with any of these constants: O_APPEND, append access; O_CREAT, create a file named name if one does not exist (with permissions indicated by mode); and O_EXCL, which, when used in conjunction with O_CREAT, causes open() to fail if a file named name exists. To combine constants, the | operator is used. The following fragment shows myfile being opened (created if necessary) for write-only access.

Choose only one of:

O_RDONLY	Read-only access
O_WRONLY	Write-only access
O_RDWR	Read/write access

Optional flags:

O_APPEND	Append access
O_CREAT	Create file if doesn't exist
O_EXCL	Fail if file exists (with O_CREAT)

Figure 13.5 Flag constants for open()

```
int filedesc;
filedesc = open( "myfile", O_CREAT | O_WRONLY, 0600 );
if ( filedesc < 0 ) {
  printf( "Error opening file.\n" );
}
```

If successful, this call either creates `myfile` if it does not already exist, giving it permissions 0600 (read and write for the owner only), or simply opens the file if it exists, without changing its permissions. (Recall that UNIX permission modes were discussed in Chapter 3.)

To close a file, the function **close()** is used. Its prototype is

```
int close( int filedesc );
```

where `filedesc` is the value returned by `open()` when the file was opened. The return value of `close()` is zero if successful and –1 if not. To close `myfile` from the previous example, the fragment

```
if ( close( filedesc ) == -1 ) {
  printf( "Error closing file.\n" );
}
```

checks the return value and prints an error message if unsuccessful. Although open files are closed automatically if a program terminates, it is a safer practice to close files explicitly.

Reading, Writing, and Seeking

The `read()` and `write()` functions transfer data as byte strings. As with binary files, this data must be typecast to the format needed by the program before it can be used. Alternatively, a large string (character buffer) can be used to hold data until the cast can be performed.

The prototypes for `read()` and `write()` are quite similar:

```
ssize_t read( int filedesc, void *buffer, size_t num_bytes );
ssize_t write( int filedesc, void *buffer, size_t num_bytes );
```

In each case the first parameter is the file descriptor returned from `open()`, the second parameter holds the data, and the third indicates the number of bytes to be transferred. The return value tells how many bytes were actually transferred. If this value is –1, then an error occurred. Otherwise, if the value equals `num_bytes`, the requested bytes were successfully transferred; if the value is positive but less than `num_bytes`, some data was transferred; and if the value is zero, the end of the file has been reached. Note that both `size_t` and `ssize_t` are defined as `int`s in `<sys/types.h>` and that the data buffer has the type `void *`, necessitating a type cast for the actual argument.

To illustrate the use of `read()` and `write()`, the following file copy program `mycopy.c` copies the contents of one file into another. The program expects two command line parameters indicating the name of the file to be copied and the name of the new file to be created. The code uses a 8192-byte character buffer, a common size for file blocks on UNIX systems.

```c
#include <stdio.h>
#include <sys/types.h>
#include <sys/stat.h>
#include <fcntl.h>
#define BUFSIZE  8192                   /* File block size        */
#define NAMESIZE 80                     /* Name string size       */
typedef char buffertype[ BUFSIZE ];    /* Character buffer type  */
typedef char nametype[ NAMESIZE ];     /* Name string type       */
main( int argc, char *argv[] ) {
  buffertype buffer;         /* Character buffer        */
  nametype   first_name,     /* Name of file copy       */
             second_name;    /* Name of target          */
  int        first_desc,     /* First file descriptor   */
             second_desc,    /* Second file descriptor  */
             size;           /* Bytes transferred       */
  /* Check for two command line parameters */
  if ( argc != 3 ) {
    printf( "Usage: mycopy <file1> <file2>\n" );
    exit( 0 );
  } /* if argc */
  /* Copy the file names and open the files */
  strcpy( first_name, argv[1] );
  strcpy( second_name, argv[2] );
  first_desc  = open( first_name, O_RDONLY );
  if ( first_desc < 0 ) {
    printf( "Error opening %s\n", first_name );
    exit( 0 );
  } /* if open() */
  second_desc = open( second_name, O_CREAT | O_WRONLY, 0600 );
  if ( second_desc < 0 ) {
    printf( "Error opening %s\n", second_name );
    exit( 0 );
  } /* if open() */
  /* Read and write until end of file */
  size = read( first_desc, (void *) buffer, BUFSIZE );
  while ( size  > 0 ) {
    if ( write( second_desc, (void *) buffer, size ) != size ) {
      printf( "Error writing to %s\n", second_name );
      exit( 0 );
    } /* if write() */
    size = read( first_desc, (void *) buffer, BUFSIZE );
  } /* while size */
  /* Close the files */
  close( first_desc );
  close( second_desc );
} /* main() */
```

The program performs error checks for the correct number of command line parameters, for a correct return value from each call to `open()`, and for a correct return value from `write()`. The return values from the `close()` calls are ignored. The `while` loop continues until zero is returned from `read()`, indicating that the end of the first file has been reached.

Chapter 5 contained an example that used a compound expression that both assigned a value to a variable and tested that value using `if`. At the time, we recommended against using the style to avoid possible confusion. Because this construct is used by many C programmers, it is shown here, but again with the warning that the straightforward method is superior. The assignment of `size`, the calls to `read()`, and the `while` loop condition could be expressed using the single line

```
while (( size = read( first_desc, (void *) buffer, BUFSIZE )) > 0 ) {
    ... and so on ...
```

This statement first assigns `size` the value returned by `read()`, then tests whether this value is greater than zero. Since the call to `read()` is done at the top of the `while` loop, the call at the bottom of the loop is no longer necessary.

Before reading or writing, it may be necessary to move to a specific position in a file. For this purpose the **`lseek()`** function is provided. To use it, the files `<sys/types.h>` and `<unistd.h>` must be `#included`. Its prototype is

```
off_t lseek( int filedesc, off_t offset, int from_where );
```

where `off_t` is an alias for `long`. The first parameter is the file descriptor, and the second is the target position. The third parameter tells from where `offset` should be counted using the constants previously discussed in connection with the buffered `fseek()` function: The constant SEEK_SET (defined as 0) indicates counting `offset` bytes from the beginning of the file; SEEK_CUR (1) indicates the current position; and SEEK_END (2) indicates the current end of the file. When using SEEK_CUR and SEEK_END, the `offset` may be positive or negative. The return value of `lseek()` is the new file position, and `-1` indicates an error.

UNIX Processes

UNIX is a multiuser operating system, since many users can be logged in simultaneously. The system's resources, including the computing power, are shared among users. Moreover, UNIX is a *multiprogramming* system. Many programs may be "running simultaneously." Although on a system with one CPU only one program can be executing in the CPU at a time, while other programs wait for the CPU to become available, for input or output, or for various other reasons, we will mostly ignore these distinctions; the programs that are ready to use the CPU take their turns at it so quickly and frequently that from a user's point of view they all appear to be running. In fact, multiprogramming is what allows UNIX to support many users at the same time.

A running program is called a *process*. Recall that each time a user logs in, a shell is started. A shell is a program that accepts commands from a user and arranges for execution of the program(s) that carry out those commands. UNIX handles this by creating, for each command request, a new process to carry out the work while the shell continues its normal processing. This type of process creation is known as the *fork* procedure, named after the **fork()** C function that creates clones (exact duplicates) of processes.

For example, when a user types ls at the command prompt, the shell forks a new process (a clone of the shell), finds the code for ls, copies this code over the clone's code, and tells the system that the new process is ready to execute. Because the old process was cloned to create the new one, the processes are referred to as *parent* (old) and *child* (new).

As in previous chapters, we focus on the C shell and its commands. The Bourne and Korn shells have similar commands for process management.

Process Information

At any given time, many processes are running on a UNIX system. Most work for the system, performing chores such as managing the system's resources, maintaining network connections, and so on, but some processes belong to users. The **ps** command provides information on running processes. Without parameter flags, ps lists only those processes owned by the user. For example, typing ps might produce the following output.

```
PID TT      S  TIME COMMAND
2567 pts/2  O  0:00 ps
2391 pts/2  S  0:01 /bin/csh
```

The listing indicates two running processes: the C shell (/bin/csh) and the ps command itself. The first column, PID, is the process identification number assigned to each process by the system.

Common flags for ps are -e, which requests information on all system processes (a potentially large and time-consuming request); -l, the long listing; and -a, which limits the listing to processes associated with a terminal (roughly, those initiated by users).

Processes may run in either the *foreground* (interactively) or in the *background* (batch or noninteractive programs). While only one process may run in the foreground, many processes may run in the background, up to a system-defined limit. Running a process in the background allows two (or more) jobs to be executed at once. Most system processes run in the background, for example. Only a foreground process can accept input from the terminal.

The mechanism for running a job in the background is to type an ampersand, &, at the end of a command. For example, consider the following command.

```
ps -e > mypslist &
```

After the user presses the enter key, the shell again presents a command prompt. Note that the output from ps is being redirected to a file to ensure that it really is a noninteractive job. When the process finishes, a "done" message is printed on the screen. While the job is running, it shows up on a ps listing, although this particular example finishes so quickly that the "done" message is probably displayed before any other commands can be entered. The following compound command is contrived to run long enough that other commands can execute simultaneously:

```
(sleep 60; ps -e > mypslist) &
```

This set of commands first sleeps (does nothing) for 60 seconds, then runs the `ps` command, all in the background. Typing `ps` while the compound command is executing produces a display similar to

```
PID TT      S  TIME COMMAND
3268 pts/2  O  0:00 ps
3267 pts/2  S  0:00 sleep 60
3221 pts/2  S  0:00 /bin/csh
```

which shows `sleep 60` executing.

The **jobs** command shows only jobs that are running in the background, displaying the job number (*not* the PID) and an indication whether the job is actively running, stopped (temporarily suspended), or done. A job number is used to refer to a process in the following commands using the syntax %*num*. The `-1` flag causes `jobs` to display the PID in addition to the job number.

A running foreground job may be stopped by pressing control-Z, after which the job will appear in a `jobs` listing. Both background and stopped jobs may be terminated with the command **kill** %*num*. Alternatively, any job a user owns may be terminated by `kill` *PID*, as in `kill 3267`. The `kill` command also accepts parameters. The most useful one is `-9`, called the "sure kill," which always gets its process. For example,

```
kill -9 3267
```

kills a process listed in the previous display. A stopped job may be resumed in the foreground by the command **fg** %*num* or resumed in the background by the command **bg** %*num* (see Figure 13.6).

Programming Processes

Besides the `fork()` function, there are many other C functions that facilitate process management on a UNIX system. Most are beyond the scope of this text; see [Stevens] for a detailed discussion of process programming, including interprocess communication. Instead, we discuss a small subset of the larger list of functions.

The `fork()` command, as noted earlier, creates a clone or child process. If not used carefully, `fork()` can create havoc for a user and a system administrator. Before attempting to use it, you should be knowledgeable in the use of the `kill` command so that unwanted processes can be terminated.

The `fork()` function takes no parameters. Since it creates a child process, there are two return values: zero to the child, and the child's PID to the parent. If `fork()` is unsuccessful

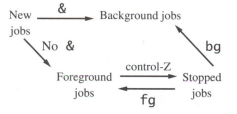

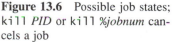

Figure 13.6 Possible job states; `kill` *PID* or `kill` %*jobnum* cancels a job

in creating the child, then -1 is returned to the parent instead. More that one child can be created using multiple calls to fork(). Children can create new children to become parents in their own right; many levels of a family tree can be created in this manner. The files <sys/types.h> and <unistd.h> must be #included to use fork().

Once a child is created, it has a complete set of code and variables identical to its parent's at the time of the fork() call. These are *not* shared variables but copies, local to the child. File descriptor values, however, have the same meaning in the parent and the child; therefore, any files that were opened by the parent are accessible to the child via their file descriptor variables. Additionally, the new child process begins execution at the same place the parent is executing. That is, the child begins running at the first statement after the fork() call. The statements before the fork() call are ignored; in particular, the child's execution does *not* begin at main().

A typical scenario is as follows. The parent initializes variables (remember that the child gets a copy of the variables and their values), then calls fork(). Depending on the return value, the parent executes one set of instructions (possible by calling a function that contains the parent's code) while the child executes another set. The two processes may finish at different times or the parent may call the **wait()** function to wait until the child finishes. The prototype for wait() is

```
pid_t wait( int *status );
```

where the return value is the PID of the first child that finishes and status is a pass-by-address parameter that, on return, contains the child's exit status (the argument to exit()). See Figure 13.7.

When a parent creates several children, the fork() call is often contained in a loop. In this case each child begins execution inside the loop. Care must be taken to prevent a child from continuing the loop and creating new children by calling fork(). Usually, the return value from fork() is tested. A value of 0 indicates that the process is a child, and either a break statement is used to exit the loop or a call is made to a function containing the child's code. The following fragment shows the second option:

```
for ( count = 0; count < NUMBER_OF_CHILDREN; count++ ) {
  ret_value = fork();
  /* Check for error condition */
  if ( ret_value == -1 ) {
    printf( "Error calling fork.\n" );
    exit( 0 );
  /* Otherwise, branch to the child code if this is the child */
  } else if ( ret_value == 0 )
    child_function(); /* must terminate with exit() */
} /* for count */
/* Rest of parent code would follow here */
 . . .
```

A child created inside the for loop begins executing at the test of ret_value. If ret_value is 0, then the process is a child and calls child_function(). In this way, only a child calls child_function(), while the parent continues executing the for loop. One other detail

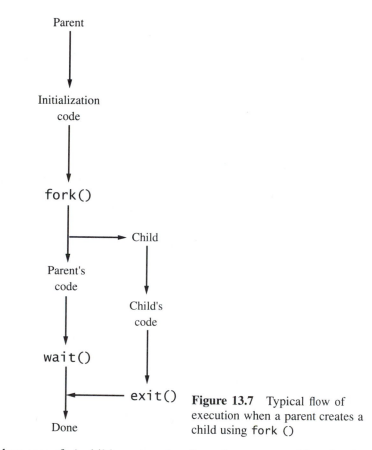

Figure 13.7 Typical flow of execution when a parent creates a child using fork ()

must be taken care of: A child must *not* be allowed to return to this point, because if it did, it would resume execution of the loop. Thus, the function `child_function()` *must* terminate with a call to `exit()` rather than with a `return` statement or by falling through to its closing brace.

What work should the child do? In the following example the child calls one of the `exec` family functions to execute a UNIX command. More generally, some problems can be divided into parts, and each process can work on one part. Most problems require that the processes communicate with each other. This can be accomplished, but not well, using files. Alternatively, UNIX provides *pipes*—interprocess communications facilities, which have already been introduced but will be discussed further in a later section—for processes to exchange data. It is also possible for processes running on different machines to communicate. UNIX provides (among other mechanisms) *sockets* (similar to pipes) for this purpose. Communicating, cooperating processes are also needed for processing on parallel and distributed systems, but they are well beyond the scope of this book.

Example: Independent Child

The following example program shows how a parent can create a child (using `fork()`) that performs work independently of the parent; that is, there is no need for communication between parent and child. Additionally, the code sections for parent and child are both contained in `main()`, because each is quite simple.

The program uses the **execlp()** function, one of six functions in the exec family. All the functions have a similar purpose: to overlay executable code onto an existing process and execute it. Usually the process will have been just created using fork(). The differences among the exec functions are mainly in how parameters are specified. The prototype for execlp() is

```
int execlp(
    char *filename, char *arg0, char *arg1, ..., char *argn, char *0 );
```

The first parameter is the name of an executable file; it may be a pathname. The parameters arg0, arg1, up to argn are the executable file's command line arguments. Note that if filename is not a pathname, then filename and arg0 will (usually) be the same. The last argument simply indicates the end of the parameter list.

Once the overlay and execution are complete, the process terminates. If a child was created to call execlp(), there is no return to the code in the child process—that is, the execlp() call is the last statement of the child's code that is executed. Making the overlay destroys the original child code.

The following program uses date as the executable file run by the child. The child and parent print several values to illustrate the functions used.

```
#include <stdio.h>
#include <sys/wait.h>
#include <unistd.h>
main(){
  int fork_value;         /* Return value from fork() */
  int child_status;       /* Status on child exit()   */
  int child_return_value; /* Return value from wait() */
  /* Create one child */
  fork_value = fork();
  /* Check for error */
  if ( fork_value == -1 ) {
    printf( "Fork failed\n" );
    exit( 0 );
  } /* if error */
  /* Check if child or parent */
  if ( fork_value == 0 ) {
    /* CHILD CODE */
    printf( "Child: fork_value = %d\n", fork_value );
    /* Execute the date program */
    execlp( "date", "date", (char *) 0 );
    /* Child should not get this far */
    printf( "Child: if this statement is printed, something is wrong!\n" );
    exit( 0 );
  } else {
    /* PARENT CODE */
    child_return_value = wait( &child_status );
    printf( "Parent: fork_value        = %d\n", fork_value );
```

```
      printf( "Parent: child_status       = %d\n", child_status );
      printf( "Parent: child_return_value = %d\n", child_return_value );
      exit( 0 );
   } /* else parent */
} /* main */
```

The output from this program should be similar to the following display:

```
Child: fork_value = 0
Fri Jun 20 16:36:58 EDT 1995
Parent: fork_value         = 2704
Parent: child_status       = 0
Parent: child_return_value = 2704
```

The second line and the status value returned into child_status are the result of the date command.

Example: Cooperative Child

In order for a parent and its children to communicate, UNIX provides the **pipe()** function. A call to pipe() creates two one-way channels: one for reading information and one for writing information. The format of the information is entirely up to the processes. Pipes behave similarly to files. Our code uses the read() and write() functions for data transfer. When attempting to read from an empty pipe, a process waits for data to arrive, much the way a scanf() or getchar() behaves in reading keyboard entries. This pipe behavior can be changed, however; see [Stevens] for details.

The prototype of pipe() is

```
 int pipe( int filedesc[ 2 ] );
```

where the parameter is an array of two integer file descriptors, and the return value is 0 if the call is successful and –1 if not. The file descriptor filedesc[0] is used for reading only, and the descriptor filedesc[1] is used for writing only. Use of the pipe() function requires <unistd.h>.

Once a pipe is created, a process may read from descriptor 0 and write to descriptor 1. Normally, though, pipes are used by two (or more) processes to communicate, so some systematic method for reading and writing is needed. Usually, one pipe is created for and associated with each process. A given process reads only from its pipe using descriptor 0. Other processes send it messages by writing to the given process's descriptor 1.

Recall that a parent and child share the descriptors of open files. If a pipe is opened before a process fork()s a child, then parent and child can use this pipe to send messages. After the fork, though, each process has its own copy of the original file descriptors and may operate on them independently. In general, there may be several children. Figure 13.8 shows one possible method for structuring parent-child communication (we ignore child-child communication).

In this method, unused channels are closed after the children are created. Since the file descriptors are local to each process, closing one channel does not affect other processes' use of the pipe. The parent creates one pipe for itself and closes the write channel (because the

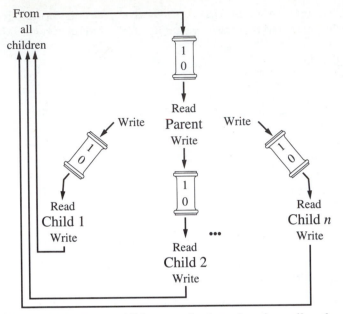

Figure 13.8 Parent-child communication using pipes; all reads
are done from 0 descriptors, and all writes are done to 1 descriptors

parent does not send messages to itself). The children always write to this pipe but close
its read channel (because children do not read messages sent to the parent). The parent also
creates one pipe for each child and closes the read channel (because the parent does not read
the children's messages). Each child reads from its pipe and closes the write channel (because
a child does not send messages to itself). This method simplifies the parent's chores, because
all messages appear on only one pipe. However, the children are now required to identify
themselves in their messages so that the parent knows to whom to reply.

The following code uses the method just described, but is somewhat simpler, because
only one child is created. Sample data is transferred using a `struct`. The child sends three
data records and then signals "all done" to the parent. No processing is done except to print
values received, because we are illustrating only communication using pipes. Keep in mind
that because of the `if` statement that distinguishes parent from child, each process runs only
one version of the communication code. The alternative design, which would put the child's
code into a function, would necessitate passing the pipe variables as parameters or making
them global to `main()`.

```c
#include <stdio.h>
#include <sys/wait.h>
#include <unistd.h>
typedef struct {  /*  Data record:    */
    int whoami;   /*     child number */
    int data;     /*     data value   */
} datagram;
main(){
```

```
/* fork() and wait() variables */
int fork_value;
int child_status,
    child_return_value;
int done;             /* Loop flag     */
int count;            /* Loop counter  */
datagram mydata;      /* Data struct   */
int parentpipe[ 2 ], /* Parent's pipe */
    childpipe[ 2 ];  /* Child's pipe  */
/* Open parent pipe */
if ( pipe( parentpipe ) == -1 ) {
  printf( "Error opening parent pipe.\n" );
  exit( 0 );
} /* if pipe */
/* Open child pipe */
if ( pipe( childpipe ) == -1 ) {
  printf( "Error opening parent pipe.\n" );
  exit( 0 );
} /* if pipe */
/* Create a child */
fork_value = fork();
if ( fork_value == -1 ) {
  printf( "Fork failed\n" );
  exit( 0 );
}
/* Which code are we in? */
if ( fork_value == 0 ) {
  /* CHILD CODE: could place this in a function */
  /* Close unneeded channels */
  close( parentpipe[ 0 ] );
  close( childpipe[ 1 ] );
  for ( count = 0; count < 3; count++ ) {
    /* Send some sample data to the parent*/
    mydata.whoami = 1;
    mydata.data = count;
    write( parentpipe[ 1 ], (void *) &mydata, sizeof( datagram ));
    /* Read the reply */
    read( childpipe[ 0 ], (void *) &mydata, sizeof( datagram ));
    printf( "Child received %d\n", mydata.data );
  } /* for count */
  /* Send all done message */
  mydata.data = -1;
  write( parentpipe[ 1 ], (void *) &mydata, sizeof( datagram ));
  /* Commit suicide */
  exit( 0 );
} else {
```

```
/* PARENT CODE */
/* Close unneeded channels */
close( childpipe[ 0 ] );
close( parentpipe[ 1 ] );
done = FALSE;
/* Read child messages until done */
while ( !done ) {
  read( parentpipe[ 0 ], (void *) &mydata, sizeof( datagram ));
  printf( "Parent received %d\n", mydata.data );
  if ( mydata.data == -1 )
    done = TRUE;
  else {
    /* Send some sample return data */
    mydata.whoami = 0;
    mydata.data = mydata.data + 10;
    write( childpipe[ 1 ], (void *) &mydata, sizeof( datagram ));
  }  /* else not done */
}  /* while !done */
/* Wait for the child to exit */
child_return_value = wait( &child_status );
printf( "Parent fork_value = %d\n", fork_value );
printf( "Parent child_value = %d\n", child_status );
printf( "Parent child_return_value = %d\n", child_return_value );
exit( 0 );
}  /* else parent */
}  /* main */
```

Because the child's code is brief, we did not place it in a function. If we had done so, recall that a call to `exit()` would be needed in lieu of a `return` statement.

Output from one sample run of this program is shown next:

```
Child received 10
Child received 11
Child received 12
Parent received 0
Parent received 1
Parent received 2
Parent received -1
Parent fork_value = 2808
Parent child_value = 0
Parent child_return_value = 2808
```

Note that the interleaving of child and parent messages may not seem right. The execution of parent and child depends on system scheduling. Different interleavings are possible on other runs of the same code. When multiple processes are cooperating, it is the programmer's job to ensure proper synchronization—often a difficult task, and beyond this text's scope.

References

Abrahams, Paul W. and Bruce R. Larson, *UNIX for the Impatient,* Addison-Wesley, Reading, MA., 1992.

Sedgewick, Robert, *Algorithms in C,* Addison-Wesley, Reading, MA, 1990.

Stevens, W. Richard, *Advanced Programming in the UNIX Environment,* Addison-Wesley, Reading, MA, 1992.

Chapter Summary

■ **C Commands**

Recursive Functions

```
void g( FILE *file_ptr )
/* This is a recursive function */
{   static count = 0;
    int ch;
    ch = fgetc( file_ptr );
    if ( feof( file_ptr ) )   /* Base case      */
      printf( "The file has %d characters:\n", count );
    else {                    /* Recursive call */
      count++;
      g( file_ptr );
      printf( "%c", ch );
    }
}
```

Function Pointers

`int (* fn1)( double x );`	Prototype for a function pointer `fn1`; `(* fn1)()` returns an `int`
`int *(* fn2)( double x );`	Prototype for a function pointer `fn2`; `(* fn2)()` returns an `int` pointer
`int (* fn3)( const void * );`	Prototype for a function pointer `fn3`; `(* fn3)()` has one generic pointer parameter and returns an `int`

`void qsort( void *, size_t, size_t,`
`  int (*)( const void *,`
`  const void * ));`
	Prototype for `qsort`, a quicksort function in `<stdlib.h>`

Low-Level File Processing

`file_desc = open( longfile,` `  O_RDONLY );`	Open `longfile` for read-only access; assign the file descriptor value to `file_desc`
`file_desc = open( longfile,` `  O_WRONLY | O_APPEND );`	Open `longfile` for write-only access; append new data at end of file

`file_desc = open( longfile,` `  O_RDWR | O_CREAT, 0664 );`	Open `longfile` for read/write access; create the file if necessary; allow user and group to have read and write access; allow world to have read access only
`lseek( file_desc, -6, SEEK_END );`	Move to a position 6 bytes before the end of the file having descriptor `file_desc`
`num_bytes = read( file_desc,` `  (void *) buffer, BUFFERSIZE );`	Read as many as BUFFERSIZE bytes from the file having descriptor `file_desc` into `buffer`, an array of size BUFFERSIZE (or greater); assign the actual number of bytes read to `num_bytes`
`num_bytes = write( file_desc,` `  (void *) buffer, BUFFERSIZE );`	Write as many as BUFFERSIZE bytes from `buffer`, an array of size BUFFERSIZE (or greater), into the file having descriptor `file_desc`; assign the number of bytes written to `num_bytes`
`close( file_desc );`	Close the file having descriptor `file_desc`

Process Management

`fork_value = fork();`	Create a clone (child) of the current process (parent); return the child's PID to the parent and return 0 to the child

`#include <unistd.h>`
`int parentpipe[ 2 ];`
`pipe( parentpipe );`
	Create a pipe having two channels: `parentpipe[ 0 ]` for reading and `parentpipe[ 1 ]` for writing

`child_PID = wait( &child_status );`	Suspend execution of the (parent) process until a child process has finished; return the child's PID and exit status in the integer variables `child_PID` and `child_status`

■ UNIX Commands

Process Management

`ps`	List all processes (and their PIDs) owned by the user
`ps -l`	List processes in long detail
`a.out &`	Run process `a.out` in the background
`(sleep 30; a.out) &`	Wait 30 seconds, then run `a.out` in the background
`control-Z`	Stop (that is, suspend) the current foreground job
`jobs`	List stopped jobs (and their job numbers)
`jobs -l`	List stopped jobs (display both job numbers and PIDs)
`fg %1`	Resume job number 1 in the foreground
`bg %1`	Resume job number 1 in the background
`kill %1`	Try to kill (permanently stop) job number 1

| `kill 3232` | Try to kill the job with PID 3232 |
| `kill -9 3232` | Kill the job with PID 3232, with certainty of success |

Review Problems

1. Write a program to test the function `g()` given in the Chapter Summary. Write documentation to describe what this function does.
2. Write a program to find the current value of `MAXFACTVALUE`, the maximum value of *n* for which *n*! is representable by an `int` variable.
3. Write a recursive function to traverse the nodes of a linked list in reverse order.
4. Write the prefix and postfix version for each expression:
   a) 2 * (3 + 4)
   b) (2 - 3) * (4 + 5)
   c) 2 * (3 + (4 - 5))
5. Draw a binary search tree, in the manner of Figure 13.4, for each numerical expression:
   a) 2 * (3 + 4)
   b) (2 - 3) * (4 + 5)
   c) 2 * (3 + (4 - 5))

Programming Problems

1. Write a `merge()` function to accompany the `MergeSort()` function of this chapter; then write a program to test the `MergeSort()` function.
2. Write a nonrecursive function to traverse the nodes of a linked list in reverse order; then write a program to test this function.
3. (Infix Numerical Expressions) Write a program to evaluate numerical expressions stored in the manner of Figure 13.4. Carefully document assumptions regarding input.
4. (Postfix Numerical Expressions) Write a program to represent and evaluate numerical expressions in the following manner. For input, accept expressions stored in a binary tree as shown in Figure 13.4. Use a preliminary function to traverse the tree and return the corresponding postfix expression. Then use a second function to evaluate the postfix expression.
5. (Quicksort–Integers) Quicksort, also known as *partition exchange sort*, is a particularly efficient algorithm for sorting randomly arranged arrays.
   a) Write the following two functions, which, used together, implement the quicksort algorithm to sort integer arrays.

   The first function rearranges a given subarray; it selects a splitting value, in this case the first value of the input array, and rearranges the array so that smaller values come first, then the splitting value, and values larger than the splitting value last. Write a function that does the described rearrangement for arrays of integers, using the first value of the input subarray as the splitting value. The function should also output the index (within the rearranged array) of the splitting value.

   For example, suppose the array {6, 5, 4, 8, 4, 3, 1, 9} is given along with the subarray whose first index is 1 and whose last index is 7; that is, the subarray is { 5, 4, 8, 4, 3, 1, 9}. Then the splitting value is 5, the algorithm gives a rearranged array, such as {6, 4, 4, 3, 1, 5, 8, 9}, and also returns the number 5, the new index of the splitting value. Note that other rearrangements, such as {6, 3, 4, 1, 4, 5, 8, 9 }, also meet the condition that smaller values precede the splitting value and larger values succeed the splitting value within the given subarray.

For the first function, use the header

```
int ReArrange( int MyArray[], int first, int last, int *SplitIndex )
/* ReArrange processes the subarray that begins with              */
/* MyArray[ first ] and ends with MyArray[ last ].                */
/* Defining SplitValue as the value of MyArray[ first ],          */
/* the subarray is rearranged so that after the function call     */
/* is completed: MyArray[ SplitIndex ] = SplitValue,              */
/* index < SplitIndex implies MyArray[ index ] <= SplitValue, &   */
/* index > SplitIndex implies MyArray[ index ] >= SplitValue.     */
```

Have this function return a code of zero if `first` < `last`, and a code of 1 in all other cases. *Note*: The efficiency of this function determines the overall efficiency of the sorting algorithm; you may need to consult references for guidance.

The second function sorts a given subarray by executing the foregoing function to rearrange the input subarray and then recursively calling itself to sort the left and right parts of the rearranged subarray. For example, if the array {6, 5, 4, 8, 4, 3, 1, 9} is input along with `first` = 0 and `last` = 7 (indicating a subarray consisting of the entire given array), the quicksort function calls `ReArrange()` to obtain the output array {5, 4, 4, 3, 1, 6, 8, 9} along with `SplitIndex` = 5, rearranges the left subarray, {5, 4, 4, 3, 1}, and then rearranges the right subarray, {8, 9}. Use the header

```
int QuickSort( int MyArray[], const int first, const int last )
```

The general case of `QuickSort()` is

```
if ( ReArrange( MyArray[], first, last, &SplitIndex ) == 0 ) {
  QuickSort( MyArray[], first, SplitIndex - 1 );
  QuickSort( MyArray[], SplitIndex + 1, last );
}
```

b) Write a program to test the `QuickSort()` function and compare its output with that produced by the `qsort()` library function.

6. (Quicksort—Strings) Adapt the `QuickSort()` function described in the previous problem to sort a ragged array of strings rather than an array of integers. Then write a program to test the modified `QuickSort()` function and to compare its output with that produced by the `qsort()` library function.

7. (Flood Fill Algorithm) Here is a simplified version of the computer graphics problem of filling a specified region with a specified color. Consider a two-dimensional array of integers. Each pair of row and column indices represents one pixel on a digital screen. Each array value represents a color, with -2 representing the color of a pixel in the region's exterior, -1 designating the color of a pixel on the region's boundary, and 0 representing the original color of a pixel in the region's interior. The purpose of the algorithm is to change the color of each interior pixel from 0 to 1. The flood fill algorithm is given by the following recursive function.

```
#define EXTERIOR -2
#define BOUNDARY -1
#define INTERIOR 0
#define FILL 1
```

```
typedef int RegionType[ NumROWS ][ NumCOLS ];
/* NumROWS and NumCOLS must be positive integer constants. */
void FloodFill( RegionType region, int r, int c )
/* The input values of r and c must                          */
/* designate an interior pixel. This algorithm               */
/* assumes that there are no gaps or holes in boundary.   */
{
   if ( region[ r ][ c ] == INTERIOR ) {
     region[ r ][ c ] = FILL;
     FloodFill( region, r, c + 1 );
     FloodFill( region, r, c - 1 );
     FloodFill( region, r + 1, c );
     FloodFill( region, r - 1, c );
   }
}
```

a) Test this algorithm by hand on several small regions. Note that changing the first index effects a vertical move to a new row (unlike geometric coordinates, where changing the first coordinate causes a horizontal move). Likewise, changing the second index effects a horizontal move to a new column.

b) Write a program, using a printout of array values to represent the screen, to implement and test the flood fill algorithm. For testing purposes, modify the algorithm so that it fills interior pixels with successively larger integers. This modification permits you to trace the order in which the interior pixels are changed.

8. (Parent-Child Cooperation) Write a program, based on parent-child cooperation, where the parent process offers a menu whose options are to display the current date, display the calendar for the current month, list files in the current working directory, or quit. For any choice other than quit, the parent should create a child process that uses execlp() to execute the necessary UNIX command, and the parent should execute wait() to allow the child process to finish before presenting the menu again. When the user chooses to quit, the parent process should terminate.

Chapter 14

Advanced Design Methods

In this chapter we discuss the concept of the *abstract data type* (ADT), first discussed in Chapter 6. An ADT is used to design reusable generic code modules. Since ADTs are one step away from objects, we also look briefly at C++, the language that has evolved from C for object-oriented programming. Our UNIX discussions so far have focused on using standard UNIX on character-based terminals. Most UNIX environments offer some type of graphical interface, usually based on X Windows. The UNIX sections include a short discussion of X and other UNIX windowing systems. In addition, several network access programs are presented.

Abstract Data Types

In the discussions of data structures and programming in previous chapters, we have emphasized encapsulation, data hiding, and modularity. Recall that an abstract data type, or ADT, employs these ideas in both the design and coding phases to create more robust data structures.

A data structure can be viewed in two ways:

1. The *internal* view shows details of the structure that are implementation-dependent. Whether a linked list, for example, is coded using dynamic memory allocation (where a link is an address) or using an array (where a link is an array index) is an internal aspect of the data structure and is decided during the detailed design phase of the software life cycle.
2. The *external* view is the way other functions see the data structure based on their use of it. How the linked list is viewed by functions that use it is, or ideally should be, independent of the implementation. If this is so, later changes to the internal details will not affect other parts of the program. The external view is defined during the high-level design phase.

An ADT emphasizes the external, implementation-independent, view.

Implementation independence is modularity in its most useful form. In practice, independence depends on the definition of the operations provided on the data structure and on the performance characteristics of those operations. Choosing one data structure over another, after all, is a choice about performance. For example, if the speed of searching for a key value in a data set is critical to a program, then a binary search tree is probably a better choice than an unordered linked list. This combination of operations and performance permits a data structure to be presented as a package of services that other functions or modules may use.

An ADT is defined by its interface (the list of functions that the ADT is providing as services) and by the performance of the ADT implied in its name. A linked-list ADT, for example, might include the operations to insert, delete, search, initialize, and destroy. The fact that it is a list promises no more than $O(n)$ search performance.

When coding data structures in our examples, we have defined data types, usually using `structs`, that comprised the units of data stored in the structure. An ADT stores generic data so that its services can be offered to a larger set of clients. Thus, a linked-list ADT is not defined by storing employee data, student records, or some other application-specific data but rather by *being* a linked list that stores data.

In summary, an ADT is a logical data type, defined during high-level design. Its implementation, while important, is not of concern at this phase. Instead, the focus is on how the ADT interacts with other parts of the program. The ADT's interface determines these interactions. The logical operation of the ADT is an abstraction—hence the name—of a data structure and its algorithms.

The next section examines one particular ADT—a list ADT—to illustrate these ideas. An ADT is usually coded in one module. In C, that means it is contained in one `.c` file. The interface is provided in a `.h` file. Generic data must be handled using the `void *` data type.

ADT for Linked Lists

As an example of the ADT concept, this section shows how to define an ADT for a linked list. The full implementation of the ADT's functions is not shown but should be clear, given the code examples of Chapter 10.

We first decide on the operations provided by the list ADT. These include the same operations discussed in Chapter 10: insertion of a node, deletion of a node, search for a particular node given a key value, and initialization and traversal of the list. To this we add an operation for the destruction of the entire list. Note that we did not include the allocation operation; this is used by insertion, but not by outside client functions, so it is not part of the interface. For each operation, we need to write a function prototype that names the operation and lists the parameters and return types.

In order to be generic, the linked list cannot use nodes containing any particular kind of data. Therefore, the "data" stored in each node is a `void *` pointer to the actual data. Our list nodes are then defined as

```
typedef struct node { /* Generic linked list node:    */
  void          *data;  /*    Pointer to the actual data */
  struct node *next;  /*    Link to the next node      */
} ListNode, *ListADT;
```

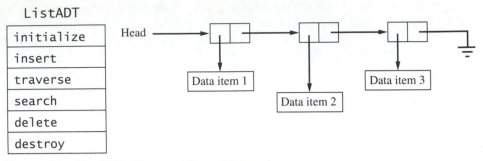

Figure 14.1   ListADT with several list and data nodes

We assume that both this definition and the prototypes in the next paragraph are placed in the header file `list.h`.

Given the definition of `ListNode` and `ListADT`, we can define prototypes that are similar to the list functions covered in Chapter 10, although there are important differences (see Figure 14.1). The prototypes are

```
void initialize( ListADT *head );
void insert( ListADT *head, void *rec );
void traverse( ListADT head, void (*fn)( void * ));
void *search( ListADT head, void *key, int (*fn)( void *, void * ));
void delete( ListADT *head, void *key, int (*fn)( void *, void * ));
void destroy( ListADT *head );
```

Each occurrence of `void *`, either as a parameter or as a return value, references generic data. Additionally, `traverse()` accepts a function pointer. (Recall that function pointers were discussed in Chapter 13.) The argument passed in this position should be a function that processes one node of actual data. Similarly, the `search()` and `delete()` functions also have a function pointer parameter. In this case, the argument should be a function that compares a key value to a field in an actual data node and returns 0 if the key and field are equal, -1 if the key is smaller than the field, or 1 if the key is larger.

We do not show the implementation for the `initialize()`, `destroy()`, and `delete()` functions. The code for `initialize()` simply sets the `head` pointer to NULL. The code for `destroy()`, which calls `free()` for each list node, is similar to `traverse()`. The code for `delete()` is similar to `insert()`, shown below. The utility function `allocate()`, similar to the `allocate()` in Chapter 10, calls `malloc()` to request a portion of memory large enough to store a `ListNode` and returns a pointer of type `ListPtr`. The `allocate()` function is not part of the ADT interface, since it is called only by `insert()`, not by outside functions.

The `insert()` function performs the easiest kind of insertion, placing a new node at the beginning of the list. Except for the data types, the following code is identical to the insert function in Chapter 10.

```
void insert( ListADT *head, void *rec ) {
  ListADT ptr;    /* Pointer to new node. */
  /* Allocate a new node */
  ptr = allocate();
```

```
    /* Copy in the data pointer */
    ptr->data = rec;
    /* Link the new node to the rest of the list */
    ptr->next = *head;
    *head     = ptr;
} /* insert */
```

Again, note that the parameter rec and the field ptr->data are void * pointers. The field ptr->next is typed as ListPtr and is filled by the call to allocate().

The traverse() function processes the linked list one node at a time from head to tail. Since the list ADT has no information concerning the type of data stored, the processing is done by passing a function pointer that references the actual processing function.

```
void traverse( ListADT head, void (*fn)( void * ) ) {
   ListADT ptr;    /* Pointer to walk the list */
   /* Initialize the pointer */
   ptr = head;
   /* Loop until the end of the list */
   while ( ptr != NULL ) {
      fn( ptr->data );     /* Process the data for this node */
      ptr = ptr->next;     /* Move to the next node         */
   }  /* while ptr */
}  /* traverse() */
```

The function that calls traverse() passes a function as an argument for fn() to carry out the processing on each node's data.

The search() function cannot compare a key value to a data field; the type is unknown to the list ADT. Therefore, search() accepts a function pointer as a parameter to do this job. The parameter key and the parameters in the function pointer prototype are of type void *. It is the responsibility of the argument function matched with *fn() to carry out the type casts that convert each void * pointer to an actual data node.

```
void *search( ListADT head, void *key, int (*fn)( void *, void * )) {
   ListADT ptr;    /* Pointer for list traversal */
   int     done;   /* Flag for the search loop   */
   /* Initialize the flag and pointer */
   done = 0;
   ptr = head;
   /* Loop until key is found or loop ends */
   while (( !done ) && ( ptr != NULL )) {
     /* Call the comparison function */
     if ( fn( key, ptr->data ) == 0 ) {
       done = 1;            /* Found a match */
     } else {
       ptr = ptr->next;  /* Get next node */
     } /* else */
   }  /* while */
```

```
    /* Why did the loop terminate? */
    if ( done )
      return( ptr->data );  /* Found     */
    else
      return( NULL );        /* Not found */
  }  /* search() */
```

The return value of search() is a void * pointer. NULL is returned if the search is unsuccessful; otherwise, a pointer to a data node is returned.

We now examine how to use the list ADT. Besides providing functions to use as arguments where function pointers are required, it is also necessary to typecast actual data to void
* and back. The sample code below uses the simple record defined by

```
typedef struct {  /* Sample data record:    */
   int count;       /*    integer field       */
   double amount;   /*    floating point field */
} DataNode, *DataPtr;
```

The DataNode structure is used only for illustration; an actual application would have a more
complicated record type.

Two argument functions are needed by the list ADT. The traverse() operation requires a function that processes a DataNode. The search() operation needs a function to
compare a key value to a data field; we will use the count field of DataNode for searches.
The function process(), shown next, casts its void * parameter to a DataPtr, then prints
the data fields of a record.

```
void process( void *record ) {
   DataPtr ptr;
   /* Type cast record to a DataPtr */
   ptr = (DataPtr) record;
   /* Print a heading and the record's fields */
   printf( "Record data:\n" );
   printf( "count = %d\n", ptr->count );
   printf( "amount = %lf\n", ptr->amount );
}  /* process() */
```

Other processing functions could be substituted for process(), provided each uses void as
its return value and uses void * as its parameter's type.

The next function, compare(), casts its parameters to DataPtr pointers, compares the
count fields of each record, and returns either 0, −1, or 1, depending on whether the first
record's count value is equal to, less than, or greater than the second record's count value.

```
int compare( void *generic1, void *generic2 ) {
   DataPtr first,    /* First data record  */
           second;   /* Second data record */
   int     value;    /* Return value       */
```

```
/* Cast the generic data to DataPtr */
first  = (DataPtr) generic1;
second = (DataPtr) generic2;
/* Compare the count fields, return 0, -1, or 1 */
if ( first->count == second->count )
  value = 0;
else if ( first->count < second->count )
  value = -1;
else
  value = 1;
return( value );
}  /* compare() */
```

As noted in Chapter 13, the details of type casting, while messy, are the price of writing generic code.

Finally, the following fragment shows how some of the list ADT functions are called. A sample data record is constructed for the call to insert(), and a sample key value is used as an argument to search().

```
#include "list.h"  /* The header file for the list ADT */
ListADT head;       /* Declare a list ADT           */
DataNode mynode;    /* Actual data record           */
DataPtr  myptr;     /* Pointer to a data record */
int      key;       /* Sample key value             */
/* Initialize the list ADT */
initialize( &head );
/* Set some sample data values and insert into the list */
mynode.count  = 47;
mynode.amount = 21.5;
insert( &head, (void *) &mynode );
/* Process the list */
traverse( head, process );
/* Set a key value and search the list for it */
key = 47;
myptr = (DataPtr) search( head, (void *) &key, compare );
/* If not found, say so; otherwise, process the data */
if ( myptr == NULL ) {
  printf( "%d not found.\n", key );
} else {
    process( (void *) myptr );
}
```

This fragment constitutes a client of the list ADT. There is no reason for this code to access the nodes of type ListNode or ListPtr stored in the list ADT; this information is hidden from the client.

As a reusable module, the list ADT could be used in multiple projects regardless of the type of application. A programmer using the ADT must adhere to the casting and function pointer conventions but needs no knowledge of the internal workings of `insert()`, `traverse()`, and the other functions in the list ADT interface.

Beyond C

An ADT attempts to enforce good software engineering practices using encapsulation, modularity, and data hiding. To implement an ADT in C requires more work than does standard C coding. Function pointers, type casting, and careful module interfaces are more cumbersome in C than they should be. For this and other reasons, alternatives to C have been developed. Foremost among them is C++, developed by Bjarne Stroustrup at AT&T in the mid-1980s and currently offered by various vendors. (See [Stroustrup] for full details of C++ coding.)

C++ is a programming language based on object-oriented methods (discussed briefly in Chapter 6). C++ is a *superset* of C; that is, a C++ compiler can compile C programs. While object-oriented programming can be used to implement a program based on any design method, object-oriented technology, to be most effective, should be applied to all phases of the software life cycle. In fact, an object-oriented life cycle has been developed that takes advantage of the features provided by object-oriented languages. C++ is only one of a number of object-oriented languages in use. Others include Smalltalk, Common LISP Object System, and various versions of object-oriented C and Pascal.

Object-Oriented Design

An object can be thought of as an extension of an ADT. Objects encapsulate data and functionality, but unlike ADTs, functions are *part of* an object, not separate entities that operate on an object. That is, an object contains data (both private and public), and functions (also private and public). Object data is usually declared as *private* to provide data hiding. Other objects that need access to private data can do so only if the called object has a function that returns a copy of private data to the caller.

A *class* is a template or pattern for objects. Much like a `struct` definition, a class definition describes the data structures that an *instantiated* object (one derived from a class) has. In addition, a class contains function definitions; those that are *public* are the ones that an instantiated object can perform when called by other objects. In other words, the public functions are an object's interface.

The class concept can be seen in another way. Since a class contains the defining properties of all objects of this class, it is a generalization of those objects. This idea can be taken further. If two or more classes share some properties among them, then those properties form a generalization of the classes. A `parent` class can be defined, containing only those common properties. The `child` classes are specializations of the parent, adding new features that the parent lacks. Applying this relationship recursively, classes can be organized into a *class hierarchy* or tree, where the most general class is the root and very specialized classes are the leaves. Thus, an important activity associated with object-oriented design is designing the class hierarchies appropriate to an application.

A child class *inherits* the parent's data types and function definitions. Inheritance is a way to define more specific classes based on more general ones. It is also a way to decrease the amount of code needed to implement new classes, because an object instantiated from a child class can use the parent's code and data structures in addition to those defined in the child class. This code reuse and the consequent decrease in development time and cost are important factors in the current popularity of object-oriented design and programming.

Since several class hierarchies may be needed for a particular program, another important design activity is choosing objects (instantiated from classes in the hierarchies), which will determine the modules of a program. The interaction of these objects is accomplished through their interfaces (public functions).

For example, suppose that we define an employee class containing fields for the employee name, age, and address, plus functions to set each field, to return each field, and to display each field (see Figure 14.2). Next we derive two child classes from the employee class to represent salaried employees and hourly employees. The salaried class also has a data field for monthly salary, functions to set the monthly salary, and functions to compute and return the yearly salary. The hourly class also has a field for the hourly wage rate and functions to set the hourly rate, to return the rate, to deduct union dues, and to deduct a health insurance premium. Refining the salary class, the manager class inherits salary information and functions, adds fields for department name and the number of employees supervised, and provides functions that set, return, and display this new data.

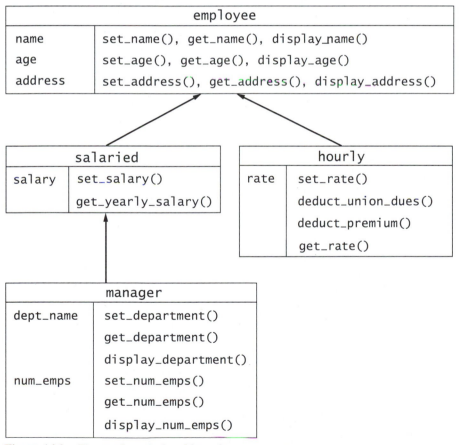

Figure 14.2   The employee class hierarchy

An object instantiated from the hourly class to represent an hourly worker responds to the specialized function `deduct_union_dues()`. A manager object responds to the function `display_department()`. Both objects respond to the function `set_name()`, since both have the traits inherited from the employee class.

Classes and objects can have other relationships besides parent-child and instantiation. For example, a class can contain objects as part of its data, as in a department class consisting of employee objects. A class can provide an organization method for objects, as in an array class or a linked-list class. An important part of the design phase is to recognize and model the relationships among classes and objects.

The objects that make up the program work together by sending requests to and receiving requests from other objects. Determining the network of possible interconnections is the second part of the high-level design. Also important in this phase are the timing of events (*when* function calls and other actions occur) and defining the changes that occur in the internal state of each object.

See [McGregor and Sykes] for a complete description of object-oriented design.

C++ Coding

C++ provides methods to implement classes and objects. The `class` definition is similar in syntax to a C `struct`, but includes function prototypes and mechanisms to make data and functions public or private. Objects are declared as variables, using the class name as the type identifier. Data fields of an object are referenced like `struct` fields, and functions are referenced in the same manner.

The following example shows the definitions (but not the implementation) of an employee class and a salaried worker class.

```
// Employee class:
class employee {
  // Public interface:
  public:
    // Two constructor functions - each makes an object
    void employee( void );
    void employee( char *myname, int myage, char *myaddress );
    // Functions to set the fields
    void set_name( char *myname );
    void set_age( int myage );
    void set_address( char *myaddress );
    // Functions to return the fields
    char *get_name( void );
    int  get_age( void );
    char *get_address( void );
    // Functions to display the fields
    void display_name( void );
    void display_age( void );
    void display_address( void );
  // Private data:
  private:
```

```
      char name[ 80 ];
      char address[ 255 ];
      int  age;
};
// Salaried worker class, child of employee class
class salaried: public employee {
  // Public interface:
  public:
    // Constructor
    void salaried( void );
    // Set the salary
    void set_salary( double sal );
    // Return the salary
    double get_salary( void );
  // Private data:
  private:
    double salary;
};
```

These class definitions would typically be placed in a `.h` file. The class definition syntax is similar to a `struct`, but note the use of the `public` and `private` keywords. Also, a new comment symbol, `//`, is used; it identifies everything to the right of it on the line as a comment.

The following fragment uses the class definitions for `employee` and its child `salaried` to declare one object of each type. Several calls to `public` functions are also illustrated.

```
  // Declare two objects
  employee person1( "Jones", 38, "123 Main Street" );
  salaried person2;
  // An int to hold a return value
  int      this_age;
  // Some employee references:
  person1.display_age();
  this_age = person1.get_age();
  // Some salaried references:
  person2.set_age( 47 );
  person2.display_age();
  this_age = person2.get_age();
  person2.set_salary( 100000 );
} /* main() */
```

The declaration of `person1` uses the second of `employee`'s two *constructor* functions. A constructor, which always uses the same name as the class, is a utility function for instantiating objects. The first `employee` constructor has no parameters. The second, which `person1` uses, takes three parameters. This function's implementation will simply set the `private` data fields of `person1` to `Jones`, 38, and `123 Main Street`. Having several constructors in a class allows for default data to be filled in when some fields are not yet known.

The first three `person2` function calls refer to functions inherited from the `employee` class. The call to `set_salary()` is unique to the `salaried` class.

It is also interesting to note several cases of illegal references. A call to `person1.set_salary( 85000 )` is not correct because `set_salary()` is not part of `employee`. Any reference to the data of either class is illegal because in this example all the data fields are declared as `private`. Thus, the statement `this_age = person1.age;` is illegal.

The implementations of classes rely both on C++ constructs and on standard C code. Obviously, there are many other C++ features in addition to those mentioned here.

Programming in a Graphics Environment

This text has focused on writing C code for a character-based display. The input and output functions typically produce strings of characters, not graphics output. Many UNIX systems provide graphical environments using high-resolution color displays running windowing software. Writing code that utilizes such hardware and software requires knowledge of graphics programming and access to a graphics package. The most popular windowing/graphics software for UNIX systems is X Windows, originally developed at MIT.

X provides an extensive basic set of functions, data structure definitions, and utility programs centered around the Xlib library. The functions in Xlib allow precise control over the creation and manipulation of windows, menus, icons, and a wide variety of graphics operations.

Some programmers feel that *too* much control is provided. Xlib is somewhat difficult to use, if only because of its size. For that reason, other utilities have been built on top of Xlib, notably the Xt Intrinsics library. The functions in the Xt library allow compound graphical objects, such as scroll boxes and slider controls, to be constructed with far fewer commands than are required when using Xlib. In turn, Xt has been used as the basis for other toolkits, such as Motif.

X works on the *client-server* model of computing, whereby client programs or processes seek services from local or remote (on other machines) servers. With X, an application program is the client, which uses an X display (through Xlib functions) as a server for its graphics needs. Additionally, programs may take advantage of even higher-level X services to operate in the Motif windowing environment. For more details on programming with X and its libraries, see [Johnson and Reichard].

Beyond UNIX

UNIX has existed for some two decades and has evolved from a small, relatively unknown operating system into a large, widely used, and commercially successful system with many variants. In our discussions, we have focused on a core set of UNIX commands and principles that are applicable on nearly any UNIX system.

Discussion of the variations among the commercial versions of UNIX can fill and have filled numerous books. Most major computer manufacturers try to present their versions as better than their competitors'. Standardization of UNIX has been achieved to some degree recently, but more remains to be done.

The current movement to graphically based windowing systems is one way that vendors distinguish their products, but even in this area some agreement has been reached on using

Motif. Motif is based on X Windows, by way of Xt, and is offered by many UNIX workstation vendors.

Distributed Systems

UNIX systems made use of computer networks long before the current popular interest in networks arose. As discussed in Chapter 13, C in a UNIX environment provides the means for interprocess communication, either between processes running on the same system (via pipes) or between processes running on different systems (via sockets). These facilities make client-server applications possible. A current trend in database systems, for example, is to have multiple data servers running on a network. Client processes provide access to data in a highly distributed environment, thereby increasing availability to data. Of course, there is also a concomitant increase in the complexity of programs that provide these capabilities.

Using distributed systems and parallel processing systems (containing more than one CPU in the same machine) can be more difficult than using single-processor systems. Some systems, however, look just like UNIX to the user. For example, the Mach operating system, while very different from UNIX internally, can run a UNIX environment as its user interface. Whether file access or system services are being provided locally or on a remote system is not known, and probably unimportant, to the user. (See [Tanenbaum] for more details.)

Programming on distributed and parallel systems is almost always more difficult than on a single-CPU system. Interprocess communications (pipes, sockets, and so on), synchronization methods (to ensure correct timing of program actions), and data distribution and integrity play key roles in supporting distributed and parallel applications, including client-server methods. For example, two challenges in a distributed database program are the ability to locate particular tables among multiple sites, and keeping remote copies of tables up to date in response to changes in local data. The tools necessary to write programs for distributed systems are beyond the scope of this book.

Internet Access

With network connections comes the ability to access the international collection of networks known as the Internet. Newsgroups, information services, and data repositories are among the attractions to users of the Internet, along with electronic junk mail, intrusive advertising, viruses, and security threats. (See [Krol] for more details.)

The `mail` program discussed in Chapter 11, when used to send electronic mail to users on other systems, is an example of a program that uses network facilities. Another example is the `rn` command, provided on most UNIX systems. The `rn` utility accesses *Usenet News*, a large collection of newsgroups on the Internet. Among the thousands of newsgroups are `comp.lang.c`, used for discussions about C, and `comp.unix` and `comp.unix.questions`, two groups (among many) used to discuss UNIX.

The `ftp` (file transfer protocol) program, mentioned briefly in Chapter 11, transfers files from one machine to another. When a user has accounts on two different machines, `ftp` can be used to move files from one account to the other. The `ftp` command takes the full network name of the remote machine as a parameter. For example, to access a hypothetical machine named `yogi.myuni.edu`, use the command `ftp yogi.myuni.edu`. Once connected, a prompt appears for a user id (on the remote machine, which may be different than on the local machine) and password.

Once logged in, the `ftp` prompt (not the regular UNIX prompt) is displayed. The set of `ftp` commands is displayed by typing `help` or `?`. Among those commands are two UNIX commands: `ls`, which displays the contents of the working directory on the remote machine, and `cd` *directory*, used to change the working directory on the remote machine. The working directory on the local machine is changed by `lcd` *directory*.

Files are transferred using the `put` and `get` commands; note that a user must have valid UNIX read and write permissions to retrieve or send files. For example, to fetch `farfile` from the remote machine, the command

```
get farfile localfile
```

names the local copy `localfile`. (Some versions of `ftp` insist on the presence of the second file name; others do not and create a local file of the same name as the remote file.) Similarly, the command

```
put herefile therefile
```

transfers the local file `herefile` to the remote site, naming the copy `therefile`. When transferring binary files—either data files stored as binary files (as discussed in Chapter 9) or executable files—the `bin` command should be issued before using `put` or `get`. The commands `mput` and `mget` transfer groups of files, using metacharacters in the file name parameters. For example,

```
mget thisfile*
```

fetches all files with the prefix `thisfile`. Confirmation is requested before files with matching names are transferred, a feature that is toggled by the `prompt` command.

Another common use of `ftp` is known as *anonymous* `ftp`, which allows public access to many remote sites. For example, the command

```
ftp wuarchive.wustl.edu
```

will open a connection to the large public archive of programs and information maintained at Washington University in St. Louis. Use `anonymous` as the response to the request for a user id, and your local user id as the password. If accepted (public sites often limit the number of simultaneous connections), only limited access to the file system is possible. Most public sites have a directory named `pub` or `public` that contains public access directories and files.

The `ftp` utility is used to transfer files, not to run programs on remote machines. To log in to an account on another machine, the commands `rlogin` and `telnet` are often available. These commands have similar syntax, using the remote machine name as a parameter. For example, after a user issues the command `rlogin yogi.myuni.edu`, prompts for user id and password appear. After the user logs in, a regular UNIX session begins. The equivalent `telnet` command is `telnet yogi.myuni.edu`. As with `ftp`, there are many public access sites available through `telnet`, such as `lias.psu.edu`, a library catalog at Penn State University. Many UNIX systems offer more user-friendly network access programs, such as the menu-driven `gopher` program and Mosaic, which runs under a windowing system such as X or Motif.

References

Johnson, Eric F. and Kevin Reichard, *X Window Applications Programming,* 2nd ed., MIS Press, New York, 1992.

Krol, Ed, *The Whole Internet,* 2nd ed., O'Reilly and Associates, Sebastopol, CA, 1994.

McGregor, John D. and David A. Sykes, *Object Oriented Software Development: Engineering Software for Reuse,* Van Nostrand Reinhold, New York, 1992.

Stroustrup, Bjarne, *The C++ Programming Language,* 2nd ed., Addison-Wesley, Reading, MA, 1991.

Tanenbaum, Andrew S., *Modern Operating Systems,* Prentice Hall, Englewood Cliffs, NJ, 1992.

Chapter Summary

■ **Abstract Data Types**

An *abstract data type* (ADT) is a data structure designed for flexibility and reuse, with emphasis on the interface (the list of functions that the ADT provides as services). For example, an ADT for a linked list offers services such as initialize, insert, traverse, search, delete, and destroy. Moreover, it should be defined using generic parameters, such as function pointers and variables of type `void *`.

■ **Internet Access**

`ftp pebbles.bedrocku.edu`	Attempt to log on to the machine `pebbles.bedrocku.edu` in order to transfer files using `ftp`
`help`	Display available `ftp` commands
`cd cfiles`	Change to directory `cfiles` on the remote machine
`lcd cfiles`	Change to directory `cfiles` on the local machine
`get greatstuff mycopy`	Transfer file `greatstuff` on the remote machine to file `mycopy` on the local machine
`put masterpiece telltheworld`	Transfer file `masterpiece` on the local machine to file `telltheworld` on the remote machine
`bin`	In subsequent transfers, transfer all files as binary files
`unbin`	Undo the `bin` command; in subsequent transfers, transfer all files as text files
`mget great* great*`	Transfer all files with the prefix `great` from the remote machine to the local machine
`mput great* great*`	Transfer all files with the prefix `great` from the local machine to the remote machine
`rlogin barney.bedrocku.edu`	Attempt to log on to the machine `barney.bedrocku.edu`
`telnet wilma.bedrocku.edu`	Attempt to log on to the machine `wilma.bedrocku.edu`

Programming Problems

1. (Stack ADT) Design an abstract data type to offer a generic stack data structure and stack operations.
2. (Queue ADT) Design an abstract data type to offer a generic queue data structure and queue operations.

Summary of C Commands

Operations

Binary Boolean Operators (Chapter 3)

<, <=, >, >=	$<, \leq, >, \geq$
==, !=	Equal, not equal
&&, ||	*And*, *or* (inclusive *or*)

Unary Boolean Operator (Chapter 3)

!	*Not* (negation)

Bit Operations (Chapter 12)

c = a & b;	Assign to c the integer value whose individual bits are 1 only when both corresponding bits of a and b are 1
c = a | b;	Assign to c the integer value whose individual bits are 0 only when both corresponding bits of a and b are 0
c = a ^ b;	Assign to c the integer value whose individual bits are 1 only when both corresponding bits of a and b are unequal
c = ~a;	Assign to c the integer value whose individual bits are 1 only when the corresponding bit of a is 0
#define MASK 127	In binary, the constant MASK = 0111 1111

```
c = a & MASK;                  Assign to c the integer value represented by the seven low bits of a

c = a & ( ^MASK );             Assign to c the integer value represented by the highest bit of a

c = ( MASK >> 4 );             Shift the bits of MASK four places to the right and assign this integer to c;
                               in binary, c is 0000 0111 and MASK is still 0111 1111

c = ( MASK << 4 );             Shift the bits of MASK four places to the left and assign this integer to c;
                               in binary, c is 1111 0000 and MASK is still 0111 1111
```

Flow Control

Branching Statements (Chapter 3)

```
if ( condition )               condition is a boolean expression, statement is a sim-
    statement ;                ple or compound statement (enclosed in parentheses),
                               and statement is executed if and only if condition is
                               true


if ( condition )               statement1 is executed if and only if condition is true;
    statement1 ;               statement2 is executed if and only if condition is false
else
    statement2 ;


switch ( variable ) {          variable is of integer type, and each statement is a
    case value1 : statement1 ; simple or compound statement (not enclosed in paren-
              break;           theses); each value is an integer constant; if variable
    case value2 :              contains value1, then statement1 is executed; if vari-
    case value3 : statement2 ; able contains value2 or value3, then statement2 is ex-
              break;           ecuted; if variable contains anything else, then state-
    default:    statement3 ;   ment3 is executed
              break;
} /* end of switch */
```

Conditional Expressions (Chapter 3)

```
( condition ) ? value1 : value2 ;   condition is a boolean expression; the expression has
                                    value1 if and only if condition is true; the expression
                                    has value2 if and only if condition is false
```

Loops (Chapter 3)

```
/* a loop to output the first 10 positive integers */
for ( count = 1; count <= 10; count++ )   /* Initialization,    */
                              /* Continuation check and Change  */


    printf( "%d\n", count );  /* Loop body                      */

/* a second loop producing the same output */
count = 1;                    /* Initialization                 */
```

```
while ( count <= 10 ) {        /* Continuation check        */
  printf( "%d\n", count );     /* Loop body                 */
  count++;                     /* Change loop control variable */
}

/* a third loop producing the same output */
count = 0;                     /* Initialization            */
do {
  count++;                     /* Change loop control variable */
  printf( "%d\n", count );     /* Loop body                 */
} while ( count < 10 );        /* Continuation check        */
```

Stopping Commands (Chapter 3)

`break;` Stop the loop or `switch` statement, and execute the next statement

`exit( 0 );` Stop the program and return 0 as the status parameter

Process Management (Chapter 13)

`fork_value = fork();`

Create a clone (child) of the current process (parent); return the child's PID to the parent and return 0 to the child

```
#include <unistd.h>
int parentpipe[ 2 ];
pipe( parentpipe );
```

Create a pipe having two channels: parentpipe[0] for reading and parentpipe[1] for writing

`child_PID = wait( &child_status );`

Suspend execution of the (parent) process until a child process has finished; return the child's PID and exit status in the integer variables `child_PID` and `child_status`

Constants

Compiler Constants (Chapter 12)

`const int time_limit = 20;` Create a read-only variable `time_limit` and assign to it the value 20

```
const char daychars[ 5 ] = {
  'M', 'T', 'W', 'R', 'F' };
```
Define a constant array of characters to label the five days of a standard work week

Enumerated Types (Chapter 12)

`typedef enum { M, T, W, R, F } daychars;` Define the type `daychars`; variables of this type can be assigned any of the five given characters

Precompiler Definitions

Precompiler Macros (Chapter 12)

`#define MAX 99`   Replace MAX by 99 before compiling the program

`#define SamIAm system( "whoami" )` Define SamIAm, a macro to report the current userid; `<stdlib.h>` must have been included

`#define lg( x ) ((( x ) > 0 ) ? ( log( x ) / log( 2 )) : log( x ))`

A macro for the base-2 logarithm function; `<math.h>` must have been included

Precompiler Constructs for Conditional Compilation (Chapter 12)

```
#if ( VERSION > 1 )
   #define ARRAY_MAX 1024
#else
   #define ARRAY_MAX 256
#endif
```
Define ARRAY_MAX depending on the value of the VERSION at the time of precompilation; VERSION must already have a defined value

```
#if ( VERSION == 2 )
   #define ARRAY_MAX 1024
#elif ( VERSION == 3 )
   #define ARRAY_MAX 2048
#endif
```
Define ARRAY_MAX depending on the value of the VERSION at the time of precompilation; but only if VERSION is 2 or 3

```
#ifdef VERSION
   #define ARRAY_MAX 2048
#else
   #define ARRAY_MAX 1024
#endif
```
If the constant VERSION has been defined, then define ARRAY_MAX to be 2048; otherwise, define ARRAY_MAX to be 1024

```
#ifndef FALSE
   #define FALSE 0
#endif
```
If FALSE has not yet been defined, at this time define FALSE to be 0

```
#ifndef TRUE
   #define TRUE !FALSE
#endif
```
If TRUE has not yet been defined, at this time define TRUE to be !FALSE

```
#ifndef MYMACROS
   #define MYMACROS
     #define TIME_LIMIT 20
     #define ERROR_LIMIT 3
#endif
```
Define macros included in the macro MYMACROS only if these definitions have not yet been made

`#undef MYMACROS`   Delete the definition of the macro MYMACROS

`#error "Type 1 error has occurred"`   Display an error message and stop precompilation

Input/Output

Command Line Arguments (Chapter 8)

```
main( int argc, char *argv[ ] )
```
Header for the `main()` function of a program using command line arguments

Opening and Closing Text Files (Chapter 5)

```
FILE *fptr
```

```
fptr = fopen( "file1", "r" );
```
Open the text file for reading; return a pointer to `file1` if opening is successful, otherwise return NULL

```
fptr = fopen( "file1", "w" );
```
Create (overwrite if necessary) a text file and open it for writing

```
fptr = fopen( "file1", "a" );
```
Open the text file for writing and set file position pointer at the end of the file

```
fptr = fopen( "file1", "r+" );
```
Open the text file for reading and writing; return a pointer to `file1` if opening is successful, otherwise return NULL

```
fptr = fopen( "file1", "w+" );
```
Create (overwrite if necessary) a text file and open it for writing and reading

```
fptr = fopen( "file1", "a+" );
```
Open the text file for writing and reading and set file position pointer at the end of the file

```
fclose( fptr );
```
Close the file to which `fptr` is pointing

```
feof( fptr );
```
Return TRUE if EOF has been read

Text Input (Chapter 5)

```
ch = getchar( );
```
Read the next character from the standard input stream and assign that character to the variable `ch`

```
ch = fgetc( file_ptr );
```
Read the next character from the text input stream to which `file_ptr` is pointing and assign that character to the variable `ch`

```
gets( str );
```
Read the next line of characters from the standard input stream and assign those characters to the string variable `str`

```
fgets( str, n, file_ptr );
```
Read the next (n − 1) characters from the text input stream to which `file_ptr` is pointing and assign them to the string variable `str`

```
scanf( "%c %s %d %lf",
  &ch, str, &i, &x );
```
Read the next character, a string, an integer, and a `double` from the standard input stream and then assign these to the variables whose addresses are &ch, str, &i, &x, converting them from text format to specified formats; the function reads over any white space (usually spaces or newlines) preceding the

`scanf( "%c %s %d %lf",` `  &ch, str, &i, &x );`	string, integer, or `double`, and terminates conversion of each of these when a white space is reached
`fscanf( file_ptr, "%c %s %d %lf",` `  &ch, str, &i, &x );`	Read a character, a string, an integer, and a `double` from the text input stream to which `file_ptr` is pointing, and assign them as described for `scanf()`

Text Output (Chapter 5)

`putchar( ch );`	Write the character `ch` to the standard output stream
`fputc( file_ptr, ch );`	Write the character `ch` to the text output stream to which `file_ptr` is pointing
`printf( " %c%7s% 7d%-7.2lf",` `  ch, str, i, x );`	To the standard output stream, write a space, the character `ch`, the string `str`, the integer `i`, and the `double` x; the string, integer, and `double` will be converted to text format and printed in a field of at least seven columns; if the integer is positive, it will be preceded by a space; the `double` will be left-justified in its field and will be printed with two decimal places
`fprintf( file_ptr, " %c%7s% 7d%-7.2lf",` `  ch, str, i, x );`	To the text output stream to which `file_ptr` is pointing, write a space, a character, a string, an integer, and a `double` as described for `printf()`

Binary Files (Chapter 9)

`FILE *fptr`	
`fptr = fopen( "file1.bin", "rb" );`	Open the binary file for reading; return a pointer to `file1.bin` if opening is successful, otherwise return NULL
`fptr = fopen( "file1.bin", "wb" );`	Create (overwrite if necessary) a binary file and open it for writing
`fptr = fopen( "file1.bin", "ab" );`	Open the binary file for writing and set file position pointer at the end of the file
`fptr = fopen( "file1.bin", "r+b" );`	Open the binary file for reading and writing; return a pointer to `file1.bin` if opening is successful, otherwise return NULL
`fptr = fopen( "file1.bin", "w+b" );`	Create (overwrite if necessary) a binary file and open it for writing and reading
`fptr = fopen( "file1.bin", "a+b" );`	Open the binary file for writing and reading and set file position pointer at the end of the file
`fread( (void *) &Item1,` `  sizeof( MyRecordType ), 1, fptr );`	Read one item from the file to which `fptr` is pointing and store it in `Item1`

`fwrite( (void *) &Item1,` `   sizeof( MyRecordType ), 1, fptr );`	Write the contents of `Item1` as one item in the file to which `fptr` is pointing
`rewind( fptr );`	Set the file position pointer to the beginning of the file to which `fptr` is pointing
`fseek( fptr, 0, SEEK_SET );`	Equivalent to `rewind( fptr );`
`fseek( fptr, 0, SEEK_END );`	Set the file position pointer to the end of the file to which `fptr` is pointing
`fseek( fptr, -sizeof( MyRecordType ),` `   SEEK_CUR );`	Set the file position pointer to the record prior to the current record
`fflush( fptr );`	Send any remaining buffered data to the output stream (file) to which `fptr` is pointing
`fclose( fptr );`	Close the binary file to which `fptr` is pointing

Low-Level File Processing (Chapter 13)

`file_desc = open( longfile, O_RDONLY );`	Open `longfile` for read-only access; assign the file descriptor value to `file_desc`
`file_desc = open( longfile,` `   O_WRONLY | O_APPEND );`	Open `longfile` for write-only access; append new data at end of file
`file_desc = open( longfile,` `   O_RDWR | O_CREAT, 0664 );`	Open `longfile` for read/write access; create the file if necessary, allow user and group to have read and write access, and allow world to have read access only
`lseek( file_desc, -6, SEEK_END );`	Move to a position 6 bytes before the end of the file having descriptor `file_desc`
`num_bytes = read( file_desc,` `   (void *) buffer, BUFFERSIZE );`	Read as many as BUFFERSIZE bytes from the file having descriptor `file_desc` into `buffer`, an array of size BUFFERSIZE (or greater); assign the actual number of bytes read to `num_bytes`
`num_bytes = write( file_desc,` `   (void *) buffer, BUFFERSIZE );`	Write as many as BUFFERSIZE bytes from `buffer`, an array having size BUFFERSIZE (or greater), into the file having descriptor `file_desc`; assign the number of bytes written to `num_bytes`
`close( file_desc );`	Close the file having descriptor `file_desc`

Structured Types

Arrays (Chapter 7)

```
#define ROWS 3
#define COLUMNS 4          (Constants to define the following array type)
```

`typedef double` `ArrayType[ ROWS ][ COLUMNS ];`	Define a template for arrays with room to store 12 doubles (total capacity of the array equals `ROWS * COLUMNS`)
`ArrayType table;`	Declare a variable whose name is `table` and whose type is `ArrayType`; for `0 <= i <= ( ROWS - 1 )` and `0 <= j <= ( COLUMNS - 1 )`, `table[ i ][ j ]` accesses the same `double` as does the pointer expression `*( table + i * COLUMNS + j )`
`table = { 0.0 };`	Set all values of `table` to zero
`table[ 0 ] = { 0.0 };`	Set all values to zero in the first row of `table`

`void FirstFn(`
  `double list[ ],`
  `int ListSize )`
	Header for a function that can access `list` as a one-dimensional conformant array of `double`s whose actual size is specified by the parameter `ListSize`

`void SecondFn(`
  `double table[ ][ COLUMNS ],`
  `int TableSize )`
	Header for a function that can access `table` as a two-dimensional conformant array of `double`s whose actual size is specified by the parameter `TableSize`

Declaration of String Variables (Chapter 8)

`#define  ITEMS 3`
`char *ptr_menu[ ITEMS ] = {`
  `"1st Choice", "2nd Choice",`
  `"3rd Choice" };`
	Declare and assign three menu strings to `ptr_menu`, a ragged array of 33 characters

`#define MAXSIZE 20` `typedef char ItemType[ MAXSIZE ];`	A template with room for a string of length at most 19 characters
`typedef ItemType MenuType[ ITEMS ];`	A template with room for 3 strings

`MenuType menu = {`
  `"1st Choice", "2nd Choice",`
  `"3rd Choice" };`
	Declare and assign three menu strings to a two-dimensional array

`char Astr[ MAXSIZE ], Bstr[ MAXSIZE ];`	Declare two untyped string arrays with room for at most 19 characters in each

String Functions in `<string.h>` (Chapter 8)

`strlen( Bstr );`	Return the number of characters in `Bstr`
`strcpy( Astr, Bstr );`	Assign `Bstr` to the string variable `Astr`
`strncpy( Astr, Bstr, 4 );`	Assign at most four characters of `Bstr` to `Astr`
`strcat( Astr, Bstr );`	Concatenate the string `Bstr` at the end of `Astr`
`strncat( Astr, Bstr, 4 );`	Concatenate at most four characters of `Bstr` to `Astr`
`strcmp( Astr, Bstr );`	Compare (show lexical relation of) `Astr` and `Bstr`
`strncmp( Astr, Bstr, 4 );`	Compare at most four characters of `Astr` and `Bstr`
`strchr( Astr, ch );`	Return pointer to first occurrence of `ch` in `Astr`, or return NULL if `ch` is not in `Astr`
`strstr( Astr, Bstr );`	Return pointer to first occurrence of `Bstr` in `Astr`, or return NULL if `Bstr` is not in `Astr`

String Input/Output Functions in `<stdio.h>` (Chapter 8)

`scanf( "%s", Astr );`	Read `Astr` from standard input, stop at white space
`fscanf( f_ptr, "%s", Astr );`	Read `Astr` from file to which `f_ptr` is pointing
`sscanf( Astr, "%d", &i );`	Read the integer i from the string `Astr`
`gets( Astr );`	Read `Astr` from standard input, stop at `'\n'`
`fgets( Astr, n, f_ptr );`	Read into `Astr` at most n characters from the file to which `f_ptr` is pointing
`printf( "%s", Astr );`	Write the string `Astr` to standard output stream
`fprintf( f_ptr, "%s", Astr );`	Write `Astr` to file to which `f_ptr` is pointing
`sprintf( Astr, "%d", i );`	Write the integer i to the string `Astr`
`puts( Astr );`	Write `Astr` and `'\n'` to the standard output
`fputs( Astr, f_ptr );`	Write `Astr` to the file to which `f_ptr` is pointing

Declarations and Assignments of Structure Variables (Chapter 9)

`typedef struct {`
`  double my_real;`
`  int my_integer;`
`  char *my_string;`
`} MyRecordType;`
	Define a `struct` template with room for
	    one `double`, *and*
	    one `int`, *and*
	    one (untyped) string

`MyRecordType Item1;`	Declare a `struct` variable that has type `MyRecordType`
`MyRecordType Item1 = { 1.0, 1, "one" };`	Declare and assign fields of a `MyRecordType` variable
`Item1.my_real = 2.0;`	Assign a value to the first field of `Item1`
`MyRecordType *Item2;`	Declare `Item2`, a pointer to a `MyRecordType` variable
`&Item2->my_real = 2.0;`	Assign a value to the first field of `Item2`

`typedef union {`
`  double my_real;`
`  int my_integer;`
`  char *my_string;`
`} MyUnionType;`
	Define a `union` template with room for:
	    one `double`, *or*
	    one `int`, *or*
	    one (untyped) string

`MyUnionType Item3;`	Declare a `union` variable that has type `MyUnionType`
`Item3.my_real = 1.0;`	Erase any currently active field of `Item3` and assign a value to the field `my_real`

`typedef struct {`
`  char ch;`
`  MyUnionType Item;`
`} ImprovedUnionType;`
	Define a data structure that allows the use of `ch` as a discriminator variable to indicate the currently active field of `Item`

Dynamic Variables

Managing Dynamic Memory (Chapter 10)

```
#include <stdlib.h>

double *ptr1, *ptr2, *ptr3;
```

`ptr1 = (double *) malloc(` `  sizeof( double ));`	Allocate heap space for one `double`
`ptr2 = (double *) calloc(` `  2, sizeof( double ));`	Allocate heap space for two consecutive `doubles` initialized to zero
`ptr3 = (double *) realloc( ptr2, 4 );`	Allocate heap space for four consecutive `doubles`, the first two of which have starting address given by `ptr2`
`free( (void *) ptr2 );`	Release the heap memory whose starting address is `ptr2`, making it available for further allocation

Function Pointers (Chapter 13)

`int (* fn1)( double x );`	Prototype for a function pointer `fn1`; `(* fn1)()` returns an `int`
`int *(* fn2)( double x );`	Prototype for a function pointer `fn2`; `(* fn2)()` returns an `int` pointer
`int (* fn3)( const void * );`	Prototype for a function pointer `fn3`; `(* fn3)()` has one generic pointer parameter and returns an `int`
`void qsort( void *, size_t, size_t,` `  int (*)( const void *, const void * ));`	Prototype for `qsort`, a quicksort function in `<stdlib.h>`

Appendix

Standard Library Header Files

This appendix describes many functions in selected standard libraries. Note that some functions are actually implemented as macros, that some details are omitted, and that there may be some differences across different machines and different versions of UNIX. Also, the usage of most functions is omitted; refer to the text for more details.

<assert.h>

Assertions—boolean conditions that should be true at particular points in a program's execution—are made with the function assert(). If the assertion is not valid, the program is aborted.

assert()

Prototype: void assert(*expression*);

Meaning: *expression* is a boolean expression. If *expression* evaluates as true, no action is taken; if false, a statement to the effect assertion failed: <*expression*>, file *x*.c, line *yy* is printed on stderr, then the function abort() is called to terminate the program.

Usage:
```
assert( x >= 0.0 );   /* Ensure that x is not negative */
y = sqrt( x );        /*    before calling sqrt()      */
```

<ctype.h>

The following utility functions are provided for ease of processing character input. Although most parameters are of type int, the arguments passed are meant to be of type char.

isalnum()

Prototype: `int isalnum( int ch );`

Meaning: Returns 1 if ch is a digit or letter, 0 otherwise.

Usage: `ch = getchar();`
`      i = isalnum( ch );`

isalpha()

Prototype: `int isalpha( int ch );`

Meaning: Returns 1 if ch is a letter, 0 otherwise.

iscntrl()

Prototype: `int iscntrl( int ch );`

Meaning: Returns 1 if ch is a control character, 0 otherwise.

isdigit()

Prototype: `int isdigit( int ch );`

Meaning: Returns 1 if ch is a digit, 0 otherwise.

islower()

Prototype: `int islower( int ch );`

Meaning: Returns 1 if ch is a lower case letter, 0 otherwise.

isprint()

Prototype: `int isprint( int ch );`

Meaning: Returns 1 if ch is printable, 0 otherwise.

Usage: `if ( isprint( ch )) {`
`        printf( "Character = %c\n", ch );`
`    else`
`        printf( "Character is not printable.\n" );`

ispunct()

Prototype: `int ispunct( int ch );`

Meaning: Returns 1 if ch is a punctuation mark, 0 otherwise.

isspace()

Prototype: `int isspace( int ch );`

Meaning: Returns 1 if ch is a white space character, 0 otherwise.

isupper()

Prototype: `int isupper( int ch );`

Meaning: Returns 1 if ch is an upper case letter, 0 otherwise.

tolower()

Prototype: `int tolower( int ch );`

Meaning: If ch is an upper case letter, the equivalent lower case letter is returned; otherwise, ch is returned.

Usage:
```
/* Convert str's characters to all lower case */
for ( i = 0; i < strlen( str ); i++ )
    str[ i ] = tolower( str[ i ] );
```

toupper()

Prototype: `int toupper( int ch );`

Meaning: If ch is a lower case letter, the equivalent upper case letter is returned; otherwise, ch is returned.

<error.h>

The variable `errno` is defined in <error.h> as type `extern int`. `errno` is set to a value by some functions when an error occurs. See `ferror()` and `perror()` in <stdio.h>.

<float.h>

A few of the constants describing the size and capacity of floating-point numbers are shown below, taken from the authors' machine.

```
#define FLT_EPSILON   1.192092896E-07F
#define FLT_MIN       1.175494351E-38F
#define FLT_MAX       3.402823466E+38F
#define DBL_EPSILON   2.2204460492503131E-16
#define DBL_MIN       2.2250738585072014E-308
#define DBL_MAX       1.7976931348623157E+308
#define LDBL_EPSILON  1.925929944387235853055977942584927319E-34L
#define LDBL_MIN      3.3621031431120935062626778817321752603E-4932L
#define LDBL_MAX      1.1897314953572317650857593266280007016E+4932L
```

<limits.h>

A few of the constants describing integer numbers are shown below, taken from the authors' machine.

```
#define SCHAR_MIN (-128)              /* signed char     */
#define SCHAR_MAX 127
#define UCHAR_MAX 255                 /* unsigned char  */
#define SHRT_MIN  (-32768)            /* short           */
#define SHRT_MAX  32767
#define USHRT_MAX 65535               /* unsigned short */
#define INT_MIN   (-2147483647-1)     /* int             */
#define INT_MAX   2147483647
#define UINT_MAX  4294967295U         /* unsigned int   */
#define LONG_MIN  (-2147483647L-1L)   /* long            */
#define LONG_MAX  2147483647L
#define ULONG_MAX 4294967295UL        /* unsigned long  */
```

`<math.h>`

The functions described in this section are the C implementations of common mathematical functions. Rules pertaining to domain and range restrictions are generally the same as they are for the mathematical functions themselves. For example, `sqrt()` accepts only nonnegative arguments. Note that the type `double` is used for parameters and return values.

`acos()`

Prototype: `double acos( double value );`

Meaning: Returns the arccosine of `value`.

Usage:
```
y = acos( 0.5 );              /* Compute arccosine of 0.5, in radians */
x = ( y * 3.14 ) / 180.0;   /* Convert to degrees.                   */
printf( "Arccosine( 0.5 ) = %lf\n",  x );
```

`asin()`

Prototype: `double asin( double value );`

Meaning: Returns the arcsine of `value`.

`atan()`

Prototype: `double atan( double value );`

Meaning: Returns the arctangent of `value`.

`ceil()`

Prototype: `double ceil( double x );`

Meaning: Returns the next integer value greater than or equal to x.

`cos()`

Prototype: `double cos( double value );`

Meaning: Given `value` in radians, returns its cosine.

cosh()
Prototype: `double cosh( double x );`
Meaning: Returns the hyperbolic cosine of x.

exp()
Prototype: `double exp( double x );`
Meaning: Returns e raised to the x power.

fabs()
Prototype: `double fabs( double x );`
Meaning: Returns the absolute value of x.
Usage: `y = sqrt( fabs( x ));`

floor()
Prototype: `double floor( double x );`
Meaning: Returns the next integer less than or equal to x.

log()
Prototype: `double log( double x );`
Meaning: Returns the natural logarithm of x.

log10()
Prototype: `double log10( double x );`
Meaning: Returns the base-10 logarithm of x.

pow()
Prototype: `double pow( double x, double p );`
Meaning: Returns x raised to the p power.

sin()
Prototype: `double sin( double value );`
Meaning: Given value in radians, returns its sine.

sinh()
Prototype: `double sinh( double x );`
Meaning: Returns the hyperbolic sine of x.

sqrt()
Prototype: `double sqrt( double x );`
Meaning: Returns the square root of x.

tan()

Prototype: `double tan( double value );`

Meaning: Given `value` in radians, returns its tangent.

tanh()

Prototype: `double tanh( double x );`

Meaning: Returns the hyperbolic tangent of x.

<signal.h>

Exceptions are error flags kept by the system. A C program can check for errors and raise an exception when one occurs. A program can be aborted on an error, or a special function, called an *exception handler*, may be called. The following functions describe these mechanisms.

signal()

Prototype: `void ( *signal( int signl, void (* fn)( int )))( int );`

Meaning: Registers the function pointed to by `fn` as an exception handler to be called when `signl` is sent by `raise()` or when a system signal is received by the program. The function sent in place of the second parameter must take an integer parameter and return nothing (that is, `void`). Default handlers may be used in place of the function `* fn` by using one of the following constants as the second parameter: `SIG_DFL`, default signal processing (usually abort); `SIG_IGN`, ignore the signal; and `SIG_ERR`, which causes `errno` to be set. The `signal()` function returns a pointer to a function that takes an `int` parameter (note the last `( int )` in the prototype); this return value is often tested against `SIG_DFL` or `SIG_IGN`. Possible values of `signl` include `SIGABRT`, abnormal termination of the program; `SIGFPE`, arithmetic error; `SIGINT`, interrupt detected; `SIGTERM`, a termination request was sent to the program.

Usage:
```
/* ... */
signal( SIGFPE, myfunc );
x = 1.0 / 0.0;
/* ...  */

void myfunc( int signl ) {
  printf( "Received %d\n", signl );
  exit( 0 );
}
```

raise()

Prototype: `int raise( int signl );`

Meaning: Sends `signl` to the program to be handled according to the function registered by `signal()`. Returns nonzero if unsuccessful.

<stdio.h>

The file record `FILE` is defined in `<stdio.h>`. File variables are declared as type `FILE *` and used to reference open files (we use the shorthand notation `fptr` for "the file referred to by the file variable `ftpr`"). Three standard files are opened automatically for each program: `stdin`, normally associated with the keyboard; `stdout`, associated with the display terminal; and `stderr`, associated with the terminal and used for error output. The constant EOF is returned by several functions to indicate end of file.

fclose()

Prototype: `int fclose( FILE *fptr );`

Meaning: Close `fptr`. Returns 0 if no error is detected, nonzero otherwise.

feof()

Prototype: `int feof( FILE *fptr );`

Meaning: Returns a nonzero value if the end of file of `fptr` has been reached.

ferror()

Prototype: `int ferror( FILE *fptr );`

Meaning: Returns a nonzero value if an error has occurred.

fflush()

Prototype: `int fflush( FILE *fptr );`

Meaning: Clears the file buffer of `fptr`. Returns 0 if no error is detected, nonzero otherwise.

Usage: `fflush( stdin );`

fgetc()

Prototype: `int fgetc( FILE *fptr );`

Meaning: Reads the next character from `fptr`.

fgets()

Prototype: `char *fgets( char *str, int num, FILE *fptr );`

Meaning: Reads a line of input from `fptr`, including the newline character.

fopen()

Prototype: `FILE *fopen( const char *filename, const char *mode );`

Meaning: Opens a file named `filename` with access indicated by `mode`; returns the file pointer, which is NULL if an error occurs. See Chapter 5 for `mode` details.

Usage:
```
fptr = fopen( "myfile", "r" );    /* Open myfile for reading */
    if ( fptr == NULL ) {          /* Check for error          */
      printf( "Error opening myfile.\n" );
      exit( 0 );
    }
```

fprintf()

Prototype: `int fprintf( FILE *fptr, const char *format, ... );`

Meaning: Writes to `fptr` using the same format conventions as `printf()`.

fputc()

Prototype: `int fputc( int ch, FILE *fptr );`

Meaning: Writes one character, ch, to `fptr`. Returns ch if successful, EOF otherwise.

fputs()

Prototype: `int fputs( const char *str, FILE *fptr );`

Meaning: Writes the string `str` to `fptr`. Returns the number of characters actually written, or EOF on error.

fread()

Prototype: `size_t fread( void *ptr, size_t size, size_t count, FILE *fptr );`

Meaning: Reads `count` items each of `size` bytes from `fptr` into the buffer pointed to by `ptr`. Returns the number of items read or EOF on error. Used for binary files (files of records).

freopen()

Prototype: `FILE *freopen( const char *filename, const char *mode, FILE *fptr );`

Meaning: Closes `fptr`, then opens the file named `filename` with access indicated by `mode`. Returns the file pointer, which is NULL on error.

fscanf()

Prototype: `int fscanf( FILE *fptr, const char *format, ... );`

Meaning: Formatted read from `fptr`, using the same conversion characters as `scanf()`. Returns the number of successful conversions or EOF on error.

fseek()

Prototype: `int fseek( FILE *fptr, long offset, int whence );`

Meaning: Changes the file position to `offset` bytes counted from the place indicated by `whence`, using the code 0 for the beginning of `fptr`, 1 for current position, and 2 for the end of `fptr`. Returns nonzero on error. Used for binary files (file of records).

ftell()

Prototype: `long ftell( FILE *fptr );`

Meaning: Returns the current file position.

fwrite()

Prototype: `size_t fwrite( void *ptr, size_t size, size_t count, FILE *fptr );`

Meaning: Writes `count` items of size `size` to `fptr` from the buffer pointed to by `ptr`. Returns the number of items actually written or EOF on error.

getc()

Prototype: `int getc( FILE *fptr );`

Meaning: Returns the next character from `fptr` or EOF on error.

getchar()

Prototype: `int getchar( void );`

Meaning: Returns the next character from `stdin`.

gets()

Prototype: `char *gets( char *str );`

Meaning: Reads the next line from `stdin`, replacing the newline character with \0. Returns `str` or NULL if end of file occurs.

perror()

Prototype: `void perror( const char *str );`

Meaning: Prints the string `str` and the system-defined error message corresponding to `errno` on `stderr`.

Usage:
```
if ( fseek( fptr, offset, 0 ) != 0 ) {
    perror( "Error in fseek." );
    exit( 0 );
}
```

printf()

Prototype: `int printf( const char *format, ... );`

Meaning: Writes to `stdout` according to the format conventions explained in Chapter 5.

Usage:
```
int    i = 5;
double x = 10.1;
printf( "i = %d, x = %lf\n", i, x );
```

putc()

Prototype: `int putc( int ch, FILE *fptr );`

Meaning: Writes ch to `fptr`. Returns ch or EOF on error.

putchar()

Prototype: `int putchar( int ch );`

Meaning: Writes ch to `stdout`.

puts()

Prototype: `int puts( const char *str );`

Meaning: Writes the string `str` and a newline to `stdout`. Returns EOF on error, nonnegative integer otherwise.

remove()

Prototype: `int remove( const char *filename );`

Meaning: Deletes the file named `filename` (that is, the C equivalent of the UNIX command `rm filename`); returns nonzero value if the deletion fails.

rename()

Prototype: `int rename( const char *previous, const char *newname );`

Meaning: Renames the file named `previous` with the name `newname` (that is, the C equivalent of the UNIX command `mv previous newname`); returns nonzero on failure.

rewind()

Prototype: `void rewind( FILE *fptr );`

Meaning: Changes current file position to the beginning of the file; equivalent to `fseek( fptr, 0L, 0 );`.

scanf()

Prototype: `int scanf( const char *format, ... );`

Meaning: Formatted input from `stdin` using format conventions explained in Chapter 5. Returns the number of successful conversions, or EOF on error.

Usage:
```
int    i;
double x;
scanf( "%d%lf", &i, &x );
```

sprintf()

Prototype: `int sprintf( char *str, const char *format, ... );`

Meaning: String print; same as `printf()`, but output is placed in the string `str`.

sscanf()

Prototype: `int sscanf( char *str, const char *format, ... );`

Meaning: String scan; same as `scanf()`, but input is obtained from the string `str`.

ungetc()

Prototype: `int ungetc( int ch, FILE *fptr );`

Meaning: Replaces `ch` in `fptr`. Returns `ch` if successful, EOF otherwise.

<stdlib.h>

The functions described in this section are utility functions, including memory allocation and deallocation routines.

abort()

Prototype: `void abort( void );`

Meaning: Causes abnormal termination and a call to `raise( SIGABRT );`

Usage:
```
if ( errno > 0 ) {
    printf( "Ending program.\n" );
    abort();
}
```

abs()

Prototype: `int abs( int value );`

Meaning: Returns the absolute value of `value`.

atof()

Prototype: `double atof( const char *str );`

Meaning: Converts the string `str` to a `double`.

Usage:
```
double x;
x = atof( "13.5" );
```

atoi()

Prototype: `int atoi( const char *str );`

Meaning: Converts the string `str` to an `int`.

atol()

Prototype: `long atol( const char *str );`

Meaning: Converts the string `str` to a `long`.

bsearch()

Prototype: `void *bsearch( const void *key, void *start, size_t count, size_t size, int (*compare)( void *keyval, void *value ));`

Meaning: Performs a binary search for the data item referred to by `*key` in the array pointed to by `start` (containing data items of size `size`) from `start[ 0 ]` to `start[ count - 1 ]` using the comparison function pointed to by `*compare()`. Returns a pointer to the data item if found, `NULL` otherwise.

calloc()

Prototype: `void *calloc( size_t count, size_t size );`

Meaning: Returns a generic pointer to an area of memory large enough for `count` items each of size `size`; returns `NULL` on error. The area is initialized to zeros.

exit()

Prototype: `void exit( int status );`

Meaning: Causes program termination. The `status` value is returned to the operating system; a zero value indicates normal termination.

free()

Prototype: `void free( void *ptr );`

Meaning: Deallocates the area of memory pointed to by `ptr`.

labs()

Prototype: `long labs( long value );`

Meaning: Returns the absolute value of `value`.

malloc()

Prototype: `void *malloc( size_t size );`

Meaning: Returns a generic pointer to an area large enough for `size` bytes. Returns `NULL` on error. The area is not initialized.

Usage:
```
int *i;
    i = (int *) malloc( sizeof( int ));
```

qsort()

Prototype: `void qsort( void *base, size_t count, size_t size,`
`int (*cmp)( const void *, const void * ));`

Meaning: Performs the quicksort algorithm on the array pointed to by `*base` of `count` items, each of size `size`, using the comparison function pointed to by `*cmp()`.

rand()

Prototype: `int rand( void );`

Meaning: Returns a pseudorandom integer in the range from 0 to `RAND_MAX`.

realloc()

Prototype: `void *realloc( void *ptr, size_t size );`

Meaning: Changes the size of the area of memory pointed to by `ptr` to `size` bytes. Returns a generic pointer to the new area or `NULL` on error.

srand()

Prototype: `void srand( unsigned int seed );`

Meaning: Uses seed to initialize the `rand()` generator.

system()

Prototype: `int system( const char *str );`

Meaning: Requests that the operating system execute the command `str`.

<string.h>

The following string functions assume that strings are legally terminated with the character \0 and that the target string has enough space to store added characters. Most of the functions return a redundant pointer to the first string argument.

strcpy()

Prototype: `char *strcpy( char *target, char *str );`

Meaning: Copies the legally terminated string `str` into the string `target`.

Usage: `char target[ 20 ];`
   `strcpy( target, "Hello" );`

strncpy()

Prototype: `char *strncpy( char *target, char *str, int count );`

Meaning: Copies at most `count` characters from `str` to `target`.

strcat()

Prototype: `char *strcat( char *target, char *str );`

Meaning: Concatenates `str` to the end of `target`.

strncat()

Prototype: `char *strncat( char *target, char *str, int count );`

Meaning: Concatenates at most `count` characters of `str` to the end of `target`.

strchr()

Prototype: `char *strchr( char *str, char ch );`

Meaning: Searches for the first occurrence of `ch` in `str`, returning a pointer to that position or `NULL` if not found.

strstr()

Prototype: `char *strstr( char *str, char *pattern );`

Meaning: Searches for the string `pattern` in `str`, returning a pointer to the beginning position if found and `NULL` otherwise.

strcmp()

Prototype: `int strcmp( const char *first, const char *second );`

Meaning: Compares the two string arguments. Returns 0 if equal, a positive integer if `first` is lexicographically before `second`, and a negative integer otherwise.

strncmp()

Prototype: `int strncmp( const char *first, const char *second, int count );`

Meaning: Compares at most `count` characters of the two string arguments. Returns 0 if equal, a positive integer if `first` is lexicographically before `second`, and a negative integer otherwise.

strlen()

Prototype: `size_t strlen( const char *str );`

Meaning: Returns the length of `str`.

<time.h>

The `time` family of functions accesses the system clock for reports on time in various formats. The types `clock_t` and `time_t` are usually aliases for `long`. The `struct` type `tm` is defined as

```
struct tm {
  int tm_sec;   /* seconds                      */
  int tm_min;   /* minutes                      */
  int tm_hour;  /* hours (24 hour clock)        */
  int tm_mday;  /* day (1-31)                   */
  int tm_mon;   /* month (0-11)                 */
  int tm_year;  /* year since 1900              */
  int tm_wday;  /* weekday (0 = Sunday)         */
  int tm_yday;  /* yearday (0-365)              */
  int tm_isdst; /* Daylight Savings Time flag */
}
```

The constant `CLOCKS_PER_SEC` is used to convert clock ticks to seconds.

asctime()

Prototype: `char *asctime( const struct tm *tptr );`

Meaning: Returns a string containing the time indicated by the structure pointed to by `tptr` using the format <dayname monthname daynumber hours:minutes:seconds year >.

Usage:
```
struct tm *time_st;  /* Pointer to a tm struct */
time_t    mytime;    /* Long for ticks         */
mytime = time( NULL );                          /* Get the time            */
time_st = (struct tm *) localtime( &mytime ); /* Convert to local time */
printf( "Time = %s\n", asctime( &time_st )); /* Write the time string */
```

clock()

Prototype: `clock_t clock( void );`

Meaning: Returns the processor time used by the program to this point.

Usage: `printf( "Seconds of execution = %ld\n", clock()/CLOCKS_PER_SEC );`

localtime()

Prototype: `struct tm *localtime( const time_t *tptr );`

Meaning: Returns local time by converting the calendar time `tptr`.

time()

Prototype: `time_t time( time_t *tptr );`

Meaning: Returns the current time (in ticks) or -1 on error. If `tptr` is not NULL, the return value is also assigned to `tptr`.

Appendix
C

Summary of UNIX Commands

Elementary UNIX Commands

Logging In and Out (Chapter 1)

`login`   Start a shell, (such as the C shell) an environment in which the user can execute UNIX commands

`logout`   Stop the shell program

UNIX Help (Chapter 1)

`stty -a`   Show all terminal settings

`man cc`   Allow the user to scroll through the manual page describing the UNIX command `cc`

`apropos passwd`   Show UNIX commands related to `passwd`

Compilation

Compiling Programs (Chapter 2)

Note: Your system may use another command, such as `acc` or `gcc`, to call an ANSI C compiler.

`cc filename.c`   Compile the C program in the file named `filename.c` and produce an executable file named `a.out`

`cc filename.c -o filename`	Compile the C program in the file named `filename.c` and produce an executable file named `filename`
`cc filename.c -lm -lf`	Compile the C program in the file named `filename.c`; include the `<math.h>` and `<float.h>` libraries, and produce an executable file named `a.out`

Executing Programs (Chapter2)

`a.out`	Execute the C program that has been compiled into the executable file named `a.out`

Executing Programs with Command Line Arguments (Chapter 8)

`a.out my_file`	Run the executable program `a.out` with `argv[ 0 ]` = `a.out` and `argv[ 1 ]` = `my_file`

File Management

Listing Files (Chapter 1)

`ls ToPort`	List `ToPort`; that is, list visible files in the directory named `ToPort`
`ls`	List visible files in the working directory
`ls -a`	List all files in the working directory
`ls -l`	List visible files using long form of listing (include sizes, dates, and so forth)
`cat NMouse`	Show all contents of the file `NMouse`
`more ToCome`	Show contents of the file `ToCome`, allowing the user to scroll forward (`Space`, d, or `Enter`), scroll backward (b), or quit (q) at any time
`lpr AlphabetSoup`	Print the contents of the file `AlphabetSoup`

Moving Files (Chapter 1)

`cp oldfile newfile`	Copy the contents of `oldfile` to `newfile`; there will be two files with identical contents
`mv oldfile newfile`	Move the contents of `oldfile` to `newfile`; this is a renaming command—there will still be exactly one file
`rm WaxBuildup`	Remove the file `WaxBuildup` from the working directory
`rm -i WaxBuildup`	Remove `WaxBuildup` interactively, prompting the user to confirm the action

File Permissions (Chapter 3)

`chmod o+rw file1`	Grant others (o) permission to read (r) and write (w) to `file1`, a file in the working directory
`chmod o-w file1`	Deny others (o) permission to write (w) to `file1`
`chmod o+r-w file1`	Grant others permission to read `file1`, and deny others permission to write to `file1`
`chmod o+x file2`	Grant others permission to execute (x) `file2`

File Information (Chapter 4)

`wc MyFile`	Display the counts of lines, words, and characters in `MyFile`
`sort MyFile`	Display the lines of `MyFile`, sorted by the first field on each line and using the ASCII sequence
`sort +1 -4 MyFile`	Display the lines of `MyFile`, sorted by the second through fourth fields on each line and using the ASCII sequence
`sort -n +5 -6 MyFile`	Display the lines of `MyFile`, sorted by the numerical value of the sixth field on each line
`grep myword MyFile`	Display the lines of `MyFile` that contain the string "myword"

Archiving Files (Chapter 11)

`tar -cvw mydir/file1 mydir/file2`	Create (c) a new archive file on the default device and write `mydir/file1` and `mydir/file2` onto the archive file (assuming that `mydir` is a subdirectory of the current working directory), using verbose instructions (v) and waiting (w) for confirmation
`tar -cvwf package mydir file1 file2`	Same as in the previous example, but write to a new file `package` in the current working directory, instead of writing to the default device
`tar -cvw mydir`	Archive all files in `mydir`
`tar -rf package file3`	Append `file3` to the existing archive file `package`
`tar -uf package file4`	If `file4` has not previously been archived in package, do so now
`tar -tf package`	List all files archived in `package`
`tar -xf package file1`	Extract `file1` from `package`
`tar -xf package`	Extract all files from `package`
`tar -xf -`	Extract all files from standard input (used with piped input)

Compressing Files (Chapter 11)

`compress greedyfile`	Replace the file `greedyfile` by a compressed file `greedyfile.z`
`uncompress frugalfile.z`	Replace `frugalfile.z` by an uncompressed file `frugalfile`

Encrypting Files (Chapter 11)

`crypt enigma < cleartext > mush`	Translate the file `cleartext` to an encoded file `mush`; use the coding key `enigma`
`crypt enigma < mush > cleartext`	Translate the file `mush` to a decoded file `cleartext`; use the coding key `enigma`

File Editing

Pattern Matching (Chapter 8)

`fgrep exit my_file`	Search `my_file` for lines containing the substring `exit`
`fgrep -f patterns my_file`	Search `my_file` for *fixed strings* listed (without quotes and separated by `'\n'`) in `patterns`
`grep exit my_file`	Search `my_file` for lines containing the substring `exit`
`grep '^exit' my_file`	Search `my_file` for lines beginning with `exit`
`grep '^e' my_file`	Search `my_file` for lines beginning with `'e'`
`grep '^[a-z]' my_file`	Search `my_file` for lines beginning with a lower case alphabetic character
`grep '^.[ab]' my_file`	Search `my_file` for lines whose second character is `'a'` or `'b'`
`grep '\.$' my_file`	Search `my_file` for lines whose last character is `'.'`
`grep ';$' my_file`	Search `my_file` for lines ending with `';'`
`grep ';;*$' my_file`	Search `my_file` for lines ending with one or more occurrences of `';'`
`grep ')[^;]$' my_file`	Search `my_file` for lines ending with `')'` followed by any character other than `';'`
`grep '(.*)' my_file`	Search `my_file` for lines containing expressions (possibly empty) enclosed in parentheses
`egrep ';+' my_file`	Search `my_file` for lines containing one or more occurrences of `';'`
`egrep 'my(_)?word' my_file`	Search `my_file` for lines containing `myword` or `my_word`
`egrep '(myword)|(my_word)' my_file`	Search `my_file` for lines containing `myword` or `my_word`
`egrep -f patterns my_file`	Search `my_file` for *expressions* listed (without quotes and separated by `'\n'`) in `patterns`

String Substitutions (Chapter 8)

`sed 's/myword/my_word/' file1`	Substitute `my_word` for the first occurrence (per line) of `myword` in `file1`
`sed '1,4s/myword/my_word/' file1`	Substitute `my_word` for the first occurrence (per line) of `myword` on lines 1 to 4 of `file1`
`sed 's/myword/my_word/g' file1 file2`	Substitute `my_word` for all occurrences of `myword` in `file1` and `file2`

`sed 's/myword/my_word/gw changes' file1`	Substitute my_word for all occurrences of myword in file1; append revised lines to the file changes
`sed 's/myword/my_word/g' file1 >> file2`	Substitute my_word for all occurrences of myword in file1; append the entire revision to file2
`sed '3,5d' file1`	Delete lines 3 through 5 of file1
`sed '3,5d' file1 >> file2`	Delete lines 3 through 5 of file1; append the entire revision to file2
`sed '/start/,/stop/d' file1`	Delete lines from first start to next stop in file1
`sed '/\{/,/\}/d' file1`	Delete lines from first '{' to next '}' in file1
`sed '1,/spot/d' file1`	Delete lines from first line to next spot in file1
`sed '/\./,$d' file1`	Delete lines from first '.' to the end of file1
`sed -f comfile my_file`	Make substitutions in my_file according to the instructions contained in the command file comfile
`10a\` `printf( "OK" );`	A command file that will append the line "printf("OK");" after the tenth line
`1i\` `/* filename: MyFile */`	A command file to insert the following line "/* filename: MyFile */" before the first line

`1i\`
`/* filename: MyFile */\`
`/* date: __/__/__ */`
	A command file to insert two lines before the first line

`1c\` `/* filename: MyFile */`	A command file to change the first line to "/* filename: MyFile */"

Directory Management

Directory Names (Chapter 3)

`/`	Root directory
`/usr`	Pathname of user directory, a subdirectory of root
`/usr/bin`	Pathname of bin, a subdirectory of /usr
`/usr/home/prog1.c`	Pathname of prog1.c, a file contained in the directory /usr/home
`~bob`	Home directory of a user named bob
`pwd`	Have the operating system report the full pathname of the working directory

Directory Maintenance (Chapter 3)

`mkdir sub1`	Make a new directory, `sub1`, a subdirectory of the current working directory
`rmdir sub1`	Remove the subdirectory, `sub1`, which must be an *empty subdirectory* of the working directory
`mv myfile sub1`	Move `myfile` to the subdirectory `sub1`
`cd sub1`	Change the working directory to `sub1`
`cd ..`	Change the working directory to the parent of the current working directory
`cd ../..`	Change the working directory to the grandparent of the current working directory
`cd`	Change the working directory to the home directory

Control

Program Input/Output (Chapter 5)

`MyProg < in_file`	*Redirect input* to the program `MyProg` from the file `in_file`, rather than from the standard input stream
`MyProg > out_file`	*Redirect output* from the program `MyProg` to the file `out_file`, rather than to the standard output stream. If `out_file` already exists, it is overwritten or an error message is given.
`MyProg >> out_file`	*Redirect output (and append, if necessary)* from the program `MyProg` to the file `out_file`, rather than to the standard output stream
`FirstProg	SecondProg`	Execute the programs `FirstProg` and `SecondProg`; *pipe* the output stream from `FirstProg` to the input stream for `SecondProg`
`FirstProg	tee SecondProg`	*Tee* the output of the program `FirstProg` into the program `SecondProg`, *as well as* to the standard output stream

Program Linking and Debugging (Chapter 6)

`cc -c prog1.c`	Compile the C code contained in the file `prog1.c`, and create an object file named `prog1.o`
`cc prog1.o prog2.o -o LinkedCode`	Link the object files `prog1.o` and `prog2.o`, and create an executable file named `LinkedCode`
`cc -c -g prog1.c`	Compile the C code contained in the file `prog1.c`, and create an object file `prog1.o` that is also suitable for analysis by the `dbx` command
`cc -g prog1.c -o buggy`	Compile the C code contained in the file `prog1.c`, and create an executable file named `buggy` that is also suitable for analysis by the `dbx` command
`dbx buggy`	Use the interactive debugging utility `dbx` to analyze the executable file named `buggy`

`make`	Compile and link separate source code files according to the instructions contained in the file `makefile` (or `Makefile`, if `makefile` does not exist)
`make -f MyMakeFile`	Compile and link separate source code files according to the instructions contained in the file `MyMakeFile`
`lint filter.c`	Use the debugging utility `lint` to analyze the source code file named `filter.c`

Process Management (Chapter 13)

`ps`	List all processes (and their PIDs) owned by the user
`ps -l`	List processes in long detail
`a.out &`	Run process `a.out` in the background
`(sleep 30; a.out) &`	Wait 30 seconds, then run `a.out` in the background
`control-Z`	Stop (that is, suspend) the current foreground job
`jobs`	List stopped jobs (and their job numbers)
`jobs -l`	List stopped jobs (display both job numbers and PIDs)
`fg %1`	Resume job number 1 in the foreground
`bg %1`	Resume job number 1 in the background
`kill %1`	Try to kill (permanently stop) job number 1
`kill 3232`	Try to kill the job with PID 3232
`kill -9 3232`	Kill the job with PID 3232, with certainty of success

C Shell Scripts (Chapter 10)

`#!/bin/csh`	Begin a shell script
`#!/bin/csh -f`	Begin a shell script but do not read `.cshrc`
`#!/bin/csh -vx`	Begin a shell script; use verbose mode (`-v`) to echo each shell command, and (`-x`) to echo each command with its variables expanded
`echo 'myvar = ' $myvar`	Print the string `'myvar = '` followed by the value of the variable `myvar`
`echo "myvar = $myvar"`	Print the given string, but recognize the $ as a shell script operator and print the value of `myvar` after the equals sign
`echo -n 'Enter a filename: '` `set mystr = $<`	On one line, prompt the user and await input of a string value for the variable `mystr`
`set mystr = 'myfilename'`	Assign the string `myfilename` to `mystr`

```
set mystr = `whoami`
```
Execute the shell command `whoami` and store the resulting string in the variable `mystr`

```
set mystr = ($str1 $str2)
```
Concatenate `str1` and `str2`, assign the new string to `mystr`

```
shift mystr
```
Discard `$mystr[1]` and shift succeeding elements toward the front of `mystr`

```
@ mynum = $<
```
Await input of an integer value for `mynum`

```
@ mynum = 2001
```
Assign an integer constant to `mynum`

```
#comment: make an assignment
if ( $#argv == 0 ) then
  filename = 'default_file'
  exit
else
  set filename = $argv[1]
  exit
endif
#comment: make a report
echo "filename has been set to $filename"
```
A fragment that will assign either the string `default_file` or the first command line argument to the variable `filename`

```
switch ( $variable )
  case value1:
            echo case 1, line 1
            echo case 1, line 2
            breaksw
  case value2:
  case value3:
            echo case 2 or 3
            breaksw
  default:
            echo default case
            breaksw
endsw
```
A fragment illustrating the `switch` statement

```
@ count = 1
while ( $count <= 5 )
  echo $count
  @ count++
end
```
A loop to print five positive integers, one per line

```
foreach number( 1 2 3 4 5 )
  echo number
end
```
A loop to print five positive integers, one per line

```
onintr TerminationLabel
while( 1 )
  echo Press Control-C to stop program
TerminationLabel:
echo program is stopping
exit
```
A fragment allowing user to stop the program

```
echo Press S to stop program
echo Press any other key to continue
set response = $<
if ( $response == S )
  echo Program is stopping
  exit
endif
echo Program is continuing.
```
A fragment allowing user to stop program

Environment Information

User Information (Chapter 4)

who	Display the ids of users currently logged in
w	Display the ids and current commands of users currently logged in
whoami	Display your own id
finger nail	Display a variety of information about the user whose id is nail

General Information (Chapter 4)

cal 2 1900	Display the calendar for February 1900
echo $SHELL	Display the current shell
echo $term	Display the current terminal setting (C shell)
echo $path	Display the current directory search path (C shell)
set	Display all shell variables (C shell)
set term = vt100	Temporarily reset term to vt100 (C shell)
set	Display all environment variables (Bourne shell)
TERM=vt100	Temporarily reset TERM to vt100 (Bourne shell)

C Shell System and Environment Controls (Chapter 9)

set	Display current values of all shell variables
setenv	Display current values of all environment variables
ls ~/subdir1	List files in subdir1, a subdirectory of the home directory
ls *.out	List files ending with the suffix .out
ls *.?	List files ending with a period followed by a single character
set noglob	Turn off recognition of filename wildcard characters
unset noglob	Turn on recognition of filename wildcard characters
set filec	Turn on the filename completion feature

`unset filec`	Turn off the filename completion feature
`alias workdir cd ~userid/dir1/dir2`	Define an alias for changing the directory to the subdirectory given by the indicated pathname
`unalias workdir`	Discard the alias `workdir`
`set history = 40`	Keep the 40 most recent commands; discard this list at the end of the current session
`set savehist = 40`	Keep the 40 most recent commands, save this list at the end of the current session
`history`	Display recent commands
`!1`	Execute command number 1 on the `history` list
`!ca`	Execute the most recent command beginning with the string `"ca"`
`!ca:s/old/new/`	Execute the most recent command beginning with the string `"ca"`, and substitute `new` in place of `old` in the command
`dirs`	Display the directory stack
`pushd dir1`	Push `dir1` onto the top of the directory stack and change the working directory to `dir1`
`popd`	Pop the top directory from the directory stack, and change the working directory to that directory

Mail, File, Transfer, Remote Access

Electronic Mail (Chapter 11)

`mail`	Report any incoming messages; if there are messages, display the header list and continue the mail program
`mail thw`	Mail a message to user `thw`; enter the message, terminated by control-D or a period at the start of the last line or aborted using two control-Cs
`write thw`	Send an immediate message to `thw`, terminated as with `mail` (this works only if `thw` is logged on and is accepting such messages)
`talk dew`	Attempt to initiate interactive conversation with `dew`; use control-C to terminate the conversation
`mesg y`	Accept interactive messages
`mesg n`	Refuse to accept interactive messages
`mail thw < toms_letter`	Mail the file `toms_letter` to user `thw`; `thw` must be a valid userid on the same machine
`mail dew@email.psu.edu < urgent`	Mail the file `urgent` to user `dew` at the machine with Internet address `email.psu.edu`

Responses to the Mail Program Prompt (Chapter 11)

 & ?   Display a summary of `mail` commands

 & p 1   Print the contents of the first message

 & s 1   Save the contents of the first message

 & d 1   Discard the first message

 & h   Redisplay the header

 & r 1   Reply to the sender of the first message; enter the response, terminated by control-D or a period at the start of the last line, or aborted using the sequence of two control-Cs

 & m thw   Mail a message to user `thw`; enter the message, terminated by control-D or a period at the start of the last line, or aborted using two control-Cs

 & q   Quit the `mail` program, saving changes to mail list

 & x   Exit the `mail` program without saving changes

Internet Access (Chapter 14)

`ftp pebbles.bedrocku.edu` — Attempt to log on to the machine `pebbles.bedrocku.edu` in order to transfer files using `ftp`

`help` — Display available `ftp` commands

`cd cfiles` — Change to directory `cfiles` on the remote machine

`lcd cfiles` — Change to directory `cfiles` on the local machine

`get greatstuff mycopy` — Transfer file `greatstuff` on the remote machine to file `mycopy` on the local machine

`put masterpiece telltheworld` — Transfer file `masterpiece` on the local machine to file `telltheworld` on the remote machine

`bin` — In subsequent transfers, transfer all files as binary files

`unbin` — Undo the `bin` command; in subsequent transfers, transfer all files as text files

`mget great* great*` — Transfer all files with the prefix `great` from the remote machine to the local machine

`mput great* great*` — Transfer all files with the prefix `great` from the local machine to the remote machine

`rlogin barney.bedrocku.edu` — Attempt to log on to the machine `barney.bedrocku.edu`

`telnet wilma.bedrocku.edu` — Attempt to log on to the machine `wilma.bedrocku.edu`

Summary of
vi Commands

General Commands

Mode Changes (Chapter 2)

Command	Description
vi filename.c	Start the vi editor in normal command mode and view filename.c
i	Change from command to input mode, insert at cursor
a	Change from command to input mode, insert after cursor
I	Change from command to input mode, insert at beginning of current line
A	Change from command to input mode, insert at end of current line
o	Change from command to input mode, open new line below current line
O	Change from command to input mode, open new line above current line
Escape key	Change from input to command mode
:	Change from command to ex mode
Escape key	Abort ex command and return to command mode
Return key	Execute ex command and return to command mode
:w	Save file (using the name given when vi was started)
:w newname	Save file using the name newname
:q	Quit vi without saving file (assumes no changes have been made)

:q!	Quit vi without saving file, even if changes have been made
:wq	Save (revised) file and then quit

Other Commands (Chapter 7)

:set number (:set nonumber)	Set line numbering option on (off)
:set autoindent (:set noautoindent)	Set automatic indentation option on (off)
view filename	Start the vi editor in read-only mode, and view filename
:q!	Quit viewing in read-only mode, if characters have been typed (in other modes, :q! quits without saving changes)
vi filename	Start the vi editor in normal command mode and view filename
vi +50 filename	Start the vi editor in normal command mode and view filename beginning at line 50
vi + filename	Start the vi editor in normal command mode and view the end of filename
vi -r filename	Start vi and recover latest version of filename following system crash
:!ls	Interrupt vi and list working directory

Mode Actions

Input Mode Actions (Chapter 2)

Return key	End current line and begin a new line
i, return key, escape key	Split current line into two lines
Control-H	Backspace one position
Escape key	Change from input to command mode

Insert Mode Cursor Movement (Chapter 7)

w (b)	Move cursor froward to next *word* (backward to previous word)
$ (0)	Move cursor forward to end of *line* (backward to beginning of line)
:2 or 2G	Move to line 2 of the file
G	Move to last line in the file
:f	Display current line number on the status line

Command Mode Actions (Chapter 2)

Arrow key	Move cursor one character/line in indicated direction
l (h)	Move cursor one character to right (left)
Space bar	Move cursor one character to right
k (j)	Move cursor one line up (down)
Return key	Move cursor one line down
Control-B (control-F)	Move one screen backward (forward)
x	Delete current character
dd	Delete current line
dw	Delete current word (from cursor to end of word)
2x	Delete 2 characters (current character and character to right)
2dd	Delete 2 lines (current line and next line)
p	Put back most recently deleted text
u	Undo most recent change
U	Undo all recent changes on current line
J	Join current line and next line

File Editing

Search (Chapter 7)

/pattern /($pattern$)	Search forward (backward) for first occurrence of *pattern*
/ \[/	Search forward for first occurrence of a left bracket followed by a space
/x.z/	Search forward for first occurrence of an x, followed by any character, followed by a z
/[xy]*[^a-z]/	Search forward for the first occurrence of an x or y, followed by a star, followed by any character other than a lower case letter
/^for(/	Search forward for first occurrence of for(at the beginning of a line
/)$/	Search forward for first occurrence of a right parenthesis at the end of a line
/+ [0-9][0-9]*/	Search forward for first occurrence of + followed by a space followed by one or more digits
%	Search for a matching parenthesis, bracket, or brace

Replacement (Chapter 7)

`:1,4 s/int/double/c`	Search lines 1 through 4 and offer to replace the first occurrence of `int` with `double`
`:1,. s/int/double/g`	Search from line 1 to the current line and replace all occurrences of `int` with `double`
`:1,. s/int/double/cg`	Search from line 1 to current line and *offer* to replace all occurrences of `int` with `double`
`:1,$ s/</(/g`	Search all lines and replace all occurrences of < with (
`ra`	Replace current character with `a`
`Rabc<esc>`	Replace current and next two characters with `abc`
`~`	Replace current lower case character with corresponding upper case character or vice versa

Cut and Paste (Chapter 7)

`"by`	Yank (copy) current line to buffer b
`"b3y`	Yank (copy) 3 lines to buffer b
`"13y`	Yank (copy) 3 lines to buffer 1
`"1dd`	Delete current line and store in buffer 1
`"b33dd`	Delete 33 lines and store in buffer b
`"133dd`	Delete 33 lines and store in buffer 1
`"1p`	Put (paste) contents of buffer 1 at current cursor position
`ma`	Mark current line with label a
`:'a, 'b w CopyFile`	Store a copy of lines a through b in `CopyFile`

Operator Precedence Chart

The following operators are evaluated according to priority, listed from highest to lowest, and within a given priority level, either left-to-right or right-to-left.

Level 1: (Left to right)

() [] . -> ++ (postfix) -- (postfix)

Level 2: (Right to left)

++ (prefix) -- (prefix) ! ~ sizeof + (unary) - (unary) & (address) * (dereference)

Level 3: (Left to right)

* / %

Level 4: (Left to right)

+ -

Level 5: (Left to right)

<< >>

Level 6: (Left to right)

< <= > >=

Level 7: (Left to right)

== !=

Level 8: (Left to right)

&

Level 9:   (Left to right)

∧

Level 10:   (Left to right)

|

Level 11:   (Left to right)

&&

Level 12:   (Left to right)

||

Level 13:   (Right to left)

?   :

Level 14:   (Right to left)

=   +=   -=   *=   /=   %=   >>=   <<=   &=   ∧= |=

Level 15:   (Left to right)

, (comma)

Index

443